The Praxis of Alain Badiou

Anamnesis

Anamnesis means remembrance or reminiscence, the collection and re-collection of what has been lost, forgotten, or effaced. It is therefore a matter of the very old, of what has made us who we are. But *anamnesis* is also a work that transforms its subject, always producing something new. To recollect the old, to produce the new: that is the task of *Anamnesis*.

a re.press series

re.press

The Praxis of Alain Badiou

Paul Ashton, A. J. Bartlett and Justin Clemens, editors

re.press Melbourne 2006

First published 2006 by re.press

Published by re.press
14 Henry St
Seddon, 3011
Melbourne, Australia
http://re-press.org

Typeset by A&R in *Baskerville*
Printed on demand wherever it is desired.

British Library Cataloguing in Publication Data
A catalogue record for this book is available from the British Library.

National Library of Australia Cataloguing-in-Publication entry

The praxis of Alain Badiou.

Bibliography.
Includes index.
ISBN 9780980305203.

ISBN 0 9803052 0 9.

1. Badiou, Alain. 2. Events (Philosophy) - History. 3. Ontology - History. 4. Philosophers, French. I. Ashton, Paul, 1974- . II. Bartlett, A. J. (Adam John). III. Clemens, Justin. (Series : Anamnesis).

III

This publication benefited from a small grant from the Institute for Community Engagement and Policy Alternatives (ICEPA) at Victoria University, Australia.

Contents

POLITICS

Abbreviations

C	*Conditions*
CT	*Court traité d'ontologie transitoire*
D	*Deleuze: The Clamor of Being*
E	*Ethics: An Essay on the Understanding of Evil*
EE	*L'être et l'événement*
BE	*Being and Event*
HI	*Handbook of Inaesthetics*
IT	*Infinite Thought: Truth and the Return to Philosophy*
LM/LOW	*Logiques des mondes: l'être et l'événement, 2*
LS	*Le Siècle*
M	*Metapolitics*
MP	*Manifesto for Philosophy*
NN	*Le Nombre et les nombres*
OB	*On Beckett*
P	*Polemics*
SP	*Saint Paul: The Foundation of Universalism*
TO	*Briefings On Existence: A Short Treatise on Transitory Ontology*
TC	*The Century*
TS	*Théorie du sujet*
TW	*Theoretical Writings*

Acknowledgements

The production of a collection of essays such as this is a laborious process at the best of times. When it is an 'Open Access' publication, however—that is, as free as possible from the constraints of commerciality and the restrictive property ownership regime of copyright—these labours multiply significantly. Consequently, we have relied on the generosity and support of a number of friends and colleagues. We would like to thank them here. We thank the contributors for their work, as well as those who responded to our initial call for papers but did not make the final volume due to the sheer number of responses. This made for many difficult choices. We would like to thank Helen Johnson for the free use of her image *The Centre for the Study of Adhocracy: The Library*, which appears on the cover of this volume, and the Sutton Gallery in Melbourne for making this possible. We thank also the thinkers who have contributed to the production process or offered intellectual support in one form or another. These include Russell Grigg, Sigi Jöttkandt, Dominiek Hoens, Rachel Hughes, Angela Cullip and our blind reviewers (the unnameable backbone of all such collections). We would like to give a special mention to the Melbourne Badiou Reading Group (they know who they are). Finally, we thank Alain Badiou for his permission to translate 'What is a Philosophical Institution?' and for the terrifying claim that he will 'read every article'.

The essays in this book first appeared in the open access journal *Cosmos and History: The Journal of Natural and Social Philosophy* (C&H). Paul Ashton, as one of the 'organizing' editors of *Cosmos and History*, would like to thank the other key organizers of the journal for their work in creating the context in which projects like this can take place: Arran Gare, Roberto Schiavo Lena and Claire Rafferty.

Paul Ashton
A. J. Bartlett
Justin Clemens
Melbourne 2006

introduction

1

Masters & Disciples:
Institution, Philosophy, Praxis

Paul Ashton, A. J. Bartlett & Justin Clemens

'Discipline, comme tu saignes!'
—René Char

'Consequently, a true master [*Meister*] is at bottom only he who can provoke the other to transform himself through his act'.

—Slavoj Žižek

I. THE SITUATION

This book, *The Praxis of Alain Badiou*, collects texts first published in a special issue of the online journal *Cosmos & History*. Our call for submissions to that issue read as follows:

> To mark the English translation of *L'Être et l'événement* as *Being and Event*, the journal *Cosmos and History* will publish a special issue on the work of the philosopher Alain Badiou. The approach of this journal is to publish work that goes beyond the merely exegetical and to this end we would like contributors to take up the challenge Badiou raises in *Being and Event* when he says:
>
> 'The categories that this book deploys, from the pure multiple to the subject, constitute the general order of a thought such that it can be *practised* across the entirety of the contemporary system of reference. These categories are available for the service of scientific procedures just as they are for those of analysis or politics. They attempt to organize an abstract vision of the requirements of the epoch.'

> We invite contributors to this special issue to respond to Badiou's
> challenge and deploy his categories in thinking a particular
> situation—be it political, artistic, scientific or amorous.

Although it has taken nearly two decades for *Being and Event* to become
available in English, there are already an enormous number of conferences,
articles, translations, introductions and monographs dedicated to Badiou
and his work (see the bibliography in this volume). We find works of
Badiou translated directly from the French editions (*Deleuze, Ethics, Saint
Paul, Metapolitics, Handbook of Inaesthetics, Briefings on Existence, Manifesto for
Philosophy, Being and Event*); essays or extracts from existing publications,
on a variety of matters (politics, art, etc.) and appearing in a range of
journals (e.g., *Diacritics, Lacanian Ink*, etc.); created or assembled works not
appearing in such form (such as *Infinite Thought, On Beckett* or *Theoretical
Writings*); interviews and new pieces written especially for translation (e.g.,
the many 'Author's prefaces' now available).

If one casts an eye over the existing commentries, they seem
preponderantly to fall into a small number of significant categories.
First, the introductions, ranging from the extended and well-informed
monographs to shorter articles in specialist journals. Second, the critiques,
which tend to focus either on Badiou's general tendencies, or on particular
claims that he makes (e.g., *Think Again*, most of the essays in *Communication
and Cognition* Vols. 36 & 37, and in *Polygraph* 17, etc.). Third, the assimilation
of Badiou's terminology and themes into more general projects, as a kind
of grab-bag of general concepts for use in varying situations. But what we
were calling for was something a little different, a fourth way: a *systematic*
deployment of Badiou's categories.

It's not that this hasn't been attempted. Oliver Feltham, the English
translator of *Being and Event*, and a contributor to this collection, has done
so in regard to a local Australian political event in 'Singularity Happening
in Politics: The Aboriginal Tent Embassy, Canberra 1972'.[1] But such an
'application' has been surprisingly rare, to the point where it seems people
might appear chary of being mistaken for a merely uncritical disciple,
dogmatist, or dinosaur. (It is noteworthy that such accusations have,
in the Anglophone world at least, been flung at 'Lacanians', a state of
affairs about which Slavoj Žižek has often fulminated).[2] It has been, as we

---

1. In *Communication & Cognition*, vol. 37, nos. 3 & 4, 2004, pp. 225-245. See also Barbara
Formis, 'Event and ready-made: Delayed sabotage', in the same volume, pp. 247-261.
2. For example, see the recent film *Žižek!*, in which our eponymous hero has a go at an
off-screen deconstructionist on precisely this point.

have said, much more the case that critics have wanted to pose different questions, or try to get different things out of Badiou's corpus to date.

II. MASTERS & DISCIPLES ≠ FRIENDS & ENEMIES ≠ FATHERS & SONS

This brings up the rather boring relationship between a master's writings, a systematic philosophy, discipleship and commentary. Badiou's great treatise *Being and Event* has just become available in English, so the system-building volume at the base of his reputation will be accessible to a new audience. This adds to the already-existing books translated straight from the French, the anthologies composed of occasional writings, 'exclusive' interviews, and essays extracted from other volumes, all subjected to the exigencies of commodity-production, legal entitlement and bio-physical limitations. This situation—hardly worth mentioning in itself, it may seem, simply the banal conditions of contemporary book marketing—should, on the contrary, force us to reappraise Badiou's own accounts of the dissemination of thought, philosophical thought. Indeed, Badiou is undoubtedly one of the few contemporary philosophers to factor in the problem of the dissemination of thought into his thought itself.

A tiny article—which, to our knowledge, *nobody* in the Anglophone world has yet translated, anthologized, or even adequately discussed—is crucial here. This article, entitled, 'What is a philosophical institution? Or: address, transmission, inscription' can be found in *Conditions*.[3] In this article of less than eight pages, Badiou elaborates an entire theory of the transmission of philosophy. Without an institution, no transmission; without transmission, no philosophy. How to think, however, this institution outside, first, established actualities such as the university which captured philosophy after Kant, and, second, without simply abstracting from or returning to classical forms of philosophical institution (the Academy, the Stoa, the Garden, etc.)? Moreover, how to think the role of the *disciples* or of the *friends* of philosophy? And so, third, how to avoid characterizing a philosophical institution in the *religious* terms—however admirable and radical—of a Quaker 'society of friends'?

For Badiou, a philosophical institution can have no instrumental value, precisely because one can never apportion ends, aims or finalities to philosophy. Philosophy must, despite its most stringent and rigorous

---

3. Alain Badiou, *Conditions*, Paris, Seuil, 1992, pp. 83-89. The translation of this essay, which appears in this volume, was translated into English with Badiou's permission by A. J. Bartlett for the special Badiou issue of *Cosmos and History*, vol. 2, nos. 1-2, 2006 pp. 9-14.

conclusions, testify to what he calls 'the interminable imperative of continuing'.

If philosophy itself institutes nothing but the void of an address, the transmission of a philosophy requires its disciples to invent new modes of thinking adequate to supporting the singularity of this empty address; these disciples work to transform the emergence of this void address into letters, into marks that subsist and can circulate along routes and through places that previously would have found these marks unthinkable and/or unacceptable. And these letters can only move as conflict, as antagonism, as committed incomprehension: a philosophical disciple doesn't really know (though he or she may desperately want to know), and knows that, though he or she can never know they know, they must place their names and bodies behind the work of their own obscure enquiries. The disciple often demands that the master be the One, even as he poses the master the most infuriating problems, induces the master to cover himself further, to drape the possibility that the garment might gape to reveal...what? The nothing beneath?[4] Disciples must *force* something, illegitimately, into being.

Yet it is not publicity at which such disciples and institutions aim, but *inscriptions*, knotted, difficult, forever being done, undone, redone. It is only by such means that a philosophy becomes what it is—in transformed institutions by which it can encounter *other* philosophies. Hence a philosophical institution 'is not the guardian of philosophy, but of its historicity. It is thus the guardian *of* philosophies. It is the knotted plural of philosophies as resistance in time, which often means: resistance to the times'. It is in such institutions-in-process—'truth-bodies', perhaps, in the language of Badiou's new book *Logiques des mondes*—that disciples read, translate, re-edit the texts of the master; squabble about the philosophy in question; relate it to classical problems in the history of thought; relate it to other philosophies; to the world as they find it transfigured in the unprecedented dark light of these new little letters, etc.

But, in what one might call this 'adherence' (we don't use the word 'fidelity', for reasons which will become apparent) of the disciple—an adherence which does not, of course, preclude vicious and unforgiving attacks on their master's texts—they can tend towards becoming policemen of the state of philosophy, the place in which all the *elements* of

---

4. See, for instance, Badiou's 'Afterword', subtitled 'Some replies to a demanding friend', in Peter Hallward, (ed.), *Think Again*, London and New York, Continuum, 2004, pp. 232-237; and his 'Author's Preface', to *Theoretical Writings*, ed. and trans. R. Brassier and A. Toscano, London and New York, Continuum, 2004, pp. xiii-xv.

(a) philosophy, having been torn from their original situations, are turned into new sets, verified, legitimated, *included*. Using the terms of Badiou's own schematization of set-theory, one can say that disciples can end up doing the work of the *state* of philosophy, the transformation of what's presented into representation, through their ceaseless unbinding, and re-countings of the philosopher's words. In this sense, the operations of disciples can be schematized by the power-set and union operations of set-theory; if disciples are the source of philosophy's growth and dissemination, they are also potential agents of its 'statification'. The putative universality of philosophy must always run the risk of the state.

Yet, in his 'Author's Preface' to *Theoretical Writings*, Badiou seems to modify the position of 'What is a philosophical institution?'

> [I]n what sense can this present book really be said to be one of my books? Specifically, one of my books of philosophy? Is it not rather a book by my friends Ray Brassier and Alberto Toscano? After all, they gathered and selected the texts from several different books, which for the most part were not strictly speaking 'works' but rather collections of essays (xiv).

If the question of *forms of writing* is critical in this context, it is because a philosophical institution must always bind itself to the singularity of a philosopher's *dicta*, and it is thus no accident that Badiou himself is very attentive to such a necessity. Each philosopher invents or constructs his or her own form (and the aforementioned 'Preface' accordingly opens with a list of major philosophical forms). We want to suggest that, although Badiou is a systematic philosopher, his own system is one that complicates the difference between 'central works' and 'occasional essays'. Certainly, his major works to date are *Being and Event* and, now, the just-released *Logiques des mondes*. Yet, as Badiou put it in a recent talk in Melbourne, these books are like 'atomic bombs', quite useless as effective weaponry in themselves. It is their mere existence, or, rather, the ongoing research that produced them, that supports the truly engaged and effective interventions evident in the shorter books, articles and interviews.

Philosophy would be nothing without its masters; yet a master requires disciples to be a master at all. Recently, Badiou has started to refer explicitly to this work of discipleship under the rubric of 'friendship', a very interesting nominal shift. If it's probably a bit rich (presumptuous?) for a living philosopher to refer to his living disciples *as* disciples, and if the rubric of 'friendship' itself has an impeccable philosophical pedigree, this nonetheless opens a question as to the true subjects of thought. In fact, we detect a double division here within Badiou's thinking of an institution:

the division between *master and disciples*, on the one hand, and between *friends and enemies*, on the other. Both are to be distinguished from *fathers and sons* (and not only for the sexist implications of the latter).

This, however, suggests another way of thinking about the relation between master and disciple, a wavering and uncertain line of division *within* philosophy and its institutions.[5] Some indications: 1) the difference between 'friends' and 'disciples'; 2) the difference between 'philosophy' and 'history of philosophy'; 3) the difference between 'situation' and 'state'; 4) the difference between 'forms of writing' and their 're-presentation'. After all, for Badiou, the very exemplum of a subject engaged in a militant fidelity to an event is Saint Paul, the greatest of all 'disciples', the one who invents the first known universal institution in human history. It is not Christ who is the hero of subjectivity for Badiou, but Paul. On the other hand, as Badiou notes, explicating St. Paul: 'Philosophy knows only disciples. But a son-subject is the opposite of a disciple-subject, because he is one whose life is beginning'.[6] The problem here is, then, the relation between 'disciples' and 'friends'.

Since, as Badiou insists at the beginning of *Being and Event*, a contemporary philosophy must circulate between ontology, modern inventions of subjectivity and its own history, the *disciples and their work must be treated as integral to the elaboration of philosophy itself.* A philosophy must attend to the problem of its own institution, to philosophical institutions, to the creation of new forms of institution. It must attend to the problem of friends and disciples. Following this mobile line takes us directly to questions at the heart of Badiou's philosophy, to his refashioned concept of *praxis*.

III. THE CONCEPT OF PRAXIS

For Badiou, we say, praxis composes a knot: it is simultaneously thought, act and category. The subject, a category that can be deployed 'across the entirety of the contemporary system of reference', does the work of tying and retying the strands of thought and act. The subject, whose being is void, constitutes in and as itself the locus of praxis which brings 'thought and being' together under the injunction of the Same.

5. This immanent division seems to be borne out by Badiou himself when in 'What is a philosophical institution?' he suggests that 'in the circumstances of writing, the master makes a disciple of himself', p. 87.
6. Alain Badiou, *Saint Paul: The Foundation of Universalism*, trans. Ray Brassier, Stanford, Stanford University Press, 2003, p. 59.

The subject is what it is to think and to be at the same time—the 'junction of a disjunction'.

Praxis is in the service of scientific procedures, artistic configurations, emancipatory politics and love. But as the knot constituted of categories, concepts and acts, praxis is in no way the predicate of the functioning of this knot nor the determinant of the existence of its strands. Rather, these three strands of the knot demand both their compossibility and their name. Praxis is the composition of, and the name for, the service of the subject whose procedure will have been decided by the situation. This situation (all situations being founded through the event) is that which endures despite the attentive recounting of what it counts by the state. It is the situation then which 'decides' the praxiological conditions for the subject. Or, to put it another way, the situation decides, qua situation, for which procedure the category of the subject is the contingent and finite support.

Like walking slowly, praxis, for the Greeks, was the privilege of 'free men'. Marx considered praxis in a similar way, though perhaps not as the privilege of free men but more as that which both constituted and supported man as free. So our knot knots together thought and act, the category of the subject, the situation for which this subject is subject, and the free man in the temporality of the *future anterior*. But what *is* a 'free man'? It is certainly not a subject; and yet it most certainly is. The trivial yet compulsive liberal definition of freedom attests only to a limitless dispersal, a casting off of all that is not 'the free man'—the (therefore) sovereign *individual*. The individual always *knows* 'that which it is not'— and by extension 'what must not be'—which is why it is sovereign. In passing we can see that 'deciding for the exception' is a banal rather than exceptional concept. The subject, our subject is, as we can see, subject to the discipline—the cruel discipline—of certain conditions: the pure multiple, the event, the situation, the practice of the procedures and their sustaining under the category of the 'same' or truth. 'Our' free man, which is to say man *as* free, is in truth a subject, whereas 'the individual, in truth, is nothing'. The subject 'knows' nothing, in the liberal sense of the word. Rather, the subject is the extent of its enquiries conditioned absolutely by its conditions. It has no knowledge to speak of. It is not a bridge between predicate and end, just as justice is not located at the 'end of a state program'. Praxis, we can say, knows no ends. Its being is infinite and the truth for which it is the support is likewise eternal.

So why praxis? Perhaps symptomatically, we have not yet mentioned that category which is critical to any praxis today, that of *courage*. What does this courage amount to? It amounts to continuing. Courage is the courage to continue in praxis, to act to sustain and extend any series of situated enquiries across the entirety of a situation—a situation that knows no end. To be a subject is to be the courageous support of a truth. It is through the courage of the subject that the thought of truth is given being as a thought-practice. As such, courage amounts to the practice of thought. And a 'thought is nothing other than the desire to have done with the exorbitant excesses of the state'. Praxis is thus the courageous work of a *free* man under the condition of a truth against the state. Above all, praxis is a name for risk. It is a throw of the dice by those who are nothing, but chance to be everything.

IV. IN THIS COLLECTION

One must beware the Sirens yearning to lure the philosophic voyager onto the rocks, even if one is a Mallarméan and finds that Sirens have considerable poetic appeal. The articles collected in this volume certainly attempt to avoid this deleterious end, whether through lashing themselves to the mast(er), or through plugging their ears with wax. Here then, without revisioning summary or summarily re-presenting, we present the names of those who have practiced-thought in response to our call: A. J. Bartlett, Lorenzo Chiesa, Justin Clemens, Oliver Feltham, Zachary Fraser, Sam Gillespie, Lindsey Hair, Alex Ling, Toula Nicolacopoulos and George Vassilacopoulos, Nina Power, Brian Anthony Smith and Alberto Toscano. We also thank Alain Badiou for permission to publish the essential article from *Conditions*. And—on the basis that no Platonist can be allowed to escape into Ideas entirely unscathed by Poetry—we have included a poem by Dominique Hecq, entitled 'follysophy', which responds directly to Badiou's work. Finally, we also include a comprehensive bibliography compiled by Paul Ashton.

If one must be an *activist* (a 'militant') in a truth process, the creation of a philosophical *system* is itself a protracted *act*—and this act itself is something that scrambles the polarities of closed and open, centre and margins, structure and occasion, continuation and punctuation. As Badiou notes early in *Saint Paul*, the hostility of the contemporary world to philosophy is evident in the repression of the very names of philosophy's conditions. Thus 'culture' obliterates 'art', 'technology' obliterates 'science', 'management' obliterates 'politics', and 'sexuality' obliterates 'love': 'The system: culture-technics-management-sexuality—that has the immense merit of being homogenous to the market, and of which all the terms, at least, designate a rubric of commercial presentation—is the nominal modern recovery of the system art-science-politics-love...' [7]

Thus the unavowed system of anti-systematic thought is in some way homogeneous with the system of the times; declarative systematic thought (philosophy), as we said above, attempts to rupture with the system of the times. Or, again, the latter attempts to take account of the thoughts that do attempt such a rupture (the four conditions). Thus 'system' is integral to philosophy. Not every system is philosophical, of course, but every philosophy, every true philosophy, must aim at systematicity. Hence the importance of the 'and' in the title of *Being and Event*; 'and' is precisely *the* philosophical injunction, the injunction of system. *Chez* Badiou, being is dealt with by mathematics, while events are the province of the conditions. Neither are, strictly speaking, the proper job of philosophy. What philosophy must do is construct a way of bridging the gap without reduction. Philosophy is the *ampersand* composing a discourse of, if we may, cosmos and history.

But let there be no confusion: there can be no simple opposition between a 'closed' system and an 'open' becoming. Whether covertly moralized or not, such denominations are insufficient to treat the novelty of a philosophical system in act. Badiou's system is produced in an endless circulation through the conditions, returning to them again and again, in different forms (extended treatises, handbooks, articles, oral presentations, etc.), constantly permitting them to norm and re-divert existing propositions of his philosophy.

It thus seems to us that there is no *principled* difference between the 'original' 'meditations' of and in *Being and Event* and the varied articles re-collected in other volumes and other languages: all are part of the ongoing *act of system*, whether or not Badiou himself actually envisaged these articles one day sitting together in an English translation. This act is novelty itself, insofar as no existing names or concepts are adequate to capturing the shape or rhythm of its elaboration. This system-act, integral to the definition of philosophy, is what tries to validate the contemporary compossibility of philosophy's conditions—that is, their heterogeneous sheltering, a void peace of their discontinuity.

In other words, there is no philosophical system without disciples, or, at least, a seething and active host of bizarre patchwork creatures traversed by the mobile line of the friend-disciple division. If they can get it together, knotting inscriptions against the tendency to representation,

---

7. Badiou, *Saint Paul*, p. 13.

a new philosophical institution may well emerge. To parody the jingle from the popular Australian soap-opera *Neighbours*—with all the horror that the very word and concept may conjure up—*that's when good disciples become good friends.*

We would therefore like to thank our contributors for their dedication and their courage, through which, to again quote Badiou in Melbourne in 2006: 'finally, we have always to become the contrary of our masters'.

2

What is a Philosophical Institution?
Or: Address, Transmission, Inscription[1]

Alain Badiou

I would like to attempt here something of a deduction in regard to the destiny of all philosophical institutions. I would like to explore the possibility of submitting to the concept our institutional intuition. The danger is easily imagined. It is certainly less than that to which Saint-Just was exposed when he maintained that only institutions could prevent the Revolution from ending with the pure rising of its event. The risk I take is only this: by reversing a materialist order whose own effect is that of immersing thought in the density of the social and the organic, I propose that the determination of philosophy as such prescribes an institution appropriate to it.

What's at stake, uncertain and brief as it is, is the transcendental deduction of any possible philosophical institution. Concerning actual institutions, of first rank and unique to the world being the *Collège international de philosophie*, we accept that their problems, their worries, their internal competitions and their elected authorities, as is reasonable, are anything but transcendental.

---

1. Except for some final improvements, this is the text first presented, in 1989, as a colloquium intervention at the *Collège international de philosophie* itself. We know today, by way of its constant reforms and by way of the aporias that pertain to the name 'Europe', that the question of institutions impassions many philosophers. I cannot say that it impassions me, but, since this injunction exists, I support it, and so I give my concept.

TN. This text is taken from Alain Badiou, *Conditions*, Paris, Éditions du Seuil, 1992, pp. 83-90. I would like to thank Justin Clemens for his help in preparing this text and Alain Badiou for his permission to publish this translation.

We begin with the negative dialectic. The institutional prescription of philosophy does not take the form of causality. Nor does it take the form of an incarnation. No institution can pretend to be an effect of philosophy; none can suggest its body, nor make philosophy into a body, a Great Body, as the specialists of French institutional sociology say. Neither does the institution have only instrumental value, in the sense of directing philosophy toward its end. This for the essential reason that its ends are non-existent. I do not say that philosophy is without destination. But I don't think that we can distribute that destination within the domain of ends or finalities. Philosophy, far from proposing ends, means always, in one way or another, to have done with ends, and even to end with *the* end. The greatest virtue of philosophy, however, is that, in not ceasing to conclude, it attests to the interminable imperative of continuing. It therefore requires no other means for abolishing ends.

No effect, no body, no instrument. What, then, is a philosophical institution? Of course, we could maintain that they do not exist, but, from the ancient schools of thought to the college that I extolled a moment ago, it is the opposite that is empirically attested. And on no account will I be entering into an interminable process of deconstruction, which would establish at the limit of the concept that these empirical institutions organize only a forgetting of their destination. No, these institutions exist and have an established connection with philosophy. But what connection?

I maintain that what the institution traces is not a *line* of causality; nor the *volume* of a body; and nor is it the *surface* of a planned operation. It is a knot, which the institution's job is to keep tied; and the only risk to this same institution is that this knot might be cut. A philosophical institution is a procedure for the conservation of a knot, at risk of the cut which would be the dispersal of its elements. A good institution is knotted, opaque, cannot be untangled: A poor one is segmented, dispersed, parliamentary. The first, the good, is tight and obscure. The second, dangerous, counts votes and separates functions in such a way that they can only reassemble in the barely philosophical form of the colloquium. Being the guardian of a knot is hardly compatible with this sometimes prudent, sometimes violent, management of factional equilibrium.

What is at stake in this knot? My subtitle declares: address, transmission and inscription. What can be said of these three strands of the knot, each of which holds together the other two that would accord with that figure bestowed on us to contemplate by my master Jacques Lacan?

Firstly I name 'address' not with regard to who or to what philosophy addresses itself but with regard to the subjective position that is proper to its address. Yet that which characterizes this position is purely and simply *void*. As a first definition, then, we can say that philosophy is without specific address. No community, real or virtual, is in relation to philosophy. No statement of philosophy is addressed as such to anyone. This is what we mean when we repeat that the question is what matters. The questioning is simply a name for the void address. The celebrated awkwardness [*maladresse*] of philosophy—its misaddress [*maladresse*]—is in its essence, the non-address, the absence of address. All philosophical texts are in *poste restante*, and it is necessary to know in advance that something can be found there even though it has not been *sent* to you.

Secondly, I call the transmission of philosophy the operation by which it propagates itself on the basis of the void address. It is well known that this propagation is carried out by those, few in number, who, against all evidence, decide that it is they who have been addressed. Thus, those who endure the void of the address form themselves in such a void. This small number never constitutes a public, as a public is always precisely that which fills the address. Philosophy cannot be transmitted by way of this filling [*par les voies de ce plein*], of this over-filling [*trop-plein*]. As always, its transmission is not at all dependent on the extension of a public, but on the figure, restrained and unfigurable [*infigurable*], of the disciple. The disciple is whoever endures this coinciding with the void address. The disciple knows it does not constitute a public but supports a transmission.

Lastly, I call inscription of philosophy all that changes the void of the address into a subsisting mark, all that philosophy writes. In itself, philosophy, as void address, is subtracted from the written, without being for all that devoted to the voice. Philosophy is that which, detained in the void of the address, obeys the temporalized injunction of the categories of being and event, on this side of the voice and the written. It is by remaining this side of the voice and the written that we name as always, thought, to which the void of the address accords. Inscription is the marking of this void, the interminable procedure of a subsisting suture with the subsistent, the effectivity of the void. Unlike the address, which is void, and transmission, which is proposed to some-ones, inscription is open and offered to all.

Notice that it may well be that the knot of which I speak cannot be knotted. If this is the case—henceforth undecidable—there may be some philosophies, but not *a* philosophy. Only the knot confers on philosophy the historicity of its existence. Only it decides that there is some philosophy that takes the form of a philosophy.

The historicity of philosophy thus demands that there be an address (in general this is covered by the proper name of a philosopher); that there are disciples (in general covered by the proper names of other philosophers who, when the time comes, after having endured the place of the void, will produce such a place); and that there are books, generally covered by those public instances which are the sequence of commentary, publications and reprints. These three instances are also that of the void (the address), that of the finite (its disciples), and that of the infinite (the inscription and its gloss).

Clearly, this knot is Borromean and therefore we consider it foundational to the *historicity* of philosophy. Without the knot, philosophy, reduced to the void address, would be only the point of indistinction between thought and being. In fact only the inscription collects, within time, the address and the transmission. And since it is only encountered in the book, inscription is that by which a new disciple comes to the void site prescribed by an ancient address. This book is encountered precisely as that which is offered to all, and which accords to the infinity of inscription. It is no less clear that only the address brings together transmission and inscription, since only it attests to that for which a disciple is a disciple, the void place that the disciple has occupied, and whose inscription perpetuates existence.

It is thus the void which, here as elsewhere, sutures the finitude of transmission to the infinity of inscription. And finally it is certain that it is solely transmission that assembles the address and the inscription, since the book can only be written from *the view-point of the disciple*, even if, in the circumstances of writing, the master makes a disciple of himself. But very often as we know (look at Aristotle, or Hegel, or Kojève or even Leibniz, or Nietzsche, or Husserl, check their archives, the transcripts of their lessons, the severe disorder of their notes and papers) very often, yes, it is the finitude of disciples that exposes the void address of philosophy to the infinity of inscription.

A philosophical institution is a proposition for the preservation of the knot. It is not the guardian of philosophy but of its historicity. Therefore it is the guardian of philosophies. It is the knotted plural of philosophies as resistance in time, which often means: resistance to the times.

What secondary imperatives are required by the first? What are the functions and the limits of an institution for philosophy such that, in accordance with its destination, it preserves the Borromean knot of the address, transmission and inscription: which is also the knot of the void, the finite and the infinite?

The first derived imperative is evidently that such ins
pate in the detection and existence of the three strands
separately. And this, if I can say so, without separating t

In what is of concern to the address, which is the sut
to being, there is nothing of the institution. This is becau
not those for which, as Parmenides says, 'The Same, indeed is at once to
think and to be'.[2]

This 'same' that is 'at once' is undoubtedly the mark of the void, and
the void is precisely definable as that whose institution is impossible. So
while we understand it as false that nature abhors a void, we are certain
that institutions do have this horror. Their unceasing tendency is toward
over-filling [*trop-plein*], and this is precisely what gives them their extremely limited natural allure.

But what the philosophical institution can and thus must do for philosophers is protect them from their misaddress, which is a consequence
of their void address. It must give the void an address proper to it; it must
be the address of the void address. What this means is that this institution must authorize him to find himself at home in it, he who nothing
registers [*recommande*] and, above all, is neither registered [*recommandé*] nor
registrable [*recommendable*].[3] How can this institution recognize whoever
presumes to philosophize, and therefore has no address? It cannot, it can
only address them. It should, quite simply, test this indiscernible, providing its address. Permit me to call this first function of an institution for
philosophy a *poste restante* function. It is thanks to this institution, contrary
to that which goes by PTT, that our unregistered mail chances to arrive
at its destination.[4]

---

2. TN. I have chosen to use the translation made by Louise Burchill in her translation of
Badiou's book on Deleuze. It better accords with the lines that immediately follow. For an
explanation of Badiou's usage of this excerpt from Parmenides see Louise Burchill's note
in *Deleuze: The Clamor of Being*, Minneapolis, University of Minnesota Press, 2000, p. 137,
note 1 to chapter 7.

3. TN. In this passage Badiou is playing on the ambiguity of the French term *recommande*.
It is obviously meant to align with the metaphor of the post-office and so we have chosen
to use the term 'register'.

4. TN. PTT is the acronym for *Poste, Téléphone et Télécommunications* the state service co-
ordinating delivery and maintenance of these services. Once upon a time Australia had
an equivalent: The PMG, Post-Master General, affectionately known as Pigs, Monkeys
and Gorillas. Today, broken in pieces, dispersed, neo-liberalized, the Pigs, Monkeys and
Gorillas goes by a name somehow meant to evoke intensities, flows and desirings for astral
travel and all the while free-floating on the stock exchange—'Telstra'!

In that which concerns transmission, it is clear that the institution must multiply the chances of having disciples occupy the void place of address. It must proliferate disciples. It is necessary therefore that it is an open house, vacant, where those whose destinies are tied to the void of a singular address can pass through. What this 'general pass' declares is that there is no criterion for presence, or, as is the rule at the *College Interna-tional*, that participation in the seminars is absolutely free, that *closed* semi-nars do not exist. Permit me to call the second function of a philosophical institution a 'clearing-house' function.

Finally, in that which concerns the inscription, it is certain that the resources of the ordinary edition cannot suffice. These editions reason in terms of the public, not to say of publicity, and these do not conform to the essence of philosophic inscription, whose infinity is measured in cen-turies, and is not automatically exhausted in its first print run. In essence my claim is that an institution for philosophy prints, edits and distributes collections, editorials, marks and books. And as it is about the editing of that which is not registered or registerable, of distributing void addresses and of the obscure turmoil of disciples, all of this being for the public incalculable and dodgy [*louche*], at least this is what we hope. Permit me then to name this third function of a philosophical institution as having the function of a 'clandestine print-works'.

Such an institution organizes at its centre a *poste restante*, a clearing-house and a clandestine print-works.

But its second great task is to be the guardian of these three stands of the knot, tightening, while not, under the pretence of its disparate func-tions, cutting this borromean knot of the historicity of philosophy. For this, it is necessary that the guarantors of the institution, those who con-stitute its kernel always exist, and are themselves able to circulate while attending to the knot; that they have a care and concern for its 'holding together'; that they comprehend for themselves the paradoxical connec-tions between address and transmission, inscription and address, and in-scription and transmission. And that what they know to articulate is not the finitude of needs and opportunities, but the triplet of the void, the finite and the infinite. What they really desire to be, without discontinuity or visible caesura, are inspectors of the *poste restante*, tenants of the clear-ing-house and printers working in secret. I can hardly see for this task any-thing other than a kind of philosophers' convention, 'convention' being understood in the sense given to it by the people of the revolution of 1792; itself a collective body captive to the seriousness of the decision, which is as such the place of the decision, and which at the same time designates great committees, invested with great powers, all of which the convention oversees with gravity. The law of such an assembly cannot be that of majorities, for this law is that of the knot, of the historicity of philosophy, the law of the *current moment* for philosophy. Only this philosopher's convention can avoid the incessant cutting of the knot, the ruin of all historicity, the risk of the *flattening* [*mise à plat*] of philosophy, in short, that terrible and classic instant where the institution that was for philosophy deviates into anti-philosophy. We know the name of this danger: it is liberalism, which seeks to undo everything and by this ensnares all in dispersion, competition, opinion and the despotism of the public and publicity.

On one of his good days, Nietzsche noted that the laws were not made against the criminals, but against the innovators. Undoubtedly the inspectors of the *poste restante* stray, the tenants of the clearing house leave and the clandestine printers are generally taken for criminals. Still, it is these innovators that a philosophical institution requires, and thus they are at risk of falling under the blows of the law, including those which the institution considers as its own necessary safeguards. But the conventional rigorous discipline—convent-like even—of a philosophical institution, supposing it were good, connects what it is to a knot, that one must guard, tighten, and must itself be retied with new combinations of the void, of the finite and of the infinite, which are themselves a cruel discipline put to the service of such innovators. Undoubtedly only chance can provide it. A good philosophical institution will therefore be that which proposes, in opposition to the criminal, who for philosophy can only be the declared enemy of all thought and therefore of all being, the very broadest power of chance, that is to say the void power of the address.

Let us conclude as one should, with a wish: when some philosophical institution is beginning to form its conventions and to settle as the new guardian of the knot, when philosophy is submitted to the ordeal of a collective decision, let us wish that no throw of the dice from the criminals can abolish the chance of its rare occurrence.

Translated by A. J. Bartlett

science

3

The Law of the Subject:
Alain Badiou, Luitzen Brouwer and the Kripkean
Analyses of Forcing and the Heyting Calculus

Zachary Fraser

'There are two labyrinths of the human mind: one concerns
the composition of the continuum, and the other the nature
of freedom, and both spring from the same source—the
infinite'.[1]

—G.W. Leibniz

One of the central tasks of Badiou's *Being and Event* is to elaborate a
theory of the subject in the wake of an axiomatic identification of ontology
with mathematics, or, to be precise, with the Zermelo-Fraenkel axiomatization of classical set theory. In accordance with this thesis, every presentation of what there is—every *situation*—is held to be thought 'in its being'
when thought has succeeded in formalizing that situation as a mathematical *set*.[2] The formalization of the subject, however, proceeds somewhat

---

1. Gottfried Wilhelm Freiherr von Leibniz, 'On Freedom', in G.H.R. Parkinson (ed.),
Philosophical Writings, trans. Mary Morris and G.H.R. Parkinson, London, J.M. Dent &
Sons, Ltd., 1973, p. 107.

2. cf. Alain Badiou, *Being and Event*, trans. Oliver Feltham, London, Continuum, 2005, p.
130: 'Set theory, considered as an adequate thinking of the pure multiple, or of the presentation of presentation, *formalizes* any situation whatsoever insofar as it reflects the latter's
being as such; that is, the multiple of multiples which makes up any presentation. If, within
this framework, one wants to formalize *a* particular situation, then it is best to consider *a*
set such that its characteristics—which, in the last resort, are expressible in the logic of the
sign of belonging alone, $\in$—are comparable to that of the structured presentation—the
situation—in question'. Further citations of this source will be abbreviated BE.

differently. Badiou insists that set theory alone cannot furnish a complete theory of the subject, and that for this task one needs the essentially non-mathematical concepts of time and the event. It is nevertheless possible, Badiou maintains, to determine the set-theoretical form of the subject's ontological infrastructure—the form of its 'facticity', to borrow a term from Sartre.[3] In *Being and Event*, the sought-after structures are declared to be found in the two concepts that Paul J. Cohen develops in his work on the continuum hypothesis: *genericity* and *forcing*. In a nutshell, a *generic subset* is one that cannot be discerned by any formula expressible in the model of which it is a subset. Badiou employs the notion of a generic subset to formalize the ontological structure of what he calls 'truths'. A truth, in brief, is a multiplicity that is fully immanent to the situation of which it is a truth, but which is not individuated as an element of the situation, and cannot be discerned by the linguistic and epistemic regimes proper to the situation in question. The point at which the concept of truth diverges from the concept of the generic consists in the fact that the elements of a truth will have been connected, through the work of a subject, to an *event* (*i.e.*, a rare ontological dysfunction in which the immanent consistency of a situation is partially unhinged). The subject is conceived as a temporally unfolding, but always finite, *part* of such a truth—which is, in itself, always infinite (as a necessary precondition of its genericity). *Forcing* is a relation defined between certain sets belonging to the model in which the generic subset is articulated, and statements bearing upon an *extension* of this model, constructed on the basis of the generic subset in question. For Badiou, forcing expresses the 'law of the subject', the abstract form of the activity through which the subject transforms the situation on the basis of the truth in which she participates. These concepts provide Badiou with the mathematical framework of a vision of the subject as a figure initially 'subtracted' from language and from knowledge, but whose acts will come to have a transformative effect on both through its fidelity to the truth that it bears.

---

3. Historically, the term 'facticity' was first brought into philosophical currency through Martin Heidegger's early work. The sense in which I employ it here, however, is essentially Sartrean. The facticity of the for-itself (roughly: the subject) is the for-itself 'insofar as it *is*', which is to say, abstracted from its nihilating and transcending activity. See Jean-Paul Sartre, *Being and Nothingness*, trans. Hazel Barnes, New York, Philosophical Library, 1956, Part II, Chapter I, § II, pp. 79-84. Likewise, the being of the Badiousian subject is schematized by ontology as a finite part of a generic subset, but the subject must nevertheless be thought as transcending this ontological base; it is 'always in non-existent excess over its being', BE p. 235.

Badiou was not the first to conceive of the subject in this way; we find a strikingly analogous doctrine of the subject expressed in the work of Luitzen Egbertus Jan Brouwer.[4] Brouwer, too, envisions the subject as a temporal process expressed in mathematical concatenations subtracted from law and language, and whose manifestations 'within the bounds and in the forms peculiar to this life are irruptions of Truth'.[5] For Brouwer, the truth borne by the subject is none other than temporal unfolding of mathematics itself—or, rather, mathematics as it *ought* to be understood, once it is recognized in its proper essence as an autonomous subjective construction. This recognition necessitates a thorough transfiguration of existing mathematics, and results in a new discipline of mathematical thought which Brouwer calls 'intuitionism'. As Brouwer once remarked, some time into the course of this project,

> The Intuitionist intervention has had far-reaching consequences for mathematics. Indeed, if the Intuitionist insights prevail, considerable parts of the mathematical structure built so far are bound to collapse, and a new structure will have to be erected of a wholly new style and character; even the parts that remain will require thorough reconstruction.[6]

An inevitable result of this intervention is that, in the field deployed by the intuitionist subject, much of the classical apparatus in which Badiou

---

4. I am aware of only one other discussion in print on the relations between the thoughts of Badiou and Brouwer. It consists in a brief but insightful endnote to Peter Hallward's *Badiou: A Subject to Truth*, and is worth reprinting here in full:

> Badiou's vehement opposition to intuitionism obscures the several things he has in common with Brouwer's original orientation. Like Badiou, Brouwer insists that 'there are no non-experienced truths' (Brouwer, 'Consciousness, Philosophy and Mathematics', in *Collected Works*, vol.1, p. 488). Like Badiou, Brouwer firmly 'separates mathematics from mathematical language, in particular from the phenomena of language which are described by theoretical logic' ('Historical Background', pp. 509-10). Like Badiou, Brouwer conceives of genuine thought as subtraction from the petty negotiation of mundane interests. He seeks 'liberation from participation in cooperative trade and from intercourse presupposing *plurality of mind*' (p. 487, [my emphasis]). Also like Badiou, Brouwer pronounces the worldly calculation of 'security' to be unworthy of thought, and argues that any genuine philosophy works against 'cooperation' with the way of the world: 'In particular, [philosophy] should not cooperate with the state' (p. 487). Hallward, *Badiou: A Subject to Truth*, Minneapolis, University of Minnesota Press, 2003, p. 379, n.22.

5. L.E.J. Brouwer, 'Life, Art and Mysticism', in *Collected Works, Vol. 1*, Arend Heyting (ed.), Amsterdam, North-Holland Publishing Co., 1975, p. 7.

6. Brouwer, 'Mathematics, Science and Language', in Paolo Mancosu (ed.), *From Brouwer to Hilbert*, Oxford, Oxford University Press, 1998, p. 52.

articulates the material foundation of his doctrine of the subject is dissolved. Neither the classical 'fidelity' of deduction nor the Cantorian doctrine of actual and extensionally determined infinities survives intact. In intuitionistic mathematics, mathematical existence becomes inseparably fused with subjective construction, and mathematical veracity becomes one with the demonstrative trajectory of the intuitionist subject.

Brouwer's vision of the nature of mathematical reality is, indeed, in stark opposition to Badiou's entire architectonic. In the last instance, however, this opposition boils down to a single point, concerning the place of the subject. Whereas Badiou axiomatically places mathematical reality *before* the subject, insofar as mathematical reality is the very form of presentation in general, the intuitionist subject *generates* this reality through the course of its temporal existence. Unlike Badiou's professedly materialist project, Brouwer conceives both mathematics and its subject along thoroughly idealist lines: rather than being a diagonal procedure imbricated in an already-existent, mathematically formalized situation, the subject is the generator of the situation in which it bears its truth.

When I say that the difference between the two theories of the subject is primarily a difference concerning the *place* of the subject, I mean this quite literally. As will be seen, both thinkers envision the *form* of the subject in strikingly similar terms. Everything hinges on the precise manner in which the subject is positioned with respect to the field of mathematical intelligibility, and on the precise orientation that this positioning gives to the closely interwoven themes of the subtraction from language and the procedural bearing of truth. We would remain in the dark, however, and possess little more than rather vague intuitions about this relation between the two theories, were the stage for their genuine encounter not presented to us by Saul Kripke's groundbreaking work in intuitionist semantics. In his 1963 paper, entitled 'Semantical Analysis of Intuitionistic Logic I', Kripke provides a model-theoretic interpretation of intuitionist logic. Among the results presented in that paper is an illustration of how Cohen's forcing-relation is isomorphic to intuitionistic entailment so long as the forcing conditions are not generic, in which case the relation behaves classically (obeying the Law of the Excluded Middle). The genericity of the sequence of forcing conditions, of course, is contingent on their forming a completed, infinite set. This does not take place at any point in the irreducibly temporal procedure by which the Badiousian subject faithfully adumbrates its truth.

The purpose of the following enquiry is to elucidate the intuitionist theory of the subject and the logical revolt that it proposes in mathematics, and to shed light on the enigmatic relations that obtain between the intuitionist and the Badiousian doctrines of the subject, particularly with respect to their logics, and the aforementioned isomorphy that Kripke discovered between them. I will begin with Brouwer and his cause.

§ 2

Near the beginning of the twentieth century, classical mathematics found itself beset with a number of antinomies, irrupting amidst efforts to provide analysis with a rigorous foundation in mathematical logic and a general theory of sets. The ensuing 'foundational crisis' became, in Badiou's eyes, an archetypical *event* for mathematics. A number of distinct interventions were taken up in response, each prescribing a careful reworking of mathematical 'fidelity', that is, of the disciplinary requirements necessary in order to preserve the integrity and consistency of mathematical truth. Among the more prominent schools of thought were that of logicism, originally headed by Frege and later championed by the young Russell and Whitehead in their *Principia Mathematica*, and the formalist school, whose greatest light was (and remains) David Hilbert. As Michael Dummett recounts, both sought to remedy the critical anomalies that had surfaced by supplying classical mathematics, as it currently existed, with a rigorous, but supplementary, foundation. The logicists would do this by producing a new logical infrastructure for mathematics, such that the latter would come to be understood as an extension of logic itself, as 'the manhood of logic' as Russell once quipped.[7] The formalists sought to supplement mathematics through a painstaking process of axiomatizing the existing mathematical disciplines and installing the resulting axiomatics within a 'metamathematical' superstructure in which their consistency would be evaluated.[8] Neither of these interventions cut as deeply into the

---

7. 'Mathematics and logic, historically speaking, have been entirely distinct studies. Mathematics has been connected with science, logic with Greek. But both have developed in modern times: logic has become more mathematical and mathematics has become more logical. The consequence is that it has now become wholly impossible to draw a line between the two; in fact, the two are one. They differ as boy and man: logic is the youth of mathematics and mathematics is the manhood of logic'. Bertrand Russell, *Introduction to Mathematical Philosophy*, London, George Allen, 1963, p. 194.

8. Both of these programmes, incidentally, have since disbanded. 'In both cases', Dummett recounts,

> the philosophical system, considered as a unitary theory, collapsed when the respective mathematical programmes were shown to be incapable of fulfillment: in Frege's case, by Russell's discovery of the set-theoretic paradoxes; in Hilbert's, by Gödel's

tissue of mathematical practice as the one carried out by Brouwer.[9] As
Dummett observes,

> Intuitionism took the fact that classical mathematics appeared to
> stand in need of justification, not as a challenge to construct such
> a justification, direct or indirect, but as a sign that something was
> amiss with classical mathematics. From an intuitionistic standpoint,
> mathematics, when correctly carried on, would not need any
> justification from without, a buttress from the side or a foundation
> from below: it would wear its own justification on its face.[10]

What is amiss in classical mathematics, Brouwer conjectured, is a clear
ontological insight into the nature of mathematical truth and existence.
Such insight has been systematically obscured by a logico-linguistic apparatus that has been abstracted from properly mathematical relations
obtaining within certain finite systems, and, by force of habit, come to
acquire the authority and prestige of a set of *a priori* laws.[11] In time, these
laws had come to usurp genuine mathematical construction, and men
had come to believe that mathematical truths could be arrived at, and
mathematical existences disclosed, by what Mill once called an 'artful
manipulation of language'.[12] Classical mathematics had mistaken the
shadow for the prey; thought had subordinated itself to theoretical logic,
and the mathematical study of infinite systems proceeded according to
laws appropriate only for finite collections. Such is Brouwer's account of
the road leading to the paradoxes.[13]

---

second incompleteness theorem. Of course, since the mathematical programmes were
formulated in vague terms, such as 'logic' and 'finitistic' the fatal character of these
discoveries was not inescapably apparent straight away; but in both cases it eventually
became apparent, so that, much as we now owe both to Frege and Hilbert, it would
now be impossible for anyone to declare himself a whole-hearted follower of either.
Michael Dummett, *Elements of Intuitionism*, Oxford, Clarendon Press, 1977, p. 2.

9. For an outstanding historical account of the intuitionist intervention through the lens
of the Kuhnian theory of science, see Bruce Pourciau, 'Intuitionism as a (Failed) Kuhnian
Revolution in Mathematics', *Studies in the History and Philosophy of Science*, vol. 31, no.2, 2000,
pp. 297-339. For a discussion on the relations between Kuhnian revolutions and Badiousian events, see Peter Hallward, *Badiou: A Subject to Truth*, pp. 210-214.

10. Dummett, *Elements of Intuitionism*, p. 2.

11. cf. Brouwer, 'Consciousness, Philosophy & Mathematics', in *Collected Works*, p. 492.

12. As quoted in Gottlob Frege, *The Foundations of Arithmetic*, trans. J.L. Austin, New York,
Harper and Bros., 1960, §16, p. 22.

13. See Brouwer, 'Historical Background, Principles and Methods of Intuitionism', in *Collected Works*, p. 508-515.

§ 3

Brouwer's intervention began with the gesture that he would retrospectively refer to as the First Act of Intuitionism. The First Act of Intuitionism, in Brouwer's words,

> *completely separates mathematics from mathematical language, in particular from the phenomena of language which are described by theoretical logic, and recognizes that intuitionist mathematics is an essentially languageless activity of the mind having its origin in the perception of a move of time, i.e. of the falling apart of a life moment into two distinct things, one of which gives way to the other, but is retained by memory. If the two-ity thus born is divested of all quality, there remains the empty form of the common substratum of all two-ities. It is this common substratum, this empty form, which is the basic intuition of mathematics.*[14]

The First Act seeks to wrest mathematical thought away from the reign of language, and found it in the subject, whose primordial form is given by a temporally conditioned 'two-ity'. The phenomenon of the two-ity, is understood as the primitive intuition of *'invariance in change'* or of *'unity in multitude'*[15] that manifests itself in time. This phenomenon is absolutely irreducible to more primitive terms; neither the One nor the subject itself is prior to it. Brouwer is quite explicit on this point, arguing that it would be inconceivable to posit the One as primary, in that any pretension of generating either a thinking subject or the field of numericity on the basis of a single term must begin by installing this term in a duality that exceeds it.[16] On the basis of the twoity unfolds the very being of the subject, whose initial trajectory consists in the articulation of the infinitely proceeding sequence of natural numbers, and of the laws which govern this sequence. It is here that arithmetic has its origin, as a movement wholly interior to the trajectory of the subject.

The absolutely primordial character of arithmetic is essential for Brouwer. Arithmetic, as Brouwer understands it, is virtually consubstan-

---

14. Brouwer, 'Historical Background, Principles and Methods of Intuitionism', in *Collected Works*, p. 508. Brouwer's italics.

15. Brouwer, *Collected Works*, p. 96.

16. 'The first act of construction has *two* discrete things thought together (also according to CANTOR, Vortage auf der Naturforscherversammlung in Kassel 1903); F. Meyer (Verhandl. internat. Math. Congr. Heidelberg 1904, p. 678) says *one* thing is sufficient, because the circumstance that I think of it can be added as a second thing; this is false, for exactly this *adding* (i.e. setting it while the former is retained) *presupposes the intuition of two-ity*; only afterwards this simplest mathematical system is projected on the first thing and the *ego which thinks the thing*', *Collected Works*, p. 96, n.1.

tial with the subject's very existence. In a few of his more speculative texts, Brouwer insists that prior to the apprehension of the two-ity in which arithmetic is grounded, the subject as such has not yet taken form.[17] Brouwer legitimates the subtraction of mathematical thought from language by appealing to the absolute *priority* of subjective mathematical construction to the installation of the subject in language. Language itself is conceived as something entirely secondary to the existence of singular subjects; in its essence, it is a vast apparatus of 'will-transmission', and where it attains an appearance of stability and rigour—as in the 'artificial' languages employed by the sciences, including mathematical logic—Brouwer sees only a crystallization of the social bond, a 'subtle form of ideology'.[18] Insofar as mathematics presents itself as a rigorous and highly structured form of thought that is prior to and eludes the ideological apparatus of language, it is, moreover, 'never without a social cause'.[19] When conducted rightly—intuitionistically—this cause is essentially subtractive, insofar as it restores a rigorous freedom to thought that 'transgresses the straightjacket of language'.[20] When mathematical practice is falsely subordinated to linguistic artifice, however, the causes it serves become bound up in the apparatuses of power, making these apparatuses all the more 'cunning'. Along these lines, Brouwer seeks to invest intuitionism with an ethical impetus.

§ 4

Any reader familiar with *Being and Event* will immediately notice several points of resonance between Brouwer's intervention and the Badiousian theory of the subject. Gathered together in a single statement of intervention we find the familiar themes of a subject subtracted from language, an irreducible and originary Two, and a 'discipline of time'. It will be possible to shed more light on these similarities once we have completed our analysis. For now, let us make note of a few key points.

First of all, the basis for the intuitionist subject's subtraction from language lies in the priority of subjective mathematical constructions to any linguistic artifice. Language only comes to mathematics 'after the fact', and 'plays no other part than an efficient, but never infallible or exact,

---

17. cf. 'Consciousness, Philosophy and Mathematics', in *Collected Works*, pp. 480-494.
18. Vladimir Tasić, *The Mathematical Roots of Postmodern Thought*, Oxford, Oxford University Press, 2001, p. 48. Tasić provides a well-informed and lucid account of Brouwer's theory of language in §2 of chapter 4 of this text.
19. Brouwer, 'Signific Dialogues', in *Collected Works*, p. 450.
20. Tasić, *The Mathematical Roots of Postmodern Thought*, p. 47.

technique for memorizing mathematical constructions, and for suggesting them to others; so that mathematical language by itself can never create new mathematical systems'.[21] By contrast, Badiou conceives of the subtraction from language in entirely inverted terms, with the subject only coming into effect amidst an already existent linguistic apparatus. This subject, moreover, subtracts itself from language, at least in part, by means of language, in a process of diagonalization across the field of linguistic determination. For the Badiousian subject, the subtraction from language is grounded entirely a posteriori. For all his insight into a certain ethic that undeniably underlies Badiou's thought, Hallward's diagnosis of the Badiousian subject as a 'singularity' that 'creates the proper medium of its existence'[22] is thus somewhat inexact. This title is better reserved for the Brouwerian subject, the 'creative subject' of intuitionistic mathematics, who, as we will see, generates the medium of mathematical existence in a process reminiscent of the Pythagorean cosmogony, where the 'Indefinite Dyad', in a dialectic with the One, gives rise to the entire universe of Number. Unlike the Pythagorean doctrine, of course, the 'intuitionist cosmogony' is immaterial, subjectively generated, and possesses the crucial structural difference of declaring the Dyad prior to the One.

Badiou's divergence from Brouwer, with respect to the subtraction from language of the truth-bearing subject, is intimately bound up with one of the cardinal ambitions of Badiou's project: namely, to re-envision the concept of the subject in a manner 'homogeneous' with the forms that it has taken in our era,[23] which Badiou declares 'a second epoch of the doctrine of the Subject' (BE 3). The subject that is presented to us in this epoch, claims Badiou,

> is no longer the founding subject, centered and reflexive, whose theme runs from Descartes to Hegel and which remains legible in Marx and Freud (in fact, in Husserl and Sartre). The contemporary Subject is void, cleaved, a-substantial, and ir-reflexive. Moreover, one can only suppose its existence in the context of particular processes whose conditions are rigorous. (BE 3)

---

21. Brouwer, 'Historical Background, Principles and Methods of Intuitionism', in *Collected Works*, p. 141.

22. Peter Hallward, 'Alain Badiou et la déliason absolue', in Charles Ramon (ed.), *Alain Badiou: Penser le multiple: Actes du Colloque de Bourdeaux 21-23 octobre 1999*, Paris, L'Harmattan, 2002, p. 296.

23. cf. BE, p. 2: '[I]t will be agreed that no conceptual apparatus is adequate unless it is homogeneous with the theoretico-practical orientations of the modern doctrine of the subject, itself internal to practical processes (clinical or political)'.

It is not difficult to place the Brouwerian conception of the subject squarely within the 'first epoch', which is essentially the era initiated by Descartes. The Brouwerian subject is essentially prior to the processes in which its active existence is affirmed, and of which it forms the reflexive centre as the guarantor of their validity and existence (*i.e.*, their constructibility). The conditions within which the Badiousian subject is traced come essentially *before* the subject. They are not given for the sake of the subject, nor is the subject conceived as their centre or guarantor. Hence there is a fundamental distinction in Badiou between the temporal unfolding of truth initiated by a subjective procedure and the axiomatically posited ontological context through which the truth-bearing subject proceeds. This context is conceived *classically*, as a pre-given and fully actual backdrop whose ontological structure is expressed by axiomatic set theory. In contrast to the subjective truth procedures that are explored by both thinkers, this axiomatically posited field has no need of being autonomously constructed by a subject of truth in order to be counted as existent. On this point Badiou holds fast to the strictly anti-Cartesian and anti-Kantian theory of science that he advanced in his youth, that 'one establishes oneself within science from the outset. One does not reconstitute it from scratch. One does not found it'.[24] Nothing could be further from the foundationalist thesis that 'mathematics is an essentially languageless activity of the mind having its origin in the perception of a move of time'.[25] Indeed, it is not unreasonable to suggest that it is with Brouwer that mathematics reaches its Cartesian apex. Never before has there been such a concerted effort to derive the entire edifice of mathematics from pure subjective introspection.

Certain resonances may also be traced between the respective roles played by temporality and the figure of the Two in the two doctrines of the subject. Both Badiou and Brouwer understand the subject as a temporally unfolding existence initiated in an irreducible occurrence of the Two. Here Badiou once again reverses the order of Brouwer's terms: the Two erupts into the pre-subjective fabric of consistent presentation in the form of an *event*, and gives rise to both the subject and to the temporality in which the subject articulates and produces the truth that it bears.[26] The

---

24. Alain Badiou, *Le Concept de modèle*, Paris, Maspero, 1972, p. 42.
25. Brouwer, 'Historical Background, Principles and Methods of Intuitionism', in *Collected Works*, p. 510.
26. The structure of the event itself, like its extra-intuitive placement in a pre-subjective and material reality, bears little resemblance to anything encountered in the Intuitionistic field. Formally, it is conceived as a non-wellfounded multiplicity, a multiple whose ele-

essential divergence between the two theoreticians on the question of the twoity that initiates the subject, however, does not primarily concern the order of operations. It more concerns the place of the Two's occurrence. For Badiou, the dyadic event inaugurating the subject is not an omnipresent intuition, common to all experience. It is a rare ontological 'dysfunction' that takes place in the remotest corners of certain concrete situations. Far from being the founding intuition of mathematics, insofar as the event is an ontological dysfunction, it is 'external to the field of mathematical ontology' (BE 184), mathematical ontology being, for Badiou, classical mathematics itself (and particularly set theory). Insofar as every subject is initiated by an event, the event's exteriority to mathematics separates Badiou's theory of the subject from his mathematical ontology. The Badiousian subject is thus *not* primarily a mathematical structure, any more than mathematics is a subjective construction. Of course, as I have already stated, Badiou does seek to determine what is mathematically structured *in* the subject, but this cannot coincide with the Badiousian subject itself.

§ 5

Before proceeding any further in a comparison of the two doctrines of the subject, we must examine the intuitionist theory of constructive mathematics in greater detail, for it is there that the logic and the structure of the Brouwerian subject, and the intuitionist theory of truth, are deployed in full. Let us begin by examining what Brouwer means by *mathematical construction*. The simplest way of doing this is to contrast intuitionist mathematics with its classical counterpart.

Among the theorems of classical mathematics, the intuitionist recognizes as valid only those which can be made evident through explicit and

---

ments consist of those of its site of occurrence X and of itself (Badiou outlines its form in the inscription $e_x = \{x \in X, e_x\}$). Such a multiple, Badiou observes, is manifestly non-constructible, for the self-membership that characterizes the event requires a certain 'antecedence to self' that is 'constructively impossible' (BE 304); one can construct the evental multiple only on condition that one has already done so. Heyting explicitly rules out the possibility of non-wellfounded sets (or 'species') in intuitionism, given that '[c]ircular definitions are excluded by the condition that the members of a species S must be definable independently of the definition of S; this condition is obvious from the constructive point of view. It suggests indeed an ordination of species which resembles the hierarchy of types', Arend Heyting, *Intuitionism: An Introduction*, 3rd ed., Amsterdam, North-Holland Publishing, 1971, p. 38. My focus, here, however, is not so much the (para)ontological substructure of the event, but what Badiou alternatively calls its 'essence' or its 'position', and names the 'Two' (cf. BE, 206).

finitely given algorithms. In other words an assertion can only be held to be true once one has provided 'an intuitively acceptable proof, that is, a certain kind of *mental* construction'.[27] Provability, truth, and existence are, in intuitionistic mathematics, inseparably fused together. The intuitionist decision to interpret mathematical being as, in every case, a matter of subjective construction is made in order to clear away the metaphysical trappings within which classical mathematics (as intuitionism understands it) has become ensnared. These trappings, moreover, are held to be responsible for the intuitive obscurity and the antinomies that have come to haunt the mathematical tradition. As Arend Heyting has it,

> [i]f 'to exist' does not mean 'to be constructed', it must have some metaphysical meaning. It cannot be the task of mathematics to investigate this meaning or to decide whether it is tenable or not. We have no objection against a mathematician privately admitting any metaphysical theory he likes, but Brouwer's program entails that we study mathematics as something simpler, more immediate than metaphysics. In the study of mental mathematical constructions 'to exist' must be synonymous with 'to be constructed'.[28]

What the intuitionist mission of distilling mathematical existence down to what is subjectively constructible gains for mathematics in clarity, it looses in scope, and 'full of pain, the mathematician sees the greatest part of his towering edifice dissolve in fog'.[29] The intuitionist, content to pluck out the eye that offends him, accepts the ensuing 'mutilation of mathematics' as a price that must be paid if mathematics is to remain faithful to the intuition which produced it. 'It can also be seen', reflects Heyting, 'as the excision of noxious ornaments, beautiful in form, but hollow in substance'.[30]

For the intuitionist, the identification of existence and subjective construction deploys a field of mathematical thought in which 'axioms become illusory'.[31] Where anything resembling axiomatization appears in intuitionist mathematics, it is only to provide a heuristically useful, but essentially secondary analytical task—as in Heyting's 1925 axiomatization of intuitionistic projective geometry (which was, incidentally, his dissertation project and was written under Brouwer's supervision). The intuitionist 'disaxiomatization' of mathematics marks another strong divergence

---

27. Dummett, *Elements of Intuitionism*, p. 7.
28. Heyting, *Intuitionism*, p. 2.
29. Weyl, 'On the new foundational crisis of mathematics', in Mancosu, p. 136
30. Heyting, *Intuitionism*, p. 11.
31. Brouwer, 'The Effect of Intuitionism on Classical Algebra of Logic', in *Collected Works*, p. 551.

from Badiou's thought. While Badiou, like Brouwer, insists on liberating mathematics from the superstitious supposition that it concerns objects that are 'external' to mathematics, and identifying mathematical truth with the very movement of its thought, for the former, the axiom is precisely the point at which mathematical intuition in concentrated. Taking a position which he sees himself as sharing with both Gödel and Plato, Badiou insists that what we must understand by 'intuition' is precisely 'a decision of inventive thought with regard to the intelligibility of axioms'.[32] For Badiou, the decisional aspect of mathematical intuition is primary and continuous, and so

> it is pointless to try to reduce it to protocols of construction or externally regulated procedures. On the contrary, the constraints of construction (often and confusingly referred to as 'intuitionist' constraints, which is inappropriate given that the genuine advocate of intuition is the Platonist) should be subordinated to the freedoms of thinking decision.[33]

Badiou's identification of his position as a 'Platonism' deserves some comment here. Badiou's reading of Plato is at quite a distance from the 'platonism' that haunts the textbooks of the philosophy of mathematics (as well as a number of the intuitionists' essays—Dummett's text is a good example[34]). This textbook platonism, as Badiou sees it, simply gets Plato's thought wrong,

> because it presupposes that the 'Platonist' espouses a distinction between the internal and the external, knowing subject and known 'object'; a distinction which is utterly foreign to the genuine Platonic framework. [...] Plato's fundamental concern is a desire to declare the immanent identity, the co-belonging of the knowing mind and the known, their essential ontological commensurability.[35]

In many significant respects (which seem to have been as unclear to Badiou in his appraisal of intuitionism as they have been to Dummett in his appraisal of Platonism[36]), Badiou's version of Platonism mirrors the intui-

---

32. Badiou, 'Platonism and Mathematical Ontology', in *Theoretical Writings*, ed. and trans. Ray Brassier and Alberto Toscano, London, Continuum, 2003, p. 52.

33. Badiou, 'Platonism and Mathematical Ontology', p. 52.

34. For a clear example of the 'textbook platonism' that Badiou is opposing, cf. Dummett's synopsis of platonism on page 7 of *Elements of Intuitionism*: '[T]he platonist picture is of a realm of mathematical reality, existing objectively and independently of our knowledge, which renders our statements true or false'.

35. Dummett, *Elements of Intuitionism*, p. 49.

36. In a discussion of intuitionistic logic that I will examine later in this essay, Badiou

tionist vision of mathematics. It is nevertheless clear that something quite different is at stake in Badiou's understanding of the term 'intuition'. In the last analysis, this difference has everything to do with the fundamental unity of intuitionist mathematics, and its rootedness is the primordial intuition of the twoity. The movement of truth proper to intuitionism consists entirely in unfolding the truth of the twoity, that is, of time. Decisions which do not follow from this original intuition are not called for; when new decisions are necessitated, it is to more faithfully express this original ontological event. Cavaillès grasped this dimension of intuitionism quite clearly, when he wrote that for the intuitionist,

> mathematics is an autonomous becoming, 'more an act than a becoming', for which a definition at the origin is impossible but whose moments in their necessary interdependence betray an original essence. From the dyad to the elaborated theories, there is continuity and unpredictability.[37]

Whereas it is the nature of axioms to be, as far as is possible, separable from one another, and thus apprehensible as discrete decisions, every modification imposed upon intuitionist mathematics is prescribed by a fidelity to its 'original essence'. It is thus at least conceptually inadequate to refer to the 'Acts' of intuitionism as axioms in the classical sense. The essential unity that the intuitionist seeks to preserve in rejecting the axiomatic method does not trouble the Badiousian Platonist, however. For Badiou—who sees himself as following in Plato's footsteps on this point—mathematical thought required no greater unity than what is guaranteed for it by the logical exigency of non-contradictority. Against the intuitionist cloverleaf that lashes together being, thought and constructibility, Badiou proposes the classical (or better, Hilbertian) axiom that identifies 'being, thought and *consistency*'.[38] The axiomatic leaps and bounds that defy constructibility do not take leave of this broader sphere, which for the Platonist, Badiou writes, is governed not by an imperative of constructive coherency but by 'that of maximal extension in what can be consistently thought'.[39]

---

writes that 'intuitionism is a prisoner of the empiricist and illusory representation of mathematical *objects*', BE, p. 249.

37. Jean Cavaillès, 'On Logic and the Theory of Science', in Joseph J. Kockelmans and Theodore J. Kisiel (eds.), *Phenomenology and the Natural Sciences*, trans. Theodore J. Kisiel, Evanston, Northwestern University Press, 1970, p. 367.

38. Badiou, 'Platonism and Mathematical Ontology', p. 54. Emphasis added.

39. Badiou, 'Platonism and Mathematical Ontology', p. 54.

One of the most immediate and dramatic consequences of the intuitionist position is a rejection of the Cantorian concept of actually infinite multiplicity, insofar as the existence of such multiplicities can only ever be the thesis of an axiom.[40] Within intuitionist mathematics, where every existence is subjectively constructed by finite means, 'all infinity is potential infinity: there is no completed infinite'.[41] This thesis 'means, simply, that to grasp an infinite structure is to grasp the process which generates it, that to refer to such a structure is to refer to that process, and that to recognize the structure as being infinite is to recognize that the process will not terminate'.[42] Such a thesis sets intuitionism at a clear distance from the set-theoretical underpinnings of Badiou's enterprise, in which the primacy of extensionality and the ubiquity of actual infinities reign supreme. It is interesting to observe, however, that the intuitionists frequently defend this thesis on the same grounds upon which Badiou defends the opposite position, namely, on the grounds that one must not denature the infinite by confusing its essence with that of the finite. For the intuitionist, the Cantorian 'destroys the whole essence of infinity, which lies in the conception of a structure which is always in growth, precisely because the process of construction is never completed;' in speaking of actual infinities, the Cantorian speaks of an infinite process 'as if it were merely a particularly long finite one'.[43] For Badiou, it is the advocates of a strictly potential conception of infinity who denature the infinite by viewing it only through the lens of finitude. Insofar as it 'determines the infinite within the Open, or as the horizonal correlate for a historicity of finitude',[44] the intuitionist disposition, by Badiou's lights, remains enslaved to the Romanticist tradition,[45] a tradition that must be overcome if thought is to unshackle itself from the 'cult of finitude'.

What is at stake in this dispute is, again, the centrality of the subject in the field of mathematical existence. So long as the (finite) subject is conceived as the central guarantor of every mathematical existence, the essence of such existences must be conceived with respect to their relation

---

40. See Meditation 14 of BE.

41. Dummett, *Elements of Intuitionism*, p. 55.

42. Dummett, *Elements of Intuitionism*, p. 56.

43. Dummett, *Elements of Intuitionism*, p. 52.

44. Badiou, 'Philosophy and Mathematics: Infinity and the End of Romanticism', in *Theoretical Writings*, p. 25.

45. For an extended analysis of the relations between Brouwer's intuitionism and the Romantic tradition, see chapter 4 of Vladimir Tasić's *The Mathematical Roots of Postmodern Thought*.

to the subject. From this perspective, the infinite *is* the outstripping of subjective construction. For the Cantorian, the infinite is deployed in its essence irrespective of the subject's position. The subject, here, does not participate in the construction of the infinite, but only its traversal.[46]

§ 6

The intuitionist identification of mathematical existence with construction, and of truth with demonstration, has consequences that penetrate through to the logical structure of mathematical reason itself. Because the intuitionist identifies the truth of a statement with the construction that validates it, and the falsity of a statement with the construction that demonstrates its absurdity, he no longer has any grounds for maintaining that a given statement *A* is either true or false prior to the effectuation of the relevant construction. To uphold the contrary, he would have to maintain that a certain construction had been constructed *prior to its having been constructed*, which is nonsensical.

The most dramatic single effect of this orientation in thought is intuitionism's well-known rejection of the Law of the Excluded Middle (LEM). LEM states that, given a statement *A*, either *A* is true or else ~*A* is true, *tertium non datur*. The proposition '*A* or ~*A*' is thus classically valid for any *A* whatsoever. Within an intuitionistic context—where a statement must be proven if it is to be true—the general assertion, '*A* or ~*A*', 'demands a general method to solve every problem, or more explicitly, a general method which for any proposition **p** yields by specialization either a proof of **p** or a proof of ~**p**. As we do not possess such a method of construction, we have no right to assert the principle'.[47] The intuitionist rejection of LEM entails the rejection of its corollary, the principle of double negation. This principle states that ~~*A* is true if and only if *A* is, and legitimates a

46. cf. Badiou, *Le Nombre et les nombres*, Paris, Éditions du Seuil, 1990, §3.17: 'Even if we can only *traverse* the numeric domain according to laws of progression, of which succession is the most common (but not the only one, far from it), why must it follow that these laws are constitutive of the being of number? It is easy to see why we have to 'pass' from one number to the next, or from a series of numbers to its limit. But it is at the very least imprudent to thereby conclude that number is defined or constituted by such passages. [*sc.* cf. NN, §3.18: "Certainly, the intuitionists adopt this impoverished perspective."] It may well be (and this is my thesis) that number itself *does not pass*, that it is immemorially deployed in a swarming coextensive to its being. [...] For the domain of number is rather an ontological prescription incommensurable to any subject, and immersed in the infinity of infinities'.

47. Heyting, *Intuitionism*, p. 101.

method of argument (quite common in classical mathematics) known as *apogogic* or *indirect* proof, whereby one takes to demonstrating the truth of A by demonstrating the absurdity of the absurdity of A (*i.e.* by demonstrating $\sim\sim A$). While intuitionism rejects the universal validity that classical mathematics gives to LEM and its consequences, it does, nevertheless, admit their legitimacy is certain special circumstances. Firstly, LEM holds for A whenever A is already a negative proposition (say, $A = \sim B$): either $\sim B$ or $\sim\sim B$ must be true, and $\sim\sim\sim B$ implies $\sim B$. This is due to the fact that the intuitionist accepts as self-evident the rule that B implies $\sim\sim B$ as well as the rule that if we have $A \rightarrow B$ then we also have $\sim B \rightarrow \sim A$. Of greater theoretical interest is the fact that LEM is also held to be valid in cases where one is operating in a strictly finite domain. The reason for this is that

> every construction of a bounded finite nature in a finite mathematical system can only be attempted in a finite number of ways, and each attempt can be carried through to completion, or to be continued until further progress is impossible. It follows that every assertion of possibility of a construction of a bounded finite character can be judged. So, in this exceptional case, application of the principle of the excluded third is permissible.[48]

Brouwer argues that the universality and a priority that have long been attributed to LEM are precisely due to habits acquired from reasoning within the bounds of finite situations.[49] Once mathematics turns to the

---

48. Brouwer, 'Historical Background, Principles and Methods of Intuitionism', in *Collected Works*, p. 510.

49. In 'Intuitionist Set Theory', Brouwer claims that LEM and the axiom of solvability (that every problem has a solution),

> are dogmas that have their origin in the practice of first abstracting the system of classical logic from the mathematics of subsets of a definite finite set, and then attributing to this system an a priori existence independent of mathematics, and finally applying it wrongly—on the basis of its reputed a priori nature—to the mathematics of infinite sets. ('Intuitionistic Set Theory', in Mancosu, p. 27, n.4)

Elsewhere, in 'Consciousness, Philosophy and Mathematics', he writes that

> The long belief in the universal validity of the principle of the excluded third in mathematics is considered by intuitionism as a phenomenon of history of civilization of the same kind as the old-time belief in the rationality of π or in the rotation of the firmament on an axis passing through the earth. And intuitionism tries to explain the long persistence of this dogma by two facts: firstly the obvious non-contradictory of the principle for an arbitrary single assertion; secondly the practical validity of the whole of classical logic for an extensive group of *simple every day phenomena*. The latter fact apparently made such a strong impression that the play of thought that classical logic originally was, became a deep-rooted habit of thought which was considered not only

investigation of the infinite—by which Brouwer always means, that which is forever incomplete—LEM immediately loses its intuitive ground.

Badiou devotes a few pages in Meditation 24 to a consideration of the intuitionist rejection of LEM and the correlate principle of double-negation. Badiou's position on this matter is (as one might expect) resolutely classical. His argument proceeds by first assuming the axioms of set theory as the common ground of the debate. Since every set-theoretical proposition is essentially reducible to a statement that is either of the form 'a set x exists, such that…' or of the form 'a set x, such that… does not exist', Badiou argues that to suppose that a certain statement is neither true nor false is to suppose that a certain, determinate multiplicity is neither existent nor non-existent. Such a position is insupportable, Badiou reasons, insofar as we are unable 'to determine, 'between' non-existence and existence, any specific intermediary property, which would provide a foundation for the gap between the negation of non-existence and existence' (BE 250). There is a subtle but significant error here. It lies in taking intuitionist logic to be determinately trivalent, that is, to be a logic with three determinate truth values. Only if this were the case could there be any grounds for rejecting intuitionist logic for want of an ontological 'foundation for the gap' between double negation and assertion. This is to mistake the very nature of the intuitionist identification of truth with demonstration and of existence with subjective construction. For the intuitionist, a negation $(\sim P)$ is founded by a constructive demonstration of absurdity, and an affirmation (P) is founded by a constructive demonstration of veracity. When the intuitionist asserts $\sim\sim P$ but cannot assert P, it is because he has produced a construction demonstrating the absurdity of any construction demonstrating the absurdity of P, but has not (yet) constructively demonstrated P. What we have here is an existential foundation for $\sim\sim P$ alongside a *lack of foundation* for P. The existential correlate of the logical gap between $\sim\sim P$ and P is not an determinate intermediary between existence and non-existence, but a simple *indetermination* of existence, by which the intuitionist always means subjective construction. Badiou elides this point by situating the argument from the outset in the context of axiomatic set theory, where existence and non-existence are distributed universally and bivalently.

This elision may be permissible within the context of Badiou's enterprise, which takes as its ontological backdrop the entirety of classical set theory. It is possible to read Badiou's remarks on intuitionistic logic as an

---

as useful but even aprioristic. *Collected Works*, p. 492

explanation of why the Law of the Excluded Middle, and consequently the deductive method of apogogic proof, is valid within the (meta)ontological framework of *Being and Event*. What is less acceptable is his rather vacuous claim that in the rejection of **LEM**,

> intuitionism has mistaken the route in trying to apply back onto ontology criteria of connection which *come from elsewhere*, and especially from a doctrine of mentally effective operations. In particular, intuitionism is a prisoner of the empiricist and illusory representation of mathematical objects. (BE 249)

The claim that intuitionism draws its rules from the study of mentally effective operations is fair enough; indeed, on this point Badiou is in consensus with most active intuitionists (including, it seems, both Brouwer and Heyting). The claim that these rules come from 'elsewhere' than the domain of ontology, however, simply reasserts Badiou's axiomatic thesis that ontology *is* classical set theory; in this respect, the claim is a trivial one, since no one is arguing that intuitionist logic naturally emerges from classical set theory. But let us not move too quickly here—after all, the initial thesis of *Being and Event* is that '*mathematics*, throughout the entirety of its historical becoming, pronounces what is expressible of being qua being' (BE 8). Whether this mathematics is classical or intuitionistic demands a second decision; it is not decided in advance by Badiou's arguments (which are themselves more like axioms) that the presentation of being is intelligible only in terms of pure multiplicity. Intuitionist mathematics, too, proposes an ontology in which every existence is realized as multiplicity, drawing out a sort of idealist Pythagorean cosmogony without an originary One (but rather a Two). In any case, the fact that intuitionism can be said to derive its rules from mentally effective operations does not preclude the thesis that these rules correctly prescribe what is *expressible* of being; the intuitionist ontologist would have no difficulty in turning the tables here, for she is always entitled to retort that the classical ontologist applies, onto being, rules which come from a doctrine of *mentally effective operations regarding finite collections*, an accusation which is twice as damning when the rights to an ontology of infinite multiples are at stake. Badiou's suggestion, which is not taken any further than what is quoted here, that intuitionistic logic remain beholden to 'the empiricist and illusory representation of mathematical objects' is rather queer. The entire intuitionist programme takes its point of departure in seeking to overcome the 'observational standpoint' that had become the spontaneous philosophy of mathematicians, and which treated mathematical judgments as if they

were judgments concerning *objects*.[50] The whole intuitionist effort is to remain faithful to a vision of mathematics as an autonomous activity of the
subject, without reference to any external object. It is strange that Badiou
neglects to mention this; he shares essentially the same project.[51]

§ 7

The full consequences of the intuitionist position concerning the non-
predeterminacy of truth can most easily be grasped by illustrating a model for this logic, such as Kripke has done in his 1963 paper, 'Semantical
Analysis of Intuitionistic Logic I'. In this text, Kripke develops a model-
theoretic treatment of Heyting's formalization of intuitionistic logic.[52] In
all justice, before proceeding any further, we must note that both Kripke
and Heyting's endeavours are, in a certain sense, external to intuitionism
proper. They are formal abstractions made on the basis of intuitionist
mathematics, and, according to the intuitionistic ethos, cannot be taken
as expressing the essence of intuitionist mathematics itself. The remarks
that Heyting makes to this effect at the beginning of his 'Formal Rules of
Intuitionistic Logic' are worth repeating here. 'Intuitionistic mathematics',
he writes,

> is a mental activity [*Denktätigkeit*], and for it every language,
> including the formalistic one, is only a tool for communication. It
> is in principle impossible to set up a system of formulas that would
> be equivalent to intuitionistic mathematics, for the possibilities
> of thought cannot be reduced to a finite number of rules set up
> in advance. [...] For the construction of mathematics it is not
> necessary to set up logical laws of general validity; these laws are
> discovered anew in each single case for the mathematical system
> under consideration.[53]

Motivated by the wish to 'facilitate the penetration of intuitionistic concepts and the use of these concepts in research',[54] Heyting nevertheless
proceeds to abstract the general deductive structure from intuitionistic

---

50. Brouwer, 'Historical Background, Principles and Methods of Intuitionism', in *Collected Works*, p. 508.
51. This is the nature of Badiou's 'Platonism', as discussed in § 5 above. (cf. Badiou, 'Platon-ism and Mathematical Ontology', pp. 49-58.
52. Kripke provides a model for both the propositional and the predicate calculus for intui-tionistic logic. In what follows, however, we will restrict our attention to the propositional calculus for the sake of simplicity and brevity.
53. Heyting, *Intuitionism*, p. 311.
54. Heyting, *Intuitionism*, p. 311.

mathematics. The result is a propositional and a predicate calculus, presented in the familiar symbolic style, in which the logical consequences of the intuitionistic position are systematically unfolded. Kripke's project arose as an effort to provide a model theory for Heyting's logical calculi, and in doing this he veered even further from the orthodox path of intuitionism by constructing his model within classical mathematics. But even the embeddedness of Kripke's model in a classical framework is not the essential problem here. Kripke himself provides several indications on how the construction of the model may be conducted 'intuitionistically', and his decision to employ classical procedures is primarily a matter of expediency (it is almost always simpler to produce a classical demonstration than an intuitionistic one). It is rather that, for the intuitionist, the entire notion of a *model* is altogether secondary. But what is this notion?

Briefly put, the role of a model (in formal semantics) is to determine the veracity and soundness of a mathematical or logical system by producing a 'model structure' in which the sentences of the system can be shown to be true when they are interpreted as referring to the objects in the domain. A mathematical model thus consists of a formally specified domain of 'objects' (usually sets, subsets and relations) and a function of correspondence, called the *interpretation* of the model, established between these objects and the syntactic elements of the system in question. As Badiou recognizes in *Le Concept de modèle*, the model-theoretic schematization of truth as ruled correspondence comes deceptively close to the empiricist or 'observational' paradigm, which makes of truth a correspondence with external objects.[55] This is precisely the orientation in thought that intuitionism seeks to overcome by identifying truth with the subjective movement of demonstrative construction, without reference to any external object. Nevertheless, Badiou, for his part, seeks to rescue the concept of the model from its empiricist appropriation, and forcefully argues that what is at issue in the mathematical employment of models is in no sense a reproduction of the 'observational' or 'empiricist' dichotomy between propositions and objects. Model theory does not concern the relation between mathematics and its exterior. Essentially, this is because both the model structure and the interpretation by which the formal system in question is evaluated are themselves produced entirely *within mathematics.* 'Semantics', accordingly,

> is an *intramathematical* relation between certain refined experimental
> apparatuses (formal systems) and certain 'cruder' mathematical

---

55. See Badiou, *Le Concept de modèle*, chapters 4 & 5.

> products, which is to say, products accepted, taken to be
> demonstrated, without having been submitted to all the exigencies
> of inscription ruled by the verifying constraints of the apparatus.[56]

The use of models, in this view, is nothing other than a mode of mathematics' historical reflexivity, and is fully immanent to mathematical thought; nowhere does mathematics call upon 'external' objects to ratify mathematical knowledge.

Insofar as the use of Kripke's semantical analysis nevertheless deviates somewhat from the spirit of intuitionism, this deviation only facilitates our own enquiry. It allows us to establish a common mathematical terrain on which certain formal aspects of both Badiou's and Brouwer's theories of the subject can be drawn out. The presentation that we will give of Kripke's semantics will, necessarily, be an abbreviated one.

Like any model, Kripke's consists of two distinct components. First, we have the *model structure*, which is defined as a set **K**, a designated element $\mathbf{G} \in \mathbf{K}$, and a reflexive, transitive relation **R** defined over **K**. **G** is uniquely specified as the 'root' of the relation **R**, so that there exists no **H** in **K** such that **HRG** (**G** is '**R**-minimal' in **K**). Second, we have the *interpretation function* $\phi(P, \mathbf{H})$, where P ranges over propositions in the Heyting calculus and **H** ranges over elements of **K**. The values of this function range over the set $\{\mathbf{T}, \mathbf{F}\}$ (make no hasty assumptions here!). We also impose the condition that, given any two elements **H** and **H'** such that **HRH'**, $\phi(P,\mathbf{H}) = \mathbf{T}$ implies $\phi(P,\mathbf{H'}) = \mathbf{T}$. That is to say, the relation **R** preserves truth-values.

We will assume that ϕ has assigned a value from $\{\mathbf{T}, \mathbf{F}\}$ to each atomic proposition in the logic. In doing this, however, it is crucial to note that while the value **T** serves to represent intuitionistic truth (demonstrability), **F** *does not immediately represent intuitionistic falsity* (demonstrable absurdity). It signifies only the *absence* of a construction verifying the proposition in question (call it P), an absence which will only crystallize into the knowledge that P is *intuitionistically false* once it has been ascertained that no **H** exists such that $\phi(P,\mathbf{H}) = \mathbf{T}$... but this comes later. The point to be made here is that the exhaustive assignment of truth-values to the atomic formulae of the logic does not contradict the intuitionist rejection of the classical vision of pre-determinate truth on which LEM rests. The formulae receiving the assignment **F** are precisely those whose truth has not yet been determined as either true or false.

---

56. Badiou, *Le Concept de modèle*, p. 53.

The semantic values for complex sentences are defined by induction over the length of formula, in accordance with the following rules for the connectives in the logic. These are defined as follows:

    a. $\phi(A \ \& \ B, \mathbf{H}) = \mathbf{T}$ iff $\phi(A, \mathbf{H}) = \phi(B, \mathbf{H}) = \mathbf{T}$; otherwise, $\phi(A \ \& \ B, \mathbf{H}) = \mathbf{F}$.

    b. $\phi(A \ or \ B, \mathbf{H}) = \mathbf{T}$ iff $\phi(A, \mathbf{H}) = \mathrm{T}$ or $\phi(B, \mathbf{H}) = \mathbf{T}$; otherwise $\phi(A \ or \ B, \mathbf{H}) = \mathbf{F}$.

    c. $\phi(A \rightarrow B, \mathbf{H}) = \mathbf{T}$ iff for all $\mathbf{H'} \in \mathbf{K}$ such that $\mathbf{H}R\mathbf{H'}$, $\phi(A, \mathbf{H'}) = \mathbf{F}$ or $\phi(B, \mathbf{H'}) = \mathbf{T}$; otherwise, $\phi(A \rightarrow B, \mathbf{H}) = \mathbf{F}$.

    d. $\phi(\sim A, \mathbf{H}) = \mathbf{T}$ iff for all $\mathbf{H'} \in \mathbf{K}$ such that $\mathbf{H}R\mathbf{H'}$, $\phi(A, \mathbf{H'}) = \mathbf{F}$; otherwise, $\phi(\sim A, \mathbf{H}) = \mathbf{F}$.[57]

As Kripke notes, the conditions for conjunction ('&') and disjunction ('*or*') are 'exact analogues of the corresponding conditions on classical conjunction and disjunction' (94). The conditions for implication and negation, however, significantly differ from their classical counterparts. For example, in order to assert the negation of *A* with respect to such and such a structure, it is necessary to ascertain that no possible extension of this structure is capable of verifying *A*. This particular point should be born in mind; we will encounter it again elsewhere. The condition imposed on implication serves to provide the *if... then...* relation with a certain intuitive concreteness which, as any undergraduate student in philosophy will no doubt testify, is lacking in classical logic. Intuitionistically, we may only affirm propositions of the form 'if *A* then *B*' when it is possible to constructively transform any construction verifying *A* into one verifying *B*. In Kripke's semantics, this notion is expressed by allowing $A \rightarrow B$ to be verified by a structure **H** only when any extension **H'** of **H** preserves this implication.

It is possible to illustrate these logical structures, as Kripke does, by means of a diagram. The tree-like structure in *figure 1* is an intuitionistic model for a formula *A* comprised of the above connectives and the atomic sub-formulae *P, Q,* and *R*.[58]

---

57. I quote these conditions almost verbatim from Kripke's text, altering only a few of the connective symbols to conform to the rest of this paper and the logical notation used by Badiou.

58. *Figure 1* is taken from Kripke, 'Semantical Analysis of Intuitionistic Logic I', p. 98.

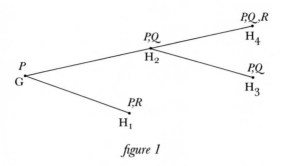

figure 1

In the model diagrammed above, we have taken $\mathbf{G}$, $\mathbf{H_1}$, $\mathbf{H_2}$, $\mathbf{H_3}$, and $\mathbf{H_4}$ to be the elements of $\mathbf{K}$. Here, they are the nodes of our tree. The relation $\mathbf{R}$ is represented by lines of succession in the tree, so that when $\mathbf{HRH'}$ we have a pathway proceeding from $\mathbf{H}$ to $\mathbf{H'}$. Note that the $\mathbf{R}$-minimal element $\mathbf{G}$ is at the 'root' of the tree. In the diagram, the letter of an atomic formula F is written above a node $\mathbf{H_n}$ when we have $\phi(\mathrm{F}, \mathbf{H_n}) = \mathbf{T}$; when $\phi(\mathrm{F}, \mathbf{H_n}) = \mathbf{F}$, F does not appear above $\mathbf{H_n}$. As Kripke has it,

> We intend the nodes $\mathbf{H}$ to represent points in time (or 'evidential situations'), at which we may have various pieces of information. If, at a particular point $\mathbf{H}$ in time, we have enough information to prove a proposition A, we say that $\phi(A,\mathbf{H}) = \mathbf{T}$; if we lack such information, we say that $\phi(A,\mathbf{H}) = \mathbf{F}$. If $\phi(A,\mathbf{H}) = \mathbf{T}$ we can say that A has been *verified* at the point $\mathbf{H}$ in time; if $\phi(A,\mathbf{H}) = \mathbf{F}$, then A has *not been verified* at $\mathbf{H}$. [...] If $\mathbf{H}$ is any situation, we say $\mathbf{HRH'}$ if, as far as we know, at the time $\mathbf{H}$, we may later get information to advance to $\mathbf{H'}$.[59]

Kripke's apparatus succeeds in capturing the temporal dimension that, intuitionism insists, must condition any logical reasoning adequate to subjectively constructed truths. Truth, which, here, is meant only to index the existence of constructive demonstrations, is not such that it is immemorially decided for every possible proposition; propositions receive truth only when the necessary constructive verification comes to pass. An

---

59. Kripke, 'Semantic Analysis of Intuitionistic Logic I', p. 98. Kripke goes on to inform the reader of the point we have made above. It nevertheless bears repeating:

Notice, then, that $\mathbf{T}$ and $\mathbf{F}$ do not denote intuitionistic truth and falsity; if $\phi(A,\mathbf{H}) = \mathbf{T}$, then A has been verified to be true at the time $\mathbf{H}$; but $\phi(A,\mathbf{H}) = \mathbf{F}$ does not mean that A has been proved *false* at $\mathbf{H}$. It simply is not (yet) proved at $\mathbf{H}$, but may be established later. (p. 98)

interesting feature of the intuitionist notion of logical time (if we may call it that), is that while truth is always something which must be produced through the activity of a subject in time, once produced, the truth is held to be eternally valid. The language of intuitionist mathematics, as opposed to any metalanguage through which we may wish to analyse it, is therefore 'tenseless', despite the irreducible temporality of the procedures that constitute its truths. Dummett provides a helpful example on this point.[60] For the intuitionist, in 1882, through the work of Lindemann, the statement 'π is transcendental' became true. Prior to 1882, no such truth existed; it is nevertheless inadmissible to claim that in 1881, say, π was *not* transcendental, for to do so employs a non-constructive form of negation: no procedure existed in 1881 that was capable of demonstrating the non-transcendental nature of π, nor did any means exist of demonstrating that no procedure *could* exist that would establish that π may be transcendental. In 1881, neither the statement 'π is transcendental' nor the statement 'π is not transcendental' were true, but neither were they false. As for the statement 'it is indeterminate whether π is transcendental or not'—this is simply not a mathematical statement.[61] It is a statement of the metalanguage. By admitting as mathematical statements only those which declare the existence of a constructive procedure, intuitionism avoids encountering contradictions between tenseless propositions concerning temporally conditioned events. In this way, intuitionism produces a logic of truths that are at once eternal and created.

Dummett's example serves also to illustrate the behaviour of negation in the Kripke model, and in intuitionistic logic in general. As I have indicated, the reason why, in 1881, it was not legitimate to affirm the non-transcendental nature of π is that no procedure existed that was capable of showing that Lindemann's proof (or some other to the same effect) was not forthcoming. This state of affairs is expressed quite well by the semantic interpretation of negation in Kripke's tree-model. 'To assert $\sim A$ intuitionistically in the situation **H**', Kripke writes,

> we need to know at **H** not only that A has not been verified at **H**,

---

60. The following example is a paraphrase of Dummett, *Elements of Intuitionism*, p. 337.

61. cf. Heyting, *Intuitionism: An Introduction*, p. 19: 'Every mathematical assertion can be expressed in the form: "I have effected the construction A in my mind". The mathematical negation of this assertion can be expressed as "I have effected a construction B in my mind, which deduces a contradiction from the supposition that the construction A were brought to an end", which is again of the same form. On the contrary, the factual negation of the first assertion is: "I have not effected the construction A in my mind"; this statement has not the form of a mathematical assertion'.

but that it cannot possibly be verified at any later time, no matter how much information is gained; so we say that $\phi(\sim A,\mathbf{H}) = \mathbf{T}$ iff $\phi(A,\mathbf{H'}) = \mathbf{F}$ for every $\mathbf{H'} \in \mathbf{K}$ such that $\mathbf{HRH'}$. (99)

The intuitionist assertion of a negative proposition is thus not merely a statement of what is not actually the case (the 'case' being the current state of what has been constructed); it is a statement on what *cannot* be the case. This 'modality of the negative' is characteristic of the intuitionistic understanding of truth and its subjective essence. We will encounter it again elsewhere.

§ 8

In Meditation 27 of *Being and Event*, and again in 'La mathématique est un pensée',[62] Badiou outlines the three great 'orientations in thought', and designates them as Constructivist, Generic and Transcendent Thought, respectively. To anyone familiar with this taxonomy, it is immediately tempting to place intuitionism under the rubric of 'Constructivist Thought'. On a purely mathematical register, there is much to recommend situating intuitionism within the constructivist orientation, and it is common practice in the literature to use the expressions 'constructive mathematics' and 'intuitionist mathematics' more or less interchangeably.[63] Neither the intuitionist nor the constructivist (in Badiou's sense of the term) recognize the existence of structures which cannot be constructed on the basis of a finite algorithm, and both schools of thought insist on the restriction of all quantification to domains of already-constructed entities.[64] But we need not read far into Badiou's exposition of constructivist thought to realize that this category is somewhat ill-suited to Brouwerian intuitionism. Constructivist thought, as Badiou understands it, is 'in its essence [...] a logical grammar. Or, to be exact, it ensures that language prevails as the norm for what may be acceptably recognized' as an existent multiplicity (BE 287). Nothing could be more anathematic to Brouwer's thought. As we have seen, Brouwer's founding gesture (the First Act of Intuitionism) was to announce an uncompromising secession of genuine mathemati-

---

62. Alain Badiou, *Court traité d'ontologie transitoire*, Paris, Éditions du Seuil, 1998, pp. 39-54.

63. cf. Errett Bishop, *Foundations of Constructive Analysis*, New York, McGraw-Hill, 1967.

64. For the constructivist, Badiou writes, 'if one says "there exists...", this must be understood as saying "there exists a term named in the situation"; and if one says "for all...", this must be understood as, "for all named terms of the situation"' (BE 287). In this text, a 'name' is taken to mean a finite algorithm by which the multiple in question can be constructed.

cal activity from language.[65] This is not the heart of the matter, however. There are difficulties that must be overcome before placing intuitionism within *any* of Badiou's three orientations.

All three major orientations of thought that Badiou addresses, insofar as they can be exhibited in mathematics, are demarcated according to their treatment of Cantor's continuum problem. This problem concerns the quantitative relation between the set of natural numbers ω_o and the real number continuum, or, more generally, between a given transfinite set ω_α and the set of its subsets $\wp(\omega_\alpha)$. The question that it poses is, on the surface, quite simple: how many points are in a line? Or, equivalently, how many subsets are included in the set of natural numbers? In 1963, Cohen showed this problem to be undecidable on the basis of the axioms of set theory. The quantitative errancy of subsets over elements in any infinite set cannot be given any measure whatsoever, but nor can it be sealed over; Cantor's theorem alone tells us that there are unconditionally more subsets in any given set than there are elements. Badiou, who in the set-theoretic axioms sees the Platonic Ideas of ontology, interprets this mathematical impasse as a real and irreducible gap in being as such, a gap which can only be provisionally surmounted by means of a pure, subjective decision. The three great orientations in thought each propose a means of sealing this fissure, or, at the very least, a means of accounting for its origin (BE 283). The Transcendent orientation 'searches to fix a stopping point to errancy by the thought of a multiple such that it organizes everything which precedes it' (BE 283); in the context of set theory, this tendency is exhibited by the invention of axioms instituting the existence of 'large cardinals', transfinite numbers vastly outstripping anything that can be produced by means of the ordinary set-theoretic axioms. As Badiou understands it, this practice is a mathematical analogue to hav-

---

65. Moreover, the entire 'statist' ideology that Badiou seeks to connect to the constructivist orientation of thought is quite foreign to Brouwer, who only ever held the state in the greatest suspicion and hostility, and insisted on a necessary distance to be held between true thought and the state. cf. 'Consciousness, Philosophy and Mathematics', in Brouwer, *Collected Works*, p. 487: 'Of course art and philosophy continually illustrating such wisdom cannot participate in the cooperation, and should not communicate with cooperation, in particular should not communicate with the state. Supported by the state, they will lose their independence and degenerate' (*Collected Works*, p. 487). The reason why mathematics is not included in this prescription is clear enough from Brouwer's previous remarks on the matter: mathematics, by its very nature, subtracts itself from the worldly concerns of the state. By its very nature, 'the basic intuition of mathematics is left to free unfolding. This unfolding is not bound to the exterior world, and thereby to finiteness and responsibility', *Collected Works*, p. 484.

ing recourse to the 'eye of God'. By introducing such colossal infinities
into the set theoretic axiomatic, one hopes to deploy the resources that
are necessary for providing an exact measure of $\wp(\omega_0)$. The Constructive or 'grammarian' orientation proposes a solution to the same problem
through the aforementioned restriction of the existent to the predicatively
specifiable. In set theory, this orientation is manifested in Gödel's constructible model for the axioms. This model is a hierarchical construction, which takes the empty set as its primitive stratum and generates
each subsequent stratum by taking as elements all subsets of the previous
stratum that can be specified by a formula restricted to that stratum.[66]
The result is a standard model for set theory that validates the equation
$|\wp(\omega_n)| = \omega_{n+1}$, stating that the power set of any transfinite cardinal ω_n is
precisely the next largest transfinite cardinal. The third orientation, which
Badiou names Generic Thought, does not so much seek to seal the gap in
being so much as it seeks to disclose the 'origin' of the 'mystery of excess'
(BE 283). 'The entire rational effort' of this orientation 'is to dispose of
a matheme of the indiscernible, which brings forth in thought the innumerable parts that cannot be named as separate from the crowd of those
which—in the myopic eyes of language—are absolutely identical to them'
(BE 283). The Generic Orientation finds its mathematical expression in
Cohen's work on the continuum problem, which proceeds to show that if
we admit certain carefully delineated 'indiscernible' or 'generic' sets into
a model for set theory, we produce new models in which the power of the
continuum exceeds that of the natural numbers by 'as much as one likes',
so that the power set of ω_0 may be assigned any cardinality at all that is
greater than ω_0 (with the single exception that the cardinal selected not be
cofinal with ω_0; that is, it cannot be $\omega\omega_0$).[67]

---

66. See Meditation 29 of BE for a more comprehensive treatment of Gödel's proof. Gödel's
own presentation of his results can be found in volume 2 of his *Collected Works*.
67. Badiou presents Cohen's results in Meditations 33, 34 and 36 of BE. Cohen's most accessible presentation of his work is to be found in: Paul Cohen, *Set Theory and the Continuum
Hypothesis*, New York, W.A. Benjamin, 1966.
  Of the three Great Orientations, the Generic Orientation comes closest to Badiou's
own project, and he seizes upon Cohen's concept of generic subsets in order to provide
the subject and the truth that it expresses with its ontological infrastructure. Nevertheless,
Badiou wishes to distance himself somewhat from the Generic Orientation as such, and
sees his own work as pursuing a fourth way, one that is 'transversal to the three others',
and which

> holds that the *truth* of the ontological impasse cannot be seized or thought in imma-
> nence to ontology itself, nor to speculative metaontology. It assigns the un-measure
> of the state [*sc.* the set of subsets, or the real number continuum when the set under

The chief difficulty that confronts us in placing intuitionism under any of Badiou's three (or four) rubrics is that the impasse to which they respond, understood as Cantor's continuum problem, is strictly speaking, is *invisible* to intuitionist mathematics.[68] This is because the problem is premised on the hypothesis that it is legitimate to treat the continuum as a completed, transfinite set of discrete entities, be they points or subsets of natural numbers. The intuitionists hold this hypothesis to be inadmissible.[69] Their position on this matter draws its force from their insistence on the unbridgeable nature of the gaps between finitude and the infinite on the one hand, and between the discrete and the continuous on the other.[70] For the intuitionist, the classical image of the continuum as an ac-

---

consideration is ω_0] to the historial limitation of being [...]. Its hypothesis consists in saying that one can only *render justice* to injustice from the angle of the event and intervention. There is thus no need to be horrified by an un-binding of being, because it is in the undecidable occurrence of a supernumerary non-being that every truth procedure originates, including that of a truth whose stakes would be that very unbinding. (BE pp. 284-5)

68. Pourciau, p. 317.

69. B. Madison Mount has produced an outstanding essay on Badiou's notion of constructivism and his application of this category to Leibniz's thought. Mount uncovers a state of affairs that is not unlike the one we find here:

The continuum, for Leibniz, is in no way made up of points: monads, which, as Badiou notes, are sometimes equated to 'metaphysical points', are the true substratum of the spatiotemporal extensa that 'exist' only illusorily. But this does not mean, as Badiou claims, that the monad is that which can be multiplied over transfinitely to reach the continuum, subjugating the 'discontinuities' to the 'commensurable' by way of language.

Instead [...] the continuum persists in its incommensurability; its 'ideality' is not a simple negation of the real, but a positive quality *in actu* which prevents the adequacy of any linguistic representation [...]. If it is necessary to find a successor for Leibniz in modern philosophy of mathematics, it may be less the 'constructivist orientation' than the intuitionism of Brouwer and Heyting, for whom the continuum was paradoxically best described as a *dis-continuity*, a jump beyond numeration for which no mathematical schema can fully account—'the "between," which is not exhaustible by the interposition of new units and which therefore can never be thought of as a mere collection of units'.

Brouwer, 'Intuitionism and Formalism', in Paul Bernacerraf and Hillary Putnam (eds.), *Philosophy of Mathematics: Selected Readings*, 2nd ed. Cambridge, Cambridge University Press, 1983, p. 80. B. Madison Mount, 'The Cantorian Revolution: Alain Badiou on the Philosophy of Set Theory', *Polygraph*, vol. 17, 2005, p. 87.

One is left to wonder on whose foot the constructivist shoe fits.

70. On the second of these two gaps, cf. Weyl, 'On the new foundational crisis of mathematics', in Mancosu, p. 95: 'The question whether the continuum is denumerable cannot seriously arise in this theory, for, according to it, there is an unbridgeable gulf between the continuum and a set of discrete elements, a gulf that excludes any comparison'.

tual and determinate, infinite set of points (or of sets of natural numbers) is cursed twice over. The question concerning the 'quantity' of such a set is therefore never raised within the intuitionist field. It would nevertheless be wrong to assume from this that intuitionism ignores the continuum altogether, or places it outside the legitimate field of mathematical thought. On the contrary, it is with respect to the older and more general problem regarding what can be said of the relation between the continuum and the natural numbers that intuitionism has produced many of its most significant innovations. And, true to the spirit of Badiou's text, it is in this field that intuitionism finds itself driven to elaborate its doctrine of the mathematical subject in such a way as to outstrip the grammarian apparatus, which otherwise, against all intentions, it weakly imitates.

§ 9

In order to have a firmer grasp on what is at stake here, let us examine a fairly simple numerical model of the linear continuum, classically understood. Consider the binary tree β, whose nodes are marked by either os or 1s, and whose levels are enumerated by the natural numbers (the elements of ω_o). We will call a *branch* of β any sequence of nodes running from the 'root' of the tree ($< >$) and proceeding infinitely. Subsets α of ω_o are then defined by the branches b_α of β, according to the following convention: $n \in \alpha$ if and only if b_α has a o in its nth place (i.e. $b_\alpha(n) = o$). So long as we are operating within classical mathematics, we may consider β to be an *actually infinite* structure, one which has completely traversed all of the natural numbers n. Each branch b_α thus completely defines a subset of ω_o (*i.e.*, a subset of the natural numbers). Now, each subset of ω_o can be made to correspond with a sequence of rational numbers defining a real (Cantor has shown that the rationals are denumerable, so we assume such a denumeration has taken place and correlate each subset of natural numbers with a subset of the rationals). Since there are two distinct possibilities for extension at every stage of development for each branch of the tree—namely, $b_\alpha(n) = 1$ and $b_\alpha(n) = o$—the number of subsets in ω_o must be equal to $2 * 2 * 2 *...$ *ad infinitum*, or 2^{ω_o}, a classical formulation of the power of the continuum.[71] Cantor's celebrated theorem that the power of any set S is necessary less than the power of the set of subsets of S tells us that 2^{ω_o} cannot be quantitatively equal to ω_o itself, but beyond

---

71. I borrow this construction from Mary Tiles, *The Philosophy of Set Theory: An Introduction to Cantor's Paradise*, Oxford, Basil Blackwell, 1989, pp. 66-67.

this, classical mathematics reaches a point of profound indeterminacy. Everything hinges on what is taken to be a legitimate subset of ω_0, or, to put it another way, a legitimate pathway through β. It is here that the grammarian-constructivist orientation in set theory would impose its restriction of the existent to the linguistically constructible, admitting only subsets which can be given a predicative definition with respect to what has been constructed thus far.

The early intuitionists—those working within the field deployed by the First Act—as well as a number of 'pre-intuitionists'[72] like Borel and Poincaré, managed the real number continuum in a way that was effectively similar to the 'grammarian' approach, despite a very different theoretical motivation. While they accepted that the intuitive continuum may well be beyond the reach of mathematical intelligibility, they pragmatically circumscribed the limits of what they called the 'reduced' or the 'practical' continuum, consisting of a set of points definable by constructive means. This limitation was, in part, imposed by the fact that the intuitionists could only treat multiples (*e.g.*, subsets of ω_0 defining reals) as being effectively infinite if a constructively knowable law expressed their principle of generation. The point-set that the early intuitionists accepted as constructible was even smaller than the continuum outlined by the grammarian orientation; its power did not exceed the denumerable and so it could not be identified, even provisionally, with the power set of the natural numbers.[73] It does, however, suffice for a limited but serviceable extent of mathematics.

The poverty and intuitive inadequacy of the practical continuum was nevertheless troubling to the intuitionists. The desolate horizon of the reduced continuum was, for Brouwer, an obstacle that must be overcome. His response, rightly called revolutionary,[74] was to overhaul the entire

---

72. 'Pre-intuitionist' is a term given by Brouwer to a pre-eminently empiricist group of mathematicians including Poincaré, Borel and others, with whom Brouwer shared a number of sympathies, especially prior to the development of his mature intuitionist programme. See 'Historical Background, Principles and Methods of Intuitionism', in *Collected Works*, p. 509.

73. Mark van Atten, 'Brouwer, as Never Read by Husserl', *Synthese*, vol. 137, no. 1-2, pp. 3-19, p. 3.

74. Hermann Weyl, a German philosopher and mathematician who was once one of Brouwer's more significant allies, once famously exclaimed: 'Brouwer—that is the revolution!', Vladimir Tasíc, *The Mathematical Roots of Postmodern Thought*, p. 54. In his article on intuitionism and phenomenology, Mark van Atten writes, in a similar vein: 'Around 1917, two revolutions took place, one fake, and one true. The true one happened in mathematics, and consisted in the introduction of choice sequences by Brouwer', in 'Brouwer, as

conceptual apparatus in which the problem of the continuum was posed. The new theory of the continuum exploits the two fundamental principles that had kept intuitionism at a distance from the classical set-theoretical treatments of the continuum—their refusal to treat the continuum as a point-set of *any* power, and their insistence on the irreducibly *potentiality* of the continuum's inexhaustibly infinite nature. In order to do this, Brouwer recognizes, it is necessary to surpass the conceptual disposition proposed by the First Act. A Second Act of Intuition is therefore declared. This Act

> *recognizes the possibility of generating new mathematical entities:*
>
> *firstly in the form of infinitely proceeding sequences p_1, p_2, ..., whose terms are chosen more or less freely from mathematical entities previously acquired; in such a way that the freedom of choice existing perhaps for the first element p_1 may be subjected to a lasting restriction at some following p_2, and again and again to sharper lasting restrictions or even abolition at further subsequent p_r's, while all these restricting interventions, as well as the choices of the p_r's themselves, at any stage may be made to depend on possible future mathematical experiences of the creating subject;*
>
> *secondly, in the form of mathematical species, i.e. properties supposable for mathematical entities previously acquired, and satisfying the condition that, if they hold for a certain mathematical entity, they also hold for all mathematical entities that have been defined to be equal to it...*[75]

The Second Act dramatically increases the power of intuitionist mathematics, and provides the groundwork for what Brouwer calls 'Intuitionist Set Theory', a discipline which, like its Cantorian counterpart, sets itself the task of charting a course through the labyrinth of the continuum. Both the path and the gauge of the Brouwerian trajectory are entirely different than those chosen by Cantor, however. If the principle challenge that Cantor selected for his theory of sets was that of providing an exact quantitative measure of the linear point set with respect to the natural numbers, the task proper to intuitionist set theory is that of mathematically thinking the continuum in its very *indeterminacy* and errancy *vis-à-vis* discrete numeration, and to do this without letting the continuum dissolve into an unintelligible mystery. The errancy of the continuum, dispelled by the grammarian orientation, becomes a locus of mathematical investiga-

---

Never Read by Husserl', p. 2.

75. Brouwer, 'Historical Background...' in *Collected Works*, p. 511.

tion in intuitionism, and finds expression in the irreducibly unfinished and unforeseeable progression of free choice sequences.

In order to show how this is possible, it is necessary to specify a few of the concepts that the Second Act bequeaths us. The two new structures which the Act explicitly puts forth are *choice sequences* and *species*. A species is essentially a class, and, conceptually bears little difference from the classical notion, save for what is at issue are classes of intuitionistically admissible structures. Of choice sequences, there are two essential types. *Lawlike sequences* are infinitely proceeding sequences of natural numbers—or any other constructible mathematical structure—prescribed by a determinate algorithm or 'law'. The notion is close to what Badiou calls *discernible* sets—but we will come to this later. *Free choice sequences* are infinitely proceeding sequences that are not determined by any law or algorithm. Between the two, any variety of intermediate forms are possible, and laws may be imposed upon and removed from free choice sequences at any stage in their development as the subject so chooses. A *spread* is a species of choice sequences possessing a common 'root' or first term, and which is governed by two laws (which we will often collapse into one for the sake of brevity): first, there is the *spread law*, noted Λ_X where X is the spread in question. This law determines the admissibility of *finite initial segments* of choice sequences into the spread. Every spread law must: (1) admit the empty sequence < > as the root of the spread, (2) not admit any choice sequence possessing an inadmissible initial segment, and (3) for each admissible initial segment, admit at least one possible extension of this segment into the spread, so that every admitted segment may proceed indefinitely along at least one path. Further restrictions may be imposed to produce spreads of the desired form. The second law is called the *complementary law* of the spread, as is designated Γ_X. This law permits us to produce spreads of mathematical entities other than the natural numbers by assigning, to every admitted sequence of the spread, some other intuitionistically constructed structure. The only restriction on this law is that it be effectively decidable for every assignment.

We are now in a position to produce the intuitionistic construction of the continuum. Whereas the classical continuum is conceived as a determinate set of real numbers, the intuitionist continuum is composed of *real number generators*. There are many possible forms of these; here we will consider infinitely proceeding sequences of rational numbers $\{r_n\}$ such that $|r_n - r_{n+1}| < 2^{-n}$. Real number generators, in intuitionist mathematics, are analogous to the classical definitions of real numbers. The crucial difference lies in the fact that they are not conceived as completed infinite sets, but as intensionally determined, infinitely proceeding sequences. The intuitionist continuum is now constructed as follows: we begin by assuming an enumeration of the rational numbers $r_1, r_2, \ldots$; we then define a spread of natural numbers by the spread law Λ_C: 'Every natural number forms an admissible one-member sequence; if $a_1, \ldots, a_n$ is an admissible sequence, then $a_1, \ldots, a_n, a_{n+1}$ is an admissible sequence if and only if $|ra_n - ra_{n+1}| < 2^{-n}$.[76] The *complementary law* for the spread C, noted Γ_C, assigns the rational number ra_n to every admissible sequence $a_1, \ldots, a_n$. The spread C thus comprises of every possible real number generator that may be given by lawlike algorithms. Beyond these lawlike generators, however, there exists an innumerable plurality of unspecified and underdetermined choice sequences which do not yet determine, but which never cease to approach, real numbers. It is thus that 'we have here the creation of the "continuum," which, although containing individual real numbers, does not dissolve into a set of real numbers as finished beings; we rather have a *medium of free Becoming*'.[77] Let us note that this is a medium created by the very subject who traverses it, a subject properly called 'singular'.[78]

It is in the Second Act that we can situate a clear break between grammarian-constructivism and intuitionism, within the mathematical framework of the latter. A free choice sequence is an intuitionistically constructible entity that is *not* constructible in the grammarian sense. By definition, a free choice sequence is determined by any constructible algorithm or predicative formula. With respect to the current enquiry, these structures are significant for the fact that, even if the subject wholly pervades intuitionistic mathematics, at no point is it more exposed than in Brouwer's theory of free choice sequences. Everywhere else, the idealist mandate of constructibility has all the same effects as a fairly weakened strain of grammarian thought. Here alone do we have a constructive form that can be generated *only* by way of subjective decisions. It is the point where intuitionism bares its subjective essence beneath its accidentally grammarian attire.

Once outside of the scope of grammarian thought, the concept of free choice sequences would seem to direct us, instead, towards the Generic Orientation, insofar as it is the business of free choice sequences to trace out a 'random conglomerate' in a spread, unlegislated by any lawlike parameters beyond those that deploy the spread itself. To be more precise,

---

76. Heyting, *Intuitionism*, p. 36.
77. Hermann Weyl, 'On the new foundational crisis in mathematics', in Mancosu, p. 94.
78. cf. Hallward, 'Alain Badiou et la déliason absolue', p. 296.

we may say that the direction in which these sequences lead us more closely approaches Badiou's subject-theoretic employment of the generic than the thought of the generic itself. In the theory of the subject presented in *Being and Event*, what we find is an attempt to mediate the mathematical concept of genericity via a concrete, subjective procedure that is infinitely proceeding in time, but which is at any moment finite. It is, in fact, not the generic at all that provides the most accurate mathematical schema for the structure of a subjective truth procedure *qua* procedure. For this we must look elsewhere.

§ 10

A subject's existence, as Badiou has it, is always temporal, and, beginning with an act of intervention that forms an indecomposable dyad with an event, consists in traversing an infinitely complex situation through an inexhaustible process that Badiou calls a *fidelity*. The business of a fidelity consists in performing a series of *enquiries* regarding the possible 'connections' that may or may not obtain between such and such an element of the situation (schematized as a set) and the event to which the subject seeks to remain faithful. A fidelity is said to be a *truth procedure* if the projected infinite subset of the situation consisting of all the elements positively connected to the event will have been *generic*. Briefly put, a generic subset is one which cannot be separated or discerned by any formula restricted to the situation—or, more precisely, restricted to the model structure S in which the situation's ontological form is expressed. This means that within the situation, there exists no law that would be a necessary and sufficient condition for belonging to the truth. Now, given that the procedure always occurs *in time*, 'at every moment, an eventally fidelity can be grasped in a provisional result which is composed of effective enquiries in which it is inscribed whether or not multiples are connected to the event' (BE 234), and this provisional result is always *finite*. Nothing of the genericity of the fidelity (its ontological 'truthfulness') can thereby be grasped in any such result, for so long as a set is finite it is always possible to compose a restricted formula that would be a necessary and sufficient condition for membership in that set, even if this formula is as rudimentary as [$\alpha_i \in \mathbf{a}$ & ... & $\alpha_n \in \mathbf{a}$] where n is the number of elements in $\mathbf{a}$. Only an infinite set has any chance of being generic, given that a formula can only be of finite length (of course, not *all* infinite sets are generic, by any stretch). If we wish to capture the mathematical essence of the Badiousian truth-procedure *in the act*, then it is clear that a strictly extensional apprehension of the subject's fidelity is insufficient, and 'in truth [...] quite useless' (BE 235). In order to adequately think the essence of a fidelity, we must attend to its temporality, and thus to its 'non-existent excess over its being' and the 'infinity of a virtual presentation' towards which it projects itself.

The essentially intensional and temporal notion of choice sequences, as developed by Brouwer and his school, is of far greater worth to us here than anything offered by the atemporal and extensionally determined landscape of classical set theory. So long as we remain within time—as every subject must—it is possible to capture the ever-incomplete unfolding of the generic procedure in terms of an Brouwerian choice sequence. I now propose to do just this.

Let us begin by circumscribing the domain in which the subject will operate. According to Badiou's exposition, this consists of a set of *conditions*, noted ©, that is both an element and a subset of the fundamental situation *S* inhabited by the subject. For the sake of simplicity, let us follow Badiou's initial example and take © to consist of the empty set Ø, and sets of countable, but possibly infinite, ordered sequences of 1s and 0s (although © may be of far greater complexity in some cases). These sets are called the 'conditions' in ©. Following Badiou's notation, we will indicate such sets by the letter π, differentiating them with numerical subscripts when necessary. The generic truth that expresses the completed subjective procedure is a form of a more general type subset defined over ©, called a 'correct subset'. The configuration of these subsets is governed by two rules, noted Rd_1 and Rd_2. Rd_1 requires that if a condition π_1 belongs to a correct subset δ, then any condition π_2 that is a subset of π_1 (that is 'dominated' by π_1, as Badiou puts it) is also an element of δ. Hence, if we have $\{<1>, <1,1>\} \in \delta$, then we must also have $\{<1>\} \in \delta$ and $Ø \in \delta$. Rd_2 requires that the elements of correct sets satisfy a relation a *compatibility* amongst one another. Two conditions π_1 and π_2 are said to be *compatible* if and only if either π_1 is a subset of π_2 or π_2 is a subset of π_1. For example, $\{<1>, <1,0>\}$ is compatible with $\{<1>, <1,0>, <1,0,1>\}$ and with $\{<1>, <1,0>, <1,0,0>\}$, but not with $\{<1>, <1,1>, <1,1,1>\}$. In order to ensure that all of the elements of a correct subset are compatible with one another, Rd_2 requires that for every conditions belonging two δ there exists a third, also belonging to δ, of which the first two are both subsets. Formally, these two rules are written:

$$Rd_1: [\pi_1 \in \delta \ \& \ \pi_2 \in \pi_1] \rightarrow \pi_2 \in \delta$$

$$Rd_2: [(\pi_1 \in \delta) \ \& \ (\pi_2 \in \delta)] \rightarrow (\exists \pi_3)[(\pi_3 \in \delta) \ \& \ (\pi_1 \subset \pi_3) \ \& \ (\pi_2 \subset \pi_3)]$$

So far we have not yet parted ways with Badiou's own mode of exposition.[79] We will do this now, by defining a *spread* of correct subsets over ©, which we will call Δ.

In order to capture the incremental development of the correct subsets, among which those capable of characterizing truth procedures will figure, let us introduce some additional notation to Badiou's apparatus. We will write $\delta(n)$ to indicate a correct subset with n elements. This 'n' will also designate the distance of the sequence in question from the root of the spread. $\delta(m)$ will be considered an initial sequence of $\delta(n)$ when $\delta(m)$ $\subset \delta(n)$ and $m < n$. If two sequences are not compatible (if one is not an initial sequence of the other), we will differentiate the two by subscripts (*e.g.* $\delta_1(n)$ and $\delta_2(m)$). As stated above, a spread is given to us by its *spread law* and its *complementary law*. Here, for the sake of concision, we will conflate the two, skipping the construction of a natural number spread and proceeding directly with the formation of a spread over ©; our conflated law will be denoted $\Lambda\Gamma_\Delta$. What we wish to do here is to define a spread whose sequences will all be correct parts of ©. Its law must, therefore, imply the two 'rules of correctness', Rd_1 and Rd_2. This law takes the form of a function, whose domain is the set of subsets of © (*i.e.* $\wp(©)$) and whose range is the set $\{1,0\}$. This function is constructed to return a 0 when its argument is admissible, and a 1 when it is not. The law $\Lambda\Gamma_\Delta$ is formulated as follows:

$$\Lambda\Gamma_\Delta(\delta(n)) = 0 \qquad \textit{iff} \qquad [\delta(n) = \{\varnothing\}] \textbf{ or}$$

$$[\Delta(\delta(n\text{-}1)) = 0 \ \& \ \delta(n\text{-}1) \subset \delta(n) \ \& \ (\forall\pi_1 \in \delta(n\text{-}1))(\exists\pi_2 \in \delta(n))(\pi_1 \subset \pi_2)]$$

$$\Lambda\Gamma_\Delta(\delta(n)) = 1 \qquad \textit{otherwise}$$

It is a fairly simple exercise to ascertain that any sequence $\delta(n)$ admitted by this law obeys the two rules of correctness stated above. A small portion of the resulting spread is diagrammed in *figure 2*.

---

79. The entire theory of correct subsets is to be found in section 3 of Meditation 33 of BE.

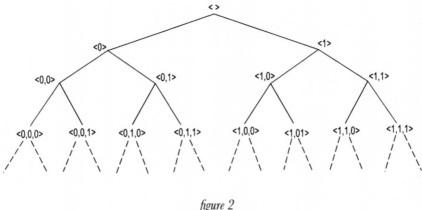

figure 2

The next step in our construction consists in delineating a *potentially generic* sequence in Δ. It must be understood that the genericity of the sequence must always remain *potential*, so long as we are operating within an intuitionist spread, for only an actually infinite sequence can be truly generic. This state of affairs is no different than that which we find in any concrete truth procedure, according to the argument advanced in *Being and Event*. The infinite multiplicity proper to a concrete exercise of fidelity—a truth-procedure—is always only 'virtual' (BE 236) or potential. That this infinity has a fully actual locus of being in the situation itself, as Badiou understands it, does not change the fact that the truth-procedure itself is internally characterized by a *potentially* infinite progression, no less than any intuitionistically admissible sequence. Even so, a significant conceptual difference between an intuitionistic sequence and a Badiousian truth-procedure is legible here; namely, that the medium of the Badiousian subject is not its own creation.

It is clear that no *lawlike* sequence is fit to express the concept of a potentially generic procedure, since a lawlike sequence is precisely one whose elements are extracted from the spread according to a constructible principle, that is, by a formula restricted to the (pre-constructed) universe in which the spread unfolds. Lawlike sequences are, in Badiou's language, essentially *discernible* sequences. One may therefore suspect that all that needs to be done to schematize a potentially generic procedure in Δ is to define that procedure as a *free choice sequence*, a sequence whose successive choices are entirely unrestricted, so long as they remain within the boundaries set by the spread law. This too, however, is insufficient, for nothing guarantees that such an arbitrary sequence will not inadvertently (*i.e.* extensionally) fall under a 'lawlike' determinant, become discernible to the situation, and fall short of genericity. Neither the 'anarchic' nor the 'legalistic' modes of operation will be sufficient for our task. The anarchic approach does, however, come somewhat closer to what we are after here. The entire problem lies in placing the necessary restrictions on the free-dom of the sequence, in 'disciplining' the sequence in a way that does not rob it of its freedom, but which keeps it at a distance from the Law. Much of Badiou's own approach to the question of liberty can be gleaned from this problematic. Hallward is quite correct in observing that 'Badiou sees freedom as an exceptionally fragile achievement', quite unlike the those who, from Kant through to Sartre and Brouwer, see it 'as a necessary presumption'.[80] It is not a question, here, of empirical freedom, the condi-tion of not being in bondage; Badiou's thesis is that rarity and fragility are characteristic of the ontological and trans-ontological basis of freedom itself: rarity, since the prerequisite unbinding from being in itself takes place only in exceptional events, and fragility, because the freedom of the subject can only sustained so long as the subject maintains the protracted effort of subtracting itself from the law. Moreover, these two conditions support one another in their being, for 'the event is only possible if spe-cial procedures conserve the evental nature of its consequences' (BE 211). Only through the genericity of the truth procedure may an event succeed in making its mark on being. No such fragility confronts the Brouwerian subject, for even the lawlike sequences are conceived in terms of choice sequences constrained by 'self-imposed restrictions'.

In order to faithfully distil the bare subjective essence of the free choice sequence from the pseudo-grammarian dross that surrounds it, and exhibit a structure that expresses the fragile and disciplined freedom that characterizes the subjective truth procedure, we must place certain restrictions on an otherwise free choice sequence. These must be suffi-cient to 'discipline' the sequence in a such a way that it does not allow itself to be (permanently) captured by any existing lawlike sequence, with-out consigning the subject to a newly invented lawlike sequence of its own. The rule that we will impose will be the following: for any lawlike sequence λ, if $\lambda(n) = \female(n)$ then there must exist some m such that $\lambda(m) \neq \female(m)$. Given that $\female$ is denumerable (even when conceived as an actually infinite subset) and can always be effectively enumerated on the basis of the natural order germane to all correct subsets, it follows that wherever $\female$ differs from a discernible correct subset, the point at which it differs can

---

80. Peter Hallward, *Badiou*, p. 167.

be indexed by a finite ordinal. The index m of this point, moreover, will always be constructible, since the means for its determination are already constructively given to us in the comparison of an algorithmically gener-ated lawlike sequence and a subjectively constructed choice sequence.

An unsettling practical consequence of this prescription, which suffi-ciently captures the potential genericity of any concrete procedure, is that a potentially generic procedure can, consistently, remain lawlike *indefinitely*: it is always possible to procrastinate its divergence from any given lawlike sequence. It has, so to speak, 'all the time in the world' to become generic. It is therefore impossible to decide, based on empirical evidence, whether any procedure is or is not generic. Strictly speaking, the *truthfulness* of a procedure does not disclose itself in extensionally determinate evidence; it can be testified to only in the interiority of the sequence, with respect to its projected intension. Any declaration concerning the existence of a truth must, therefore, always remain hypothetical and anticipatory, without the hope of sufficient evidence ever arriving. For as long as a procedure is conceived as a stepwise concatenation of discrete elements of a situation, it is clear that never will this procedure achieve historical completion. The condition of genericity, like the holiness to which the Kantian subject as-pires, is 'a perfection of which no rational being of the sensible world is ca-pable of at any moment in his existence. Since, nevertheless, it is required as practically necessary', if the procedure is to be affirmed as a *truth*, 'it can only be found in a *progress in infinitum* towards that perfect accordance', or rather that pure *discordance*, with the Law.[81] No less than Kant, Badiou is forced to postulate a form of 'immortality' for the subject. Badiou does not balk at this exigency, and insists that in its essence, 'subjectivation *is* immortal.'[82] The immortality avowed here, however, is not that of the 'hu-man animal' who bears the truth in question, but the *progress in infinitum* of which the subjective procedure itself is, in principle, capable, and which the truth that it serves demands of it. This illuminates a significant point concerning the Badiousian subject that we have not yet mentioned: the subject is not identical with the individual as such, but with the procedure in which the individual is engaged. There may therefore be collective subjects, just as there may be epochal subjects, whose scope far exceeds that of any single participant. All this is quite different from Brouwer's

81. See Immanuel Kant, *Critique of Practical Reason*, trans. T.K. Abbott, Amherst, Prometh-eus Books, 1996, p. 148.
82. Badiou, *Ethics: An Essay on the Understanding of Evil*, trans. Peter Hallward, London, Verso, 2001, p. 12. Emphasis mine.

occasionally quite solipsistic tendencies. Nor does Brouwer's theory of the subject place any wager on the existence of an actual infinite, but this is quite in accordance with his radically immanentist vision of the subject and its mathematical task.

§ 11

The anticipatory nature of genericity does not prevent the subject from drawing conclusions regarding the postulated 'new world' that would come at the end of the truth procedure. This is where the operation of *forcing* comes into play. Before it is possible, however, it is necessary to calibrate the initial situation by defining within it a complex apparatus of 'names' for the elements of the new world, the 'generic extension' $S(♀)$ of the initial situation S. These names are defined, prior to the exact determination of their referents, as sets in the initial situation of a certain kind—namely, as ordered pairs consisting of conditions in © and other, previously constructed names. In the interest of brevity, I will forgo a detailed account of how this may be done; one such method is illustrated in Meditation 34 of *Being and Event*; another is given in Chapter IV, § 3 of Cohen's *Set Theory and the Continuum Hypothesis*, and still others are available in the existing literature on the topic. As Cohen notes, the precise method chosen for the calibration of names 'is of no importance as long as we have not neglected any set' in the generic extension (Cohen, 113). In empirical situations, moreover, it is certainly to be expected that the method should differ from one specific truth procedure to another. In any case, what is essential is that the referential value of these names is determined by the composition of ♀; more precisely, the referential value of each name is determined by the membership in ♀ of the conditions which enter into the composition of the name in question.

The constellation of names is generated by the subject figure in what Badiou calls the 'subject-language', an amalgam of the native language of the situation and the names whose reference is contingent on the composition of the generic truth ♀. This language is naturally empty or nonsensical for inhabitants of the initial situation S, since the names it employs, in general, do not have a referent in S; the situation to which they refer, moreover, has not yet fully arrived, and even here their referential function is filtered through what, for those in S, is entirely indiscernible.[83] Op-

---

83. As Badiou describes it, this state of affairs finds a peculiar resonance in Brouwer's work. As Jan von Plato observes, Brouwer's 1920 papers on intuitionistic mathematics are populated with strange and often esoteric terminology and notation. This unusual

erating within this new language, the subject is capable of making certain hypotheses of the form: '*If* I suppose that the indiscernible truth contains or presents such or such a term submitted to the enquiry by chance, *then* such a statement of the subject-language [*sc.* bearing on the new situation, the generic extension $S(♀)$] will have had such a meaning and will (or won't) have been veridical' (BE 400). The hypothetical character of these statements is gradually, but never completely, resolved throughout the course of the generic procedure, as the elements of the truth become known to the subject in question (*i.e.*, as the index n of $♀(n)$ increases). Of the projected composition of $♀$, 'the subject solely controls—because it is such—the finite fragment made up of the present state of the enquiries. All the rest', we are told, 'is a matter of confidence, or of knowing belief' (BE 400).

The rational means by which the subject of the generic procedure makes such assertions and hypotheses is governed by the *forcing relation*, which Badiou names as the 'fundamental law of the subject'. The ontological form of this relation derives from Cohen's work on the continuum problem, where forcing is used to demonstrate the existence of models for set theory in which the power of the continuum may exceed ω_o by virtually any degree at all (the only restriction being $\omega_o < |\wp(\omega_o)| \neq \omega\omega_o$). In the context of Badiou's theory of the subject,

> [t]hat a term of the situation *forces* a statement of the subject language means that the veracity of this statement in the situation to come is equivalent to the belonging of this term to the indiscernible part which results from the generic procedure. It thus means that this term, bound to the statement by the relation of forcing, belongs to the truth (BE 403).[84]

---

reconfiguration of mathematical language, von Plato informs us, has its theoretical motives in the programme of the 'Signific Circle', a philosophical group in which Brouwer participated. 'The circle', he writes, 'aimed at moral betterment of humankind through a socio-linguistic reform. Brouwer himself believed that old words contain moral connotations that can lead to evil thoughts. For him, language was in the first place a means for getting power over others. Thus the strange and specifically intuitionistic vocabulary (and notation, in part still followed by some intuitionists) is part of a utopian program of language revision'. (Jan von Plato, 'Review of Dirk van Dalen, *Mystic, Geometer, and Intuitionist, The Life of L.E.J. Brouwer vol. 1. The Dawning Revolution*', in *Bulletin of Symbolic Logic*, vol.7, no.1 March, 2001, p. 64) Indeed, Brouwer considered his intuitionist movement to be, in a subtle but significant way, of both spiritual and political importance, and part of his task of 'creating a new vocabulary which admits also the spiritual tendencies in human life to considerate interchange of views and hence social organization' ('Signific Dialogues', *Collected Works*, p. 448).
84. In more technical terms:

The forcing relation is intimately related to the logical notion of *implication* or *entailment,* as Cohen points out (Cohen, III). It determines the states of affairs that will arise on the condition that this or that set π belongs to the generic ♀ on the basis of which $S($♀$)$ is constructed. As Badiou has it, what is at stake here is the immanent logic of a subjective truth procedure. It is, in several respects, analogous to the logic of being—that is, the classical logical calculus by which set theory operates. Where forcing formally diverges from classical logic, it does so insofar as it is compelled to derive its veracities from an infinite sequence whose total composition is inaccessible to any algorithmic determination. It is no accident that these are precisely the exigencies faced by the intuitionist subject, when operating in a domain that cannot be finitely specified.

A definition for the forcing relation with respect to atomic formulae cannot be adequately presented within the limits of this paper. The curious reader may find a thorough treatment in Cohen's text, and an adequate gloss of the forcing of atomic formulae in Appendix 7 of *Being and Event.* What is more significant for us, in any case, is the logical structure which the forcing relation takes with respect to compound formulae. Here, the structural divergence of forcing from classical entailment is clearly legible. With respect to the propositional connectives,[85] the definition of forcing is as follows:

a. π forces $P \& Q$ if π forces P and π forces Q.
b. π forces P *or* Q if π forces P or π forces Q.
c. π forces $P \rightarrow Q$ if either π forces P or π forces $\sim Q$.
d. π forces $\sim P$ if for all π' dominating π, π' does not force P.[86]

As Cohen remarks, these 'definitions do not imply that for π and P we must have either π forces P or π forces $\sim P$. Also, forcing does not obey some simple rules of the propositional calculus. Thus, π may force $\sim \sim P$

-   if a condition π forces a statement on the names, then, for any generic part ♀ such that $\pi \in$ ♀, the same statement, this time bearing on the referential value of the names, is veridical in the generic extension $S($♀$)$;
-   reciprocally, if a statement is veridical in a generic extension $S($♀$)$, there exists a condition π such that $\pi \in$ ♀ and π forces the statement applied to the names whose values appear in the veridical statement in question. (BE p. 412)

85. As in the above exposition of Kripke's intuitionistic semantics, I leave out the conditions for the quantifiers $\exists$ and $\forall$. Again, this is done in the interest of brevity. The interested reader may consult Chapter IV of Cohen's text.

86. These definitions are presented in Cohen, p. 117-8. I have altered some of the notation to conform to Badiou's. This, of course, does not affect the meanings of formulae in question.

and yet not force P'.[87] To be more precise, the definitions we have here do not obey some simple rules of the *classical* propositional calculus; as an analogue of entailment, the forcing relation here defined is, in fact, highly suggestive of the *intuitionistic* calculus. Consider the definition for negation. As Cohen tells us, it is only possible for a condition π to force $\sim P$ so long as no other condition participating in the generic sequence forces P. 'In forcing', Badiou observes, 'the concept of negation has something modal about it: it is possible to deny once one is not constrained to affirm'; the certainty of non-constraint always being deferred until the sequence is completed. 'This modality of the negative', Badiou continues, 'is characteristic of subjective or post-evental negation' (BE 415)—just as it is characteristic of the temporally deployed constructions of the intuitionist subject (cf. § 7). It is not merely a superficial structural similarity that is at issue here; the formal congruence between the two subjective logics is the effect of essentially identical requirements. These requirements stem from the fact that 'both' subjects participate in the articulation of a truth which finds its full determination only in time. We have seen that Badiou's temporalization of the subjective truth procedure has the effect of translating the generic subset in which the subject participates into the intuitionistically legible form of a *potentially generic choice sequence*; we see now that this same temporalization seems to bring the logic of the post-evental subject into conformity with the logic of intuitionism.

In the same 1963 paper from which we earlier drew the semantical analysis of intuitionistic logic, Kripke confirms our suspicions (pp. 118-120). He shows that model structures of the sort presented in § 7 can be, rather straightforwardly, interpreted as modelling the forcing relation instead of the Heyting calculus for intuitionistic logic. Roughly speaking, this involves assigning *forcing conditions* to the nodes of the model structure in such a way that $\pi R \pi'$ whenever we have $\pi \subset \pi'$. For those π which are elements of ♀, we have $\phi(P,\pi) = \mathbf{T}$ or $\phi(P,\pi) = \mathbf{F}$, according to whether π forces P or fails to do so. In this model, ♀ thus appears as an infinitely long path through the tree (in the classical context of Kripke's model, we may consider this path as a completed structure).

Kripke presents us with a fascinating theorem concerning this model: if we say that ♀ forces Q whenever there exists a π in ♀ which forces Q, then for all Q, ♀ forces either Q or $\sim Q$, *if and only if* ♀ *is generic*. This theorem elegantly brings together the essential law of classical logic—the point at which its difference from intuitionistic logic is concentrated—and

---

87. Cohen, p. 118. Notation altered; see previous footnote.

the classical, non-intuitionistic concept *par excellence*: the actual completion of a extensionally determined, intrinsically non-constructible, infinite set.

Now, we must recall that throughout the entirety of $♀(n)$'s historical existence, n, which marks both the 'age' of $♀(n)$ and its cardinality, remains finite. So long as $♀(n)$ is finite, it is *not yet a generic sequence*; it is merely *potentially* generic, but extensionally considered, it is no different than any other finite set in this respect. The Law of the Excluded Middle is therefore *not* generally valid for the subject of a truth procedure, insofar as this subject remains finite. The logic of the subject is not classical. It is intuitionistic.

§ 12

It is now possible to characterize the intuitionist application 'onto ontology [*i.e.* mathematics] rules of connection which *come from elsewhere*' (BE 249) in terms more precise and more rigorously developed than the vague epithets of 'empiricism' and 'objectivism' with which Badiou dismisses intuitionistic logic in the 24th Meditation. We may now characterize the logic of the intuitionist subject in terms internal to the conceptual apparatus set out in *Being and Event*: the rules of intuitionistic logic are precisely those prescribed by the law of the subject, the logic internal to a truth procedure. If intuitionist mathematics is justified in applying these rules back onto mathematics, it is because intuitionism seizes mathematics *as a truth procedure*. Conversely, if mathematics *is* a truth procedure, then these rules cannot be said to be derived from elsewhere; they are proceed from the very subjectivity which bears ontology towards truth.

The paradox, here, is that throughout *Being and Event*, mathematics is charged with a double task. It is repeatedly summoned not only to provide the ontological lineaments of the world, but also to stand as an exemplary truth procedure—indeed, as the paradigm for an entire species of truth procedures (the scientific). Yet if mathematics is a historical and concrete truth procedure, then its logic is not classical. And if mathematics is ontology, then either its logic cannot be the intuitionistic logic prescribed by the law of the subject, or else this ontology cannot be primarily set-theoretical.

Let us tackle one problem at a time: how is it possible for the logic of the mathematical truth procedure to be classical, when its subjective law is intuitionistic? In truth, the problem does not confront Badiou in this form, for he does not make of classical deduction the *law of the ontologist subject*. Instead, deduction is conceived as ontology's *operator of fidelity*, the principle whereby the ontologist subject concatenates the elements of the truth to which it is faithful (BE med. 24). Both classical and intuitionist deduction are conceived in this way, as two bifurcating regimes of fidelity (BE 249). Is this interpretation of deduction legitimate? Under the hypothesis that a truth is generic, it would seem that it is not. A sequence of elements concatenated in such a way that each is *deducible* from the series prior to it will not become generic. Insofar as classical mathematics is held to express, in its axioms, the laws of being *qua* being, the laws which dictate the formal structure *of any presentation whatsoever*, these laws are necessarily operative in the 'ontological situation' wherein the mathematician exercises her fidelity. Any sequence there articulated in accordance with these laws would be a *discernible* or *lawlike* sequence, and hence non-generic. Of course, the same problem would confront us if we chose to select *intuitionistic deducibility* as a principle of connection, but this is not the issue here. Deduction *as such* cannot be the principle of connection for a generic procedure. The principle of connection for mathematical truth procedures thus remains obscure. Of course, this is consonant with the nature of generic sequences: by definition, the operator of fidelity cannot be lawlike. It remains an open question how the operator of mathematical fidelity is to be thought. As for deduction, it can more consistently be conceived as the subjective law corresponding to the mathematical truth procedure, that is, as a manifestation of the forcing relation. And yet, if this is done, then deduction would obey an intuitionistic logic, and ontology, if it is a truth procedure, would not be classical.

If we maintain, despite all difficulties, that mathematics is a truth procedure in the sense outlined in *Being and Event*, the next question that we face concerns its status as ontology. This is a question that is far more profound and difficult that can be adequately dealt with here. A few, tentative remarks may be made at this point, however.

First of all, if the foregoing speculations are correct, then if mathematics is at once a truth and an ontology, then it would be compelled to obey an intuitionistic logic. This is not to say that it must be intuitionistic mathematics as such—as has been mentioned already, it would be wrong to reduce intuitionism to its abstract logical form. Nevertheless, this is a seemingly viable hypothesis. If we do take intuitionistic mathematics to be that which expresses the sayable of being, however, then we face the immediate consequence of having undercut a great deal of the formal apparatus that has brought us to this point. We lose the concept of the completed generic—even if such a figure never arrives historically, and we lose the non-wellfounded multiplicity that Badiou calls the event—even if such a structure was already foreclosed from the classical ontology. Time, on the other hand, enters into a much more subtle and organic relation with intuitionist ontology than it does with its classical predecessor, for which it appears as a somewhat awkward supplement. The question also arises as to the character of an intuitionistic ontology. There is no need to assume in advance that it would compel an idealist metaontology, as opposed to the materialist doctrine that Badiou sought to draw out of classical set theory; Badiou himself, at least in principle, wishes to distinguish between being in itself and what is *sayable of being*.[88] It is possible to uphold this distinction by maintaining beyond the scope of constructive thought, an unconstructed horizon about which we can, as of yet, say nothing.

Lest we loose the thread we took up at the beginning of this essay, let us take stock of the following points: Within the immanence of their procedures, the intuitionist and the post-evental subject are indiscernible from one another. It is their positions which differ. The post-evental subject is conceptually distinct from the intuitionistic subject in that its form is articulated within a medium that it did not create, and in that it proceeds from an aleatory event that is not the root of the ontological apparatus that delivers this medium (like the Brouwerian 'two-ity'), but an exception—something less than a sapling—that remains unthought by this very apparatus. Yet the ontological apparatus is *itself* to be conceived as a subjective procedure, and so we are driven to think the form of the Badiousian truth-subject within the field deployed by another subject of truth. If the subject of ontology is to formally coincide with the ontological schema of the subject, then we are presented with a problem, for the subject schematized by ontology is *incongruent* with the subjective form of ontology as such, insofar as this ontology is classical. If we insist on congruence, we are led away from classical ontology and towards intuitionism, but to take this route would require reformulating the problem to which we are responding.

At this point, the range of possible speculative solutions to these difficulties appears as broad as it is unclear. It seems that it would be both more fruitful and more cautious to formulate the general questions that confront us here. There are two:

What would it mean for ontology to be a truth procedure?

What would it mean for this not to be the case?

---

88. cf. BE, p. 8: 'The thesis that I support does not in any way declare that being is mathematical, which is to say comprised of mathematical objectivities. It is not a thesis about the world but about discourse. It affirms that mathematics, throughout the entirety of its historical becoming, pronounces what is expressible of being qua being'.

It remains to be seen whether they can be answered within the context in which they are posed.[89]

---

89. With respect to Badiou's thought, I have intentionally restricted the focus of this paper to the system put forward in *Being and Event* (*L'être et l'événement*), and have not taken any consideration of the developments that this system has undergone in Badiou's 2006 work, *Logiques des mondes: l'être et l'événement 2*. This is a significant omission, given that the concept of the subject undergoes extensive revision in this recent work. Among the changes bearing on the above enquiry are a reworking of the subject in such a way that it is no longer simply the finite fragment of a truth, but participates in a properly infinite system of operations, as well as an explicit employment of the Heyting algebra for intuitionistic logic in the context of a theory of appearances that draws its mathematical support from category theory. A continuation of the current line of investigation into the terrain covered by *Logiques des mondes* is certainly called for, but this must await another time.

4

The Limits of the Subject in Badiou's *Being and Event*

Brian Anthony Smith

The figure of the subject in Badiou's *Being and Event*[1] is key to understanding the link between his revival of a systematic ontology, in the form of set theoretical mathematics, and his wider philosophical and ethical concerns. Through a critical examination of the subject, as it appears in *Being and Event*, and an evaluation of the categories of subjective Good and Evil, developed in his book *Ethics: an Essay on the Understanding of Evil*[2], I hope to probe the limits of this subjective model and to propose a new subjective figure that appears possible, but unexamined, in either of these works.

My analysis will focus on two main points: first, Badiou's use of the Axiom of Choice, as a key factor in his philosophy that allows for the possibility of a subject, and, second, his selective use of set theoretical forcing, which concentrates mainly on the independence of the Continuum Hypothesis.

Badiou's ethics is based on the capacity of individuals to distinguish themselves from their *finite* animal nature and to become *immortal*; to become immortal is to become a subject (E 12, 132). What constitutes this singular ability, our rationality, is the use of mathematics (E 132). Specifically it is the Axiom of Choice that elevates the human animal to the

---

1. Alain Badiou, *Being and Event*, trans. Oliver Feltham, London, Continuum, 2005 (henceforth BE).
2. Alain Badiou, *Ethics: an Essay on the Understanding of Evil*, trans. Peter Hallward, London, Verso, 2001 (henceforth E).

level of a *potential* subject. This axiom expresses an individual's freedom, a freedom equivalent to the affirmation of pure chance.[3] It is this capacity that allows an individual to affirm its chance encounter with an event; the moment of this affirmation is called *intervention* and marks the birth of a subject (BE Meditations 20 and 22).

The importance of the Axiom of Choice is clear; it provides the connection between the individual, the event and the subject. It defines the individual and provides the *condition* under which subjectivity is possible.

Badiou's appeal to Paul Cohen's theory of forcing is predominately directed toward his proof of the independence of Georg Cantor's Continuum Hypothesis. But in Cohen's book, *Set Theory and the Continuum Hypothesis*, the method of forcing is used equally to prove the independence of the Axiom of Choice.[4] For Badiou, the Continuum Hypothesis is a restrictive theorem of ontology; it confines ontology to the merely constructible and neuters the individual by reducing the power of the Axiom of Choice (BE Meditations 28 and 9). Under such a restriction the Axiom of Choice loses its independence as an axiom and becomes a theorem, a mere consequence of the system (BE 305-7). Cohen's theory of forcing is important as it shows that it is possible to construct a model of set theory in which the Continuum Hypothesis fails, thus liberating us from its restrictive bonds. In the process it not only reinstates the full power of the Axiom of Choice, the freedom of the individual, but also, through the use of this axiom, a *subject* emerges.

The mathematical theory of forcing, as it is applied to the Continuum Hypothesis, provides Badiou with the paradigmatic model for the subjective response to an event. The subjective process *emancipates* the individual, through a *correct* use of their freedom in the face of an event, from some restrictive condition of their situation. This production of a truth introduces true novelty that expands, or extends, the subject's situation. This forms the basis of Badiou's theory of ethics. Subjective endeavour, forcing the truth of an event, forms the *positive* concept of the Good and 'It is from our positive capability for Good... that we are to identify Evil' (E 16). The range of types of Evil can be identified with false, abortive or totalizing activities that try to subvert a truth procedure, the Good being

3. Alain Badiou, '*On Subtraction*' in *Theoretical Writings*, ed. and trans. Ray Brassier and Alberto Toscano, London, Continuum, 2004, p. 113.
4. Paul Cohen, *Set Theory and the Continuum Hypothesis*, New York, W. A. Benjamin, 1966, pp. 136-142.

the practice of the *virtues* of discernment, courage and moderation (E 91). The subject remains faithful to the event and its consequences.

The clarity and decisive character of Badiou's ethics is refreshing, but is it the case that the subject is always *intrinsically* good? What would happen if we examined the consequences of a valid subjective process, based on the mathematical model of forcing, which instead of liberating an individual, in the process of their subjective action, condemned them? I think the independence of the Axiom of Choice provides such an occasion. What would be the consequences of forcing a situation in which the Axiom of Choice fails, in which the freedom of the individual is denied and the competence of the subject questioned?

To be in a position to evaluate the nature of this possible subject it will be necessary to fully understand Badiou's move to equate ontology and mathematics, and to recognize that his theory of the event is more than a reduction of philosophy to mathematics.

It will therefore be necessary to examine two main areas: first, the reasons why Badiou equates ontology and mathematics, focusing on the critical distinctions this allows him to make, and, second, the importance of the Axiom of Choice for the formation of the subject, and the specific relation between the subject and the event. Special attention will be given to those concepts that separate the theory of the subject from its ontological existence, namely the matheme of the event and the concepts of History and temporality. Finally I will consider Badiou's ethics, and the types of subjectivity associated with Good and Evil and conclude with an analysis of the position and character of a subject based on the procedure of forcing a situation in which the Axiom of Choice fails.

I. ONTOLOGY, SET THEORY AND THE SPACE OF THE SUBJECT

Badiou's philosophical claim that mathematics *is* ontology forms the central thesis of *Being and Event* (BE 4). One of the main figures that motivate this approach is Heidegger and his critique of Western metaphysics. Like Heidegger, Badiou believes that philosophy can only be revitalized through a new examination of the ontological question, but he does not agree with his later retreat into poetics (BE 2, 9-10).

Badiou sees Heidegger's problem in his refusal to give any legitimacy to systematic ontology. This refusal is based on the belief that systematic ontology always begins with the move of forcing an identity between *being* and the *one*, or oneness.[5] This identity causes being to split into separate essential and existential parts; the history of metaphysics then exhausts itself in the impossible task of reconciling and rejoining these two aspects.[6] The solution to this problem is to view metaphysics as something that must be abandoned, its positive role can only be to make the question of being ever more poignant through the distress that it causes: this distress is heard as the cry elicited by the violation of being by metaphysics. The truth of being can only be understood as the simple letting be of being, exemplified by poetic thought that refrains from all analysis. Here being is thought of as a simple presencing, where the two aspects of the essential and the existential belong together in an undifferentiated shining forth, prior to any separation.[7]

Badiou's response to Heidegger is twofold: to separate philosophy from ontology and to propose a systematic ontology not based on the one. This last point gives rise to what he calls his ontological wager: 'the one *is not*' (BE 23). There is no pure presentation of being, not even the poetic active *presencing* of Heidegger, instead being is radically subtracted from all presentation (BE 10). The problem with the history of philosophy has not been its attempt to present being in a *consistent* and *systematic* way, but its attempt to present being as a *one*. For Badiou, if being is not a one, then it can only be thought of as a pure multiple: being *is*, but it is not one, therefore it must be multiple. Here we have the two key conditions for ontology: being *is* multiple and the one *is not*. Ontology must be the consistent presentation of the pure multiple of being; the problem is that consistent presentation involves the one, or oneness (BE 23-4). Badiou avoids conceding a point of being to the one by conceiving it as a pure operation, the operation of the count-as-one (BE 24). The one, for Badiou, must remain a process, therefore the one as this operation of the presentation of the count-as-one is never itself presented; it is only the structure of presentation. It is *how* the multiple is presented, not *what* the multiple is. Hence oneness is presented as the result of the operation of the count-as-one on the pure multiplicity of being, as Badiou states: 'What will have been counted as one, on the basis of not having been one, turns out to be multiple' (BE 24). This move enables Badiou to make a decisive distinction, that between *consistent* and *inconsistent* multiplicity (BE 25).

5. Martin Heidegger, *Contributions to Philosophy: from Enowning*, trans. Parvis Emad and Kenneth Maly, Bloomington, Indiana University Press, 1999, p. 146 §110:4.

6. Heidegger, *Contributions to Philosophy*, pp. 145-146 §110:2.

7. Heidegger, *Contributions to Philosophy*, pp. 145-146 §110:2.

These distinctions apply to the pure multiplicity of being as it is split apart by the operation of the count-for-one, into a retroactively designated prior *inconsistency* and a *consistent* result as a presented one.

Before examining in some detail the appeal that Badiou makes to set theoretical mathematics in order to realize this ontology, it is worth considering what he hopes to achieve by adopting such an approach. What Badiou is essentially trying to achieve is to move philosophy beyond its obsession with foundations, origins and beginnings. Philosophy should not only give up its search for foundations, but also its post-modern lament on the impossibility of such origins. For Badiou, the creation of novelty, in the form of a truth produced by subjective endeavour, does not find its source in the impossibility of presenting being, an impossibility whose trace resides in all presentation, but in fidelity to an event (BE 27). The subject affirms that something has happened and is prepared to bare the consequences, whether the event actually occurred may be undecidable but the situation provides the subject with the necessary material to not only distinguish different events, but also recognize the problem posed by the event as different from the problem of foundation.

Badiou's aim is to establish two fundamentally different concepts of non-relation that he feels have been confused in philosophy. The first is the type of non-relation described above: there must be no relation between being and the one. This is the unilateral subtraction of being from presentation: the inconsistent multiple is never presented, only ever a consistent presentation of it. This type of non-relation is a *no*-relation, ontology is a situation that presents a structure, but being has *no* structure (BE 26-7). Relations, or functions, are always consistent ontological presentations, but they do not always share the same degree of determination (BE Appendix 2).

The second type of non-relation is more of a non-determinate relation. Consistent multiples within Badiou's ontology can usually be subject to two different kinds of presentation, an *extensive* presentation, associated with a multiplicity's *cardinal* magnitude, and an *intensive* presentation, associated with its *ordinal* order. These two types of presentation form two separate number systems: the cardinal and ordinal numbers. At the finite level these two systems coincide and behave identically, but at the infinite level the two systems diverge and their relation to each other becomes indeterminate. A space is opened up at the infinite level whereby a multiplicity of possible relations can be maintained between the two systems. More importantly, for Badiou, is the possibility under certain restricted situations for multiples to exist which have no intensive presentation, only an extensive one: these multiples are called non-constructible. Such non-constructible multiples provide the material that a subject requires in order to transform a situation. What is important about this type of multiple is that it is a form of *unordered* consistent presentation. Consistent presentation is not dependent on order; it is not constrained to what can be constructed, but can encompass the minimal structure of unordered, or disordered, multiplicity. This lack of structured order is not to be confused with a lack of consistency: the disordered is *not* inconsistent.

For Badiou, ontology must be able to make this distinction between indeterminacy, in terms of disorder, and inconsistency. His recourse to set theory must therefore achieve three things: first, it must establish that an ontology based on the pure multiple is possible; second, that there is within this system of ontology indeterminate, or indiscernible, material and, third, that this material can be accessed and utilized by a subject. The event itself, which motivates a subject, is always outside and excluded from ontology (BE 189-90). The remainder of this first section will concentrate on the first two points: axiomatic set theory as a possible ontology of the pure multiple, and the significance of the infinite within set theory for introducing the concept of the non-constructible set and the indiscernible.

a) Set Theoretical Foundations

Badiou's philosophy stands or falls on whether set theory actually provides an ontology of the pure multiple that avoids the pitfalls of the one. Only after this possible use of set theory has been accepted can we begin to look at how Badiou uses it in his theory of the subject. The first few meditations of *Being and Event*, which introduce set theory, are motivated only by the desire to demonstrate that such an ontology is possible.

It is not clear how set theory can provide a theory of the pure multiple, which avoids attributing being to the one. Even if we accept that the count-for-one, as an operation, avoids presenting being as a one, and only attributes oneness to the structure of presentation, an idea that is not without its critics, this still leaves us with an empty theory.[8] Badiou thinks that the formal axiom system of Zermelo-Fraenkel set theory (ZF) avoids making what is presented in the operation of the count-for-one into *a* being by excluding any formal definition of a set (BE 30). What a set *is*

---

8. Jean-Toussaint Desanti, 'Some Remarks on the Intrinsic Ontology of Alain Badiou', in Peter Hallward (ed.), *Think Again: Alain Badiou and the Future of Philosophy*, London, Continuum Press, 2004.

cannot be defined; being is never attributed to the *concept* of a set. A set might be thought of as the collection of its members into a one, they are counted as one, but the set's members are again sets. A set is the presentation of pure multiplicity; the members of a set are multiples of multiples of multiples, endlessly. There can be no formal definition of what a set is, as our understanding of it is dependent on us already knowing what a set is, the alternative, discussed below, is to designate atomic entities that are not themselves sets. The oneness inherent in the presentation of a set is due to the operation of presentation; it is not dependent on any inherent oneness in what is being presented.

Subsequently the majority of the axioms of ZF dictate rules for the formal manipulation of sets, but they do not entail the actual existence of any set (BE 62). If an axiom cannot be given that either discerns or generates sets then, to prevent the system from being empty, it is necessary for axioms to explicitly state the existence of certain sets.

Here the danger of reintroducing the one can occur, depending on what type of sets are claimed to exist. There are many different ways of introducing sets axiomatically, but they do not all provide a pure theory of the multiple. It is not sufficient to simply use a formal axiomatic system, it is also important that the right axioms are chosen. There are many theories of set theory that introduce atomic *individuals* at the axiomatic level, which, in Badiou's eyes, would clearly constitute the presentation of being as a one.[9] The axioms that do not conform to simple rules of manipulation are the two explicitly existential axioms of the Empty Set and Infinity (BE 62). The Axiom of the Empty Set, finally, allows Badiou to claim that set theory is a theory of the pure multiple. In order to understand the significance of this axiom it will be necessary to introduce some set theoretical terminology.

Badiou's initial introduction of the concept of the pure *presented* multiple, as the result of the operation of the count-as-one, is very close to Georg Cantor's original naïve description of a set: 'By a set we are to understand any collection into a whole M of definite and separate objects m'.[10] Such a set M is written: $M = \{m\}$, or if M has more than one element, $M = \{m_1, m_2, m_3, \ldots m_n\}$. A set is therefore a collection of separate elements, which are said to *belong* to a set. This relation of belonging is the

9. Michael Potter, *Set Theory and its Philosophy*, Oxford, Oxford University Press, 2004, pp. 72-75, 291.

10. Georg Cantor, *Contributions to the Founding of the Theory of Transfinite Numbers*, trans. Philip Jourdain, New York, Dover, 1915, p. 85.

fundamental non-logical relation that structures all sets, and is written '∈'. In the set M above, for example, all the elements that appear within the brackets belong to M: $m_1 \in M$, $m_2 \in M$, and so on. For Badiou, the set is the consistent presentation of its elements. The term element can be somewhat misleading, as it seems to suggest that the elements themselves are ones, thus introducing oneness into set theory. Badiou avoids calling these terms elements and prefers to call them presented terms. I will continue to call them elements as this is the name that most commonly appears in texts on set theory. The construction of the elements of sets will make it clear that they are not atomic individuals, but rather pure multiples, which are each multiple in their own right.

The initial set, asserted to exist axiomatically, cannot have any members; nothing can belong to it. If it did, the set's members could legitimately be held to be atomic individuals. This would guarantee that the one *is*, contradicting the wager that the one *is not*. Therefore, to begin with, the only set that can be asserted to exist, without contradicting the above wager, is an empty set. Unsurprisingly, the Axiom of the Empty Set asserts that just such a set exists. Badiou's technical formulation of this axiom is:

$$(\exists \beta)[\neg(\exists \alpha)(\alpha \in \beta)]$$

This reads 'there exists a β such that there does not exist any α which belongs to it' (BE 68). The set β is void, or empty. In his formulation Badiou chooses to use the existential quantifier, $\exists$, 'there exists', twice rather than the more usual use of the universal quantifier, $\forall$, 'for all'. The more usual formulation of this axiom is:

$$(\exists \beta)(\forall \alpha)\neg(\alpha \in \beta)[11]$$

This would read: there exists a set β such that, for all α, no α belongs to β. The double existential form is important for Badiou: there *exists* β such that there *does not exist* α. There is the *presentation* of something that is *not* presented, for Badiou this is pure inconsistent multiplicity (BE 67).

With this axiom, the final requirements of a theory of the pure multiple, a form of consistent presentation without a one, is achieved. The metaontological significance of this axiom is that 'the unpresentable is presented, as a subtractive term of the presentation of presentation' (BE 67). As Badiou states: 'If there cannot be *a* presentation *of* being because being occurs in every presentation—and this is why it does not present *itself*—then there is one solution left for us: that the ontological situation be *the presentation of presentation*' (BE 27). The Axiom of the Empty Set guar-

---

11. Mary Tiles, *The Philosophy of Set Theory: An Historical Introduction to Cantor's Paradise*, Oxford, Basil Blackwell, 1989, p. 121.

antees the existence of at least one set, from which other sets can then be generated, but this set presents nothing more than presentation itself. The empty set, written $\emptyset$, can be thought of as simply an empty pair of brackets: $\emptyset = \{\}$. If a set is the formal operation of presenting its elements, then if a set has no elements all it presents is this formal operation itself: the empty set, $\emptyset$, presents nothing but presentation itself.

This *consistent* presentation is often assumed as paradoxical, or a sleight of hand: the assertion that $\emptyset$ exists means that the theory is not empty, only that the *content* of this theory *is* empty. What is being presented here is only the 'how', of how being can be presented: the operation of the count-as-one. The content of mathematical set theory is empty, although there is a great richness to the structures of presentation. The empty set in conjunction with the other ZF axioms can be used to generate an indefinite number of other sets, all of which ultimately present nothing. Therefore the theory is not empty, it is populated by the variety of empty structures of presentation, but it is still, finally, empty.

Here we can see how the two alternative phrasings 'the one *is not*' and 'being *is* multiple' are both satisfied by this axiom. Every result of a count-as-one, a set, is formed from the empty set, so that although the presentation is not empty, there is a presentation of structure, *nothing*, that is no *being*, is presented: the one *is not*. Being is therefore subtracted from all presentation of it as a one, the empty set perfectly expresses this by presenting nothing, no one, and if being is not one then it is multiple.

The final point to be made on this is that the empty set's uniqueness means that it acts as a proper name, the proper name of being. The empty set, $\emptyset$, is not the presentation of being itself, but only its proper name. The uniqueness of $\emptyset$ is immediate as *nothing* differentiates it; the uniqueness of the empty set is based on its in-difference (BE 68). The empty set, or void set as Badiou often calls it, is in-different *not* indiscernible. It is not that we cannot discern what is presented in the empty set, but rather that there is *nothing* to discern. This point is of vital importance when indiscernible sets are introduced as being central to a theory of the subject.

To conclude this section, set theory is based not on a general definition of a set, but on the assertion that a particular set does exist. The empty set, $\emptyset$, makes it possible for set theory to be an ontology of the pure multiple.

b) The Infinite as the Space of Novelty

Having established that such a form of ontology is *possible*, it is now necessary to show that it is not sterile. The space opened by set theory must not be foreclosed against novelty. The fear is that set theory will present such a formal system that it will be structurally determined and closed. Although this is true at the finite level, at the infinite level there is no absolute structure. For Badiou, the notion of the infinite does not go hand in hand with the themes of transcendence and totalization, but it is instead what makes the indeterminate and the undecidable possible. In this section I will explore how the concept of the infinite frees ontology from any single structure, and allows for the appearance of the indiscernible, or non-constructible set.

In order to make these aims clear it will be necessary to introduce more of the technical terminology of set theory of *Being and Event*.

Cantor's initial aim with his theory of sets was to introduce the most abstract mathematical objects possible: at base they should be pure multiples abstracted from both their *content* and their *order* of appearance.[12] Free from these two *intrinsic* qualities a set was presented as a pure *extrinsic* multiple. This idea remains in modern ZF set theory in the form of the Axiom of Extension, which defines the identity of a set solely in terms of its elements. A set is nothing more than the collection of the elements that it brings together, regardless of how these elements have been collected or arranged. The axiom states:

$$(\forall \gamma) \; [(\gamma \in \alpha) \leftrightarrow (\gamma \in \beta)] \rightarrow (\alpha = \beta)$$

This reads: a set α is the same as a set β if, and only if, every element of α is also an element of β, and vice versa. This extensional, or combinatorial, concept of a set is vital for Badiou; a set is a pure multiple defined by nothing more than the multiples that it presents.

Cantor called this abstract extensional presentation of a set its *power* or its *cardinal* number, but it is also possible to think of a set in terms of its *intrinsic order*, thus defining the sets *ordinal* type. If a set is *well ordered*, the ordinal type of the set becomes its ordinal number. A set is partially ordered if each element can be thought to 'have a place' relative to the other elements. For every m_1 and m_2 belonging to a set M, and $m_1 \neq m_2$, it must be the case that either $m_1 < m_2$ or $m_2 < m_1$. This equates with our general understanding of the natural, rational and, even, the real numbers. Well ordering is a slightly more strict form of order, which restricts well ordering to the type of discrete order found only in the natural numbers, each

---

12. Cantor, *Contributions to the Founding of the Theory of Transfinite Numbers*, p. 86.

number always has a direct successor with no number appearing between the original number and its successor.

Two sets α and β have the same cardinal number if there is a one-to-one relation between them; each element of α maps onto a unique element of β and vice versa. Two sets α and β have the same ordinal number if a similar one-to-one relation exists, but the relation must also preserve the well ordering of the sets.

It is this distinction between a set's cardinal and ordinal character, and the relation between these two relations, that lies at the heart of both Cantor's life long obsession with the continuum hypothesis, and Badiou's interest in set theory and the infinite.

The difference between cardinal and ordinal numbers is simple to understand, but the significance of this distinction does not become obvious until infinite sets are considered. Cardinality measures the magnitude of a set, while ordinality is a measure of degree, based on order. Take for example the set $\alpha = \{1, 2, 3, 4\}$, this set has a cardinal power of four and an ordinal degree of four. It has a cardinal power of four, as it clearly has four elements. It has an ordinal degree of four, as the highest ranked element, according to its ordering, is four. If a set has a clear order then we need only look for its highest ranked element in order to know its ordinal number.

At the finite level every set can be well ordered, also this ordering is unique: you cannot change the ordinal value of a finite set by rearranging its elements. Every finite set can only be associated with one ordinal number. This ordinal number is also identical to its cardinal power; in the above example the set α had both the ordinal and cardinal number four.

The concept of an infinite ordinal can only be reached through an extension of the method that generates finite ordinals. This is the seemingly simple notion of adding one. Badiou's approach to the construction of the ordinals begins with his distinction between belonging and inclusion. Badiou claims that this distinction provides the source of the originality of *Being and Event* (BE 81).

Given a set $\alpha = \{a, b, c, d\}$, the elements that belong to it are: a, b, c and d. But what about sets that share coincident elements, such as $\beta = \{a, b\}$ for example? Such a set is said to be *included* in α, or to be a *subset* of α, and is written: $\beta \subset \alpha$. If all the elements of a set β are also elements of α, then β is a subset of α. The Power Set Axiom then states that if a set α exists then so does the set of all α's subsets. Taking the example $\gamma = \{a, b, c\}$, the power set of γ is: $\wp(\gamma) = \{\{a\}, \{b\}, \{c\}, \{a, b\}, \{a, c\}, \{b, c\}, \{a, b, c\}, \varnothing\}$. The new set, $\wp(\gamma)$, has eight, or 2^3, elements. Perhaps the only two surprising inclusions are the empty set and the set γ itself. Given the definition of a subset above, their inclusion becomes clear. Although the original set cannot belong to itself, on pain of paradox and inconsistency, it can include itself as it obviously shares all its elements.[13] The empty set, $\varnothing$, has the unique property of being universally included in all sets; there is *no* element belonging to $\varnothing$, which is not also an element of any other set, as $\varnothing$ has no elements.

Before continuing, it is worth noting how important the Power Set Axiom is for Badiou. If sets *present* their elements, they *represent* their sub-sets. The full representation of a set is equivalent to its power set, and Badiou calls this the State of a situation (BE 95). The State represents the situation, and it will be in the minimal relation between an infinite set/situation and its power set/State that novelty will be possible.

Badiou's set theoretical universe is, to begin with, sparse; only the empty set exists. The first new set he produces is $\wp(\varnothing) = \{\varnothing\}$, a set with one element, a singleton (BE 91). This is not too surprising either, if the general rule is that the number of elements of a power set are 2^n, where n is the original number of elements, if $n = 0$ then $2^0 = 1$. From this Badiou derives the rule that given any set α, then its singleton, $\{\alpha\}$, also exists (BE 91).[14]

We are now in a position to consider the construction of the finite ordinals. The void, or empty set $\varnothing$ can be considered as the first natural ordinal 0, with its singleton $\{\varnothing\}$ corresponding to the ordinal 1. The successor of these two ordinals is the union of these two: $\varnothing \cup \{\varnothing\} = \{\varnothing, \{\varnothing\}\}$, the ordinal 2. The process of succession is to form the unity between the current ordinal and the singleton of this current ordinal. The construction of the ordinal 3 is accomplished as follows: the union of $\{\varnothing, \{\varnothing\}\}$ with its singleton $\{\{\varnothing, \{\varnothing\}\}\}$: $\{\varnothing, \{\varnothing\}\} \cup \{\{\varnothing, \{\varnothing\}\}\} = \{\varnothing, \{\varnothing\}, \{\varnothing, \{\varnothing\}\}\}$. In general if a is an ordinal the successor of a is $a \cup \{a\}$, this is equivalent to the idea of adding one. The interesting feature of this construction of the ordinals is that all the previous stages of the construction appear within the current level as elements. Every element of an ordinal is itself

---

13. Such paradoxes include Russell's paradox etc.

14. Badiou suggests this as an application of the Axiom of Replacement, where the element of the singleton $\{\varnothing\}$ is replaced by an arbitrary set α, to form the singleton $\{\alpha\}$. It also follows from the Power Set Axiom, where the singleton can be thought of as the power set of α, minus everything that is not α. For example, if $\alpha = \{a, b\}$, then $\wp(\alpha) = \{\{a\}, \{b\}, \{a, b\}, \varnothing\}$, if we remove the subsets $\{a\}$, $\{b\}$ and $\varnothing$ we are left with $\{\{a, b\}\} = \{\alpha\}$, the singleton of α.

an ordinal, it is this feature of nesting and homogeneity that qualifies as a set as *transitive*:

$$\forall\alpha\forall\beta\,(\alpha\in\gamma\,\&\,\beta\in\alpha)\to\beta\in\gamma$$

This reads, if α belongs to γ and β belongs to α, then β belongs to γ.[15] Badiou calls such transitive sets *normal* and recognizes them as the hallmark of natural situations (BE 132-4). Every ordinal number is a *transitive* set, well ordered by the relation of belonging.

This method can then be used to generate any finite number of ordinals. But it cannot be used to create an infinite set, one greater than all the finite ordinals. The nature of ordinal numbers means that an ordinal greater than all the finite ordinals would include all these ordinals as elements. It would be the set of all ordinals that could be produced using the method of simple succession, the limit of this productive procedure. This *limit* ordinal is called ω, and can only be introduced via a second existential declaration (BE 156). The Axiom of Infinity states: there exists a set ω, such that for any finite ordinal a, both a and the successor of a, $a\cup\{a\}$, belong to ω. Although there is a first infinite ordinal, there is no last finite ordinal (BE 159).

There are now two types of ordinal numbers, the finite ordinals *produced* by means of succession, and the infinite ordinal ω, stated to exist as the limit of the process of succession. Hence we have successor and limit ordinals. It is now possible to examine the profound differences between an ordinal and cardinal conception of number.

Ordinal succession can be reintroduced, without modification, at the infinite level. There is the *next* ordinal after ω, which is $\omega\cup\{\omega\}$, or $\omega+1$. Again, an infinite number of new ordinal numbers can be created, their structure being defined by the number of times the above two modes of generation are used. For example, the set of all the even numbers followed by the set of all the odd numbers, $\{2, 4, 6, 8\ldots\,;\,1, 3, 5, 9\ldots\}$, uses in its *intrinsic* structure the rule of the limit of the process of succession twice, its ordinal number is therefore $\omega\cdot2>\omega$. Cardinality, on the other hand, takes no notice of the intrinsic ordering of a set and measures the pure magnitude in terms of the number of elements. The cardinality of one set is said to be equal to that of another if a simple one-to-one relation is possible between them. This is trivial for the above example, 1 would map to 1, and 2 to 2 and so one. Therefore the cardinality of the set of even numbers followed by the set of odd numbers is equivalent to the cardinality of the set of natural numbers. It is no longer the case that

---

15. Tiles, *The Philosophy of Set Theory*, p. 134.

every ordinal set can be associated with a unique cardinal number. An infinite number of infinite ordinals share the same cardinality, all of them equivalent to ω. The cardinal number associated with ω is $\aleph_0$, aleph null, and all ordinal sets using the first two methods of construction share the same cardinality.[16]

After the rather benign and simple relation between cardinal and ordinal numbers at the finite level, their divergence at the infinite level is quite fascinating. The question now arises: what is the relationship between an ordinal set's intrinsic ordinal number and its extensive cardinality?

In order to make the ordinal number system a closed and coherent system Cantor added a third rule of ordinal generation, to add to the two rules of succession and taking the limit of a succession.[17] The first rule generates all the finite numbers, and these constitute the first class of ordinal numbers (I), the combination of the first rule with the second produces all the infinite ordinals with a cardinality of $\aleph_0$, and constitutes the second class of ordinal numbers (II). The third rule of generation, called the Principle of Limitation, states that a new class of ordinal numbers (III) can be generated by taking the aggregate of all the ordinals that can be produced using the first two rules. This new ordinal, ω_1, has a cardinality that exceeds $\aleph_0$, and is thought of as the next cardinal after $\aleph_0$ called $\aleph_1$.[18] An important feature of the ordinal ω_1 is that, because it cannot be put into a one-to-one correspondence with the denumerable natural numbers, it is non-denumerable or uncountable.

This method can be used to generate an indefinite series of ordinal number classes; the ordinals of each class have the same cardinality as the aggregate of all the ordinals in the class below. The first ordinal of each class is known as a limit ordinal and corresponds to a cardinal number: Limit Ordinals: (ω, ω_1, ω_2...), corresponding Cardinals: ($\aleph_0$, $\aleph_1$, $\aleph_2$...). Although this method also produces new cardinals, it does not produce them directly, they are the result of an ordinal construction. For the two systems to be considered as complete number systems it was necessary to find a direct method for producing infinite cardinal numbers, without reference to methods of ordinal generation.

The method that Cantor introduced to directly generate new infinite cardinal numbers is via the use of the power set function. To recall, if α is

16. This leads to the familiar proofs that the set of even numbers is equinumerous with the set of odd numbers, and that the natural numbers are equinumerous with the rationals.
17. Potter, *The Philosophy of Set Theory*, p. 106.
18. Potter, *The Philosophy of Set Theory*, pp. 106-107.

a set with β elements then $\wp(\alpha)$ will be a set with 2^β elements, and $2^\beta > \beta$. Here we have a direct method of producing new cardinal numbers. It can be shown that this holds for infinite cardinal numbers, so $\wp(\aleph_0) = 2^{\aleph_0} > \aleph_0$. In general, if $\aleph_\alpha$ is an infinite cardinal number, then $\wp(\aleph_\alpha) = 2^{\aleph_\alpha} > \aleph_\alpha$.[19] Having established this separate method, the question as to the relation between these two number systems can be addressed.

The obvious choice would be to make the two systems completely commensurate with each other. This could be achieved if $\wp(\aleph_0) = \aleph_1$, a formulation of Cantor's Continuum Hypothesis, or generally if $\wp(\aleph_\alpha) = \aleph_{\alpha+1}$. But it turns out that the only thing that can be conclusively decided about $\wp(\aleph_0)$ is that it has a cardinality greater than $\aleph_0$. This minimal determination can consistently be strengthened, both the Continuum Hypothesis and its generalization can be asserted, but so can almost any other value of $\wp(\aleph_0)$. Whereas Cantor saw this as a problem within the system of set theory, the failure of set theory to form a closed system conditioned by a single set of rules, Badiou sees it as its saving grace. This realm of undecidability opens up an immanent space within set theory for the appearance of novelty, and for the subject to act on this novelty. It is Cohen's theory of forcing, proving that the Continuum Hypothesis is independent, which opens up this possibility.

If the Continuum Hypothesis holds, then $\wp(\aleph_0)$, the set of all possible subsets of countable, natural, numbers is exhausted by the ordered methods of construction deployed by ordinal generation: $\wp(\aleph_0) = \aleph_1$, or $\wp(\omega) = \omega_1$. The question posed by this hypothesis is: what would it mean to think of infinite subsets of the natural numbers that were not *constructed* according to the ordinal rules of generation? The intuitive response would be that such sets would, in someway, embody a lack of order.

One possible argument would be that the existence of such sets is irrelevant, as they could in no way be effective. The only way that our finite minds can cope with infinite sets is that they *do* embody some order that can be codified in a *finite* way. We can only know such *infinite* sets through their *finite* structure; their members satisfy some property. This idea recalls the common philosophical theme of duality; a set has its intrinsic ordinal structure, and its purely extrinsic cardinal magnitude: an intensive form and an extensive content. At the finite level these two aspects are indistinguishable and identical, but at the infinite level things change. The Continuum Hypothesis states that the formal aspect takes precedence at the infinite level; we can only discern infinite sets that embody some

---

19. Potter, *Set Theory and its Philosophy*, p. 262.

constructible order. The extensive cardinal magnitude is only accessible through this structured order. If we assert that a non-constructible set can exist, for example if there exists infinite subsets of ω which do not belong to the second ordinal number class (II), how can we have access to them without recourse to some constructive property?

In order to exploit the potential of non-constructible sets a formal approach to sets that lack order must be developed. The Axiom of Choice provides such an approach, by developing a concept of free choice that is independent of any criteria of choice. This axiom affirms freedom and chance, it does not necessarily posit non-constructible sets, but it allows for our manipulation and use of them should they exist.

In this section I have tried to show how Badiou's approach to ontology in *Being and Event* attempts to answer two fundamental questions: how an ontology based on the 'one is not' is possible, and, now, how this ontology is not sterile, it has the potential for real novelty. Novelty can be generated immanently within a situation, due to the minimal relation between a set and its power set, or between a situation and its state representation. All that can be known is that state representation is greater than the original situation, the extent of this excess can never be *known*. But in order to fully exploit this excess of the non-constructible sets, which constitute this undecidable excess of the state, they must be accessible to a subject. The subject must be capable of deploying the consequences of affirming the existence of a certain number of non-constructible sets, without subjecting them to a complete construction or discernment.

In the next section I will introduce the idea of the event, as something that occurs *outside* mathematical ontology. However, the consequences of this event can be expressed as something novel within an ontological situation by a *subject*, this subject depends on the productive *free* affirmation of non-constructible sets. The Axiom of Choice is essential to understanding this free affirmation.

II. THE AXIOM OF CHOICE: INTERVENTION AND THE TIME OF THE SUBJECT

The central role that the Axiom of Choice plays in the subjective realization of an event's consequences depends on Badiou's separation of situations into two fundamental categories, Natural situations, introduced above, and Historical situations (BE 174).[20] Natural situations are *normal*,

---

20. These are not the only types of possible situation, Badiou mentions *neutral* situations,

this normality is provided by their transitive nature. Here the relation between a set's extensional, cardinal, existence and its intentional, ordinal,
construction share an absolute minimal relation: everything that exists is
constructible according to the rules of ordinal generation. Here the Continuum Hypothesis holds, if ω is the presentation of a natural situation,
then $\wp(\omega) = \omega_1$ is its state representation. Here every subset, or state representation, is equivalent to a formal production. The state restrictions in
a natural situation do not allow anything to 'just happen'. Historical situations, on the other hand, are ab-normal; they represent something *subtracted* from the state representation of a situation (BE 174). They present
a *singularity*, something that is presented, but not represented, something
that does 'just happen'.

A singular term, for Badiou, is one that is presented in a situation but
not represented (BE 99). The subject of an event will always be a finite
portion of an infinite procedure that attempts to represent a singular term;
this production is the production of a truth. So a singular term is not
strictly a presented term that is not represented, it has a *temporal* quality
with reference to a subject. It is a term that is *not yet* represented, or one
that *will have been* represented.

This is a recurrent theme in *Being and Event*: Badiou makes significant
philosophical distinctions by dissecting mathematical proofs and procedures, which are taken mathematically to occur all at once, and imposing
a temporal structure on them (BE 410).

This temporalization is important for Badiou's discussion of foundation, which is key to his distinction between Natural and Historical situations. Foundation is a question of origin, in a natural situation the answer
is simple and unique: natural situations are founded on the empty set, $\varnothing$.
From this set all the others are explicitly generated in a strict order, this
order can always be traced back to its foundation. This foundation is, of
course, axiomatic. The axiom itself does not justify the empty set's existence it merely asserts it. A situation's foundational element is the one that
shares nothing in common with any of its other elements. This indicates
its generative function, being the element from which all others are generated. This idea is stated in an axiom, the Axiom of Foundation:

$$\forall\alpha\exists\beta\ [(\alpha \neq \varnothing) \rightarrow [(\beta\in\alpha)\ \&\ (\beta\cap\alpha = \varnothing)]]$$

To every non-empty multiple there belongs *at least* one element that
shares nothing in common with the multiple itself; this is a foundational

---

'in which it is neither a question of life (nature) nor action (history)', BE, p. 177. As far as I
can tell, he never mentions these situations again.

set. An historical situation is one with at least one non-empty foundational set. Badiou calls such a non-empty foundational set the *site* of an event (BE 175). Clearly such a set shares much in common with the empty set, both are foundational and both are subtracted from the situation, in that they share nothing in common with it. It is these properties that lead Badiou to state that such evental sites are *on the edge of the void* (BE 175). Although they share common properties with the void, or empty set, they are distinguishable from it, if only because they are non-empty. An event is concerned with something other than the proper name of being; it is concerned with the singular specific happening of the event itself.

Badiou readily admits that it is with historical situations that the gap between ontology and thought first opens up (BE 188). Strictly speaking, historical situations can only appear ontologically if these situations are given a temporal dimension. In Cohen's theory of forcing the set that is chosen to extend the standard model of set theory is a set whose elements are non-constructible sets.[21] Here, if the initial situation is thought of as ω, and its state representation as all the sets constructible from it, then if α is a non-constructible subset of ω: $\{\alpha\} \cap \omega = \varnothing$. This *looks* like a foundational set, but we must remember that $\alpha \notin \omega$, and is therefore not foundational. The next move is typical of the kind of temporality that Badiou is introducing. This *potential* site does not belong to the initial situation, but it *could* be added to it. The new initial situation would be $\omega \cup \alpha$, it is clear now that $\alpha \in \omega \cup \alpha$, but equally clear is that $\{\alpha\} \cap \omega \cup \alpha = \alpha$. So *before* its addition to the situation it only satisfied one aspect of foundation, and after its addition it only satisfies the other condition. Only taken as a temporal entity, not solely as a timeless mathematical entity, can the non-constructible set constitute a site.

The decision as to whether this site belongs, or not, is undecidable. To affirm its belonging depends only on the event actually having happened, and the *intervention* of a subject to begin the process of making it belong. The augmented situation does not, therefore, have a site; it is only marked by the trace of a decision. Cohen's theory of forcing produces new situations, which are extensions of the old, but these new situations are natural; they are standard *transitive* models of set theory.[22] To maintain a situation as historical is to keep a process of forcing continually open by focusing on the immanent subject within the situation.

21. Cohen, *Set Theory and the Continuum Hypothesis*, p. 110.
22. Cohen, *Set Theory and the Continuum Hypothesis*, p. 130.

Here the temporal aspect is emphasized again. After a subjective intervention, a decision on the undecidable belonging of a site to a situation,
the state of this situation is still that of the old situation *prior* to this intervention. It is the work of the subject to play out the consequences of their
intervention through a constant *fidelity* to their conviction that the event
occurred. The post-evental state is never fully completed, as the infinite
task of the finite subject to extend the state of the situation can never be
completed.

The entire theory of the event rests fundamentally on this situated
and temporal appropriation of set theory. This is Badiou's philosophical
use of ontology, the concepts of the individual inhabitant of a situation,
and therefore the subject are *not* mathematical/ontological concepts (BE
411). Cohen's theory of forcing is developed 'in the absence of any temporality, thus of any future anterior, … [to] establish the ontological *schema*
of the relation between the indiscernible and the undecidable' (BE 410
my emphasis).

This helps to explain Badiou's peculiar matheme of the event. The
matheme of the event is also *not* an ontological statement; it explicitly
covets inconsistency. Badiou calls the event the ultra-one and formalizes
it in the following way:

$$e_x = \{x \in X, e_x\}$$

Here, e_x is the event occurring at the site X and it presents not only all
its elements, $x \in X$, but also itself. Badiou's use of the Axiom of Foundation
makes such a set impossible within consistent mathematical ontology; it is
being's prohibition of the event (BE 190). Self-belonging is forbidden within a system of set theory that adopts the Axiom of Foundation. The matheme acts as an inconsistent supplement outside of ontology that lets the
subject know that its task is never complete. The task of the subject is to
make the truth of the event consist within a situation, to build the relation
between the indiscernible and the undecidable (BE 428). In set theoretical
terms, the generic extension of a situation, which utilizes non-construct-
ible/indiscernible sets, can decide previously undecidable statements.
The key example is the proof of the independence of the Continuum
Hypothesis, by demonstrating that there is a consistent situation in which
this hypothesis fails. For Badiou, this process is experienced immanently
from within the situation, a subject whose endless task is motivated and
completed by this external supplement.

Central to the philosophical understanding of an individual or subject's experience within a situation is the Axiom of Choice. It provides not
only the potential of an individual to become a subject through an *interven-*

tion, but also the means to maintain subjectivity indefinitely, through the continued *fidelity* to an event.

a) The Axiom of Choice

Intervention is the *illegal* naming of an event, the wager and declaration that something, the event, *has* happened (BE 205). The *choice* of this name is not recognized by the current situation, it is a non-choice for the state (BE 205). The current state restrictions do not encompass the name of the event; this means that the presentation of the name is not constructible according to the current state laws. The name does not conform to any state law of representation. By declaring that an event has occurred, and thus naming it the state apparatus is interrupted and a subject is born.

The potential subjects of a situation are the individual inhabitants who occupy it. This potential for subjectivity is what elevates man, as rational, above the merely animal (E 58-9, 132). It is dependant on their use of mathematics, especially the Axiom of Choice, which makes them capable of intervention. This capacity is hard to define and it seems to involve the coincidence of many classical ideas: rationality, freedom, order and chance. What is interesting is that this capacity can be exercised, to the detriment of the individual, in an autonomous fashion, but it only transforms an individual into a subject when supplemented by an event (BE 230-1). I shall return to this point in the next section.

In the previous section it was the declaration that the site belonged to the current situation, which made it a foundational set, albeit only in a temporal sense. This is the decision of intervention that marks the beginning of the historical transformation of a situation. The subject chooses to affirm the event, and names its site (BE 205). Before the intervention the event occurs, later the subject affirms this event by naming its site: thus only together, an event coupled with a subjective intervention, can a foundation be established. Initially the event is undecidable, it is unpresented in the site, and after its nomination it is illegal at the level of the state representation. It will be the labour of the subject to make this illegal choice legal, to make the truth of the event consist.

The very term illegal states something outside the law, here in an ontological situation that corresponds to rules of construction. An illegal presentation would be the presentation of something not controlled or constructed according to some clear rule. This idea was introduced above with the idea of non-constructible sets. All constructible sets are at base pure extensive multiples, but they all also posses an intrinsic definition, a condition which all its members satisfy. A non-constructible set is one that cannot be given such an intrinsic definition, it can only be considered extensively. In some sense the *laws* governing constructible sets are seen as necessary if any manipulation of infinite sets is to be meaningful. They are the conceptual tongs by which infinite sets can be accessed and manipulated. No such tools are available for non-constructible sets, so either they are not intelligible entities, or they are inaccessible, or there is another way in which they can be accessed. This is what the Axiom of Choice provides, a non-conceptual means of *choosing* and manipulating non-constructible sets. If the laws of constructible sets *govern* and *dictate* the choice of elements in a set, then the Axiom of Choice states that it is possible to choose in an *unrestricted* way: the choice can be unrestricted, free and arbitrary.[23]

The theory of set theoretical forcing works by selecting a set of non-constructible sets to add to a given situation, to expand the number of possible sets constructible within the situation.[24] This initial selection corresponds to the subject's nominative intervention. After this addition the number of possible sets constructible from this new, extended, situation increases. The state representation of the situation is now capable of deciding things which were previously undecidable (BE 416-7). This extension of the state representation, based on the newly chosen and affirmed addition to the situation, does not occur all at once, nor is it ever fully completed. Mathematically it does happen all at once, based simply on it being possible, but within Badiou's philosophy the procedure of extending a situation occurs slowly. The subject is both what produces this slow extension, and the extension itself; the subject is a finite portion of a truth procedure.

This temporal extension of the mathematical procedure is sustained by the subject's fidelity to the event. The impetus to carry on the slow and laborious procedure is given by the meta-ontological matheme of the event: $e_x = \{x \in X, e_x\}$. The matheme has two terms, the elements of its site and its name. These two terms drive subjective fidelity: a fidelity to the subject's *choice* of affirming the site, and a fidelity to the name of the event.

The formal definition of the Axiom of Choice states that if a set exists it is possible to construct a new set by selecting a single *arbitrary* element

23. Tiles, *The Philosophy of Set Theory*, pp. 190-191.
24. Tiles, *The Philosophy of Set Theory*, pp. 186-187

from each of the subsets of the original set. To give an example, the subsets of a set β constitute the power set of β, $\wp(\beta)$. Now there exists a new set, defined by a choice function, which selects one element from each of the elements of $\wp(\beta)$. At the finite level there is no need for this axiom, take α = {a, b}, then $\wp(\alpha)$ = {$\varnothing$, {a}, {b}, {a, b}}. There are only two possible sets constructible by 'choice', which do not already appear in $\wp(\alpha)$: {a, b, b} = {a, b}, or {a, b, a} = {a, b}. At the finite level there is no *free* choice, all such sets coincide with one of the initial set's constructible subsets.

We can see that the Axiom of Choice is operating to extend the scope of the Power Set Axiom; it is trying to create, or name, *new* subsets. If only constructible infinite sets are allowed then the limitation on choice extends to the infinite level. A supposed 'choice' function would coincide with a constructible subset; freedom would be subordinate to the law.

The power set function marks the excess between a situation and its state representation. If this excess is legally conditioned by the restrictions of construction then it forecloses the individual inhabitants of a situation against novelty. In order to interrupt this legal conditioning an illegal declaration must be made, one which affirms freedom, accesses the novelty of the non-constructible and deploys the consequences by extending the given situation. But the Axiom of Choice does not arbitrarily affirm the existence of *all* non-constructible subsets; it affirms the existence only of those that it chooses. It allows for a certain *controlled* anarchy, although it affirms and introduces chance it does so in a selective and *ordered* way.

A consequence of this ordered introduction of chaos is that the axiom has a number of significant consequences. For example, the Axiom of Choice is equivalent to stating that every set can be well ordered.[25] This means that every set can be put into a one-to-one relation with an ordinal number, which means that it can be constructed. This might seem to contradict the fact that the axiom seems to introduce non-constructible sets, but what has to be noted is that constructability and non-constructability are *relative* to a situation. This is due, partly, to the fact that the ordinal numbers do not in their totality form a set: there is no set of *all* ordinal numbers.[26] This, for Badiou, means that although there are natural situations, there is no such thing as Nature in its totality; Nature does not exist (BE 140-1). There is no ultimate level that could either absolutely affirm or deny the non-constructible. Where non-constructible sets are affirmed to exist they represent a symptom of the situation's limits. The question is

25. Potter, *Set Theory and its Philosophy*, p. 224.
26. Potter, *Set Theory and its Philosophy*, p. 181.

whether this is a desirable symptom; is it a symptom of disease? Should the non-constructible be viewed as deficient and lacking, or should it be affirmed and incorporated?

The limit ordinals code, in their structure, a certain degree of complexity by defining all the possible sets constructible from a certain number of rules. Every situation is conditioned by a limit ordinal, which restricts the degree of constructed complexity.[27] If only constructible sets can appear within a situation there is no problem, but the Axiom of Choice can force sets to appear in a situation that present a greater degree of complexity than the current situation can condition. Therefore, in this situation the construction of these sets cannot be known and they appear random and non-constructible. A further ordinal external to the situation could provide a rule for construction, but it is not immanently available to an inhabitant of the current situation.

The Axiom of Choice also greatly simplifies cardinal arithmetic, and also dictates that every infinite cardinal number is an aleph.[28] If we recall, the rules of ordinal generation produce a limitless succession of ordinal numbers, each limit ordinal being the first number to be associated with a new cardinal number, and these cardinal numbers are called alephs. What the above idea suggests is that there *is* a minimal relation between ordinal and cardinal number production; it might not be the strict relation of the General Continuum Hypothesis: $\wp(\aleph_\alpha) = \aleph_{\alpha+1}$. But there is, nevertheless a relation, the freedom of the Axiom of Choice still chooses within limits. Every cardinal is always equivalent to some ordinal.

In this section I have explored three different uses of the Axiom of Choice. First, choice is subordinate to the current law of the situation. Anything that appears to be a free choice in fact coincides with a constructible and legal part of the current situation: nothing new is produced. Second, a subjective intervention claims that certain freely chosen non-constructible sets belong to the situation. They *extend* the current situation through the novel constructions they allow. Third, freely chosen non-constructible sets are accepted as non-constructible and novel within the current situation, but a *new* situation is posited in which they are constructible. Only the second scenario, the subjective scenario, allows the illegal sets to retain their non-constructible status. Although, during the course of a truth procedure, the *names* of the non-constructible sets *become* legal, their non-constructible nature remains. The constructible and non-

---

27. Tiles, *The Philosophy of Set Theory*, p. 187.
28. Potter, *Set Theory and its Philosophy*, p. 266.

constructible co-exist. In the first case non-constructability is denied, and in the third case it is a *problem* solved through the introduction of a *new* situation with *new* rules of construction.

The random aleatory character of non-constructible sets are not considered a deficiency by the subject, their chance nature is affirmed. This idea that the subject *extends* a situation rather than creating a *new* situation is important to Badiou (BE 417). A new situation suggests that the subject performs a transcendent role. In such a transformation the subject gains access to an ordinal number outside and beyond the current situation in order to solve the *problem* of a multiple's non-constructability. This new ordinal is of sufficient complexity to define the construction of the previously non-constructible multiple. With Badiou's theory the subject remains firmly within the current situation and transforms it immanently. His only appeal to a meta-mathematical concept is to the matheme of the event. The matheme does not provide a transcendent multiple necessary for the transformation, but opens a temporal space in which the subject operates.

Although the full theory of set theoretical forcing is necessary to appreciate Badiou's subject, I believe that it is with this concept of freedom, motivated by the Axiom of Choice, that Badiou makes his most significant ethical distinctions. The three distinctions, made above, all reappear in Badiou's book on ethics. The misuses of freedom in being subordinate to the law, or attempting to transcend a given situation correspond to Badiou's categories of Terror, Betrayal and Disaster. The good is entirely defined by a correct subjective operation. But what if a correct subjective operation undermines the freedom of the subject/individual itself, what kind of subject would that be?

b) Ethical Categories

Badiou's theory of ethics focuses entirely on a clear distinction between Good and Evil, with Evil only being possible on the basis of the Good (E 16). The Good is defined as what results from a correct subjective response to an event. This involves the occurrence of an event, and the production of novelty/truth within the situation, as the result of an initial subjective intervention and their subsequent faithful labour. Evil occurs only when some aspect of this complex arrangement goes wrong (E 60). Here, the presupposition that I find difficult to accept is that all events, and subjective responses are fundamentally Good. This might not seem problematic, affirming the creative free expression of a subject, who extends the possibilities of a situation through the production of truth, but these common themes of subjectivity, freedom and truth are completely transformed in Badiou's system. They no longer have their everyday intuitive appeal. Rather, the distinction between Good and Evil is too convenient, and seems *derived* from the system of *Being and Event* rather than expressing something true. The theory of ethics developed by Badiou seems to be *consistent* with his systematic philosophy rather than with experience.

For me, Badiou's ethics appear to be based too strongly on the notion that the theory of forcing, borrowed from Cohen, is essentially a liberating operation. In providing the final proof of an axiom's independence from the standard axiom system, set theory is liberated, or emancipated, from the constraint imposed by it. Badiou presupposes two things: emancipation from a given axiom liberates the formal system from a constraint, the system becomes more open as a result, and the potential of a future subject remains intact after a process of forcing (BE 416). It is this second idea that I want to particularly concentrate on. As I have demonstrated during the course of this essay, the Axiom of Choice is essential if a subjective response is to be possible within a situation. One of the aims of developing the theory of forcing was to prove the independence of the Axiom of Choice, that is, to force a situation in which it fails.[29] Badiou calls the future anterior situation when a truth *will have been* forced, the post-eventual situation. This is an almost Kantian 'as if' projection, to consider a situation *as if* the truth had been completely forced.[30] What is the post-eventual situation if the Axiom of Choice has been forced to fail by a subject adhering to the strictures of set theoretical forcing in strict fidelity to an event? This situation will be one in which it is impossible for a new subject to arise, the individual will be stripped of their freedom. The Axiom of Choice won't be in a dormant state subordinate to the law, as it is in the restrictive constructivist's situation. The Axiom of Choice, and therefore the individual's freedom will have been an inconsistent principle.

In order to explore this idea more fully, I will examine the ethical categories of Terror, Betrayal and Disaster in order to show that none of these covers the possibility I have suggested. The forcing of the failure of the Axiom of Choice is a positive example of an undesirable event and a subsequent, fully legitimate, undesirable subject. This, I think, posses a

---

29. Cohen, *Set Theory and the Continuum Hypothesis*, pp. 136-142.
30. Badiou, 'Truth: Forcing and the Unnameable' in *Theoretical Writings*, p. 127.

significant problem for the simple division of Good and Evil in Badiou's philosophy.

Badiou finds the *simulacrum* of an event the most dangerous form of evil due to its formal similarity to a true event (E 72). The simulacrum deploys its pseudo-subjectivity in the form of terror. The simulacrum is potentially the most interesting form of evil as it allows for degrees of terror. The concept rests firmly on the Axiom of Choice and intervention, here though, the intervention is the intervention of an individual. What the individual names as the site of the event, is only what superficially appears to be the site. Thus the individual remains an individual, and does not become a subject.

The importance of the site, prior to the subjective intervention, is that it should share nothing in common with the current situation. If S is the situation and X the potential site of an event: $S \cap X = \varnothing$, X is on the edge of the void. The site is important, as sharing nothing with the situation it is equally addressed to the whole situation, there is no privileged subset of the situation that could claim special access to the event (E 73). In the case of the simulacra this supposed site is not empty, it is not on the edge of the void (E 73). Here the intervention is not based on a radical emptiness of the site, but on plenitude.

Essentially if the intersection, $S \cap X \neq \varnothing$, is not empty then this intersection constitutes an already existent subset of the situation. A constructible subset already exists that represents, at least partially, the supposed site of the event. The event can then become *identified* with an already established group. In his example of Nazi Germany Badiou gives the example of the concept of German racial purity (E 73). The question that arises is, that although the intersection is not empty, would it be empty if the identified subset where removed? For example, if $S \cap X = \alpha$, would $S \cap (X-\alpha) = \varnothing$ and, further more, is $(X-\alpha)$ non-empty? Here is the danger inherent in simulacra, as if both of these conditions are fulfilled, then $(X-\alpha)$ could be a genuine site of an event. Here there are two possible types of terror, a terror that hijacks an actual event and one that does not.

Formally or mathematically speaking the simulacra does not occur. If $(X-\alpha)$ were a genuine site, then so would X. The appearance of α would be dismissed from the formal mathematical approach, it would be seen as the mere repetition of a constructible set and removed or ignored. But within the temporal philosophical approach, developed by Badiou, this repeated subset causes immense problems.

The pseudo-subject of a simulacrum might well be generating true novelty, but the organization of this novelty under the name of a privileged subset of the original situation strips it of its truth. The address is no longer universal; it is addressed to the preordained chosen ones. Their domination of the potentially revolutionary novelty results in a reign of terror. All true subjects are open to the potential for their event to become a simulacrum, to identify its message with a predetermined group or class.

Betrayal is possibly the simplest category of Evil; it is a renunciation of one's participation in a truth procedure, and therefore a renunciation of one's subjectivity. This renunciation cannot be in the form renouncing one's *interest* in a certain cause, but must reject the very cause itself as having ever been significant (E 73). The Axiom of Choice, again, plays a central role. Here, with respect to the truth that I used to believe in, I claim that its novelty and uniqueness were merely derivative. I affirm in my renunciation that the site, which I took to be composed of non-constructible multiples, was in fact wholly constructible. The individual accepts that their freedom is only ever apparently free from their own perspective; in actuality it is subordinate to the law. Their freedom, embodied in the Axiom of Choice, is actually nothing more than a theorem entailed by a universe restricted to constructible multiples: the Axiom of Choice loses its vital axiomatic status (E 305-7).

Finally, the Disaster is what Badiou calls an attempt to name the unnameable. Here the full power of the Axiom of Choice is deployed, in an attempt to eradicate the singularity of the event in favour of the pure autonomy of the individual's freedom. There are two ways for the Axiom of Choice to deal with the possible appearance of non-constructible sets. The first, forcing, is the method chosen by the subject, where the non-constructible aspect of an event's site are made to consist in a situation. The second uses the fact that the Axiom of Choice allows all sets to be well ordered. The ordinal required to well order the non-constructible sets are not available within the limitations of the current situation. This ordinal is an unnameable for the situation, and a disaster for truth is when the individual appeals to his freedom, in the form of the Axiom of Choice, in order to name this unnameable. As Badiou claims: 'Rigid and dogmatic (or 'blinded'), the subject-language would claim the power, based on its own axioms, to name the whole of the real, and thus to change the world' (E 83).

The random character of the event, which the subject requires in order to affect an intervention, is abandoned. The individual's free choice is exercised in an isolated and autonomous fashion, which characterizes the event as a problem to be solved. In the new situation nothing of the event is left, or preserved. This is a disaster for truth, rather than affirming the truth of a situation the individuals seek confirmation of their own autonomy and power in an appeal to a transcendent realm. In the mind of God there is no confusion, there is nothing that cannot be constructed, the individual need only make an appeal to this totalized transcendent realm in order to find a solution to the problem of the event.

All of these forms of Evil rely, in one way or another, on the 'misuse' of an individual's capacity for free choice. The individual's inability to correctly deploy the Axiom of Choice, in the face of an event prevents them from making a subjective intervention. But the proof of the independence of the Axiom of Choice clearly falls into the 'correct' use of the Axiom of Choice; it inaugurates a subject through an intervention. It is somewhat bizarre, though not inconsistent, that the Axiom of Choice is a necessary axiom in the forcing of its own failure, but this does not stop it from being a valid instance of set theoretical forcing.[31]

The forcing of the failure of the Axiom of Choice works by adding non-constructible sets of a certain type to a situation. In order for the Axiom of Choice to function in the extended situation, supplemented by these non-constructible sets, it is necessary that all the sets constructible within this situation can be well ordered. For this to be possible the added sets need to be distinguishable from each other given only a finite amount of information. It is possible to *choose* non-constructible sets where this does not happen, well ordering of the constructible sets fails and so too does the axiom of choice.[32] The subject is no longer able to cope with

---

31. Tiles, *The Philosophy of Set Theory*, p. 190. Many of the features of the Axiom of Choice's use, especially in the context of Badiou's philosophy, offer parallels with Sartre's concept of bad faith. Here, for example, the Axiom of Choice, as an individual's free capacity to choose, is employed *against* that very capacity, seeking to undermine it. But this use still requires an event to supplement it, unlike Sartre. Closer would be the concept of betrayal, seen above, here freedom denies itself as free reducing itself to a theorem who's results are governed by law. This possible relation between these two thinkers is further complicated by Sartre's later work in the *Critique of Dialectical Reason*, where a similar philosophy of the event is developed. Any substantial investigation of this relation between the Axiom of Choice and bad faith would have to address the question of what happens to the concept of bad faith in Sartre's later writings.

32. Cohen, *Set Theory and the Continuum Hypothesis*, p. 136. Badiou's technical response may be that the set used to force the independence of CH only contained *denumerable* non-con-

the truth that his intervention affirmed. The subject is not capable, even potentially, of fully deploying the truth of the event.

Badiou's argument that his theory of the subject, modelled by set theoretical forcing, brings a new rationalism to the study of the subject is undermined at this point. This rationalism is based on the subject's ability to cope with events and deploy the consequences. The faith, or fidelity, of the subject is based on the Axiom of Choice as it allows, in the model of forcing the independence of the Continuum Hypothesis, the differentiation of the non-constructible sets from any given constructible or non-constructible set on the basis of a finite amount of information. The *finite* subject's faith is *justified* on the grounds that it can differentiate sets on a *finite* amount of information, regardless of whether it achieves a specific differentiation within its own lifetime. This faith is undermined if such a differentiation is not finitely possible.

The subject that forces an event that undermines their subjectivity and the *rational* power of the Axiom of Choice to manage and produce order has an echo of the sublime about it. In encountering an event of a specific kind the subject experiences something beyond the power of his free rational power to manage. Although here this does not strengthen the subject, but threatens to destroy it. If the subject holds its fidelity to this event it then enters willingly into this nihilistic endeavour. Once the Axiom of Choice has been undermined the minimal relation between the intensive and extensive character of multiples is lost, every infinite cardinal is no longer an aleph. Extensive multiples are no longer tied to intensive multiples, not even to a range of possible intensive multiples. The relative simplicity of the set theoretical universe is somewhat complicated.

I am not sure what the possible consequences of such a subject are for Badiou's philosophy. It does complicate his ethics. A self destructive subject intent on affirming something beyond reason's control could be seen as an unwelcome return of the irrational, no longer considered as inconsistent but as exceeding the power of choice, or as a reintroduction of the sublime and the Other, something which Badiou specifically wants to avoid (E ch2). But this subject is not the product of a misuse of the Axiom of Choice, but one formed according to the model outlined in *Being and Event*. Therefore, to preserve Badiou's ethics this subject must be either denied, it is not a subject, and might possibly constitute a new category

---

structible elements, whereas the set used to force the independence of AC uses *non-denumerable* elements. This would force Badiou into accepting a limited form of AC, based on *countable* choice, but in *Being and Event* he affirms the full power to the axiom.

of Evil, or it is a subject and its activity is to be affirmed as Good. Both options do not seem to comfortably fit into the framework as it stands. If this subject is affirmed the consequences of the post-evental situation need to be addressed. Although *Being and Event* allows for the indeterminacy of non-constructible sets, their inclusion is limited to those that human individuals can cope with. The individual can only allow forms of presentation that the Axiom of Choice can manipulate, that is, those sets that can be subjected to the individual's rational power. Without this rational capacity Badiou feels that man is reduced to his animal status, and incapable of ethical practice. But in the type of situation and subjectivity described above, it could be argued that the subject is in the process of exceeding his rational limitations, acting in a selfless way in the face of something that he cannot master. Perhaps this is a more fitting figure for the ethical subject, and the post-evental situation, although it never arrives, a more interesting ethical situation?

In conclusion, Badiou's use of set theory, in his conceptualization of the subject, allows him to take a truly original approach to both ontology and philosophy. The mathematical approach gives him the ability to add great clarity and distinction to otherwise similar concepts, such as the name of the void, in general, in the form of the empty set, and those entities on the edge of the void that constitute evental sites. Here Badiou's philosophy is at its strongest, rejecting the problems of systematic philosophy and ontology as an endless problem of grounding by adopting the axiomatic method, and thus explicitly nullifying the problem. The problem of the ground, or the Axiom of the Empty Set, does not recur in ontology, what occurs, instead, are events.

But set theory is also something of a Pandora's box. There are so many clearly defined bizarre entities within this universe that many of the aspects of philosophy that Badiou wants to reject, especially in recent continental philosophy, can return from the realm of inconsistency, where he banishes them, and associate themselves with some of these more unusual and offbeat products of mathematics. In this essay I have introduced the possibility that the independence of the Axiom of Choice could reintroduce themes of the Other and the sublime right into the heart of Badiou's philosophy.

What this proves is not that Badiou's philosophy is a failure but that this approach has a huge potential for productive work, even if this may divert from, or undermine, Badiou's own singular vision for his work. The central place of the subjective in the production of novelty and truth in Badiou's philosophy of events is a position that I think needs to be questioned.

5

Had we but worlds enough, and time, this absolute, philosopher...[1]

Justin Clemens

> 'We know that mathematicians care no more for logic than logicians for mathematics. The two eyes of exact science are mathematics and logic: the mathematical sect puts out the logical eye, the logical sect puts out the mathematical eye, each believing that it can see better with one eye than with two'.
>
> —Augustus de Morgan

PREAMBLE

Alain Badiou's most recent book *Logiques des mondes* presents itself as a sequel to *Being and Event*. But what is a philosophical sequel? What are the conceptual consequences for a philosophy for which a sequel has come to seem necessary? To answer this question, I begin by identifying certain key features of Badiou's position in BE, particularly regarding the 'absoluteness' of philosophy's conditions. These conditions—science, love, art and politics—prove absolute insofar as they are inseparably *contingent* in

---

1. This article draws on the following works of Badiou:

Alain Badiou, *Logiques des mondes: L'être et l'événement, 2*, Paris, Seuil, 2006 (LOW).

Alain Badiou, *On Beckett*, trans. and ed. N. Power and A. Toscano, Manchester, Clinamen, 2003 (OB).

Alain Badiou, *Being and Event*, trans. O. Feltham, London, Continuum, 2005 (BE).

Alain Badiou, *Briefings on Existence: A Short Treatise on Transitory Ontology*, trans. N. Madarasz, New York, SUNY, 2006 (TO).

Alain Badiou, *Conditions*, Paris, Seuil, 1992 (C).

Alain Badiou, *Le Siècle*, Paris, Seuil, 2005 (LS).

Alain Badiou, *Théorie du Sujet*, Paris, Seuil, 1982 (TS).

their emergence, *immanent* to their situations, *self-supporting* in their elaboration, *indifferent* to all existing forms of self-interest, *egalitarian* in their address, and *restrained* in their extension. Philosophy is a transliteration of the
singular injunctions delivered by these conditions, and the recomposition
of these effects in a system. Several aspects of BE, however, harbour certain difficulties. For example, in regards to the details of subjective variation, the relation between events and their sites, the local status of bodies
and situations, and, above all, in leaving aside the relation between mathematics and logic. In *Logiques des mondes* (the title translated here as *Logics of Worlds*), Badiou confronts these difficulties. Using category theory,
Badiou tries to forge a 'Grand Logic' able to account for the specificity
of worlds and the local apparition of events, without abandoning his doctrine of the transmundane nature of truths. This review argues that the
attempt—though overwhelmingly brilliant—is confusing, and its execu-
tion not altogether effective. LOW wavers because it revivifies, despite
itself, Hegelian elements that, in the absence of the Hegelian dialectic,
entail treating *conditions* as *examples*. When reduced to examples, truths
are no longer *conditions of* but *objects for* philosophy; as objects, however,
these truths cannot support philosophy in the way that it requires; without
such support, philosophy collapses into a 'theory' of the logic of appearances. Or, to put this another way, LOW is an *extra*-philosophical work,
concerned to delineate the possibility *of* such situations as the ontological,
rather than working directly *with* such situations itself. Symptoms of such
a philosophical 'extraneousness' are evident in the book's escalating rhetoric, its proliferation of examples, its unclarified structure, and its creation
of new problems in the guise of resolving old ones. In a word, LOW is at
once too Hegelian and not Hegelian enough. Unlike BE, LOW no longer
simply attends to *absolutes*, but tarries with *variabilities*.

I. *WORLDS' LOGICS: BEING AND EVENT 2*; OR, PHILOSOPHY'S *SEQUELA*

The first thing you notice about LOW is its size. In its original French
edition, BE was just over 560 pages, beautifully printed on heavy paper.
LOW is 630 pages long, and the paper and printing seem thinner. The
card of LOW's cover is significantly more supple than the cover of BE.
You may also be struck that the stark minimalist cover of BE has here
been ornamented with the reproduction of a beautiful Hubert Robert
painting, of figures bathing before a neoclassical folly in dark woods, the
sky rift by sun behind the angling clouds. BE appeared in the series *L'ordre*

philosophique, then edited by François Wahl; LOW appears in the same series, which is now directed by Badiou and Barbara Cassin. It may or may not be of significance that Seuil were originally retailing BE for 200 francs, and LOW for 30 euros (though I got mine for 28.50 euros). Times have clearly changed.

The differences aren't due only to design issues and a major currency shift. The title reads: *Logiques des mondes: L'être et l'événement, 2*. This literally translates as *Logics of worlds: being and event, 2*. Initially, I was tempted to twist this into *Worlds' Logics*. Why? First, because 'de' in French can be perfectly well rendered as an English possessive, retaining the irreducible ambiguity of the genitive. Second, *Worlds' Logics* is such a rebarbative syntagm that it at once detains a force of thought (you do have to think about it), and, as such, is also a reminder that this title has a very particular and significant sense. For me, it suggests something about the pluralization of both 'worlds' and 'logics' that 'logics of worlds' may not. Note the title proper is without articles, definite or indefinite. Third, it is an opportunity to offer contemporary readers a rare example of the correct use of the apostrophe. In the end, however, I have submitted to the most straightforward rendering of the title in English—a rendering that seems to have been peculiarly unpopular to date—but which at least mimes the form of the original and, as the acronym LOW, is much richer than WL.[2]

Translation issues aside, the next thing you might notice about LOW is its peculiar organization. If you turn to the 'Table' of contents, you are immediately confronted by a labyrinth of peculiar divisions: a Preface, seven Books (each titled) and a Conclusion, each division of noticeably variable length and further subdivided; there are also scholia, technical notes, appendices, avant-propos, information, commentaries and digressions, statements, dictionaries, bibliography, index and iconography; further subdivisions, bristling with titles, sometimes even the same title repeated in different books, sometimes numbered, sometimes not (e.g., 'Existence', 'Atomic logic', 'The inexistent', etc.).

---

2. See, for example, A. Toscano and R. Brassier, 'Editors' Note' in A. Badiou, *Theoretical Writings*, London, Continuum, 2004, pp. ix, x, where they speak of *The Logics of Worlds*, whereas Norman Madarasz has recourse to *World Logics* in his translation of Badiou's 'Preface' in TO, p. xi. As for Steve Corcoran and Bruno Bosteels, they give *Logics of Worlds* in their translation of 'Logics of the Site' in *Diacritics*, vol. 33, nos. 3-4, 2003, pp. 141-150. Moreover, in their unpublished 'Postface: Aleatory Rationalism' (written 2003) to *Theoretical Writings*, Toscano and Brassier do indeed speak of *Logics of Worlds*. This already gives us, bizarrely, four possibilities for what seems an eminently straightforward title. David Bowie fans will surely appreciate the acronymic allusion here to his magnificent album of the same name.

For anyone familiar with the structure and vocabulary of BE, many of the headings here will appear unfamiliar or anomalous. BE is classically and minimally structured. It begins with an account of the philosophical conjuncture into which BE is intervening, and then proceeds, in an orderly fashion—that is, at once logically, chronologically and thematically—from Plato to Lacan, interspersed with what is essentially a course in set theory ontology. LOW, on the other hand, is not ordered classically, chronologically, minimally, or, to the naked eye, logically. In the Preface alone, one finds, alongside a polemic opposing 'democratic materialism' and the 'materialist dialectic', discussions of prime numbers *chez* the Greeks and *chez nous*, of the painted horses of the Chauvet-Pont-d'Arc grotto and Picasso, of Virgil and Berlioz, of radical Chinese political tracts. It is surely significant that LOW does not, as did its predecessor, situate itself in a *philosophical* conjuncture, but in a very generalized, global *cultural* moment (that of 'democratic materialism'). As one progresses through the book, the logic of the presentation of category theory begins to take precedence, until, finally, the formalisms tail off to end with propositions entirely in natural language. There is certainly a kind of structure here, but it is less clearly rigorous and less self-evident than its predecessor's.

I will come back to this question of structure more directly below, but I wish to broach it here by asking a particular, if perhaps unusual, question: *What does it mean to write a philosophical sequel?* In the case of Hollywood, the necessity for a sequel is very clear: it is audience receipts. In the case of philosophy, the necessity for a sequel is, on the contrary, highly obscure. It's not usually sales that determine success. As David Hume notoriously remarked of his own *Treatise on Human Nature*, 'it fell dead-born from the press'. Such a lack of public approbation, however, is hardly an argument against the value of a book (especially not one that Immanuel Kant said woke him from his 'dogmatic slumbers').[3] Still, aside from metaphors of continuing to rudely awaken people despite your demise, it's hard to know what constitutes philosophical success, let alone what sort of philosophical success might demand a sequel. If a philosophical work is a success, surely that *precludes* a sequel? You've said what needed to be said: you can now spend the rest of your life reiterating, rewriting, or recanting your program. If you add a proposed second volume, that hardly constitutes a sequel; a systematic work in no matter how many volumes is not a sequel.

---

3. Jon Roffe has alerted me to the fact that Kant may never have read Hume's *Treatise*, but relied on secondary sources for his information about the problem Hume raises in regards to causation. I would like to take this opportunity, too, to thank both Roffe and A. J. Bartlett for their comments on an earlier draft of this review.

In philosophy, a sequel perhaps implies that the 'original' was in some way a failure, somehow deficient, requiring supplementation or correction—and yet, somehow, *the* intervention you can't help but follow.

You may get something of this sense from Hegel's problems with sealing up his system. In his 'Preface to the First Edition' of the *Science of Logic*, he writes:

> As regards the external relation, it was intended that the first part of the *System of Science* which contains the *Phenomenology* should be followed by a second part containing logic and the two concrete [*realen*] sciences, the Philosophy of Nature and the Philosophy of Spirit, which would complete the System of Philosophy. But the necessary expansion which logic itself has demanded has induced me to have this part published separately; it thus forms the first sequel to the *Phenomenology of Spirit* in an expanded arrangement of the system. It will later be followed by an exposition of the two concrete philosophical sciences mentioned.[4]

The philosophical system that presents the Absolute System finds itself forced into a 'necessary expansion', determined by 'logic itself'. As Martin Heidegger glosses the transmogrification:

> Soon after the appearance of the *Phenomenology of Spirit* in 1807, Hegel began publishing a work known as the *Logic*. The first volume of this work appeared in 1812/13, and the second volume in 1816. But the *Logic* did not appear as the second part of the system of science. Or is this *Logic*, in accord with the matter at issue therein, the remaining second part of the system? Yes and no....[5]

'Yes and no': what I want to underline at this point is that Hegel, a philosopher notorious for enforcing a total and systematic approach to philosophy, is himself forced to alter his declared presentation so significantly that

---

4. G.W. F. Hegel, *The Science of Logic*, trans. A.V. Miller, Atlantic Highlands NJ, Humanities Press International, 1996, pp. 28-9.

5. M. Heidegger, *Hegel's Phenomenology of Spirit*, trans. P. Emad and K. Maly, Bloomington and Indianapolis, Indiana University Press, 1988, p. 2. As Heidegger continues, 'Why is the title *System* omitted as early as 1812? Because between 1807 and 1812, a transformation was already underway. The sign of the initial transformation in the idea of the system can be seen in the fact that the *Logic* not only loses the main heading but also stands separately, by itself—not because it turned out to be too detailed, but because the *Phenomenology* is to take on a different function and position in the fluctuating arrangement of the system. Because the *Phenomenology* is no longer the first part of the system, the *Logic* is no longer its second part', p. 4. Indeed, the entire 'Introduction' is of pertinence here, pp. 1-42. I would like to thank Paul Ashton for reminding me of these passages, as well as for his detailed commentary on these issues (personal communication).

the system that the original purports to present must itself be reorganized according to new criteria that retrospectively transform its essence. Yet this very transformation continues to pursue its singular divagation in the wake of the original. I will return below to the consequences of Hegel's systemic-reconstruction-in-process. Here, however, I want to mark just how tightly the problem of the philosophical sequel is articulated with, first, the problem of the *absolute* and, second, with the problem of *system*. One might suggest that sequels tend to force out an impossibility of articulation between the two, as they betray the intervention of new concepts. A sequel makes its predecessor the *one* that it was not (or had not been). The whole—or at least its non-existence or its impossibility—is at stake in a sequel.

Which is why it is not surprising that philosophy begins with a man who writes nothing but sequels. The same action hero returns, again and again, hurling himself enthusiastically into dangerous and extreme situations; one rediscovers familiar figures and locations, which are then rendered uncanny by the events in which they are summoned to participate; a battery of narrative special-effects are placed in the service of a ceaseless conceptual warfare. All of which makes the Platonic dialogues extremely difficult to decipher. Is Socrates the same character throughout the dialogues? How does he change? Why? How close a resemblance does he bear to the 'historical' Socrates? Especially since this Platonic character Socrates dies, then returns to life, to circumstances which are painfully fictional or rankly impossible. What are the consequences for the elaboration of concepts given this swarming of personae? And so on. The complexity of the relation between continuity and rupture in the presentation and capture of concepts is not just implicit, but itself exposed and put to work in and by such a serial presentation, to the extent that 'continuity' and 'rupture' must themselves be re-conceptualized in order to fulfil the demands of philosophy.[6]

Nor is it then surprising, given Alain Badiou's declared Platonism, that LOW, his most recent book, presents itself as a sequel to his indisputable *magnum opus*, BE. As the back cover blurb puts it, LOW 'is conceived as a sequel [*une suite*] to his previous 'great' book of philosophy'. Why? Badiou himself notes that, despite several of his books proving genuine 'bestsellers' in the wake of BE, this economic success was no index of philosophical triumph. On the contrary, his doubts only grew about sev-

---

6. To follow this line of thought, could then not Aristotle's *Physics* and *Metaphysics* be thought according to a logic of the sequel?

eral aspects of his own work. Was Badiou about to expel himself from his own paradise? In the 'Preface' to the new English translation of *Court traité d'ontologie transitoire*, Badiou puts it like this:

> From the middle of the 1990s, what slowly grew to become most evident to me were the difficulties of my undertaking. Happy times were coming to a close. I told myself: 'The idea of event is fundamental. But the theory I propose on what the event is the name of is not clear'. Or: 'The ontological extension of mathematics is certain. But, then, what about logic?' Many other doubts and questions ensued (TO, ix-x).[7]

What is striking about the problems of philosophical sequels (or, if you're happy to contract a epidemiological pun, the *sequela*) is that they constitute a *return to oneself*. Jacques Lacan notoriously called for 'a return to Freud', meaning—not a return to dogmas or doctrines of the master— but to the *impasses* of the Freudian text. It is to the turbulent traces of Freud's own failed solutions to the unprecedented deadlocks his discovery of the unconscious generated that Lacan attends. So when, in BE, Badiou proposes the clarion-call of a 'return to Plato', his call should be taken in this vein. A return to Plato is not just a return to the Platonic dogmas, but to the rifts and opacities of the Platonic text; rifts and opacities, however, that would have been unthinkable before Plato's 'interruption' of poetry by mathematics.

Yet both Plato and Freud were, for the reasons I have been implying, *already* caught up in their own process of return to their own earlier work, and it is this returning—to the impasses thrown up by a founding intervention—that constitutes the development of their work. A return always returns to return. But it does so on the basis of an interruption that exceeds any sufficient reason. In Plato, this interruption is called Socrates; in Freud, it is called the symptom. Which makes a sequel different from just another book by the same author: it is a return to one's own failures to have thought what renders possible and necessary such a return.[8]

---

7. See A. J. Bartlett's review of TO in *Cosmos and History*, vol. 2, no. 1-2, pp. 339-344. As Bartlett (and others) have noted, the English in TO can be imprecise and confusing.
8. One should then note the perhaps surprising profusion of sequels in contemporary European philosophy: I think immediately of Michel Foucault's *History of Sexuality* volumes, as well as Michel Serres's *Hermès* sequence, Deleuze and Guattari's *Anti-Oedipus* and *A Thousand Plateaus*, Giorgio Agamben's *Homo Sacer*, *Remnants of Auschwitz* and *State of Exception*, etc. Badiou himself has a little sequence of volumes entitled *Circonstances* (collections of little articles that have appeared elsewhere), and speaks of his own temptation to publish a *Conditions 2* (cf. 'Preface' to TO, p. xi). But it's necessary to be careful: not every numbered sequence constitutes a sequel in the sense I am speaking of here ; nor are unnumbered

One could give this sequaciousness of philosophy a number of different names, such as those that Badiou himself has explored in some detail elsewhere. In *Le Siècle*, he gives Chapter 8 the title of 'Anabasis', drawn from a famous memoir of Xenophon, student of Socrates, contemporary of Plato. Badiou writes: 'In the trajectory it names, anabasis leaves undecided the parts respectively allotted to disciplined invention and uncertain wandering. In so doing, it constitutes a disjunctive synthesis of will and wandering. After all, the Greek word already attests to this undecidability, since the verb αναβαυειν ("to anabase," as it were), means both "to embark" and "to return."'[9] If Badiou here invokes anabasis in the context of a discussion of Saint-John Perse and Paul Celan, it is also present—if not named as such—in the discussion in LOW, under the heading of 'referents and operations of the faithful subject':

> Let's suppose that, following the revolt of a handful of gladiators around Spartacus in 73 BCE, the slaves—or rather, *some* slaves, if in large numbers—made a body, instead of being dispersed in groups. Let's accept that the trace of the revolt-event be the statement: 'We, slaves, we want to return home [*chez nous*]'. Is the subject form the operation by which the new 'body' of slaves (their army and its dependents) joins itself to the trace?...Its materiality is the consequences drawn day after day from the evental trace, that is, from a principle *indexed to the possible*: 'We, slaves, we want to *and can* return home' (59).

Once you recognize this operation, you might begin to discern it everywhere in Badiou—if under a sequence of ever-varying names. In an essay on Beckett that first appeared in French in *Conditions*, and now appears in English in *On Beckett*, Badiou pinpoints a serious shift in Beckett's work of the 1960s. It is from this shift that Badiou is able to draw the lesson that every generic procedure 'weaves within its singular duration these four functions: wandering, immobility, the imperative, and the story' (OB 32). For Badiou, it is important not to reduce the shift in order to discern the

---

titles not necessarily sequels. Badiou : 'Let us note that *Briefings on Existence. Short Treatise on Transitory Ontology* is part of a trilogy, which is already more tentative than the unity of the *Conditions* volume. Published simultaneously with it was the *Petit manuel d'inesthétique*.... There was also the *Abrégé de métapolitique*', TO, p. xi. Moreover, a sequel is not a 'carefully orchestrated succession of works dealing with problems in a clearly discernible sequence, as in Bergson', 'Author's Preface' in *Theoretical Writings*, p. xiii. And a proposed sequel may never appear at all: where's *Being & Time 2*? There is something *unplanned* about a philosophical sequel (or its failure to appear).

9. A. Badiou, *Le Siècle*, Paris, Seuil, 2005, p. 121. I am indebted to Alberto Toscano for use of his excellent draft translation of this book, which I rely on here.

return of return; to add to our list of pertinent features of the sequel, this raises the question of *time*. The sequel's double-blow, its irreducible Twon-ess, can't help but make one think of various utterances of Badiou's, e.g. 'Time…is intervention itself, thought as the gap between two events' (BE 210) or 'the structure of the ultra-one is the Two' (BE 210); or, in LOW, drawing on the 'striking' examples of Spartacus and Archimedes, 'we will call this destination *resurrection*, which reactivates a subject in another logic of its appearing-in-truth' (74). In any case, the return or resurrection must be a return to unprecedented possibilities in and of the present, founded on the contingency of an evaporated event and its uncanny trace.

In other words, it is not the bestselling success of BE that founds the necessity for a sequel, but, beyond whatever its (perceived) errors, insuf-ficiencies, and obscurities might be, there is a truth to continue across the interruption (i.e., a cleft of non-relation). As a sequel then, LOW an-nounces itself as: a *reiteration* of certain ideas of BE, notably the proposition that 'mathematics is ontology'; a *revision* of certain claims of BE, notably the theory of the subject and event; a *replacement* of certain concepts, no-tably that of 'situation' by 'world'; an *extension* of certain tendencies of BE, notably the much fuller account given of logic; and a *supplementation* of cer-tain minimal elements of BE, notably in the descriptions of political and artistic processes. Yet there is a final aspect: LOW wishes also to *complete* BE, to fill in its holes and answer its critics. This (inexpungible but ille-gitimate) desire will, as we will see, have serious consequences for LOW's structure. Reiteration, revision, replacement, extension, supplementation, and completion: we find that Badiou himself is obsessed with the problem of the sequel, which returns throughout his post-BE work under an ex-traordinary smattering of diverse names. It is in the scattered light of this embarkation-return and disciplinary-archiving ('sequel', 'anabasis', 'resur-rection')—which, on Badiou's own account, always produces a new body and new possibilities—we will examine what becomes of BE in LOW. Whatever else one can say, Hollywood cinema and philosophical sequels clearly do have something in common. For both, sequels are a common modality of the generic.

II. PHILOSOPHY AS CONDITIONED, CONDITIONS AS ABSOLUTES

What made reading *Being and Event* such a deranging experience was that its author had clearly touched upon an *absolute*.[10] Even if you end up disagreeing with every proposition in that book, it is nonetheless impossible to read and not agree that contemporary philosophy will have to change in its wake—whether in the guise of affirmation, extension, critique, resistance, rejection, or some other operation. The asceticism of its presentation, the assuredness of its declarations, the rigour of its structure, the inevitability of its development, the universality of its ambition, all help to render BE an event in the thought of being. In this regard, Badiou's account in his 'Author's Preface' to the recent English translation of BE perhaps errs on the side of *politesse*:

> Soon it will have been twenty years since I published this book in France. At that moment I was quite aware of having written a 'great' book of philosophy. I felt that I had actually achieved what I had set out to do. Not without pride, I thought that I had inscribed my name in the history of philosophy, and, in particular, in the history of those philosophical systems which are the subject of interpretations and commentaries throughout the centuries (xi).

What makes BE such a 'great' book? Among its major claims are the following:[11]

- Plato is the founding moment of philosophy
- Plato founds philosophy insofar as he interrupts poetry's revelation of presence by means of pure mathematics
- This interruption also entails the rethinking of love and politics
- Plato therefore founds philosophy on extra-philosophical conditions
- There are four, and only four, of these conditions
- These conditions are irreducible to each other
- These conditions are mathematics, poetry, love and politics
- The conditions are truth procedures
- The foundation of philosophy was an act that organized these conditions into a system

---

10. See Roffe's review of *Being and Event* in *Cosmos and History*, vol. 2, no. 1-2, pp. 327-338.
11. Although it is true that many of these claims are only fully rendered clear, explicit and distinct in accompanying texts such as *Conditions* and *Manifesto for Philosophy*, they are implicit in BE.

- To do philosophy is to remain faithful to this founding act
- Remaining faithful to this foundation entails the construction of a system according to the contemporary directions proposed by these conditions
- These contemporary directions enjoin: attending to set theory, attending to poetry, attending to post-Revolution emancipatory politics, attending to psychoanalysis qua love
- This attention will result in ideas, such as 'mathematics is ontology', 'poetry delivers the matheme of the event', 'politics engages the universality of address', 'love is the struggle of the non-relation'.[12]

Although it is necessary to be telegraphic in the present context, there are a number of details that must be clarified, above all, the concept of 'condition'.

The concept is best explained by recourse to Badiou's claims about mathematics. Pure mathematics is the paradigm of deductive rationality. Anyone can do mathematics, yet anyone who does mathematics will be constrained to the same results; or, more precisely, to the same points of undecidability. Such mathematics has no empirical reference. Mathematics clarifies the problems about which one can rationally speak, and how one must speak of them (i.e., to invoke 'infinity' today outside of its post-Cantorian acceptation is mere *flatus vocis* or obscurantism). Its verification is *immanent* to its practice; indeed, verification and practice are *inseparable* in regard to mathematics. Mathematics is therefore in this sense indubitable, obeying only its own procedures. Anyone doing mathematics must accord with these procedures and their results. Mathematics is therefore also *egalitarian*: all are literally equalized in their submission to its procedures.

Its conditioning by mathematics means philosophy has an unbreakable commitment to the most rigorous possible form of rationality. This rationality is detached from any direct empirical influences whatsoever (i.e., not only from history, social mores, sexual, ethnic, religious differences, etc., but from the vicissitudes of natural languages themselves). Moreover, the limits of mathematics are rigorously given *within* mathematics itself.

---

12. Significantly, Badiou insists that each generic procedure has an affect proper to it. In *On Beckett*, he writes: 'Happiness also singularizes love as a truth procedure, for happiness can only exist in love. Such is the reward proper to this type of truth. In art there is pleasure, in science joy, in politics enthusiasm, but in love there is happiness', p. 33. He repeats this schema verbatim in LOW. See the excellent little Tableau 1, p. 86 (reproduced below).

These features have further consequences pertinent here. First, one cannot judge mathematics by any external criteria; only mathematics is adequate to its own reason. Philosophy must follow the lead of mathematics, not the other way around. Second, philosophy must take reason as far as it can go; if one starts to follow mathematics, one must follow it to the bitter end. Third, in doing so, philosophy must be prepared to rupture with all social prejudices, even and especially its own. Four, mathematics cannot, for all that, be permitted to totalize what happens; indeed, mathematics explicitly theorizes and prohibits its own totalization.

After all, what happens radically exceeds mathematics. How could one talk of a mathematics of love or politics or, indeed, poetry, when it is precisely their extra-deductive character that is essential to these genres? For Badiou, love, politics and art are also genres that have a genuinely thoughtful kernel—if the materials and operations by which they reason cannot be *anticipated* by deduction. As we shall see, these genre-conditions can (after the fact) be *formalized* by mathematical means by philosophy (e.g., in 'mathemes'), but their apparition is due only to ungovernable Chance and the process of their development entirely subjective. Moreover, each of these genres deals with a different aspect of human creativity: art with the problem of being emerging as absent presence; love as the problem of sustaining an encounter with a non-dialectizable 'other'; politics as the problem of non-totalizable universality.[13] And mathematics has a particular claim on our philosophical attention. Badiou notoriously declares that 'mathematics is ontology', a statement to which we will return in the next section of this review. These genres are founded in 'events', that is, as non-deducible, illegal occurrences in a situation whose consequences may come to bear on the experiences of all. Truths rupture History. For Badiou, all the genres share the following features. They are: *contingent* in their emergence, *immanent* to their situations, *self-supporting* in their elaboration, *indifferent* to all existing forms of self-interest, *egalitarian* in their address, *restrained* in their extension. It is this six-fold aspect that renders truths (or, more precisely, the event-subject-truth process) absolute. Note how contingency and restraint (non-totalization) here become

---

13. How Badiou differentiates these conditions from text to text is of extreme interest. In *The Century*, he notes that 'science…possesses problems; it does not have a project', while in *Conditions*, he shows how love and politics begin at each other's rear ends, so to speak. For Badiou, if one condition comes to dominate one or another (or indeed all) of the others, this entails what he calls a 'suture': under such conditions, philosophy itself disappears, and the conditions may start to take on the roles that are properly the province of philosophy (e.g., poetry in the post-Romantic era starts to think Being).

part of what it means to be absolute, a radically untraditional conception; note that self-supporting means 'bearing its reason within itself' and 'supported by a self [subject]'; note that indifference includes 'excepting itself from pre-existing forms of temporality', as time is usually practised as an exemplary form of self-interest; note that egalitarian is synonymous with 'bearing universal address', and so on.[14]

Philosophy is to construct a system on the basis of the four conditions, and on these four *alone*. Why? As Badiou reiterates in *Logiques des mondes*:

> The fact is that today—and on this point things have not shifted since Plato—we know only four types of truths: science (mathematics and physics), love, politics and the arts. We can compare this situation to Spinoza's report concerning the attributes of Substance (the 'expressions' of God): there are undoubtedly, Spinoza says, an infinity of attributes, but we, men, know only two, thought and extension. Perhaps there are, we will say, an infinity of types of truths, but we, men, know only four. However, we know them truly. In such a way that our relation to truths…is *absolute* (80).[15]

I have italicized the word *absolute* in the final sentence above, because it is precisely the status of our relation to the conditions as absolute that I want to emphasize here. No other 'human' practices can provide such an absolute. This 'absoluteness' is, as I have been concerned to specify, of a very precise if peculiar kind. Philosophy really must be conditioned by these absolutes. How Badiou does this will become apparent to anyone

---

14. I believe these features are plausible, even compelling, as a *description* of the peculiarities of these four 'discourses'. Empiricist and anecdotal as such a remark may be, I can verify that English political activists, Italian historians and Australian artists have also found this compelling as a description of their practices. It also strikes me that these features also constitute an immanent philosophical justification—or, to use the more bombastic term favoured in recent French thought, an 'affirmation'—of these practices. Philosophy must affirm the extra-philosophical thoughts that make it possible. Finally, this coupling of description and justification enables a third moment, an 'explanatory' one, e.g., 'mathematics is ontology'. What such statements present is a purely philosophical seizure of the status of the particular discourse. Description-justification-explanation: if you will excuse such teminology, it is still possible to accept that this is one of the knots that philosophy should tie.

15. The paragraph begins 'a truth is certainly an experience of the inhuman. However, "our" point of view that forges (in philosophy) the theory of truths and subjective figures has a price: we cannot know if the types of truths we experience are the only possible ones. Other species, unknown to us, or even our own species, at another stage of its history (for example, transformed by genetic engineering), can, perhaps, accede to types of truths of which we have no idea, and even no image', LOW, p. 80.

who reads BE carefully: he directly transliterates the operations of the conditions into philosophical jargon. There's hardly more to it than that. The axioms of set theory provide all the necessities for the ontology; the operations of poetry provide the matrix for an extra-rational thought of the event *qua* undecidable (see, in particular, Meditation 19 on Mallarmé). By means of such a transliteration, philosophy constructs its own 'ideas'. These ideas are phrased in such terms as 'mathematics is ontology'. This means that, as Oliver Feltham puts it in his 'Translator's Preface' to BE, a philosophical idea is at once 'a decision, a principle and a hypothesis' (xxii), one which could only have been generated out of some kind of confrontation with conditions. The absolute forces questioning, not any kind of belief. Indeed, 'condition' should also be given the logical flavour of the *conditional* for its subjects: *if* this event, *then* what are the consequences?

So Badiou's absolute conditions are clearly not the Hegelian Absolute. There is no Whole; there is no single overarching logic of presentation, developmental or not; there is no necessity to a truth, nor essence of truths; there is no temporalization of the concept, etc. In general, it cannot be philosophy's task to try to think everything; indeed, for Badiou, philosophy is necessarily a precarious discourse, for at least three reasons. The first of these, the 'pragmatic reason', is that, dependent as philosophy is on its conditions, not all these conditions are functional in all epochs and places: in such cases, philosophy itself must disappear. The second reason, the 'bad reason', is that philosophy, consistently tempted to think outside the square, dissolves itself in the temptation to think the non-existent 'whole', either ossifying into overweening dogmatism or reducing itself to just another way of describing the incoherent slew of empirical happenings (for example as a glorified grammarian or sociologue, as a physicist manqué or psychologist). The third, 'good reason', is that, even when these conditions are all available, they are themselves exceptionally difficult to grasp; every 'successful' philosophy is therefore, at best, built on a constitutive instability. There is no totality to think, only the contingent becomings of heterogeneous event-truths and their subjects. Philosophy tries to seize on the ideas these conditions induce, as axioms of and for action.[16] This is the fundamentally *affirmative* movement of philosophy. It is the 'void place' constructed by philosophy to enable the heterogeneous truths produced by its conditions to meet, that Badiou refers to as 'Truth'. The difficulties of doing so entails that the absolute in philosophy

---

16. See A. Badiou, *Infinite Thought*, ed. and trans. J. Clemens and O. Feltham, London, Continuum 2003, p. 54.

is not something one can relax into, like a warm bath or a reliable security system, but, on the contrary, involves the savage wrenching-away of every certainty, the embrace of incalculable risk. Worse still, this savagery of the absolute is quiet, fragile, almost indiscernible....

Despite the brevity of this summary, it should be clear how Badiou takes his distance from theology and analytic philosophy on the one hand; and the extreme affects of religious beliefs, on the other. One must not underestimate this aspect of Badiou's work, which, having pure reason as a paradigm, induces him to repudiate all forms of religious and theological thought. This does not mean that he does not engage with examples of such thought. On the contrary, he makes committed interventions into such thought, by essaying to detach what he *de facto* treats as the pure thought of such thinkers from the 'religious' impurities in which they have become enmired. In this approach, somebody like Saint Paul becomes an exemplary *political* militant and thinker, who ought to be extracted from his religious envelope, including from the history of the church.[17]

This is why I sometimes characterize Badiou's philosophy as a 'SLAP philosophy': philosophy not only integrally relies on Science, Love, Art and Politics, but it gives you a slap to awaken you from the nightmare of history. Moreover—and I apologize for the cheesy sloganizing here—one can usefully permute these letters as a handy mnemonic for Badiou's doctrines. The work of fidelity can be considered long, protracted, repetitive, difficult: it's like doing LAPS. But if one persists, one acquires PALS in this enterprise, that is, philosophical friends with whom you also engage in questioning around the status of truths and Truth. As such, you'll attain the heights of thought in those philosophical ALPS presently 'icy with forgetting and desuetude' (and maybe get some skiing in while you're there). SLAP → LAPS → PALS → ALPS: the permutations of philosophy.

I have begun with a protracted review of what may now appear, after many years of commentary, very familiar, even merely introductory, platitudes about Badiou's system. I do not, however, believe this to be the case. One of the difficulties that commentators have so far had is taking seriously the concept of 'condition'. To the extent that they do so, they miss Badiou's utter reliance on his conditions. Cantorian set-theory really *is* ontology for Badiou; Mallarmé's poetry really *does* provide the matheme of the event. These are not 'examples', no matter how subtly one thinks

---

17. See A. Badiou, *Saint Paul: The Foundation of Universalism*, trans. R. Brassier, Stanford, Stanford UP, 2003.

the problematic of the example. They are *absolutes*. As such, they are the only possible foundations for a philosophical *system*.

III. FROM MATHEMATICS TO LOGIC; FROM SITUATIONS TO WORLDS; FROM BEING TO BEING-THERE; FROM ESSENCE TO APPEARANCE; FROM SUBJECTS TO OBJECTS; FROM CONDITIONS TO TRANSCENDENTALS

As I have noted, many things remain the same between BE and LOW. Mathematics remains the science of being, and truths remain exceptions to existence. Badiou puts it like this: '*There are only bodies and languages, except there are truths*', as a kind of slogan of what he here denominates his 'materialist dialectic', to distinguish it from the common or garden kind of 'democratic materialism' dominant today. The slogan's syntax is explicitly Mallarméan—the stars its destination—to demarcate it from the repulsive 'modesties' of philosophies of finitude. Whereas democratic materialism believes that 'there are only individuals and communities', the materialist dialectic proclaims that truths are accompanied by the eclipsing of all individuation and community. Truths are eternal, infinite, generic; they are supported by depersonalized, 'inhuman', subjects. As we have seen, part of the point of conditions is to think affirmatively, i.e., proceed on the basis of positive constructions alone. BE's procedure continues in LOW. As Badiou says, 'In no way do I go back on all this' (45).

What, then, has changed between BE and LOW? As the title of this subsection announces, there are a number of key changes in the vocabulary, argumentation, organization and references. The aim for Badiou is to reconfigure his existing concerns in a different framework, that is, according to 'the singularity of worlds where [truths] appear' (45). With this in mind, Badiou elaborates a fuller account of subjective variation, a revised account of the event, a new account of appearance, a new concept of objectivity, an extended account of logic (by shifting from set theory to category theory), and so on.[18] On his own account, however, the '*most*

---

18. 'Eilenberg and Mac Lane created categories in the 1940s as a way of relating systems of algebraic structures and systems of topological spaces in algebraic topology. The spread of applications led to a general theory, and what had been a tool for handling structures became more and more a means of defining them. Grothendieck and his students solved classical problems in geometry and number theory using new structures—including toposes—constructed from sets by categorical methods. In the 1960s, Lawvere began to give purely categorical definitions of new and old structures, and developed several styles of categorical foundations for mathematics', C. McClarty, *Elementary Categories, Elementary Toposes*, Oxford, Oxford University Press, 1992, p. 1.

considerable stake of LOW is to produce a new definition of bodies, understood as truth-bodies, or subjectifiable bodies' (44). To do this, however, Badiou has to reformulate the status of logic itself. In this new dispensation, '"logic" and "consistency of appearing" are the same thing' (47), and it is from this point that he returns to the problem of the subject.

For Badiou, a subject is not a register of experience, a moral category, or an ideological fiction ('three dominant determinations' of the subject); on the contrary, it is an index of the real, born of an event, faithful to the trace. Though a political subject is as different from a subject of love as that subject is from a subject of mathematics, etc., each subject must be *formally* thought according to the same concepts. In BE, this subject is a 'finite quantity of truth'. From the standpoint of BE's conception, then, individuals that didn't assent or remained indifferent to the event were implicitly considered by Badiou to remain mere state agents, agents of inertia. As such, they were not held to be, *stricto sensu*, subjects. In BE, a political reactionary is not a subject; an academic painter is not part of a truth process; nor are the surgeons who sneered at Lord Lister's absurd obsession with hygiene, and sharpened their scalpels on their boots; nor those who reduce love to a pure biological function or a category of eu-phemistic illusion. This is a central instance of the binary minimalism of BE: if there is a subject, it must be affirmative; if it is not affirmative, it is not a subject. In LOW, however, to this basic model of the faithful subject, Badiou has added two (or three) more categories: the reactionary, the ob-scure and the resurrected. Spartacus's slave revolt is his primary example in this initial delineation.

Badiou has had to do this in order to explain how, in the responses to the emergence of a faithful subject, reactionaries too are perfectly capable of inventiveness (or, rather, are forced to be so). As he writes: 'To resist the call of the new, it is again necessary to create arguments of resistance ad-justed to the novelty itself. From this point of view, every reactive disposi-tion is contemporary with the present against which it reacts' (62). What's typical of such a subject is that it works to extinguish the present that a faithful subject has opened, denying its possibilities and powers through 'the negation of the evental trace'. Don't revolt, it's not worth it, you'll just end up getting yourself crucified on the Appian Way. Or: all things in moderation, just slow down, we'll set up some committees to look into gladiatorial affairs and maybe have a sausage-sizzle too. Here Badiou invokes André Glucksmann and his cohort of nouveaux philosophes as contemporary imagos of such reactionary moderation.

But we also find an 'obscure' [*obscur*] subject: 'What relation can a patrician of ancient Rome have to the alarming news that assails him concerning the slave revolt? Or a Vendean bishop learning of the downfall and imprisonment of the king?' (67)[19] Well, what they want is 'the pure and simple conservation of the prior order'. The obscure subject wants above all to repress the present, to repel the event in the name of a transcendent Body ('City, God, Race'), and, to this extent, obliterate the event and its trace altogether. If the reactive subject wishes to snuff the extremity of the present, the obscure subject wishes thereafter to shovel it under.

So these three figures of the subject all respond to the *present* with different operations: 'the faithful subject organizes its *production*, the reactive subject, its *denial*...and the obscure subject, its *occultation*' (70). One can immediately see how and why the doctrines of BE have been altered; this new attempt retains the method of double affirmation (philosophy affirms the conditions because these conditions are already affirmative in the real), but aims to provide a fuller and more nuanced description of some subjective features evident in reality. Moreover, it suggests why no-one can ignore or remain merely indifferent to or undecided about events. To pick up on one of Badiou's own examples, today God really is dead, and it is this event (some might prefer to call it a 'non-event') that fundamentalists want to occlude at all costs. Yet they betray the patency of God's death in their very attempts at occultation.... What's still missing from this triple figure of the subject is a crucial possibility that I have already flagged: its *resurrection*.

The problem is a very serious one for Badiou: can a truth, once broached, ever be utterly destroyed? Take the avatars of Spartacus himself. They return in the slave revolt of the French Revolution, in the 'black Spartacus' who is Toussaint-Louverture; they return in Karl Leibnecht and Rosa Luxemburg, the Spartacists; they return in Stanley Kubrick's *Spartacus*, where all declaim 'I am Spartacus'; they also return, though Badiou doesn't mention it, in Monty Python's *Life of Brian* ('I am Brian, and so is my wife'). 'Spartacus' therefore returns in very different worlds, in very different circumstances. It is the logic of this resurrection that Badiou

---

19. There is absolutely no question that Badiou has drawn this term '*obscur*' from what must be one of his favourite poems, Mallarmé's sonnet on Edgar Allan Poe, in which we read of the 'Calme bloc ici-bas chu d'un désastre obscur...' Badiou's allusions to this verse occur in all sorts of contexts: his novel is entitled *Calme bloc ici-bas*, another little volume on politics is *D'un désastre obscur*, and so on and on. Aside from the resonances of such allusions, one should undoubtedly hear in '*obscur*', not only 'unclear', or 'unknown', but 'dark' and 'gloomy', as well as 'obscuring' and 'obscurantist', etc.

is going to have to explicate, that is, how 'the multiplicity of worlds' can be articulated with 'the invariance of truths'. Resurrection is, as I will show, the key, the crucial, figure that governs the entirety of LOW—in line with the very essence of sequels.

For the moment, however, Badiou is able to give only the etiolated lineaments of this figure. These lineaments are summarized at the end of Book I in two (almost excessively) helpful diagrams, one of which I reproduce here (from 86).

Truths	Ontological background (A)	Evental trace (ε)	Body ($\flat$)	Present (local)	Affect	Present (global) (π)
Politics	State and people (representation and presentation) $A < St(A)$	Fixation of the superpower of the State $\varepsilon \Rightarrow (St(A) = \alpha)$	Organization	New egalitarian maxim	Enthusiasm	Sequence
Arts	Perceptible intensity and the calm of forms $P \leftrightarrow f$	What was formless can be form $\neg f \rightarrow f$	Oeuvre	New perceptive intensity	Pleasure	Configuration
Love	Sexuated disjunction $m \perp f$	Undetermined object (encounter) $(\exists u) [m \leq u$ and $f \leq u]$	Couple (bi-sexuated)	New existential intensity	Happiness	Enchantment
Science	Border of the world grasped or not by the letter $l(w) \mid \neg l(w)$	What rebelled against the letter is submitted to it $\neg l(w) \rightarrow l(w)$	Result (law, theory, principles…)	New Enlightenment	Joy	Theory

Table 1—The truth procedures and their singular activation[20]

---

20. Note that I have tampered with Badiou's mathemes here. The French for the 'Ontological background' of Politics is, of course, A < Et (A), that is, A < Etat (A), thus becoming A < State (A) in English ; for the Arts, 'le monde exhibe une forme singulière de la tension entre l'intensité du sensible et le calme de la forme', p. 81. I have here translated 'sensible' as 'perceptible', and hence 'S $\leftrightarrow$ f' becomes 'P $\leftrightarrow$ f'. Likewise, **m** for *monde* becomes **w** for world, and the $\flat$ for *corps* has become $\flat$ for body. I am as yet uncertain of the value of such

The 'Scholium' that immediately follows Book I, titled 'A musical variant of the metaphysics of the subject', provides a very full and interesting example drawn from the development of serial music. This section, moreover, offers some excellent summarizing propositions of Badiou's altered doctrine of the subject. Whereas the restraint of BE saw it speak very little of subjective affect—limiting itself at most to two, anxiety and courage[21]—LOW insists on a quadrature of affects, terror, anxiety, courage and justice.[22] Note that all of these affects are now considered internal and essential moments of *any* truth-process, whereas *each* truth-process has also its characteristic or signature affect. As the table above shows, politics is linked to enthusiasm, the arts to pleasure, love to happiness, and science to joy. Telegraphic as these assignations could appear, it is equally true that they find strong support within the philosophical tradition itself (e.g., think of Spinoza's joy, which is very closely linked to the practice of science; or of the pleasure Kant assigns to the arts, etc.).

---

a transliteration. In Lacan's case, his mathemes were intended to be 'integrally transmissible', that is, without any translation, e.g., 'a' for '*autre*' should remain so in English (and not become 'o' for 'other', etc.).

21. Note that the question of affects arises in BE particularly around the question of the status of poetry, and of the matheme of the undecidable that Mallarmé provides: 'Given that undecidability is a rational attribute of the event, and the salvatory guarantee of its non-being, there is no other vigilance than that of becoming, as much through the *anxiety* of hesitation as through the *courage* of that outside-place, both the feather, which "hovers about the gulf", and the star "up high perhaps",' BE, p. 198, my emphasis. It is further noteworthy that affects are identified with the subjects of truths, not with philosophy or philosophers; in fact, I cannot think of any place where Badiou discusses an affect proper to philosophy as such.

22. 'Four affects signal the incorporation of a human animal to the subjective process of a truth. The first is evidence of the desire for a Great Point, of a decisive discontinuity, that will install the new world with a single blow, and complete the subject. We will name it *terror*. The second is evidence of the fear of points, of a retreat before the obscurity of all that is discontinuous, of all that imposes a choice without guarantee between two hypotheses. Or, again, this affect signals the desire for a continuity, for a monotone shelter. We will name it *anxiety*. The third affirms the acceptance of the plurality of points, that the discontinuities are at once imperious and multiform. We will name it *courage*. The fourth affirms the desire that the subject be a constant intrication of points and openings. It affirms the equivalence, in regard to the pre-eminence of the becoming-subject, of what is continuous and negotiated, and of what is discontinuous and violent. It is only there that there are subjective modalities, which depend on the construction of the subject in a world and the capacities of the body to produce effects. They are not to be hierarchized. War can be as good as peace, negotiation as good as struggle, violence as good as gentleness. This affect by which the categories of the act are subordinated to the contingency of worlds, we will name *justice*', LOW, pp. 96-7.

But it is really in Books II, III and IV that the full project of LOW gets going. This is 'La Grande Logique', which aims to provide a general theory of the logic of appearing, of objects and their relations, subsuming under its gargantuan umbrella the 'little logic' that is the grammatical and linguistic analysis beloved of analytic philosophy (103). In order to do so, Badiou has recourse—as I have already flagged above—to category theory. If Badiou's deployment of Zermelo-Fraenkel set theory governed the entire conceptual presentation of BE, here the presentation is governed by the necessities of the algebraic proofs. Both set theory and category theory are often considered to be rival 'foundations of mathematics'. As Saunders Mac Lane, one of the doyens of category theory, has remarked, the former axiomatizes sets and their elements, whereas the latter axiomatizes functions, that is, relations—and not elements at all. For his part, Badiou will continue to affirm that set theory is ontology, but that category theory founds the logic of appearing.[23]

Book II concentrates on the construction of the concept of the 'transcendental'. This constitutes quite a severe departure from the situations of BE. In BE, being [*l'être*] was thought in its raw multiplicity; here, being is thought in its organized localization, as 'being-there' [*l'être-là*] in a 'world'. Every world must have a transcendental organization, around which multiples cohere according to their differing degrees of identity or difference. It is a classical problem—'how to conjoin, in the substance of the soul of the world, the Same and the Other?'—and immediately demands a theory of negation or rather, for Badiou, of the *reverse* [*envers*].[24] Badiou gives the reverse 'three fundamental properties':

1. The reverse of a being-there (or, more precisely, of the measure of apparition [*apparition*] of a multiple in a world) is in general a being-there in the same world (a different measure of intensity of apparition in that world).

---

23. 'In category theory, the initial data are particularly meager. We merely dispose of undifferentiated objects (in fact, simple letters deprived of any interiority) and of 'arrows' (or morphisms) 'going' from one object to another...the aim is ultimately for the 'obejcts' to become mathematical structures and the 'arrows' the connection between these structures. But the purely logical initial grasping renders the determination of an object's sense entirely extrinsic or positional. It all depends on what we can learn from the arrows going toward that object (whose object is the target), or of those coming from it (whose object is the source). An object is but the marking of a network of actions, a cluster of connections. Relation precedes Being', TO, p. 145.

24. I am translating *envers* here as 'reverse' in accordance with the existing translation in *Theoretical Writings*, e.g. pp. 213-219. It is possible that one should see some relation to the mathematics of the 'inverse', but the word for this in French is, precisely, '*inverse*'.

2. Of both the reverse and negation it can be said that a being-there and its reverse have nothing in the world in common (the conjunction of their degrees of intensity is null).

3. In general, the reverse doesn't have all the properties of classical negation. In particular, the reverse of the reverse of a degree of apparition is not inevitably identical to this degree. And again, the union of an appearing [*apparaissant*] and its reverse is not inevitably equal to the measure of apparition of the world in its entirety (117-118).

Badiou immediately proceeds to show that: there is no Whole (using an argument directly derived from Russell's critique of Frege); that an existent can only be thought insofar as it belongs to a world; that, nonetheless, there has to be some kind of minimum available, which doesn't appear in a world ('a sort of zero'); there are maximal and minimum degrees of apparition, and so on. He gives an excellent account of Hegel, a formal account of what he calls the 'three transcendental operations' (zero, conjunction and the envelope) of appearing, as well as a brilliant demonstration of the superiority of Badiou's own 'Grand Logic' over 'ordinary logic'. This section is a kind of compressed tour de force, in which the familiar operations of ordinary logic (and/or/implication/negation, the quantifiers) are derived from Badiou's new categories of minimum, maximum, conjunction and envelope. The book concludes with a notice: 'What is a classical world?' There we find that such a world has double negation and excluded middle as valid principles, that '*a classical world is a world whose transcendental is Boolean*' (200), and that—as Badiou has said elsewhere—ontology is such a classical world.[25] Note the new, subtle and formal justification of set theory as an ontology: a logic is now explicitly given to this decision, whereas in *Deleuze*, it was still being put down to a question of 'taste'.[26]

---

25. In the '*Renseignements*' at the back of LOW, Badiou notes: 'It finally appears that the two great Aristotelian principles (non-contradiction and excluded middle), such as are proposed in *Metaphysics* Γ, condition three logical types (and not two, as has been long believed). One can in fact validate universally the two principles (classical logic), or only the principle of non-contradiction (intuitionist logic), or only excluded middle (para-consistent logics)', p. 557. Badiou immediately continues : 'the canonical model of classical logic is set theory, that of intuitionist logic, topoi theory, that of para-consistent logics, category theory. These models are more and more general, and negation becomes more and more evasive', pp. 557-558.

26. 'As Deleuze would have said, in immediately taking up again, just as I would myself, the thread of the argument and the desire to seduce or to win the other over: it is a question of taste', A. Badiou, *Deleuze: The Clamor of Being*, trans. L. Burchill, Minneapolis, Uni-

Book III 'proposes an entirely new concept of what an object is' (205). The novelty of this concept derives from the fact that Badiou thereby 'constructs an object without subject', that is, that the logic of appearing must be purely *objective*. This will be done through the concept of *indexation*: 'if x and y are two elements of an existent A, and T is the transcendental of the world under consideration, indexation is an identity function **Id** (x, y) that measures in T the degree of 'appearing' of x and y. Otherwise put, if **Id** (x, y) = p, this means that x and y are 'identical to degree p' in regard to their power of apparition in the world' (206). Having established the atoms of appearance, the very minimum necessary to appear in a world at all, Badiou seeks to explore this 'articulation between the logic of appearing and the ontology of the multiple' (208). In BE, Badiou shows that the 'one' does not exist, being only the self-dissimulating result of an operation of counting; in LOW, the One is rethought as the atom of appearing, as 'the quilting point of appearing in being' (231). Appearing is always localized, it is always being-*there*, and being-there is inherently bound. If love comes in spurts (as Richard Hell and the Voidoids put it), then existence comes in degrees.

Nonetheless, these degrees of existence are founded on something absolutely real: 'In a general fashion, an atom is a certain regulated rapport between an element a of a multiple A and the transcendental of a world....The postulate of materialism is that every atom is real' (236). (With the proviso, of course, that *existence* is not a category of *being*.) This 'real synthesis' is the key to this book. Whereas Kant cannot effectively suture the phenomenal to the noumenal, except at the cost of complex sophistries or causal leaps, Badiou will insist that a real atom 'attests to an apparition, in appearing, of the being of appearing' (231). If this synthesis does not work, then being and appearance cannot be sewn together by Badiou. (This will evidently be one of the key places for commentators to intervene in future essays into the worlds of LOW.) As for the object, it receives its definition at the same time:

> *Given a world, we call an object of the world the couple formed by a multiple and a transcendental indexation of this multiple, on the condition that all the atoms of appearing whose referential is the considered multiple are real atoms of the referential multiple* (233).

The object, in other words, is what bridges 'being' and 'existence'. Even quoting such definitions, which can only hint, in their very difficulty, at the logical sequences that underpin them, it is impossible to convey the

versity of Minnesota Press, 1999, p. 92.

enchained rigour of Book III in any adequate way. It provides some of the most difficult formal passages I have read in contemporary European philosophy (I refer interested readers to 310 if they wish to marvel at the incredible little box 'Complete form of the onto-logy of worlds'). Such passages are leavened only by detailed evocations of a political rally at the Place de la République and of the aforementioned Robert painting that graces the cover. Despite the difficulties, you can't help but get the drift: 'Existence is at once a logical and an intensive concept' (285). There are a number of other noteworthy moments, such as the demonstration that phenomenology and vitalism share a non-philosophical enthusiasm for death, an enthusiasm which exposes their weaknesses: 'just like existence, death is not a category of being' (285). No, death is a category of appearing (we will return to some consequences of this below). And the book concludes with the aptly-titled 'Scholium as impressive as it is subtle', in which Badiou gives a stunning example, a 'logical evaluation' of a battle between Alexander the Great and the Persian emperor Darius....

Book IV concludes the 'Grand Logic' part of LOW, with a new thought of 'relation'. Relation must depend on objects, and not at all the other way around; this is why the Grand Logic moves from object *to* relation, and why there *is* a purely logical order at work in LOW. To allude to a statement of Deleuze, no relation here is prior to or external to its terms:

> A relation is a bond between objective multiplicities—a function—that creates nothing in the order of intensities of existence or in the order of atomic localizations that was not already prescribed by the regime of apparition of those multiplicities (317).[27]

For Badiou, the very 'infinity of a world (ontological characteristic) entails the universality of relations (logical characteristic)' (318), and that this universality be a consequence and not a postulate. This book's major examples are drawn from the world of Quebec, its objects, politics and their relations. But the point is, again, fundamentally technical. For Badiou, every world must be considered infinite, but its infinity is 'inaccessible', that is, according to the textbook formulation, if the following three conditions hold:

---

27. For 'the non-being of existence means that it is otherwise than according to its being that being is. It is, precisely, the being of an object. The object exhausts the dialectic of being and existence, which is also that of being and appearing or being-there, or finally that of extensive or mathematical multiplicity and intensive or logical multiplicity', LOW, p. 316. Note that 'relation' is here given a particular sense by Badiou, that may signal a gap between the mathematical and philosophical notions of 'relation'.

i. $\alpha > \aleph_0$;

ii. for any cardinal $\beta < \alpha$, there is $2^\beta < \alpha$;

iii. the union of less than α ordinals, each less than α, is less than α.

As Badiou notes, this definition operates a kind of 'finitization' of the infinite itself: $\aleph_0$ (aleph-zero) is the smallest infinite cardinal, 'marking the caesura between finite and infinite', and, as such, cannot be approached by operations on any natural number; an inaccessible cardinal larger than $\aleph_0$ would therefore be really pretty big....nor is it any surprise that the existence of such a cardinal cannot be proven. The inaccessible infinity of a world is absolutely inaccessible from within the world itself, and 'any "world" that pretended to less would not be a world' (353). Second, 'this impossibility is what ensures that a world is closed, without for all that...being representable as a Whole' (326). Now, this ontological closure also ensures logical completeness; it is also the case that any relation in the world must be universally exposed, objectively available.

It is with Book V 'The four forms of change' that the demonstration returns to Badiou's more familiar terminology (multiples, sets, sites, events, etc.). But it is a reconfigured account of the site and event that we are given here. For Badiou,

> The ontology of a site thus allows itself to be described by three properties:
>
> 1. a site is a reflexive multiplicity, that belongs to itself and thereby transgresses the laws of being.
>
> 2. A site is the instantaneous revelation of the void that haunts multiplicities, by its transient cancellation of the gap between being and being-there.
>
> 3. A site is an ontological figure of the instant: it appears only to disappear (389).

BE organized an entirely different disposition of the site/event couple: the site, not being a proper subset of the situation (or world), was 'the *minimal* effect of structure which can be conceived' (BE 173) and provided the condition of being for the event; the event was considered a vanishing apparition composed simultaneously of elements from the site and itself. Now, we have something like certain predicates of the site merged into certain predicates of the event, and a new hierarchy of possible changes. Once again, against the minimality of BE (event v. no event; change v. no change), we have a larger array of possibilities:

i.   A *modification* is the basic form of change as usual, without requiring a site or any transcendental modification of the world;

ii. 'A *fact* is a site whose intensity of existence isn't maximal';

iii. 'A *singularity* is a site whose intensity of existence is maximal' (393).

This is further complicated by a division *within* singularity. There we find 'weak' singularities (without maximal consequences) or what is now denominated the 'event' proper (a singularity with maximal consequences for the world). In short: at the level of *becoming*, we can have no real change (modification) or real change (site); at the level of *existence*, we can have a non-maximal existence (a fact) or a maximal existence (a singularity); at the level of *consequence*, we have a weak singularity or an event (see diagram on 395; or more technical extension on 417).[28]

The key concept in the case of the event proper turns out to be what Badiou calls 'the inexistent'. Inexistence is a concept which comes up rather quickly in LOW, in II.1.1, to do with the 'Inexistence of the Whole' (119-121) and in II.1.3, where the subtitle says it all: 'Inexistence of the Whole: to affirm the existence of a set of all sets is intrinsically contradictory' (165-167). But 'the inexistent' of an object is first properly dealt with in a conceptual and formal manner in IV.1.6 (338-341), then again in IV.3.4 (360-362). Its first formulation is as follows: '*we will call "the proper inexistent of an object" an element of the sub-jacent multiples whose existence value is minimal*' (339). Badiou continues:

> Given an object in a world, there exists a unique element of this object that inexists in this world. It is this element that we call the proper inexistent of the object. It proves, in the sphere of appearance, the contingency of being-there. In this sense, its (ontological) being has (logical) non-being as being-there (341).

The 'inexistent' is thus a dissimulating avatar in LOW of BE's 'void' (or empty set); or, at least, it is a distant relative. So it is no surprise that, just as in BE, an 'event' is integrally linked to the reemergence of the void that has been foreclosed from the situation or, in this new conceptual framework, to the uprising of the inexistent: '*An event has for maximally true consequence of its (maximal) intensity of existence, the existent of the inexistent*'

---

28. 'The four forms of change are formally defined on the basis of three criteria: inexistence or not of a site, force or weakness of singularity, the pickup [*relève*] or non-pickup of the inexistent. An ontological criterion, an existential criterion, and a criterion relative to consequences', p. 416.

(398).[29] This returns us to a pre-BE doctrine, efficiently summarized by a Heiner Müller phrase: 'for something to come, something has to go'. Death—which had in BE been purged altogether from the regime of being—is back on the agenda in LOW at the level of appearing and, of course, disappearing. As Badiou puts it here, 'the opening of a space for creation requires destruction' (418).

This primes us for the final two books of LOW, Book VI, 'The theory of points', and Book VII, 'What is a body?' These books return us, in a different vocabulary, to some key moments in BE. The 'point' is now how Badiou rethinks the production of a truth from the point of view of the subject: 'A faithful subject is the form of a body whose organs treat a worldly situation "point by point"' (421). Whereas in BE the notion of forcing, of inquiries on the generic set, was employed to give a well-founded rational account of the process of a truth, in LOW this is given through the treatment of points. A 'point' is something that confronts the subject with a binary choice. There are only two possibilities on which to decide, and one cannot not decide (contrast this with BE on the doctrine of the intervention on the event, e.g., the meditation on Pascal, BE 212-222). To choose one is to continue in the truth; to choose the other is to abandon the truth, if not to decide for disaster: 'there is a "point" when, through an operation that implies a subject and a body, the totality of the world is the stake of a coin-toss' (422). Hence a decision upon which the world depends, the 'reduction to the Two of infinite multiplicity' (423). The examples are, as elsewhere in LOW, rather diverse: key decisions in Sartre's plays, the city of Brasilia, Kierkegaard, among others. For Badiou, a subject treats points in a world, point by point, and must, as the advertizing campaign for a popular battery has it, 'keep on keeping on', despite all the difficulties. Badiou has never resiled from martial examples: 'a battle… can be abstractly defined as a point of war' (431-2). Life, as the Emperor Marcus Aurelius put it in his diaries, is war; a war, Badiou might add, of immortals. You can't drop a point, as if it were neither here nor there. It's immortality or nothing.

So the 'body' in which Badiou is interested in giving the concept of is a very peculiar body, a purified, new, immortal body of truth: 'Point by point, a body reorganizes itself, making more and more singular consequences appear in the world, which subjectively weave a truth of which

---

29. Formally: '*Given an object (A, **Id**), we call* event *the apparition/disappearance of the site A from the moment that this site is a singularity, whether **EA**=M, which really affects the proper inexistent of the object, or (**EA** ⇒ **E∅**$_d$)=M*, LOW, p. 416.

one could say that it eternalizes the present of the present' (525). I would like to underline here the term 'reorganize', as it has connotations important to Badiou: of novelty (it is a *new* body that is being produced); of metamorphosis (the novelty is *real*); of discipline (it is an *organization*, not simply a disorganization that is at stake). In line with his injunctions that a truth-body can therefore be neither individual nor communitarian, we could pun that 'nobody, newbody'. It's a materialist resurrection. But *la vita nuova* isn't always *la dolce vita*. You have to struggle for it. And since we're on this renaissance line of allusion, let's continue down the line. *Alea re-jacta est*: having crossed the Rubicon of mathematics once, Badiou has had to cast the dice of BE again in order to head for the Capitol of logic, object and relation.

IV. BE→LOW

Why, then, given its incredible range, clarity and import, can LOW feel unsatisfactory? There is a clue in one of Badiou's own admissions. In V.3.1, under the heading 'Variations in the status of formal expositions', he notes that the Grand Logic adumbrated in books II, III and IV derives directly from category theory, and that 'all this permitted the doubling of the conceptual exposition by a formal exposition supported by its concepts, and homogeneous with certain strata of deductive mathematics' (411). Yet 'it wasn't so in book I, where the formalizations of the concept of the subject were, if one can say so, *sui generis*'. Then, he continues, 'In the present book, as in books VI and VII, we have a situation intermediary between book I (stripped of para-mathematical apparatus) and the three books of the Grand Logic (homogenous with entire strata of this apparatus)' (411-412). This third variation constitutes a formal exposition that, although not deductive, seeks to flay, by means of its sharply 'uninterpretable' literality, the flesh of sense in order to expose the bones of truth.

It's clear that Badiou knows what he's doing. But that's just it: his self-knowledge forces him to present this triple variation, and it is this variation that frustrates and provokes throughout. Badiou knows it too: one finds such apologia scattered throughout LOW. In the 'Technical Note' that concludes the Preface, Badiou writes: 'From Book II, each movement of thought is presented in two different ways: conceptual (which means without any formalism, and with, each time, examples) and formal (with symbols, and if necessary, schemas and calculations). Objective phenomenology and written transpacency' (50).[30] I do not believe this gap is so easily presented as a benefit; indeed, it is quite not for Badiou himself, given the symptomatic proliferation of apologia.[31]

In BE, as I have said, we have the most rigorous minimalism. BE asks, in the most direct and rational fashion possible: what is the minimal situation of being, what are its elements, and what are the operations that can be performed upon them? This makes BE a foundational work, in the triple sense that: it takes foundations as its object (being qua the void, the Two, the undecidable, infinity, etc.); that it does this in a foundational way (according to mathematical reason, supplemented by poetic reason); and it thereby itself becomes foundational (an act of philosophical foundation). By contrast, LOW no longer treats of foundational ontology, but of transmundane variations of localization; it is no longer simply foundational, but aims to be more fully descriptive of what transpires: 'one can only fully account for these nuances of appearing through the mediation of examples drawn from varied worlds, and for the invariance of transcendental operations through the confrontation between the coherence of these examples and the transparency of forms' (47-48). Yet the persuasiveness of descriptions varies radically in this book: the early account of the painted horses is miserably deficient compared to that of Hubert Robert's painting in Book III.

This isn't a failure of style, far from it. On the contrary, Badiou is a master of the pedagogical announcement, the clarified definition, the ordered progression, the directive heading, the illuminating instance and the recapitulative slogan. I am constantly struck by the demonstrative rigour of what may initially seem to be only loose discursive gestures, but which turn out to be highly structured and carefully-placed. The examples given in LOW's preface are, for example, clearly preliminary, intended only to give intimations of claims that will be justified later. They thus provide a general rhetorical orientation. They cannot be taken as serious fodder for refutation, precisely because they serve such a clearly pedagogical func-

---

30. For example, 'The systematic meditations of BE are followed here by an interlacing of examples and calculations that directly stage the consistent complexity of worlds. The latter, in fact, infinitely diversified figures of being-there, absorb in a transcendental frame, whose operations are invariant, the infinite nuances of qualititative intensities' LOW, pp. 47-8.

31. Yet another example: in the introduction to Book III, Badiou notes, 'It's clear that, by reason of the extreme rigour of enchainments, the formal exposition is here often more illuminating than the phenomenological didactics that precede it', p. 209.

tion; moreover, their very variety is directed towards exposing the hard formal kernel that stabilizes their profusion.

Still, Badiou's demonstrations in BE were so clear and precise, so concerned to ensure the reader's understanding of extremely difficult formal materials (just as Descartes taught his manservant mathematics and wrote in the vernacular so even women might understand), that they never felt excessive or overwhelming. This is not always the case in LOW, where an enormous amount of formalism is deployed—with a much higher symbol-to-page ratio than in BE—but not always with the same clarity, nor to the same effect. One can see the unavoidability of this state of affairs. After all, in the light of LOW, BE is focussed on the elaboration of one world alone, the classical world of ontology, in which non-contradiction and excluded middle reign supreme over their binary empire like Ferdinand and Isabella over an expansionist Spain. But LOW is concerned to speak of *worlds*, of the heterogeneity of worlds (classical, intuitionist and para-consistent), and this entails much broader logical developments. The algebra is uncircumventable, and, if one cannot follow it, one cannot seriously intervene in the descriptions.

For a number of reasons, category theory is more difficult than set theory. First, there is simply the time-lag: set theory essentially dates from the end of the 19th century; category theory arises post-WWII. This temporal fact means that we've all just had more time to deal with the impact of set theory and its infinite infinities. But there's more to it than that. Category theory is, undoubtedly part of our transition to 'post-modernity' (whatever that means); it is not the accomplice of Mallarmé, Lenin and Freud, but accompanies Celan, Mao and Lacan. There is a certain difficulty, intensity and obscurity to this new world. Moreover, much of the philosophy of the 20th century has been directly inspired by and engaged with set theory in one way or another, from Bertrand Russell through Ludwig Wittgenstein to Michael Dummett. To do philosophy today is already to have encountered, even if indirectly, a set theory that has integrally shaped and been shaped by philosophy. This has not yet been the case for category theory, at least not in such a thoroughgoing and foundational way. Finally, as Badiou himself has remarked, a crucial difference between mathematics and logic emerges here. Set theory is essential mathematics: one can, at a pinch, understand the mathematical concepts, without having to *follow* the formal calculations (e.g., the innumerable accounts of Russell's Paradox endemic to first-year philosophy courses). This doesn't mean one doesn't have to do the maths. Category theory, on the other hand, bears the essential hallmarks of formal logic (albeit mathematized): as the very name suggests, one cannot quite get it unless one submits to and goes through the formal definitions and procedures step by step.[32] As Badiou says, 'logic is definitional, whereas real mathematics is axiomatic' (TO 119).

Rather, the problem is not so much a problem of style as of substance. That is, anyone who wishes to read LOW properly is going to have to follow the logic. One hopes—without any real faith—that this fact will prevent commentators from trying to dismiss Badiou's use of logic and mathematics as if these were simply rhetorical add-ons, merely smart-arse ways of presenting a message that could just as well have been presented in common language without the use of all those symbols. To date, such a position remains the most obscurantist response to Badiou's work. One can regularly read critics (both 'for' and 'against' Badiou) who seem to think, if they do not declare it directly: 'oh, the mathematics isn't really important, we can go straight to the doctrines and treat them as if they were like any other philosophical utterances'.[33] One can at least see why people are tempted to defend such a deleterious error, given they have been lucky enough to understand something thanks to the outstanding clarity of Badiou's conceptual re-presentations. Though it might be going too far to say something like 'you don't have to be a poet, mathematician, militant or lover to understand something about the thoughts they think, but you can't really get anything about the logic unless you submit to the algebra', it's still tempting to do so—on the basis of the experience of reading LOW.

This is a consequence of Badiou's unrelenting pedagogical efforts. From maxims to tables, from exegesis to argument, Badiou could not present his philosophy more clearly or rigorously. In LOW, he introduces

---

32. Badiou specifies: 'The mathematics of being as such consists in forcing a consistency, in such a way that inconsistency is exposed to thought. The mathematics of appearing consists in disclosing, beneath the qualitative disorder of worlds, the logic that holds differences of existence and intensities together. This time, it is a question of exposing consistency. The result is a style of formalization at once more geometrical and more calculative, taken to the edge of a topology of localizations and an algebra of forms of order. Whereas ontological formalization is more conceptual and axiomatic: it examines and unfolds decisions of thought of a very general import', LOW, p. 48.

33. If you will forgive the execrable taste involved in self-citation, please refer on this point to my 'Doubles of Nothing: The Problem of Binding Truth to Being in the Work of Alain Badiou', *Filozofski vestnik*, vol. XXVI, no. 2, 2005, pp. 97-111. For a stringent critique of Badiou's mathematics—one of the very few that I have seen that goes about such a critique in an acceptable way, see R. Grigg, 'Lacan and Badiou: Logic of the *Pas-Tout*', in the same edition, pp. 53-65.

each book with a summary of what is to come; he speaks of his method and its justification in ordinary language; he elucidates the technical elements of logic with an extraordinary care, and so on. His inclusion of scattered scholia and appendices, of a list of the book's 66 major statements, of a 'dictionary of concepts', of an index, is testimony to his desire not to obscure anything. The 'Renseignements' are of real interest, supplying unfailingly accessible yet incisive remarks about Badiou's references and trajectory, his antecedents and colleagues, his friends and his enemies (including a note on a genuinely hilarious compact with Slavoj Žižek, as well as allusions to two stunning formal interventions by Guillaume Destivère). Yet a certain obscurity still emerges in the gap between demonstration and conviction, between deduction and rhetoric, in the very variability of the presentation. It is precisely because Badiou must have recourse here to so many *examples* that his propos seems to waver. The radically inventive nature of LOW, which effects an almost violent technical resignification of a wide range of terms (logic, appearing, transcendental, object, relation, envelope, reverse, maximal, etc.), is strained by the very tirelessness with which Badiou surrounds the formal expositions with intuitive sketches. Yet, as Badiou repeats throughout, the descriptions are nothing without the logic and mathematics; it is the logic that must bring out the consistency binding the incoherent slew of appearances.

To put this another way, the problem is that the transliteral operations of BE, which sutured set-theoretical mathematics and meta-ontological propositions without mediation, are shown to be highly *localized* operations, good for one particular classical world but not, by definition, necessarily for any other kind. In the very attempt to specify a theory of appearing that is consistent with the theory of being in BE, Badiou needs to find *new* operators between philosophy and logic that will ensure the gap between them is not, once again, subjected to the ruses of mediation. This necessity provokes certain questions that I am not sure have yet been adequately answered by Badiou. To give some very simple examples: is the revised theory of the event-site given in LOW a more 'general' theory, one which leaves the account given in BE correct, but only for the ('special', 'restricted') ontological situation? Or is LOW correcting the theory of BE *tout court*? Or is LOW simply giving the theory of how event-sites function in appearing, saying nothing about how they function in being? This is, of course, the return of the problem of the sequel; or, for reasons I will shortly expand upon, of *resurrection*.

V. KANT OR HEGEL?

As Friedrich Nietzsche pointed out, not the least charm of certain theories is that they can be refuted; everyone believes him- or herself strong enough for the job. So mediocrity survives, slipping unrepentantly from era to era like Rameau's Nephew in search of a few small positions and a couple of coins. Certainly, works sometimes survive, not because of their refutability, but because of their irrefutability. And yet is it not always irrefutability that forces opponents to discover or invent entirely new ways to circumvent great philosophical interventions. It is something indifferent to the distinction 'refutable' and 'irrefutable'. Thus Kant's division between noumenal and phenomenal realms, his circumscription of the heterogeneous operations of thought, his elaboration of networks of categories and conditions to articulate this heterogeneity, etc., forced Fichte, Hegel and Schelling to unprecedented efforts in philosophy. If one can certainly argue with Kant on his own grounds, his establishment of these grounds completely reconfigures the previous terms of philosophical discussion in such a way that hitherto central problems come to look like false problems or, even when on the right track, are superseded by the Kantian presentation. Even then, if one later 'out-Kants' Kant himself, he has, as I have said, forced such an operation, and has done so in such a way as to ensure what we might call the impossibility of his own obsolescence. He may be out of date. He may be wrong. His ontology may have been superseded by independent developments. Yet he cannot be circumvented. We are back to the problem of the *absolute*.

Of all the philosophers (and anti-philosophers) to whom Badiou dedicates little sections of LOW—including Deleuze, Kierkegaard, Lacan and Leibniz—the two most important are undoubtedly Kant and Hegel (it is illuminating to refer to the index to see who gets the most references). As we know, this is not an idle coupling. If Badiou certainly tries to treat them independently in his discussions, this is not altogether possible. Kant and Hegel have effectively set the terms of post-Romantic philosophy to the present. The problem in this context is precisely the problem of the logics of worlds: does Badiou offer a way in LOW to circumvent the stringent division inflicted on being by Kant, without simply sewing it up again, à la Hegel? Let's examine this question by a kind of indirect comparison.

First, Kant. If Badiou dedicates an entire section of this book to an interpretation of Kant (III.2), he notes in his 'Renseignements' that 'Kant is exemplarily the author with whom I have not managed to become familiar. Everything about him irritates me, and first of all the legalism—always asking *Quid juris?* or 'Haven't you crossed the limit?'—combined, as in the United States today, with a religiosity all the more disturbing for being at once omnipresent and vague' (561). For Badiou, then, just as for Deleuze (not to mention Nietzsche), Kant is a rather unprepossessing figure. Yet Badiou will also accord Kant a 'shadowy grandeur' and, following Lacan, a 'philosophical sadism'.

This ambivalence shouldn't hide the fact that Kant is perhaps the real interlocutor throughout LOW, precisely because, in addition to his setting of the terms that still regulate contemporary philosophy, he is the philosopher who first broached the problems of appearing and of subtractive ontology: 'Kant is undoubtedly the creator in philosophy of the notion of object' (244). Moreover, Kant's creation is rigorous and precise: 'The subtractive rationality of Kantian ontology ends up placing the relation between an empty logical subject and an object that is nothing at the foundation of representation' (TO, 138). Moreover:

> What is common to Plato, to Kant and to my own attempt, is to state that the rational grasp of differences in being-there, or intramundane differences, is not deducible from the ontological identity of the existents concerned, because this identity tells us nothing of the localization of the existent (132).

Nonetheless, the Spider of Königsberg never arrived at Badiou's own 'ontico-transcendental synthesis' of the gap between 'the pure presentation of being in the mathematics of multiplicities on the one hand, and the logic of identity that prescribes the consistency of a world on the other' (239). And yet, and yet....

Against this ambivalent relation to Kant, we can array Badiou's altogether less troubled relation to Hegel: 'To my eyes in fact, there are only three crucial philosophers: Plato, Descartes, Hegel' (552). In fact, the identification with Hegel is so strong that Badiou will even declare: '*Logics of Worlds* is to *Being and Event* what Hegel's *Phenomenology of Spirit* is to his *Science of Logic*, although the chronological orders are reversed: an immanent grasp of the givens of being-there, a local traversal of figures of the true and the subject, and not a deductive analytic of forms of being' (16). A little later, Badiou will displace this comparison again: 'The "historic" companion to the present book is Hegel, thinker par excellence of the dialectical correlation between being and being-there, between essence and existence. It is against his *Science of Logic* that we measure ourself here' (110). It's Hegel over Kant, any day.

So Badiou's identification is overwhelmingly with Hegel. But in many ways his intervention is far more Kantian than Hegelian. Like Kant, Ba-

diou's most striking philosophical achievements have come relatively late
in his career. This is not simply a biographical detail; after all, 'age' and
'generation' are integral to the disposition of philosophy (think, for example, of the relation between Plato and Socrates, or the Romantic exalta-
tion of the figure of 'the child'). BE was only published in 1988, after a
long succession of extraordinary works, such as TS (1982), which remixed
philosophy, psychoanalysis, political theory, and poetry in very odd ways.
But TS is, in my opinion, a philosophical failure. It's not that it's not a brilliant book. Its ambition, inventiveness, local apercus, and range of reference are staggering (if still restricted in comparison to BE and LOW).

The point is that a book can be brilliant without being a genuine work
of philosophy. Indeed, one of the things that makes philosophy unique is
that is it sometimes even permitted to be ignorant and stupid. Badiou's
oft-stated appreciation of TS has a merely personal flavour to it; the book
does not necessarily deserve such approbation in itself, at least not as philosophy. So the question of the generation of BE must, like the first *Critique*,
entail a kind of *maturation*, that is, a leap and a rupture that is not merely
a supersession. Such 'maturation'—I give it this obscene name in honour
of Kant's own definition of Enlightenment as an exit from a self-imposed
immaturity—must further recognize itself as a leap and a rupture, at the
very moment that it retains within itself a trace of the confusions of in-
fancy from which it emerged.[34]

---

34. In fact, disciples are often reactionary or obscurantist in the guise of fidelity. If you believe that such propositions as 'Badiou has always been interested in mathematics' or 'the
key to Badiou's thought throughout is the dialectic' *norm* BE's emphasis on conditions, then
you are a reactionary. BE is thereby figured simply an extension of a pre-existing situation,
one in which the attempt to think the materialist dialectic is king. The equation *mathematics
= ontology* is thus submitted to the dictates of an alleged Ancien Régime; on such a vision,
BE did not mark any real rupture at all. This view is tantamount to believing BE *is an ad-
justment to sustain* a larger, ongoing program. It reduces BE to an extension of categories that
'were present from the start', but without—the key point—acknowledging that they have
been totally 'recast', OB, p. 15. Certainly, as Ray Brassier writes, 'Throughout Badiou's
work, mathematics enjoys a privileged status as paradigm of science and of "scientificity"
in general. This has been a constant, from his first significant philosophical intervention,
the 1966 article 'The (Re)Commencement of Dialectical Materialism', notable for the way
in which it already prefigures his subsequent (career-spanning) preoccupation with the
relation between set-theory and category-theory, to his most recent work, wherein Badiou
finally establishes a philosophical connection between these two branches of mathematics by arguing that the doctrine of being, laid out via set-theory in *Being and Event* (1988),
needs to be supplemented by a doctrine of appearance that mobilizes category-theory,
as Badiou does in his forthcoming *Logics of Worlds*', 'Badiou's Materialist Epistemology of
Mathematics', *Angelaki*, vol. 10, no. 2, 2005, pp. 135-150. All this is absolutely true; but it
would be false if one believes that this fact bears in any serious way upon the *breach* effected

It is undoubtedly also significant that Kant, having seized the work of his maturity, starts to produce sequels: *Critiques* 1, 2, and 3 (Pure Reason, Practical Reason, and Judgement). For this maturation also involves an act of radical self-restriction. Like Kant's great *Critiques*, Badiou's BE period works exhibit a certain *asceticism*. This asceticism is both enacted and thematized in the restrained selection of targets, the style of writing, not to mention the concepts themselves. It's no accident that one of Badiou's favourite slogans becomes the Mallarméan one of 'restrained action'. No less than the problem of maturity, the problem of asceticism is entirely immanent to the philosophical text.

Like Kant—but unlike Hegel—Badiou radically denies the existence of the Whole, the All. Kant is in fact so radically opposed to such totality that he refuses to vitiate the rift between phenomenal and noumenal. At best, for Kant the idea of 'totality' must remain purely regulative. If there is 'some of the One', it's subordinated to its inexistence, to irrecuperable division. For his part Badiou, mounts one argument after another against the One. In both LOW and BE, he provides nifty demonstrations derived from Russell. What this inexistence of the Whole in fact entails is a division of being and being-there. As Badiou himself says, Kant is the beginning of subtractive ontology: 'For the first time really, Kant was the one to shed light on the avenues of a subtractive ontology, far from any negative theology' (TO 139).[35] To the extent that the Hegelian Absolute is given any truck, it is as a foil for the true state of affairs: 'Like the Hegelian Absolute, a world is the unfolding of its own infinity. But, in contrast to that Absolute, it cannot construct in interiority the measure, or the concept, of the infinity that it is' (326).

Finally, like Kant, Badiou insists that philosophy is entirely *conditional*. For both philosophers, integral to the work of philosophy is the affirma-

---

by BE: before BE, Badiou (as he himself admits) was completely unable to give, in all its power and clarity, the unprecedented equation *mathematics = ontology*, and push it into the real. Brassier himself is certainly not proposing that such a continuity trumps the breach, though others are....

35. On the necessity of *division*: 'Plato must separate himself from Parmenides and identify thought otherwise than by its pure coextension to being. Descartes, by hyperbolic doubt, Husserl by the transcendental epoché, separate immanent reflexion from every position of the object. Kant, all at once, distinguishes thought (element in which transcendental philosophy proceeds) from knowledge (which determines particular objects). For my part, I distinguish speculative meta-ontology from mathematical ontology, and mathematical ontology from the logic of appearing. But, more essentially, I also distinguish thought (subjective figure of truths) and knowledge (predicative organization of truth effects)', LOW, p. 253.

tion of the very conditions it depends upon; moreover, they both insist upon the conditions' irreducible separation from one another, as well as their irreducible exteriority to philosophy. What else is the 'conflict of the faculties' in Kant? What else is the 'peace of the discontinuous' in Badiou? The conditions are self-supporting in the peculiar way that I spoke about above (e.g., their verification is intrinsic to their practice). Philosophy, by contrast, is not self-supporting, being entirely reliant on these conditions. This is why so much of Kant's text is dedicated to what seems to be an elaborate police operation: yet what is really at stake, as in the famous image of the dove, is that, unlike the bird itself, philosophical flight cannot ignore the resisting air which renders it possible. And this is why so many of Badiou's headings have to do with 'metaontology', 'metapolitics', and 'inaesthetics': the 'ins' and 'metas' are neither an index of superiority nor of negation, but the philosophical stigmata of *being conditioned*.[36]

Maturation, asceticism, division, condition: Kant and Badiou, certainly radically different in so many ways, are nonetheless aligned according to these fundamental operators. So Badiou's clear and conscious identification with Hegel not only falsifies his far more profound affiliations with Kant—but tempts him in LOW to vitiate some of the rigour of BE (LOW reads very much more like TS than like anything else Badiou has written post-1988; that is, a philosophical *omnivorum*, a gargantuan rattlebag of interesting phenomena and brilliant aperçus).[37] What are the problems that Badiou's total curiosity, not to mention his avowed identification with Hegel, and his disavowed identification with Kant, get him into?

Here are three problems that I see as deriving directly from the Kant-Hegel imbroglio: 1) the materialist dialectic; 2) the temptation of the whole; 3) the theory of change. These problems are all linked. Symptomatically, one can see the return of triads throughout LOW. For example, the dialectic of presentation of the logic of the concept of body proceeds like this: 'our trajectory can be summarized thus: subjective formalism (without object); object (without subject); objectivity of the subject (bodies)' (205). Then are the three forms of the subject (faithful, reactive, obscure), the

---

36. 'The words "inaesthetic," "transitional ontology," "metapolitics" are coined against "aesthetics," "epistemology" and "political philosophy" respectively in order to indicate the twisted relation of the condition/evaluation pairing, and, if possible, in order to deny oneself the temptation to rely on the reflection/object relation', Alain Badiou, 'Preface to the English Edition', *Metapolitics*, trans. J. Barker, London, Verso, 2005, p. xxxiii.
37. As A. J. Bartlett has suggested to me, LOW might even be better considered a *prequel* rather than a *sequel* to BE, given the number and intensity of LOW's links to TS (private communication).

three fundamental operators of objectivity (localization, compatibility, order), the three themes of the Grand Logic (transcendental, object, relation) and so on. When you start dealing with Triads, one bad guy is still the big boss, and that's Hegel. Even if you add a fourth strut to each, that is, as Zizek has often noted, Hegelian too.

For Badiou, because there is no One, nothing binds the inconsistency of worlds. The problem is: how is it that, given the patency of incommensurables, a truth can be said to be 'the same'? This is also the problem of time. For Badiou, a truth-procedure must aim at the 'present', a present that is such only as a 'future anterior', and is, thereby, 'immortal' (or 'eternal'). The two issues are linked. Take the little demonstration on prime numbers (18-25). Here Badiou reiterates:

> Must it be deduced that all is culture, including mathematics? That universality is only a fiction? And perhaps an imperialist, even totalitarian, fiction? From the same example we will, completely to the contrary, affirm:
>
> • that an eternal truth is enveloped in different linguistic and conceptual contexts (in what we will call, on the basis of Book II, different 'worlds');
>
> • that a subject of the same type finds itself implicated in the demonstrative procedure, whether it be Greek or contemporary (whether it belongs to the world 'Greek mathematics' or to the world 'mathematics after Cantor')
>
> The key point is that the truth subjacent to the infinity of prime numbers is not so much this infinity itself as what is deciphered there regarding the structure of numbers: that they are all composed of prime numbers, which are like the 'atomic' constituents—indecomposable—of numericity (20-21).

This can only work if one takes mathematics to be one world, love another world, politics another, art yet another—and that these 'worlds' are not the 'worlds' we think of when we think 'Greek theatre' or 'modernist theatre'. Against relativism ('democratic materialism'), Badiou has then, on the one hand, to affirm eternal truths; on the other hand, there is no totality, so worlds are really disjunct. The difficulty is then to explain how eternality can emerge from *within* a world, and how this eternality then communicates *between* worlds: 'I believe in eternal truths and in their fragmented creation in the present of worlds. My position on this point is completely isomorphic to that of Descartes: truths are eternal because they have been created, and not because they have been there forever'

(534). But this is to restate the problem in the guise of a conviction, supported, moreover, by an appeal to authority.

Part of the difficulty is that it isn't simply that a theory of change is lacking; it's nice to have a more elaborate theory of world-transformation, sure, but such a theory only forces out the problem more clearly. I was impressed with the account given in BE, as I am impressed with the different account of change (and the possibility of change) in LOW.[38] But perhaps it isn't enough. It's that a really convincing concept of eternity is lacking. It seems to me the kernel of the problem is this: how to seize and present *the historicity of the eternity of contingency*, the fact that eternity emerges in worlds in time. Kant wouldn't see the need to do it; Hegel could do it, but because he believed in the Whole. It may well be a trap to think that a 'materialist dialectic', an account of 'specificity' routed through category theory, or a better typology of subjective variations is going to help with this deadlock. On the contrary, we have so much trouble thinking contingency *precisely because of the ineluctability of the dialectic*.

A *resurrected* truth—whether that of prime numbers or the depiction of horses—must leap the gap between heterogeneous worlds, but a truth can only be the truth of *a* world. It is this 'sequelization' of truth that I have not yet understood in LOW.

VI. CONCLUSION

It may not be enough to pair the rigorous formal demonstrations with quasi-phenomenological talk of battles and demonstrations and paintings. But only time will tell: I have never read anything quite like LOW before, and, given that it was officially published barely a half-year ago (March 2006), I have been unable to find any substantial responses to it. None of the existing accounts have given the slightest evidence that they

---

38. As Oliver Feltham notes, BE 'can provide a theory of both the multiplicity of structures and contingent astructural change. What Badiou's philosophy adds is basically: 1) The contingency of structural incompleteness or instability: not every structure permits global change. 2) The possibility of anomalous events that occur in the register of the real, outside structure (they are not grounded in any external reality/context), and which can initiate change if there are. 3) The elaboration of structural preconditions for transformation—someone recognizes and names the event as belonging to the situation...Finally, 4) A new way of thinking subjects of change, subjects who, over time, participate in the invention of a new symbolic order by means of hypotheses and enquiries concerning the belonging of the anomalous event to a structure', 'Enjoy your stay : Structural Change in Seminar XVII', in J. Clemens and R. Grigg (eds.), *Jacques Lacan and the Other Side of Psychoanalysis*, Durham, Duke University Press, 2006, p. 192.

have so far dealt adequately with the formal logic, let alone with the real ambitions of the book. Indeed, LOW will probably prove to be among the most ambitious and wide-ranging works of philosophy of the 21st century. Who else in contemporary philosophy anywhere in the world shares Badiou's range and depth of knowledge (mathematics, logic, philosophy, great moments in politics, key developments in contemporary music, the history of theatre, etc.), let alone the ability to articulate these knowledges in such an unprecedented fashion?

Still, I cannot see what's at stake in affirming a 'materialist dialectic' today against 'democratic materialism'. These are terms from the struggles of a previous era, one that still held out hope for the Whole, even in its negation or loss (e.g., 'the Whole is the untrue', 'the end of metanarratives', 'anti-dialectics', etc.). Nothing intrinsic justifies this as a 'materialism' (why not just call it a 'realism'?), other than old fondnesses. Idealism, materialism: this has become a distinction without difference in a world where foundational physics invents incommensurable and untestable string-theories that are nonetheless each consistent; where the legacy of political activism engages local struggles that hardly require any kind of doctrine or praxis of 'materialism' for their organization or effects. What's in this 'dialectic' today that's worth saving? What's in this 'materialism' that's not a mere slogan? LOW is certainly BE2, a genuine sequel in the sense of which I spoke above. But it is in some fashion also a recoiling, a kind of return to the good old days of Badiou's pre-BE struggles. So I think the guiding opposition that opens this book, between 'democratic materialism' and 'materialist dialectics' is misleading. The challenge is rather to surpass democracy, materialism and dialectics, without succumbing to fascism, idealism and lassitude. The slogan one might brandish instead is *transliteral absolutism*.

I think this is what one should ask of philosophy: to identify, to announce, to harbour, to affirm, to practice the (or an) *absolute*. A philosophy can certainly domicile regional theories within it; but it is itself not simply a theory, or agglutination of theories. Nor can philosophy be reduced to a quasi-Wittgensteinian 'dissolution of false problems', though dissolution can certainly sometimes in itself provide some kind of absolute. But the point is that true philosophy may require no theory at all. Just an absolute. An absolute, moreover, that can even be evanescent, infirm, indiscernible.

This is what an attention to the conditions of philosophy enabled Badiou to do in BE. Badiou's undoubted personal genius—evident from *Le Concept de modèle* to *Peut-on penser la politique?*—was curbed by conditions to produce the terrible beauty of BE. There, there is no real rhetoric at all, as he is reduced to presenting the foundational interventions of other discourses, mathematics and poetry above all. BE's philosophical power derives from its Platonic attention to the incommensurable absolutes and their articulation, which had to be done in a non-dialectical fashion. BE is very explicit on this point: it is not logical negation, contradiction, antagonism, or other familiar philosophemes that are up to the mathematical thought of the foreclosure of the inconsistency of the void. It's set theory, and set theory alone. Moreover, it's not just that Badiou's philosophical ambitions can only be fulfilled by being brutally curbed; rather, everyone's ambitions are curbed as they are delivered into their secular eternity. Plato is an absolute, but, coming before Cantor, must fail to think being as infinity, having to take recourse to the figure of a dream; Rousseau is an absolute, who, despite his anti-philosophical tendencies, forges an eternal distinction between the totality of wills and the general will.

All this can be done precisely because, in the terms that LOW offers, BE largely restricts itself to a world, to a single world, the world of ontology (and to its fracturing through events). LOW, however, is about the logics (irreducibly plural) of worlds (also plural). It thus sets itself a task so grand that self-comparisons to Hegel aren't going to cut it: in the last instance, LOW provides neither the unbearable ontological intrication of the *Science of Logic*, nor the hallucinatory cavalcade of the *Phenomenology of Spirit*. Why? Precisely because there is no Whole for Badiou, the worlds can be given no overarching arché, no principle, no absolute reason. What in BE were not examples, in any sense of the word, but conditions, that is, the supports for the philosophical snatch and grab, in LOW turn once more into examples. To read LOW after BE is to read a jumbled work of genius, teeming with inventiveness at all levels. But its genius can also seem tendentious, precisely because its only restraint is to gesture towards possible exemplifications of the logical structure. What has happened to the absolutely central doctrine of such books as BE and C, where philosophy's 'historically invariant' definition involves the construction of a place in which science, love, art and politics can all encounter each other? Is this still the case? In LOW, everything verges on a Borgesian dream, moving, with a delirious energy, from prime numbers to cave paintings of horses to Spartacus to contemporary music to....

So if LOW must be read, its propositions, even when irrefutable, often appear far from absolute. Nonetheless, it never gives up on what the stakes are today for philosophy. These are, as I suggested above, to attain to a *transliteral absolute* by taking reason to the very points at which it breaks down and is transformed into something unprecedented. To literality, not materiality; to contingency, not sufficiency; to absolution, not dialectics; to submission, and not to surrender.

love

6

Count-as-one, Forming-into-one, Unary Trait, S1

Lorenzo Chiesa

> 'Let us give Lacan his due: he was the first to make a sys-
> tematic use of numericality'.
>
> —Alain Badiou

INTRODUCTION

According to Alain Badiou, psychoanalysis thinks the amorous 'procedure', one of the four procedures for the sake of which the 'abstract
categories' of his *Being and Event* have been formulated.[1] Badiou invites
psychoanalysts and psychoanalytic theorists to 'practice' these categories
in their own field.[2] Against the background of such an invitation, in this
paper, it is my intention to outline a possible application of some of the
most important conceptual propositions advanced in the first two parts of
Being and Event to the key psychoanalytic issue of the identification of the
(conscious and unconscious) subject as expounded by Jacques Lacan in
his ninth Seminar, *L'identification*. More specifically, I aim to show how Badiou's notions of the 'count-as-one' and the 'forming-into-one' can profitably be put to work in order better to understand Lacan's notions of the
'unary trait' and the S1, the 'master-signifier'. What is at stake in both cases
is the relationship between structure and metastructure, presentation and

---

1. I would like to thank Ana Alvarez Velasco, a true '*non*-working' mathematician, for her
invaluable advice. I am also grateful to Alberto Toscano for his Badiouian comments on
an early draft of this article.
2. Alain Badiou, *L'être et l'événement*, Paris, Seuil, 1988, p. 10. The English translation, which
is otherwise excellent, curiously omits this reference to psychoanalysis, replacing it with
a reference to art—which does not appear in the original, Alain Badiou, *Being and Event*,
trans. Oliver Feltham, London, Continuum, 2005, p. 4 (henceforth BE).

representation, starting from the common premise that 'the one, which is not, solely exists as *operation*' (BE 24) (Badiou), as an 'instrument' (Lacan) which is not 'the one of Parmenides, nor the one of Plotinus, nor the one of any totality'.[3] It should be noticed that, although *L'identification* arguably remains one of Lacan's most abstract Seminars, it is nevertheless the case that the topics it discusses have vast repercussions for basic technical questions concerning the cure, such as the handling of the transference and the emergence of anxiety. Applying *Being and Event* to the practice of psychoanalytic thought will thus also implicitly indicate its relevance to the practice of psychoanalytic treatment.

In *Being and Event*, Badiou endeavours to think philosophically, that is meta-ontologically, what '*circulates*' between the modern theories of the subject, *in primis* the Lacanian one, and ontology understood as axiomatic set-theory (BE 3). As Justin Clemens and Oliver Feltham rightly remark, Badiou does not merge ontology into the theory of the subject, 'rather, the *tension* between the two drives his investigations'.[4] This tension is what appears to be annulled when one 'practices' Badiou's categories across Lacanian psychoanalysis. While a significant amount of research has recently been carried out that carefully investigates the similarities and differences between Badiou and Lacan's theories of the subject,[5] less attention has been paid to the *direct* relationship between the latter and Badiou's set-theoretical *ontology*. Badiou's ontology of the One and the Multiple—the '*a priori* conditions of any possible ontology'—relies on the 'law that the one *is not*' (BE 23, 28). By Badiou's own admission on page 1 of Meditation One of *Being and Event*, this law is closely associated to Lacan's pathbreaking principle according to which 'there is [*symbolic*] Oneness' (BE 23)—or

---

3. Lesson of 29/11/61 from Jacques Lacan, *Seminar IX (1961-1962): 'L'identification'*, unpublished (henceforth Seminar IX).

4. Alain Badiou, *Infinite Thought: Truth and the Return to Philosophy*, ed. and trans. Justin Clemens and Oliver Feltham, London, Continuum, 2003, p. 6.

5. See, for instance, Slavoj Žižek, *The Ticklish Subject: The Absent Centre of Political Ontology*, New York, Verso, 2000, pp. 127-70; Slavoj Žižek, 'Foreword to the Second Edition: Enjoyment within the Limits of Reason Alone', *For They Know Not What They Do: Enjoyment as a Political Factor*, 2nd, London, Verso, 2002, pp. lxxxi-lxxxviii. See also Bruno Bosteels, 'Alain Badiou's Theory of the Subject: The Recommencement of Dialectical Materialism? (Part I)', *Pli: Warwick Journal of Philosophy*, no. 12, 2001, pp. 200-29, pp, 220-9. and Bruno Bosteels, 'Alain Badiou's Theory of the Subject: The Recommencement of Dialectical Materialism? (Part II)', *Pli: Warwick Journal of Philosophy*, no. 13, 2002, pp. 173-208, pp. 197-208; Ed Pluth and Dominiek Hoens, 'What if the Other Is Stupid? Badiou and Lacan on 'Logical Time'', in Peter Hallward (ed.), *Think Again: Alain Badiou and the Future of Philosophy*, London, Continuum Books, 2004, pp. 182-90.

better, there is *only* symbolic Oneness. What Badiou fails to emphasize in this context is that this principle is, for Lacan, confined to a theory of the subject: in spite of proposing important hypotheses about being, Lacan never really developed any ontology independently of his notion of subjectivity.[6]

My considerations should therefore always be measured against the threat of a short circuit in Badiou's *magnum opus*, which I do not intend to investigate any further in this occasion. On the one hand, Badiou's theory of the subject-event in *Being and Event* may rightly be labelled as 'beyond Lacan'—as the title of Part VIII of the book suggests—due to his rigorous philosophical appropriation of Paul Cohen's mathematical notion of forcing. On the other hand, in spite of its reliance on the radical thesis according to which 'ontology [...] is nothing other than mathematics itself' (BE xiii), Badiou's solid ontological edifice is itself amply anticipated by Lacan's own theory of the subject. The latter is indeed based on the principle that there is only symbolic Oneness—or, adopting a formula closer to Badiou's own terminology, 'there is no One except in mathematics'[7]— albeit in an often hesitant and imprecise manner. Thus, the least we can say is that, in practising the *ontological* categories made available by *Being and Event* across Lacanian psychoanalytic notions, we will not be surprised to discover a high degree of compatibility between them. The ideal result of such a practice would be nothing less than an accurate set-theoretical formalization of the relation between consciousness and the unconscious, succeeding there where Lacan's courageous attempts to demonstrate that mathematical topology *is* structure—and meta-structure—failed.[8]

COUNT-AS-ONE, ONE, PHANTOM OF INCONSISTENCY

'Everything turns on mastering the gap between the presupposition (that must be rejected) of a being of the one and the thesis of its "there is"' (BE 23). For Badiou, the one is not, yet it exists as an operation, the count-as-one. The count-as-one is not a presentation either: what presents itself,

---

6. For a discussion of Lacan's ethics as an ontological ethics, see Lorenzo Chiesa and Alberto Toscano, 'Ethics and Capital, Ex Nihilo', *Umbr(a): A Journal of the Unconscious,*, no. 1, 2005, pp. 9-25. And Chapter 5 of Lorenzo Chiesa, *Lacan and Subjectivity: A Philosophical Introduction*, Cambridge, MIT Press, 2007.

7. Lesson of 17/5/1972 from Jacques Lacan, *Seminar XIX (1971-1972)*, '...Ou pire', unpublished.

8. 'Topology is not "made to lead us" to structure. Topology is this structure' Jacques Lacan, 'L'étourdit', *Autres écrits*, Paris, Seuil, 2001, p. 483.

a situation, is multiple. However, every situation is *structured* by means of the operation of the count-as-one. Thus, the relation between the multiple and the one is *retroactive*: the multiple will have preceded the one only after having necessarily been structured by means of the count-as-one. As Badiou puts it, 'the count-as-one (the structure) installs the universal pertinence of the one/multiple couple for any situation' (BE 24). This amounts to saying that, with regard to presentation, the one is also an 'operational *result*' (BE 24, my emphasis). A concomitant splitting occurs on the side of the multiple: inconsistent multiplicities, multiples that are retroactively understood as non-one 'as soon as being-one is a result', are to be distinguished from consistent multiplicities, 'multiple[s] as "several-ones" counted by the action of structure' (BE 25). We can thus conclude that the law that 'the one is not' is at the same time the law that 'the one is a law of the multiple' (BE 25).

It is vital to stress that, according to Badiou, what is normally presented in any situation is the fact that the one *is*: all that is presented in a situation is counted-as-one, which is to say that the principle 'the one is not' cannot be presented in it. At this level, inconsistent multiplicity is 'solely the presupposition that prior to the count the one is not' (BE 52). Having said this, we should also keep in mind that the one is an operational result, and that for this reason, there must be '"something" of the multiple [that] does not absolutely coincide with the result' (BE 53). In other words, in situations, which are as such always structured, a remainder exceeds the one of consistent multiplicities, and this can be nothing other than the very operation, the law of the count-as-one, from which the one results. With regard to a given situation, inconsistent multiplicities, the pure multiple, are therefore included as an exclusion: adopting a quasi-psychoanalytic terminology whose Lacanian affinities, as we shall later see, are remarkable, Badiou suggests that this inclusive exclusion is what 'causes the structured presentation to waver towards the *phantom* of inconsistency' (BE 53, my emphasis). This phantom, a retroactive by-product of the count-as-one, cannot itself be presented, yet it is *included* in the situation 'in the name of what "would be" the presentation itself, the presentation "in-itself", if what the law does not authorize to think was thinkable: that the one is not' (BE 53). Put differently, from the structured situational standpoint for which the law is 'the one is a law of the multiple', the phantom of inconsistency amounts to the excluded law that 'the one is not'.

More specifically, the pure multiple, unpresentable insofar as it is excluded by the law 'the one is a law of the multiple', is *nothing* from the standpoint of the situation. As Badiou observes, being-nothing is different from non-being: '*There is* a being of nothing, as form of the unpresentable. The "nothing" is what names the unperceivable gap [...] between [...] the one as result and the one as operation' (BE 54, my emphasis). But be-ing-nothing *is not*, just as the one is not: the *there is* of being-nothing does not instigate any search for *the* nothing, and thus avoids falling back into an ontology of presence: 'The nothing is neither a place nor a term of the situation. For if the nothing were a term that could only mean one thing: that it had been counted as one' (BE 54). Rather, the nothing is the non-one of any count-as-one; or, the phantom of inconsistency is the name 'nothing', which is not a-nothing [*un-rien*]. At this stage, it is important to emphasize that, for Badiou, the nothing is both the pure unpresentable multiple, the name of unpresentation in presentation, *and* the operation of the count, that which exceeds the one-result.[9] The nothing, or better the void as its local—yet unlocalizable—occurrence, has a *dual* status.

Let us consider this question further. Being *qua being* is neither one *nor* multiple; although being is certainly *presented* as multiple, being indeed occurs in every presentation, being does not present *itself* (see BE 27): be-ing *qua being* 'is what presents (itself)' (BE 24), and, it is as such, 'in being foreclosed from presentation' (BE 27), that it is sayable. Thus the void is the name of being insofar as the void indicates precisely that nothing is presented; by means of the void, presentation gives us the non-access to an unpresentable (see BE 56). However, in addition to naming being as an unpresentable, a non-one 'that wanders in the presentation in the form of a *subtraction*', 'the subtractive face of the count' (BE 55, my emphasis), the void also concomitantly names being in the very operation of the count-as-one which, in exceeding the presentable one-result, *sutures* a situation to its being (a suture is quite literally an operation). Again, the void is the name of being in two inextricable ways. Both exclude the possibility that the void may be localized and thus encountered in the normal regime of structured situations: Badiou believes that, from the situational standpoint, the void as name of being is equivalent to an 'absolute "unconscious" of the void' ['*inconscience*' *du vide*] (BE 56). The phantom of inconsistency can-not be conscious.

---

9. 'The law of the count as condition for existence, which renders presentation possible by precluding the presentation of inconsistent multiplicity (i.e. being itself), is ultimately indiscernible from the ontological inconsistency whose presentation it forecloses', Ray Brassier, 'Presentation as Anti-Phenomenon in Alain Badiou's Being and Event', *Continental Philosophy Review*, 2006, [available on-line at: http://www.springerlink.com/content/k3r6782060171279/?p=1661625d348044a1b73f87e8doc3fd49&pi=4]

UNICITY, FORMING-INTO-ONE, ANXIETY OF THE VOID

Badiou states that 'there are four meanings concealed beneath the single signifier "one"' (BE 89). The first two distinguish the count-as-one from the one: as we have already seen, the one, which is not, can only be the retroactive and *fictive* effect of a structural count, the count-as-one. Since being is always presented as multiple, multiple of multiples, what is *really* counted as one through the 'nominal seal' [*sceau*] of the count-as-one is the multiple-of-multiples (BE 90): multiples are counted by the count-as-one as 'one-multiples', consistent multiplicities, 'multiples as "several ones"'. In other words, the couple one/multiple installed by the count-as-one *qua* structure should ultimately be understood as the couple one-result/one-multiple.

The third meaning of the signifier 'one' is, for Badiou, unicity. Unicity is not a being, 'but a predicate of the multiple' (BE 90). Multiples are unique: this simply means, 'a multiple is different from any other' (BE 68). What differentiates a multiple from all other multiples is its proper name, that is, being counted as one-multiple by the nominal seal of the count-as-one. A notion of unicity that has done with any filiation from the being of the one and only accepts the one as result, is what allows us to think the relationship between the same and the other in a new way: given that the one is not, 'it is in regard to themselves that the others are Others' (BE 33). A multiple is Other than any other multiple only due to its unicity. Or, 'the Other [...] cannot designate the gap between the one and the others-than-one [*autres-que-l'un*], because the one is not' (BE 33 trans. modified). Put simply, the Other is coextensive to the unicity of the others, not the one.

Finally, there is a fourth meaning of the signifier 'one', which Badiou designates as 'forming-into-one' [*mise-en-un*]. This is basically a '*second count*', 'a count of the count' (BE 83-4 my emphasis), which should be understood in two inextricable ways according to the two sides of the couple one-result/one-multiple installed by the first count, the count-as-one. Indeed, the forming-into-one indicates the concomitant possibility of both 'count[ing] as one an already counted one-multiple' and 'apply[ing] the count to the one-result of the count' (BE 90). Such an operation is possible insofar as, after the first count, the one is not really distinguishable from the multiple: given that the one is the result of the structuring count that makes the multiple consist, it remains immanent to presentation, which, as such, can present only multiples. Differently put, the *one*-multiple results from the count-as-one, and for this very reason the one-*result* can only itself be a multiple.

If we now consider that the count-as-one is, as we have already re-marked, a law that produces a name—the proper name of each multiple as unique—it also follows that the forming-into-one will be nothing other than 'submitting to the law the names that it produces' (BE 90). It is im-portant to emphasize that the resulting 'multiple of names' (BE 91), the product of the forming-into-one, is itself a multiple: even after the second count has taken place, the one is solely a retroactive fiction, albeit a more elaborate one, since it now transcends presentation into representation. At this level, the one as representation can be distinguished from presen-tation as multiple, yet it remains a *re*-presentation of a multiple and thus a fiction. On the other hand, notice that retroactive representation will necessarily have a retroactive effect on retroactive presentation: it is also in this sense that I understand Badiou's suggestion according to which 'forming-into-one is not *really* distinct from the count-as-one' (BE 91).

The relation between the two counts, the counting-as-one of pres-entation and the forming-into-one of representation, is to be conceived of in terms of a relation between structure and metastructure, situation and the state of the situation. Although Badiou insists on differentiat-ing the two counts—they are 'absolutely distinct' (BE 83)—he also af-firms that the 'reduplication' of the count is necessary—'every structure call[s] upon a metastructure' (BE 84)—and consequently structure and metastructure, situation and its state, are not really distinct. The reason for this necessity is 'countering the danger of the void', warding it off from structured presentation (BE 84): all situations are thus defined by an in-evitable 'anxiety of the void' [*angoisse du vide*] (BE 93). As we have seen, the unpresentable and unlocalizable character of the void as the name of a situation's (inconsistent) being is what guarantees the consistency of this very situation, the emergence of consistent multiplicity. That is to say, it is only insofar as a structured presentation does not encounter 'its' own void that the situational one is not ruined. However, we have also seen that, within presentation, something exceeds the count: the very operation of the structural count-as-one *qua* nothing. This means that the errant void could fix itself in the guise of structure: 'It is […] possible that, subtracted from the count, and by consequence a-structured, the structure itself be the point where the void is given' (BE 93). In order to counter the danger of the void, it is therefore necessary to structure the structure or 'that the "there is Oneness" be valid for the count-as-one' (BE 93).

Significantly, according to Badiou, this redoubling, the second count, should be understood as an *imaginarization* of the first: if the count-as-one as a (symbolic) operation retroactively produces a fictional (imaginary) one-result, the count's 'undergoing, in turn, the operation of a count' is equivalent to 'the fictionalizing of the count via the imaginary being conferred upon it' (BE 95). Put simply, while the first count symbolically produces the one, the second count, the count of the count, imaginarily *is* one.

UNARY TRAIT AS TRAIT UNIQUE, OR 'LA MULTIPLICITÉ ACTUELLE'

The central notion of Lacan's ninth seminar is arguably what, in an explicit attempt to echo the function of the one in set theory, is designated as the unary trait [*trait unaire*].[10] Generalizing and elaborating on Freud's notion of the *einziger Zug*,[11] Lacan believes that identification is ultimately based on identification with the signifier, and the unary trait is 'what all signifiers have in common', their 'support'.[12] More precisely, the one as unary trait is the '*instrument*'[13] by means of which identification is made possible: the unary trait is not a one but an operation, a count, that constitutes 'the *foundation* of the one' of identification with the signifier.[14] Simply put, the unary trait should be understood as what produces a 'stroke', /, not a unity, let alone a totality:[15] Lacan openly denies that he is taking into consideration any of the many significations of the one proposed by philosophical tradition, rather 'it is a question of the 1 [...] of the primary teacher, the one of "pupil X, write out a hundred lines of 1s for me!", namely strokes [which have] always been sufficient for minimal notation'.[16]

In describing the unary trait as a count, and even as a first count, the count-as-one, that as such is to be distinguished from a second count, I

---

10. Seminar IX, lesson of 6/12/61.
11. According to Freud, in *some* cases, 'identification is [...] partial [...] and only borrows a single trait from the person who is its object', Sigmund Freud, 'Group Psychology and the Analysis of the Ego', *The Standard Edition of the Complete Psychological Work of Sigmund Freud*, vol. XVIII, London, The Hogarth Press and the Institute of Psychoanalysis, 2001, p. 107.
12. Seminar IX, lesson of 22/11/61.
13. Seminar IX, Lesson of 29/11/61.
14. Seminar IX, Lesson of 22/11/61.
15. See Seminar IX, lesson of 29/11/61.
16. Seminar IX, Lesson of 29/11/61.

am far from forcing Lacan's own terminology. 'The unary trait begins the function of counting': this initial 'activity of counting [that] begins early for the subject' should not be confused with the activity of 'establishing collections'.[17] In other words, the count-as-one of the unary trait is what produces the one, many ones, as strokes ///; however, at this stage, there is no second count, or *addition*, that can count the strokes as 1s, or put differently, that can count the operation of the first count as *an* operation. As Lacan observes, 'the unary trait [...] supports [...] one plus one and one again, the plus being meant there only to mark well [a] difference, where the problem begins is precisely that one can add them together, in other words that two, that three have a meaning'.[18] In order to stress how / + / + / is not the same as 1 + 1 + 1, Lacan goes as far as suggesting that a child may well be able to count up to two and three *without* being able to operate with numbers: two and three are in this case nothing but a repetition of the / produced by the unary trait, and should be distinguished from the number 2 and 3 understood as 1 + 1 and 1 + 1 + 1. This 'early' counting is ineffective when dealing with numbers higher than 3: we should therefore not be surprised 'when we are told that certain so-called primitive tribes along the mouth of the Amazon were only recently able to discover the virtue of the number four, and raised altars to it'.[19] What is at stake in the gap that separates these two counts is nothing less than the birth of the subject's identification as modern Cartesian subject split between consciousness and the unconscious.[20]

In what precise sense does the + of the / + / + / 'mark a difference' between the strokes produced by the count-as-one of the unary trait? This question certainly has to do with the fact that, throughout Seminar IX, Lacan indiscriminately alternates the phrases '*trait unaire*' and '*trait unique*': put simply, a unary trait is a *single* trait. If the unary trait, as instrumental operation, is the 'most simple structural trait' in the sense that it presents 'no variations',[21] its sole property will be its *unicity*. That is to say, the + separating / from / denotes the singleness of the *trait* as such, the absence of any 'qualitative difference' in it,[22] and thus works as an indicator of 'sig-

---

17. Seminar IX, Lesson of 7/3/62.
18. Seminar IX, Lesson of 7/3/62.
19. Seminar IX, Lesson of 7/3/62.
20. For a description of the Cartesian God as the *cogito*'s unary trait, see lesson of 22/11/61.
21. Seminar IX, Lesson of 22/11/61.
22. Seminar IX, Lesson of 6/12/61.

nifying difference', 'difference in the pure state'.[23] Or, every count, every /
is absolutely different from any other / without its ever being a question of
counting the trait as a qualitatively differentiated 1: as we have just seen,
the unary trait precedes number *stricto sensu.*[24]

Two crucial specifications should be made. Firstly, the unary trait
marks 'difference as such',[25] which does not mean it *is* difference as such.
This is a straightforward way to distinguish the unary trait from the full-
fledged signifier which it 'supports'. While the unary trait is a stroke, and,
significantly enough, it is as 'letter' that it can be differentiated from all
other strokes,[26] the signifier is 'the one as difference', that is, following
Saussure, 'simply being what the others are not'.[27] Thus, unlike the unary
trait, the signifier 'implies [the] function of the *unit* [...] *qua* pure difference'.[28] According to Lacan, the *one* as difference, the emergence of 'the
one [which] as such is the Other',[29] that is the fictional big Other, necessitates the second count.

Secondly and most importantly, 'at its first appearance, the one manifestly designates actual multiplicity [*multiplicité actuelle*]'.[30] The count-as-
one of the unary trait as *trait unique* produces nothing other than consistent, that is 'actual', multiplicity: Lacan also refers to it as a 'distinctive
unity' [*unité distinctive*].[31] In order to illustrate this last point, he evokes a
scene of everyday pre-historic life:

> I am a hunter [...] I kill [an animal], it is an adventure, I kill another
> of them, it is a second adventure which I can distinguish by certain
> traits characteristic of the first, but which resembles it essentially
> by being marked with the same general line. At the fourth, there
> may be some confusion: what distinguishes it from the second, for

23. Seminar IX, Lesson of 6/12/61.
24. 'Lacan affirms that the signifier as such serves to connote difference at its purest, and,
we can add, it is all the purer because it precedes even number', M. Safouan, *Lacaniana: Les
séminaires de Jacques Lacan * 1953-1963*, Paris, Seuil, 2001, p. 193.
25. Seminar IX, lesson of 6/12/61.
26. Seminar IX, Lesson of 6/12/61.
27. Seminar IX, Lesson of 29/11/61.
28. Seminar IX, Lesson of 29/11/61.
29. Seminar IX, Lesson of 29/11/61.
30. Seminar IX, Lesson of 6/12/61.
31. Safouan even names this concept 'distinctive one' [*un distinctif*], Safouan, *Lacaniana: Les
séminaires de Jacques Lacan * 1953-1963*, p. 202. To the best of my knowledge, Lacan never
uses this expression in Seminar IX. In the lessons of 13/12/61 and 20/12/61 he also refers
to the 'distinctive trait', which I take to be synonymous with 'unary trait'.

example? At the twentieth, how will I know where I am?[32]

Like a child who 'counts' without numbers, our primitive man can initially distinguish the second adventure from the first by certain imaginary—intuitively qualitative—traits that are then symbolically presented
as a stroke / on an animal rib-bone. Yet, as soon as this occurs, his two
adventures are marked by 'the same general line', the same kind of stroke
which leads to 'signifying sameness', //. Although qualitative difference
is never eliminated completely, the fact that each 'adventure' is, for a
'limited time', 'intuitively' experienced as new proves to be all the more
secondary inasmuch as quality is precisely what is overshadowed by the
signifying in-difference of the traits //.[33] From a slightly different perspective, all this amounts to saying that the distinctive unity of the unary trait
is still *immanent* to the situation it counts, and thus runs the risk of becoming indistinguishable from the non-situation of a primitive man who is still
lacking any 'method of location'.[34] Thus, marking signifying difference as
such results in nothing other than signifying sameness, in-difference, if the
count is not itself counted, if the 'actual multiplicity' /, the one-multiple
that presents the hunter's adventure, is not itself represented as 1. We can
then understand why Lacan pays so much attention to the later appearance in pre-history of 'a *series* of strokes' carved on an animal rib-bone—
'First two, then a little interval and afterwards five, and then it recom-
mences...'.[35] It is only at this level, that of the count of the count, where 1 +
1 retroactively replaces //, that the properly human symbolic dimension
begins: this is the subject's own identification with the signifier.

Finally, it is quite remarkable that, in this context, Lacan himself draws
a comparison between the use of the / made by the primitive hunter and
the notion of the one with which set theory operates. Against what we
are taught at school—'You cannot add up oranges and apples, pears with

---

32. Seminar IX, lesson of 6/12/61.
33. Lesson of 6/12/61. Lacan concedes that, while the function of the unary trait 'is linked
to the *extreme* reduction [...] of qualitative difference', even just at the level of the imaginary
appearance of the stroke itself, 'it is quite clear that there will not be a single [trait] like
another'. Commenting on this point, Safouan rightly observes the following: 'It is clear
that the function of these notches is not more related to their [qualitative] differences than
it is to the elimination of these differences. It is not because the traits are different that they
work differently, but because signifying difference is different from qualitative difference',
Safouan, *Lacaniana: Les séminaires de Jacques Lacan * 1953-1963*, pp. 192-3.
34. Seminar IX, lesson of 6/12/61.
35. Seminar IX, Lesson of 6/12/61.

carrots and so on'[36]—the primitive hunter counts as one a multiple 'adventure' made by irreconcilable 'objects' and 'things'. In the same way, in set theory, 'you can very well add up what you want'.[37] More technically, Lacan acknowledges that 'in what one calls the elements of sets, it is not a matter of objects, or of things', it is rather a question of the multiples of a multiple. In other words, at the level of presentation, the set is a one-multiple, what Lacan refers to as 'actual multiplicity': the count-as-one of the unary trait presents a multiple-of-multiples, or to put with Badiou, a 'multiple as "several ones"' (BE 25).

In order to appreciate better the proximity between Badiou's consistent multiplicity and Lacan's distinctive unity we should not lose sight of the following convergence. Badiou's consistent multiplicity, the one-multiple, is 'initially' determined solely by its unicity, in all cases; unicity is *the* property of consistent multiplicity *qua* counted-as-one, independently of any other possible property of *a* situation (or set). What matters at the level of presentation without representation is the *proper name alpha*, a letter that 'seals' the multiple, rather than the extension of what is being presented—the terms or elements of the situation. Indeed, extension is not properly defined before the second count takes place and the state of the situation is established retroactively: only at that stage, the one-multiple will have been counted as *a* situation (or, ontologically, *all* the parts of a set will have formed the elements of *a* set as the powerset). *A* situation is not identical to what is being presented in it. Following Ray Brassier, another way to put this would be to say that presentation as such, presentation without representation—the prehistoric hunter's 'adventure'—is an anti-phenomenon.[38]

LETTER AND PROPER NAME, OR 'A IS NOT A'

The most basic formula of identification is 'A is A'. Lacan believes that its apparent simplicity conceals a number of problems. It is therefore only insofar as we question this formula that we can really grasp the difficulties involved in identification. This questioning is strictly related to 'the [signifying] function of the one' and, conversely, 'the extended use of the

---

36. This amounts to a very advanced 'definition of addition which supposes a number of axioms which would be enough to cover the blackboard' (Seminar IX, Lesson of 6/12/61).

37. Seminar IX, Lesson of 6/12/61.

38. See Brassier, 'Presentation as Anti-Phenomenon in Alain Badiou's *Being and Event*'.

signifier in mathematics'.[39] More specifically, for Lacan, 'A is A' presupposes first of all the existence of A, the emergence of the *letter*, which, as we have seen, should be understood as a unary trait, a first count. Lacan's bold propositions according to which "'A is A'" is a belief' and 'There is no tautology' are thus always to be considered against the background of the dimension of the letter. 'It is not insofar as the first A and the second A mean different things that I say that there is no tautology, it is in the very status of A that there is inscribed that A cannot be A';[40] 'A is not A' means that A is not identical to *itself*, or, to use a well-known Lacanian locution, A is barred, not that A is actually B: more precisely, the letter A as unary trait counts as one but is not *a* one.

Lacan's theory of the proper name and his theory of writing aim to show how the true nature of the proper name is the letter as unary trait, which in turn is inextricable from the written mark. The proper name cannot be understood as a 'word for particulars', a definition proposed by Bertrand Russell: this would soon lead us to paradoxes such as 'Socrates' not being a proper name since, for us, it is no longer a particular but an abbreviated description—'Socrates' is indeed Plato's master, the man who drank the hemlock, etc.—or, conversely, the demonstrative 'this' is a particular and could therefore be designated as 'John'. Relying in part on the linguist Alan Gardiner, Lacan believes that a proper name functions on the basis of the distinction between meaning and signifying material (signified and signifier); however, departing from him, he specifies that it should not be identified with a distinctive sound to which the subject pays particular attention *as* sound. From a structuralist standpoint, it is indeed a matter of fact that all language is based on the differentiality of distinctive sounds, or phonemes; what is more, 'it is absolutely not true [...] that each time we pronounce a proper name we are psychologically aware of the accent put on the sonant material as such'.[41] In other words, the problem with Gardiner's notion of proper name is that he relies on a psychologically substantialist idea of the subject: the subject is for him simply someone who pays attention to signifiers when they are proper names. On the other hand, for Lacan, the subject can be defined only 'with reference' to signifiers, not as someone underlying their functioning;[42] the central role played by proper names in the subject's identification should

---

39. Seminar IX, lesson of 29/11/61.
40. Seminar IX, Lesson of 6/12/61.
41. Seminar IX, Lesson of 20/12/61.
42. Seminar IX, Lesson of 20/12/61.

thus be explained solely in terms of the signifier, especially according to its most basic appearance, the unary trait of the letter. 'There cannot be a definition of the proper name except in the measure that we are aware of the relationship between the naming utterance and something which in its radical nature is of the order of the letter'.[43]

Most importantly, the proper name's relation to the letter as unary trait is itself dependent on the logic of the written mark. Lacan plainly points out that 'the characteristic of the proper name is always [...] linked to [...] writing'.[44] As Aaron Schuster remarks in his elegant commentary on the fourth lesson of Seminar IX:

> The crucial point for Lacan is that writing emerges first as 'the isolation of the signifying trait' (unary trait) which then becomes— again, retroactively—the basic support for the phoneticization of language, i.e. the treasury of signifiers proper. Far from being simply the translation of a more 'original' speech, it is speech itself that ultimately finds its basis in the exteriority of the written mark. 'What results from this', Lacan adds, is that the proper name qua brand [...] ought to be linked not with sound à la Gardiner, but with writing. The proof of this is found in the decipherment of unknown languages: one always begins by looking for proper names since they remain the same across all languages [...]. *In the proper name, one thus rediscovers within the synchronic order of language a signifier in its 'pure state', a state represented in diachronic (pre-)history by the primitive hunter's notched bone.*[45]

Let us dwell on these issues. It is doubtless the case that man's vocal utterings preceded writing, chronologically speaking; however, language *stricto sensu* as determined by the function of the signifier is, for Lacan, ultimately retroactively dependent on writing. Conversely, the letter as writing potential 'was waiting to be phoneticized': this is what we have at a first stage in prehistory, the simple traits, or strokes, of primitive bone etchings. Lacan is careful in specifying that, as we have already seen, the letter as unary trait always involves an initial imaginary dimension— 'something figurative'—that is soon 'effaced':[46] this is valid both for the simple stroke / carved on an animal's rib—which originally marked the image of an 'adventure'—and, even more so, the more sophisticated traits

---

43. Seminar IX, Lesson of 20/12/61.
44. Seminar IX, Lesson of 20/12/61.
45. A. Schuster, *Commentary on Lacan Seminar IX L'Identification, 20 December 1961*, unpublished (my emphasis).
46. Seminar IX, lesson of 20/12/61.

used in ideographic notation—the schematic representation of the head *
of the animal I killed during my adventure still functions as a unary trait.

At a second stage, the writing of the trait—that designates something
imaginary—is accompanied by the utterance of a phoneme; but, for the
time being, the utterance 'm' is not as yet detached from the image represented by the trait *. Put differently, phoneticization here depends on
the designation of an object via the marking of the trait. In a third and
final stage, which determines the retroactive passage from prehistory to
history, we witness the reversal of this relation: now the marking of the
trait depends solely on phoneticization. This is writing proper: the letter
is retroactively transformed into a signifier and, being an element in a
differential structure of other signifiers, acquires a life that is completely
independent of the object it used to designate.

From a slightly different perspective, we can say that writing proper—
and language *stricto sensu* with it—only really begins when the marking
of the trait * is phoneticized *as trait*, that is, *named as such*. At that point, *
becomes the support of the phoneme 'm' which was previously the mere
'sound' of the object designated by *—the mooing head of the animal I
killed. We retroactively move from the—ultimately animalic—sound 'm'
to the—human—phonematic signifier 'm' only when 'm' can *even* be regarded as a *proper name* 'M'. As Lacan has it, 'It is a fact that letters have
names', 'a' is named 'alpha'.[47] We should pay particular attention to this
apparently trivial remark which, in its expanded form, reads as follows:
it is *only* insofar as 'a' has a name, insofar as 'A' is a proper name, that the
letter 'a' can be said to be 'a', that 'a' is identical to itself (albeit as part of
a differential 'sonant structure'). The 'idiotic character'[48] of the proper
name—its meaninglessness, the fact that, as already noted by John Stuart
Mill, 'it is not the meaning of the object that it brings with it'[49]—is nothing
less than the precondition of identification: Lacan is Lacan only if 'Lacan'
is a proper name.

More specifically, 'the proper name [...] specifies as such [...] the
rooting of the subject' precisely insofar as it is 'more specially linked than
any other, not to phonematicization as such, the structure of language,
but to what in language is already ready [...] to receive this informing by
the trait'.[50] The proper name is closer to the letter than to the symbolic

---

47. Seminar IX, Lesson of 10/1/62.
48. Seminar IX, Lesson of 20/12/61.
49. Seminar IX, Lesson of 20/12/61.
50. Seminar IX, Lesson of 10/1/62.

proper: it approaches the unary trait by redoubling its operation, the idiotic in-difference of its count, and in this way guarantees the consistency of the structure of language, the differentially phonematic chain of signifiers. In other words, the proper name 'make[s] us question ourselves about what is at stake at this radical, archaic point that we must necessarily suppose to be at the origin of the unconscious', that is, primary repression.[51] And this in two complementary ways: the proper name as the redoubling of the letter, the unary trait, raises the issue of 'the attachment of language to the *real*,'[52] as well as that of *negation* as directly involved in 'the genesis of language' in the guise of an '*existential* relationship'.[53] If the letter as unary trait is that which retroactively makes the real object exist as negated (be it the killed animal or the mother's breast), the proper name is that which, operating retroactively on the letter, allows the subject's own identification by naming this very negation.

Ø = 'THERE EXISTS A NEGATION'

Although the origins of writing lie outside the concerns of Badiou's general ontological edifice, it is nevertheless profitable to begin to accommodate Lacan's reflections on the proper name to the notions made available by *Being and Event*. Using Badiou's terminology, we could suggest that, for Lacan, the proper name can be situated on two different levels, that of the situation and that of the state of the situation, while preserving the same 'sealing' function. The proper name as letter, the stroke / on the primitive hunter's bone that counts as one the multiple of the hunter's 'adventure' works exactly like the proper name *stricto sensu*, the name 'Lacan': indeed, the latter forms-into-ones the 'multiple[s] of names' (BE 91) (bluntly put, the multiples 'p.s.y.c.h.o.a.n.a.l.y.s.t.', 'd.o.c.t.o.r.', 'b.u.f.f.o.o.n.', 'f.r.e.n.c.h.', 'b.o.u.r.g.e.o.i.s.', 's.q.u.e.a.k.y.', 's.m.o.k.i.n.g.', 'e.t.o.u.r.d.i.t.' etc.) made of proper names as letters. We could also suggest that the proper name *stricto sensu* is equivalent to structure *in* the metastructure, presentation *in* representation. It amounts to the insistence of the unary trait of the first count in its meaningless unicity, the insistence of the letter, within the state of a situation—where number and meaning

---

51. Seminar IX, Lesson of 10/1/62.
52. Seminar IX, Lesson of 10/1/62. 'But what is it that inscribes [the fact] that a real exists? It is the symbolic as such. Thus, we will say that 1 is the digit of the symbolic. The 1 is the *unary trait*, that is to say, the minimal possible Other for the pure letter of the real', Alain Badiou, *Un, Deux, Trois, Quatre, et aussi Zéro*, unpublished.
53. Seminar IX, Lesson of 10/1/62.

as such are now possible. Consequently, the proper name accounts for the fact that 'the state of the situation can either be said to be separate (or transcendent) or to be attached (or immanent) with regard to the situation and its native structure' (BE 98).

At this point, there is a question we cannot postpone any longer: how does Lacan account for that which is being counted, and thus named, by the unary trait of the letter? What is involved in 'early counting'—with regard to both the phylogenetic 'adventure' of the primitive hunter and the ontogenetic emergence of number in the child—is first and foremost 'the functioning of the sensorium'.[54] This means that it is only with the / of the unary trait that something 'really exists' for the subject, that 'the judgement of existence begins'.[55] Yet, one should note that the unary trait is always necessarily associated with the retroactive effect of negation: the in-different notch on the bone presents the primitive man's adventure as effaced—significantly enough, under the sign of a killing—just as the 'early counting' of the child marks a proto-symbolic relation with an object insofar as he has been frustrated of it. In opposition to what he terms Bergson's 'naïve realism',[56] Lacan believes that negation is not the negation of a primordial affirmation which would affirm the existence of a real that is immediately given. It is doubtless the case that negation 'supposes the affirmation on which it is based' but this does not in the least entail that such an affirmation is 'the affirmation of something of the real which has been simply removed';[57] affirmation does not precede negation; negation and affirmation occur concomitantly by means of *negation*. Put differently:

> There is no more, and not at all less, in the idea of an object conceived of as not existing, than in the idea of the same object conceived of as existing, because the idea of the object not existing is necessarily the idea of the object existing with, in addition, the representation of an exclusion of this object by the present reality taken as a whole.[58]

To cut a long story short, according to Lacan, what is being counted by the unary trait is the possibility of the real (its affirmation) through

54. Seminar IX, lesson of 7/3/62.
55. Seminar IX, Lesson of 7/3/62.
56. Seminar IX, Lesson of 17/1/62.
57. Seminar IX, Lesson of 17/1/62.
58. Seminar IX, Lesson of 17/1/62.

the preservation of the 'rights of the nothing'.[59] In opposition to the false axiom for which anything real is possible, one should always start with the axiom for which 'the real takes its place only from the not possible': the possibility of affirming that something exists always relies on a law that safe-guards the nothing. But if the real, or better reality, only originates in the not possible, this not possible, presented as such by negation, is *the* real. Here, Lacan uses the term 'real' in two ways: a) as the possible that follows the not possible; b) as the not possible that originates the possible. But it is in fact possible to think these two acceptations together: the real *qua* reality 'takes its place' only from the *possibility* of the not possible, the possibility of the real as such. Indeed, 'this real exists', Lacan says, as 'exception' or 'exclusion'.[60] In other words, 'there is not only the not possible at the origin of any enunciating', but also the possibility of the not possible: the origin of any enunciating is the '*enunciation of the nothing*',[61] the affirmation of negation accomplished by the unary trait.

Badiou's philosophy thinks meta-ontologically a set theoretical ontology which relies on the very same axiom, the axiom of the empty set, which formalizes existence at its most basic level. As he writes in *Being and Event*, 'the axiom of the empty set states, in substance, that *there exists a negation*' (BE 86 my emphasis); it is necessary that the 'absolutely initial existence be that of a negation', the existence of an inexistent (BE 67). What negation as the absolutely initial existence negates is belonging: no elements belong to the void-set, not even the void. If, for Badiou's set theoretical ontology, the void presents the unpresentable as that which 'alone in-exists' (BE 69), for Lacan's theory of the subject, the possibility of the not possible affirms the real that ex-sists as exclusion. If for Badiou, the in-existent void subtractively sutures a situation to its being (inconsistent multiplicity), for Lacan the ex-sistent, or ex-timate, real—the real-of-the-symbolic—retroactively reminds a subject of the undead (an inconsistent real which was and will be not-one, barred *in itself*, before and after the presence of the symbolic).[62] If, finally, for Badiou, the void as set is abso-

---

59. Seminar IX, Lesson of 7/3/62.
60. Seminar IX, Lesson of 7/3/62.
61. Seminar IX, Lesson of 7/3/62.
62. Although the notion of the undead has been employed profitably by Žižek in a number of ways, Lacan appears to delimit it within a particular domain: the undead refers to the 'closed world' of the animal as that which is always 'already dead' from the perspective of the individual and 'immortal' from that of the species or nature, see for instance Jacques Lacan, *The Seminar of Jacques Lacan. Book I, Freud's Papers on Technique, 1953-1954*, trans. John Forrester, Jacques-Alain (ed.), 1st American ed., New York, W.W. Norton, 1988, pp. 121,

lutely 'in-different' in the sense that 'nothing differentiates it', its unicity is not based on a difference that can be attested (BE 68), for Lacan, the real-of-the-symbolic is the other side of a 'distinctive unity' whose unicity precisely resolves itself, as we have seen, into in-difference. (It is important to bear in mind that the count of the unary trait is two-sided. Moreover, this two-sidedness is somehow 'unbalanced' towards one side, that of the nothing/void: just as, for Badiou, the void as name is both unpresentation in presentation *and* the operation of the count, which as such exceeds the one-result, so for Lacan the 'enunciation of the nothing' is both the real-of-the-symbolic as the possibility of the not possible *and* the very operation of the unary trait, which as such exceeds the distinctive unity).

We must then take seriously Lacan's provocative remark according to which '"A is A" signifies nothing'.[63] Initially, there exists a negation, non-A, no element belongs to the empty set ø: in order for the set *alpha* to exist, in order for A to be A as a set to which at least one element belongs, the nothing must first be enunciated, 'signifierized'. At this stage, it is crucial to emphasize that if the 'primal fact'[64] is the enunciation of the noth-ing—the void as name, the void-set—then we witness here nothing less than the collapse of the traditional categories of unity and totality. Lacan explains this point quite clearly: 'Unity and totality appear in the tradition as solidary [...] totality being totality with respect to units [and] unity be-ing [...] the unity of a whole'; such a solidarity is what is being 'shattered' by the 'other meaning of unity' he proposes, that of distinctive unity, the -1 brought about by the enunciation of the nothing.[65] From now on, any possible *semblance* of totality (or unity for that matter) can only be based on the -1, since the primal fact is that the one is not. Note that this is exactly what is ultimately at stake from a philosophical, or better, metaontologi-cal, perspective in the revolutionary contribution of axiomatic set-theory. As Badiou remarks:

> It would not be an exaggeration to say that the entirety of speculative ontology is taken up with examinations of the connections and disconnections between Unity and Totality. It has been so from the very beginnings of metaphysics, since it is possible to show that Plato essentially has the One prevail over the All whilst Aristotle made the opposite choice.

137.
63. Seminar IX, lesson of 6/12/61.
64. Seminar IX, Lesson of 7/3/62.
65. Seminar IX, Lesson of 7/3/62.

Set theory sheds light on the fecund frontier between the whole/
parts relation and the one/multiple relation; because, at base, it
suppresses both of them. The multiple [...] for a post-Cantorian
is neither supported by the existence of the one nor unfolded as
an organic totality. The multiple consists from being without-one
(BE 81).

Interestingly enough, in this context, it is Badiou himself who bends
his fundamental ontological thesis according to which 'the one is not' towards a formulation, 'being *without-one*' [*sans-un*], that is reminiscent of
Lacan's -1, the 'one-less'. Unity and totality, the particular and the universal—or better their semblances—can only be conceived of if one begins from the multiple, which initially un-presents itself in the void-set as
being without-one. The fact that both elements and sets are multiples-
of-multiples and thus become indistinguishable collapses the traditional
distinction between unity as an element of a totality and totality as a set
of unities. Using natural language paradoxically, we could suggest that a
'particular' unity is always already a one-*multiple* whilst being an element
of a 'universal' totality which is never as yet a *one*-multiple. Thus, there
is only one possible relation between sets and elements, *belonging*, 'which
indicates that a multiple is counted as element in the presentation of another multiple' (BE 81). Besides this, all we can do is count the multiple
according to its *parts*. This is the relation of *inclusion*, 'which indicates that
a multiple is a sub-multiple [or part] of another multiple' (BE 81). Such
a relation is dealt with by the axiom of the powerset, the set of subsets,
among others: this affirms that between belonging and inclusion 'there is
at least the correlation that all the multiples *included* in a supposedly existing *alpha* [the initial set] *belong* to a *beta* [its powerset]; that is, *they form a
set, a multiple counted-as-one*' (BE 82 my emphasis). Let us dwell on this last
point, which is crucial for Badiou. According to axiomatic set-theory, the
following can be stated:

1.   inclusion is derived from belonging as the sole primitive relation
     between sets and elements, yet belonging and inclusion are
     distinct;

2.   the fact that inclusion and belonging are distinct entails that there
     is an excess of inclusion over belonging, the powerset over the set;
     this excess is an excess in belonging: there is always at least one
     element of the powerset which does not belong to the initial set;

3.   nothing belongs to the void, not even the void itself;

4. the void is a subset of any set: by the very fact that nothing belongs to the void, the void is included in everything;

5. the void possesses a subset, the void itself; hence, the powerset of the void must also exist;

6. the powerset of the void is the set to which the void alone belongs, since everything included in the void belongs to the powerset of the void; *the void, or better its name, is therefore an element of the powerset it forms while it is not an element of itself.*

Badiou can thus conclude that the powerset of the void, the set to which the name of the void alone belongs, is the first set that is able to count-as-one the result of the first count, the relation of belonging. Thus, the powerset of the void is what gives us the forming-into-one: indeed, it is only 'once [...] the forming-into-one of ø [...] is *guaranteed* via the power-set axiom applied to the name of the void [that] the operation of form-ing-into-one is uniformly applicable to any multiple supposed existent' (BE 91 my emphasis). If, on the one hand, what is presented by the form-ing-into-one is always the multiple—the effect of its operation is again a one-multiple, the same as on the level of the count-as-one—on the other hand, it is nevertheless the case that the powerset of the void accomplishes something quite remarkable, namely *counting the name of the void, the -1, as an element, a 1*. In this way the powerset of the void operates against what Badiou calls the 'errancy of the void', the fact that, after the first count, the void is included in all sets *without* belonging to them. As a consequence of this, it is inevitable that we consider the second count as an operation which, by turning the -1 into *an* element, representing the name of the void, somehow preserves the *semblance* of the distinction between unity as an element of a totality and totality as a set of unities, even though what is being counted are multiples-of-multiples.

This in no way means that, after the second count has taken place, the void does not continue to err on the level of the first count; after all, the state of a situation can be said to be 'separate' (or 'transcendent') with regard to the situation. While the retroactive effect of the forming-into-one on the count-as-one definitely makes the void 'take place' in a 'part [that] receives the seal of the one' (BE 97), its errancy is far from being interrupted within this circumscribed 'partial' place. Here, it would cer-tainly be reductive, if not misleading, to regard the situation as a mere part of the state of the situation, since, in a sense, the state is 'attached' (or 'immanent') to its structure (the powerset is still a set); rather, we should acknowledge the following: the situation as situation characterized by the errancy of the void takes place in a part of the situation as state of the situation. From a slightly different perspective, we can propose that both the initial counting of the multiple in the set and the second counting, that of the parts of the set as elements of the powerset, both structured presentation and metastructured representation, ultimately rely on the void-set—the 'initial multiple' as 'absolutely initial point of being' (BE 48)—which should always remain errant. As a matter of fact, what should be avoided at all costs as 'the catastrophe of presentation', is a 'fixation of the void', the presentation's encounter with its own void (BE 93-94).

It should be stressed that Badiou himself seems implicitly to distinguish the errancy of the void in a situation *as such*, 'the *pure* errancy of the void' (BE 96 my emphasis) from the errancy of the void *at the level* of the situation after the state of the situation has been established: this second, impure errancy is nothing other than what he refers to as the 'unconscious of the void'. Given Badiou's deliberate choice to employ psychoanalytic terms to describe the basics of his meta-ontological edifice, I do not think I am forcing his argument in finally suggesting that the 'unconscious of the void' amounts to the unconscious status of the situation under state control, or put simply, the state's unconscious. *The unconscious of the void, or, significantly enough, the 'phantom of inconsistency', is the name retroactively imposed on the name 'void', the letter ø, by state repression.* Having said this, it must be observed that Badiou fails to emphasize the following: as long as the state of a situation (consciousness) remains both separate from the situation (the unconscious) and attached to it, *repetition* is the movement that prevents the taking place of the void in the phantom of inconsistency from degenerating into a fixation of the void.[66]

---

66. Badiou's failure to account for the function of repetition in the 'phantom of inconsistency' gives rise to terminological ambiguity when he describes the difference between the 'taking place' of the void—which wards it off—and its 'fixation'—that is, 'the ruin of the One' (BE 93): how does the 'fixation' of the void, its 'becom[ing] localizable' (BE 56), differ from its 'taking place' if one does not specify that the latter still entails (repetitive, circular) movement? In *Saint Paul*, Badiou seems to suggest that repetition should rather be *associated* with fixation, a fixation of the subject's desire which is, however, a fixation *of* the law (and not aimed against it): 'The law is required in order to unleash the automatic life of desire, the automatism of repetition. For only the law *fixes* the object of desire [...]', Alain Badiou, *Saint Paul: The Foundation of Universalism*, trans. Ray Brassier, Stanford, Stanford University Press, 2003, p. 79. Beyond terminological confusion, should we not identify such a repetitive 'fixation' of the law with what *Being and Event* defines as the 'taking place' of the void? For a recent critique of Badiou's unsatisfactory notion of repetition with regards to the political subject, see Slavoj Žižek, 'Badiou: Notes From an Ongoing Debate', *Interna-

THE SUBJECT AS AN ERROR OF COUNTING

Lacan's breaking of the solidarity between unity and totality allows him to work with parts. 'Repudiat[ing] the reference to totality does not prevent one speaking about the partial'; rather, from the inexistence of totality as a one follows the possibility of thinking the part as 'partial system'. This system is, for Lacan, the unconscious.[67] At this stage, it would not be exaggerated to suggest that the Lacanian unconscious can properly be understood according to a third set-theoretical axiom, that of separation ('For any multiple supposed given, there exists the sub-multiple of terms which possess the property expressed by the formula $\lambda(a)$') (BE 46). Paraphrasing Badiou's explanation of this axiom, we could propose that, for Lacan, language separates out, within a *supposed* given existence—the undead real as not-one—the existence of a sub-multiple, the unconscious as partial system. This partial *system* is constituted from terms which 'validate' language, that is follow its metonymic and metaphoric laws—the famous thesis according to which 'the unconscious is structured like a language'. Against common accusations of idealistic structuralism, for Lacan, 'language cannot induce existence, solely a split within existence'; his notion of the unconscious 'breaks with the figure of idealinguistery' and is therefore materialist (BE 47). We are now able to see why Badiou himself briefly refers to Lacan's notions of the symbolic and the real as an exemplification of the axiom of separation: the supposed given existence of the undead real as not-one anticipates what language, the symbolic, retroactively separates out from it as implied existence, the unconscious partial system. Such an implication *concomitantly* entails conscious reality, a semblance of existence which, rather successfully, attempts to totalize the partial unconscious, turning the system—the structure—into the mirage of a one/whole.

Applying both the axiom of separation and that of the empty set, it is important to emphasize that the existence of the unconscious as partial system ultimately relies on the in-existence of the void, or, more specifically, the *existence* of the void as *part* that *in-exists* as element. Indeed, the most basic sub-multiple that language—the unary trait as first count—separates out from the undead real as not-one is the void which un-presents itself as the *part object*, the object *a*. Unsurprisingly, Lacan identifies the void as part with the breast; the 'primal fact', which, for what we have seen,

---

tional Journal of Žižek Studies, vol. 1, no. 2, 2006, http://ics.leeds.ac.uk/zizek/article.cfm?id=21&issue=3.
67. Seminar IX, lesson of 24/1/62.

should also be conceived of as the primal existence, is the 'enunciation of the nothing' as the -1 *of* the absent *mamma*. In this way, a fundamental un-presentation functions as the 'radical support' for any relationship of inclusion. More precisely, Lacan explains how we can formulate a definition of the traditional category of class—'if you really want to guarantee it its universal status'[68]—only by means of the un-presentation of the -1: the mammalian class can only be postulated on the basis of the absence of the *mamma*.

> There is first of all the absence of the *mamma* and [then] one says:
> it cannot be that the *mamma* is missing, here is what constitutes the
> mammalian class. [...] The zoologist, if you allow me to go this far,
> does not carve out the mammalian class in the assumed totality of
> the maternal *mamma*; it is only because he detaches the *mamma* that
> he can identify the absence of the *mamma*.[69]

The in-existence of the un-presented *mamma* which nevertheless exists as void-part determines both the particular existence of the *mamma* and the representation of the possible absence of the *mamma* with regard to the mammalian class taken as a *whole*. However, Lacan immediately specifies that, if the construction of the whole relies on the un-presentation of the -1, then it is the product of an '*error of counting*', and consequently universality can be regarded only as a *semblance*; in order to obtain the universal, the 'enunciation of the nothing', the void-set as -1, must necessarily be primally repressed.

More precisely, Lacan believes that it is *the subject* who necessarily makes an error of counting: there is a 'constituting necessity [that] the subject should make an error in the count'.[70] This count is a second count for the subject since, on an initial level, he is nothing other than what dis-counts itself by means of the unary trait, the very un-presentation of the -1. Put differently, initially, 'the subject as such is minus one'[71] insofar as he identifies with the absent object, first and foremost the *mamma*—'In the [first form of the] identification relationship [...] what the subject assimilates [...] is him in his frustration'.[72] It is only at a second stage, which works retroactively on the first and carries out identification proper, the splitting between the unconscious and consciousness, that 'we are going

68. Seminar IX, lesson of 7/3/62.
69. Seminar IX, Lesson of 7/3/62.
70. Seminar IX, Lesson of 7/3/62.
71. Seminar IX, Lesson of 7/3/62.
72. Seminar IX, Lesson of 24/1/62.

to rediscover the subject [as] first of all established as minus one [...] as [himself] *verworfen*', primally repressed.[73] Identification proper is then the subject's retroactive counting of himself, a - 1, as a 1. More specifically, the second count concomitantly brings about in a retroactive way the conscious subject's primal repression of himself as the un-conscious un-presented -1 *and* his unconscious 'seeking' (or, desiring) himself as that very same un-conscious un-presented -1, that is, the 'enunciation of the nothing', the void-set. (Strictly speaking, what precedes the second count is not unconscious: the unconscious, just like consciousness, is a retroactive effect of the second count on structure *qua* count of the unary-trait).

Lacan clearly states that, with regard to the subject, the fact that should most interest philosophers and psychoanalysts is that his inaugural mistake is what allows him to express, or name, himself as *a* subject. Thus, it will not be a matter of simply 'rectifying the means of knowing' in order to avoid the mistake: what is ultimately involved in it is the subject's conscious access to reality (the re-presentation of structure) and, at the same time, his endless unconscious search for 'the real *qua* not possible'[74]— since, as we have seen, the real is precisely what in-exists as 'enunciation of the nothing'. The second count has therefore a retroactive effect on the original counting of the un-conscious unary-trait $///$; more specifically, the latter should now be understood in terms of unconscious repetition, in the precise sense of a compulsion to repeat something which is as such unrepeatable.[75] Consequently, repetition is characterized by unicity, 'the unicity as such of [each] circuit of repetition', just like the counting of the un-conscious unary trait $///$.[76] As Lacan puts it, 'repetition in the unconscious is absolutely distinguished from any natural cycle, in the sense that what is accentuated is not its return', the sameness of the cycle; what is accentuated is rather the original unary trait $/$—the initial enunciation of the nothing as the real *qua* not possible—which 'has marked the subject' as -1.[77] Each circuit of repetition is unique since repetition, the making of $/$ always anew, amounts to the impossibility of repeating the signifying uniquity of the first $/$, the un-presentation of the part-object.

The subject's conscious access to reality, his knowledge [*connaissance*], presupposes a mistake, an error of counting, about which he knows noth-

---

73. Seminar IX, Lesson of 7/3/62.
74. Seminar IX, Lesson of 7/3/62.
75. Seminar IX, Lesson of 7/3/62.
76. Seminar IX, Lesson of 7/3/62.
77. Seminar IX, Lesson of 7/3/62.

ing, and which moreover forces him into an endless unconscious search for what 'preceded' it. It is important to remark that this mistake, bluntly put, the turning of -1 into 1, originates at the very moment the initial enunciation of the nothing, the void-set, is turned into the absence of the part-object, the void as part. In *Being and Event*, Badiou clarifies precisely this point when he discusses the operation from which the property 'the void is a subset of any set' is obtained, the fact that the void is omnipresent in all structured presentation, its errancy. As Badiou has it, this fundamental ontological theorem is deduced as a particular case of the logical principle '*ex falso sequitur quodlibet*': 'if a statement A is false (if I have non-A) and if I affirm the latter (if I posit A), then it follows that anything (any statement B whatsoever) is true' (BE 86-87). The void as part which is universally *included* in all sets supposed given follows from a *falso*; it relies on the negation of the true negative statement advanced by the axiom of the empty set, that is, 'there is a negation', or 'nothing belongs to the void', not even the void itself. The void as included part tacitly presumes the existence of an element that belongs to the void.

This kind of negation of negation is precisely the error, or *falso*, on which Lacan's symbolic structured like a fiction, the big Other *qua* 'one as difference', is based. As we have seen, for Lacan, initially we have non-A, which is why taking 'A is A' as the basis of identification is so problematic; the A of *l'Autre* is barred and tautology is possible only at the price of making a mistake. More specifically, in Lacan's theory of the subject, the void as part of all sets supposed given—whose existence as formed-into-one is itself affirmed only starting from the in-existence of this part as universally included—should be located on the level of what he calls the 'symbolic object'. During the dialectic of frustration between the mother and the child at the beginning of the Oedipus complex—the time of the un-conscious counting of the unary trait ///, of structure without metastructure—the symbolic object is the object which the child demands beyond the object of need, the object 'as grasped in what it lacks'. Remarkably enough, Lacan also specifies that the symbolic object '*is not nothing* since it has the property of *being* there symbolically';[78] the part-object as 'there *is* the nothing as part', the void-part, results from the falsity of the negation of the initial true 'enunciation of the nothing', the void-set. The mistaken falsification of truth as the real *qua* not possible is what allows any affirmation whatever to be symbolically true, first of all that which proclaims

---

78. Jacques Lacan, *Le séminaire livre IV. La relation d'objet, 1956-1957*, Paris, Seuil, 1994, p. 155 (my emphasis).

the existence of the void as part. This error will then be aggravated retroactively by the second count, an operation (a metaphor) which Lacan refers to as the Name-of-the-Father; through the Name-of-the-Father, the part-object as the errant, and thus potentially dangerous, void-part itself receives the seal of the one, taking its place as *a* part in the phantasy $\$$-*a*. The Name-of-the-Father operates on the extimate part-object in which the subject identifies himself as vanishing in the same way as the forming-into-one operates on the in-existent part of a situation that initially does not belong to it.

'NOUS NOUS COMPTONS COMPTANT'

While Badiou only hints at the distinction between the metastructured state of the situation and the structured situation as a distinction between consciousness and the 'unconscious of the void', Lacan attempts to delineate the two concomitant sides of the second count, the Name-of-the-Father, in a more elaborate manner. He does this precisely by thinking consciousness as both immanent and transcendent with regard to the unconscious: just as the situation will have been the 'unconscious of the void' of the state of the situation, so the un-conscious—the count of the unary trait as structure—will have been consciousness's unconscious—the phantasy $\$$-*a* as the repressed structure of repetition. The phantasy $\$$-*a* to be read as 'the subject split by the signifier in relation to the object *a*' is the unconscious result of the operational metaphor of the Name-of-the-Father. Insofar as it seals as *one* the phantasy as unconscious structure, the Name-of-the-Father can also be designated as the S_1, the master-signifier. Concomitantly, the subject's proper name, which is equivalent to the possibility of saying 'I', having an ego, will be nothing other than the conscious (metastructural) side of the Name-of-the-Father.

Note that the S_1 as the metastructure that structures the unconscious signifying chain amounts to a resumption of the unary trait at another level. Put differently, the un-conscious unary trait as structure will have been the S_1, the structural, that is unconscious, side of the metastructure. It would also be correct to suggest that the S_1 is the unary trait as repressed. Lacan himself stresses the similarity between the unary trait and the S_1 when, in Seminar XI, the first seminar to introduce the notion of the master-signifier, he openly refers the S_1 to the notch made by primitive hunters on sticks in order to signify the killing of an animal.[79]

---

79. Jacques Lacan, *The Four Fundamental Concepts of Psychoanalysis*, London, Vintage, 1998,

Let us conclude with the following remarks:

1.   Initially, the subject in-exists as -1, it is what dis-counts itself by
     means of the original unary trait as 'enunciation of the nothing';
     more precisely, at this level, the subject should be regarded as the
     gap, or cut, between the structured presentation of signifiers, or
     more precisely letters, which signify the subject's in-existence, and
     'their' inextricable void, the symbolic object. After the operation
     of the Name-of-the-Father, the second count, has taken place, the
     subject as -1 counts himself as 1; this 1 should rather be understood
     as a new gap between the structured presentation of letters, now
     turned into the signifiers of the unconscious, and metastructured
     representation, that is, conscious discourse.[80]

2.   The first gap, between structure and 'its' void, which causes the
     latter's errancy, designates the metonymic dimension of demand,
     the unstoppable sliding of the symbolic object (the object of love)
     beneath the objects of need. On the other hand, the second gap,
     between structure and metastructure, designates the metaphoric
     dimension of desire. In order to pass from the gap of demand
     to the gap of desire the subject must carry out a positivizing
     organization of the void: the void must 'take place' within the
     phantasy S-a by means of the metaphor of the Name-of-the-
     Father.

3.   The subject that counts himself as 1 is equivalent to the subject as
     the gap of desire who is *represented* in the unconscious phantasmatic
     object a as 'enunciation of the nothing'; that is, the subject is 1
     in the unconscious insofar as he appears there as not-one, -1.[81]
     More precisely, the subject *continues* to make 1 in the unconscious
     phantasy precisely because, as 'enunciation of the nothing', he
     is not-one. Differently put, the subject can name himself 'I' in

---

p. 141.

80. 'The gap between a (which counts-as-one the belongings, or elements) and $\wp(a)$ (which
counts-as-one the inclusions, or subsets) is [...] the point in which the impasse of being
resides. [...] I said that a and $\wp(a)$ were distinct. In what measure? With what effects? This
point, apparently technical, will lead us all the way to the *Subject* and to truth' (BE 83-84,
my emphasis).

81. See especially lesson of 3/6/1959 from Jacques Lacan, *Seminar VI (1958-1959)*, *'Le désir
et son interpretation'*, unpublished.

consciousness—and thus value himself [*se compter*]—only because he repeats the act of counting himself [*se compter*] as not-one in the phantasy—there where in fact the object *a* functions as a 'lost name'.[82]

4. The subject's naming of himself as 'I' is what allows him to count numbers, 1,2,3,4,...; this counting is nothing other than the conscious side of the unconscious repetitive circuit traced by the phantasy and sealed as one by the S1. While the latter manages to accomplish an organization of the void, this by no means amounts to saying that the void is eliminated: the organization of the void is thus repressed and this operation can be considered as an error of counting. At the synchronic level of the unconscious, the identifying representation of the subject as 1 in the object *a* necessarily preserves the -1 and thus gives rise to the repetitive series ////... in which each 'count' is started anew, each 'go' is absolutely unique. On the other hand, at the level of consciousness, the subject's naming of himself as 'I' mistakenly adds 1 + 1 + 1 + 1... and obtains 2, 3, 4..., which is to say, the diachronic 'temporal' continuity of his lived experience.

5. The fact that the subject as 1 is, at the same time, a subject as gap means nothing other than that the subject is himself a one-*multiple*.[83] The two counts retroactively differentiate three 'levels' of the multiple: the inconsistent undead real as not-one; the consistent multiplicity given by the metonymic slide of the objects of demand (marked as letters); the subject as split between conscious signified and unconscious signifier. The split subject's multiplicity is an empirical fact attested by the existence of the formations of the unconscious, such as symptoms, jokes, and slips of the tongue. However, the subject's multiplicity is repressed by the second count, just as the inconsistency of the multiple is un-presented by the first count. The second count both symbolizes the void and carries out, through repression, an imaginarization of the first count, that of the letters as 'pure' signifiers; the void is symbolized as phantasmatic desire, but desire is itself repressed and can be 'approach[ed] [consciously] only by means of some

---

82. Seminar VI, lesson of 3/6/1959.
83. Put differently, 'negation is irreducible' (Seminar IX, lesson of 24/1/62).

sort of demand'.[84] Finally, the phantasy where the void takes place should also be considered as a 'picture' in which anxiety is 'framed' and thus 'tamed, placated, admitted'.[85]

---

84. Jacques Lacan, *Le séminaire livre V. Les formations de l'inconscient, 1957-1958*, Paris, Seuil, 1998, p. 330.
85. Jacques Lacan, *Le séminaire livre X. L'angoisse, 1962-1963*, Paris, Seuil, 2004, p. 91. For a detailed analysis of the three logical times of anxiety with regards to phantasy, see Chapter 5 of Chiesa, *Lacan and Subjectivity: A Philosophical Introduction*.

7

Introduction to Sam Gillespie

Sigi Jöttkandt

Sam Gillespie, as Joan Copjec wrote in her moving tribute to him in *Umbr(a)* (2004), was 'one of the most gifted and promising philosophers of his generation' and this judgment has only become more pronounced with the posthumous appearance of various publications in the intervening years since his suicide in August 2003.

Sam was a leading figure in introducing Badiou to the English-speaking world. A key member of the original *Umbr(a)* collective at SUNY Buffalo, he instigated the special Badiou issue that published translations of 'Descartes/Lacan', 'Hegel', 'Psychoanalysis and Philosophy' and the hugely influential 'What is Love?' His intellectual and aesthetic influence on the journal were profound, and he continued to help set its editorial direction long after he left Buffalo, contributing essays, selecting texts by Badiou for translation, and designing the arresting covers that have helped to make *Umbr(a)* such an outstanding occasion of resistance to what Copjec, in her opening manifesto, named today's 'archival racism'.

To re-read his contributions to that first issue is to be struck again by how intensely focused Sam already was on the questions that would later make up the core of his Ph.D.,—the nature and source of novelty in the objective world, the differences between the materialism of Deleuze and Badiou, the limits of thought—paying witness to the remarkable intellectual seriousness with which he approached his early academic endeavors. It goes without saying that what one inevitably misses in such written leavings is the electric wit and sardonic humour of this anti-democratic but never inegalitarian individual who inaugurated our tradition of numbering each issue of *Umbr(a)* as One—not only as a token of what he once called the 'arduous' procedure of counting to Two but also as a formal expression of fidelity to what had escaped the previous issue's 'count'. A warm and deeply generous man, Sam was constitutionally unable to tolerate what he perceived to be injustice, and one of the last days of his life was spent protesting the imminent Iraq war with his partner Mike and friend Jason Barker who tells me that long after everyone else had given it up as futile, and the number of protestors dwindling to a trickle, Sam would be on the phone, rounding people up, never ceasing to call power on its abuses.

The essay published here for the first time is a chapter from Sam's dissertation at the University of Warwick which his brother Chris Gillespie, his partner Michael Mottram and I edited and submitted for the degree of Doctor of Philosophy, awarded in 2005. The longer work from which it is taken, provisionally titled *The Mathematics of Novelty: Badiou's Minimalist Metaphysics*, is under review at SUNY Press. A full list of his publications appears below, several of which are available as post-prints from the open access archive CSeARCH http://www.culturemachine.net/csearch. Electronic copies of Sam's dissertation can be sent on request. Please email sigij@pandora.be

PUBLICATIONS:

'Slavoj Your Symptom!', *UMBR(a)*, no. 1, 1995, pp. 115-9.

'Subtractive', *UMBR(a)*, no. 1, 1996, pp. 7-10, (available from CSeARCH).

'Hegel Unsutured (an Addendum to Badiou)', *UMBR(a)*, no. 1, 1996, pp. 57-69 (available from CSeARCH).

'Badiou's Ethics: A Review', *Pli: The Warwick Journal of Philosophy*, no. 12, 2001, pp. 256-65.

'Neighborhood of Infinity: On Badiou's Deleuze: The Clamor of Being', *UMBR(a)*, no. 1, 2001, pp. 91-106 (available from CSeARCH).

'Placing the Void – Badiou on Spinoza', *Angelaki: Journal of the Theoretical Humanities*, vol. 6, no. 3, 2001, pp. 63-77.

'Beyond Being: Badiou's Doctrine of Truth', *Communication and Cognition*, vol. 36, no. 1-2, 2003, pp. 5-30 (available from CSeARCH).

The Mathematics of Novelty: Badiou's Minimalist Metaphysics, PhD., University of Warwick, Warwick, 2004.

'Get Your Lack On', *UMBR(a)*, no. 1, 2004, pp. 9-19.

TRANSLATIONS:

Badiou, Alain, 'Hegel', trans. Marcus Coelen and Sam Gillespie, *UMBR(a)*, no. 1, 1996, pp. 27-35.

Badiou, Alain, 'On a Contemporary Usage of Frege', trans. Justin Clemens and Sam Gillespie, *UMBR(a)*, no. 1, 2000, pp. 99-115.

Giving Form to Its Own Existence: Anxiety and the Subject of Truth

Sam Gillespie

For anyone willing to accept the two primary theses of *Being and Event*—that mathematics is ontology, and that there is an inconsistency that cannot be exhausted by presentation—a number of questions immediately follow. To accept that mathematics is ontology may prove useful for one particular set of problems (for example, finding the most adequate means of understanding multiplicity), but this only opens the door to a whole series of other problems. To give only the most general and obvious example, there is an uncertainty surrounding the particular relation between mathematical being (inconsistent multiplicity) and its manifestation in particular situations. Badiou maintains that the relations between a situation and its latent being are purely subtractive insofar as presentation is an operation that presents particular beings *as multiples* and not multiplicity as such. What we are left with, then, is not so much a relation that follows from the inherent limitations of either presentation or language (however limited they may in fact be), but rather an axiomatic presupposition that the nothingness that escapes presentation is an inaugural existence. Being, in other words, is not inferred from presentation, but axiomatized.[1] And as Deleuze has shown in his reading of Spinoza, axi-

---

1. The axiomatization of being, while itself being an axiomatization of nothing, nonetheless inaugurates certain properties (say, of multiplicity or equality) which can produce decisive effects in situations. This is nowhere more true than in politics as a truth procedure for Badiou. The Lacanian, Joan Copjec, extends from Badiou's need for an axiomatic in her recent writing. 'One must start from the notion of infinity because it is impossible to introduce it by the path of the finite. And one must begin with an axiom of equality rather than foolishly trying to bring it into being through some Other who would recognize and validate individual pleasures'. One could, in a Badiouian move, substitute Copjec's 'pleasures' with 'interest'. See Joan Copjec, *Imagine There's No Woman: Ethics and Sublimation*, Cambridge, MIT Press, 2002, p. 175.

oms can just as readily generate positive manifestations (or expressions) of being.[2] This creates problems if Badiou wishes to create an effective connection between axiomatized being and its manifestation in situations (through presentation or forcing).

The difficulty of an axiomatization raises a set of particularly puzzling questions concerning why Badiou confers existence onto nothing (a supposition that, for Cunningham, is the acme of nihilism[3]). Furthermore, it also overlooks any inquiry into the particular process that informs the manifestation of being-qua-being in possible or particular situations. Of course, when this is posed as a problem, what is overlooked is the fact that Badiou accords an extreme importance to the operations of both presentation (the count) and representation as the means by which particular situations and worlds are formed. The difficulty, however, is that for Badiou, presentation is not a direct presentation of being-qua-being; it is rather a constitution of a situation from which being-qua-being is subtracted. And with respect to the fact that presentation is simply the operation of the count as one, Badiou maintains that the one does not exist at all: it is purely the result of an operation. What this assumes is that only sets have an existential validity—operations don't. As a theory, this hardly seems consistent with John Van Neumann's belief that an axiomatic set theory can depart from the existence of functions alone—the existence of sets will follow from them.[4]

My aim here is not to argue for an ontological principle of unity in Badiou but to ask why the operation of the count, the material support of number, has any less ontological validity than the existence of the void? The operations of thought, for example, are certainly capable of producing thoughts that together constitute a multiplicity, but this is very different from positing thought as something that is irreducibly infinite. In the process of the constitution of thought, singular thoughts come first. It becomes difficult, furthermore, to separate an ontological theory of multiplicity from any unifying principle of presentation if we interrogate the

---

2. Gilles Deleuze, *Expressionism in Philosophy: Spinoza*, trans. Martin Joughin, New York, Zone Books, 1991.

3. Cunningham has written that Badiou's philosophy is an attempt 'to have the nothing as something; to be without being'. See Conor Cunningham, *A Genealogy of Nihilism: Philosophies of Nothing and the Difference of Theology*, London, Routledge, 2002, p. 243.

4. '[…] it is formally simpler to base the notion of set on that of function than conversely'. John Von Neumann, 'An Axiomatization of Set Theory', in Jean Van Heijenoort (ed.), *From Frege to Gödel: A Source Book in Mathematical Logic, 1879-1931*, Cambridge, Harvard University Press, 1967, pp. 393-413, p. 396.

status of the term inconsistency. In a strict set-theoretical sense, nothing is inconsistent in and of itself: something is inconsistent only insofar as it cannot follow a principle of well-ordering which departs from a principle of presentation and ordering under the count as one. From this perspective, it is difficult to then grant multiplicity an ontological primacy over and against the one. My basic starting point for the following will be that the situation, the subject and the event are categories of experience that depend upon a theorization of the one as much as they do upon any notion of transfinite infinity. Badiou's displacement of a theory of the one runs the risk of contempt of those domains of experience on which his philosophy ultimately depends.

What is missing is thus an account, on the one hand, of the process through which possible situations or possible worlds are formed, as well as the various categories that are transitive to both ontology and the situation itself, on the other. This is not to say that mathematics does not provide an adequate foundation for ontology, and by extension, a philosophical system. It is rather that something is required in addition to that framework that can come to constitute situations, subjects and events. Badiou's mathematical formalism, which is perfectly capable of weaving complex multiplicities and rules out of nothing, is simply an empty game of manipulating symbols. The problem is not simply that of giving the operation of presentation the same ontological validity as sets; rather, what is needed is an analysis of why being must depend upon presentation as its material support, and what sort of framework may be necessary for such a dependency. One can put this more simply: in talking about material objects (a chair, say), one would not say that it is a presentation of a chair—it is a chair. Presentation, that is, is not a direct presentation of the inconsistency of being, but rather the material instantiation of being. This holds even for a number, for which there is no ontic/ontological doubling between the being and its Being. In other words, being-qua-being is nothing apart from its material instantiation, and this nothing then becomes the rudimentary means through which being can be mathematically ordered by set theory. Even the number zero is not a direct presentation of nothing, but a mark of that nothing that enables it to become ordered as multiplicity. This is where Badiou's reader enters a quandary: if there is an excess of inconsistency which is, in itself, nothing, can it become manifest over and above presentation? This, I believe, is where Badiou was led to posit his theory of the event. The only direct presentation there could be is the event, which is simply the eruption of nothing into the situation. The pressing question, then, is how nothing comes to announce itself.

If we are to make any kind of move from ontology to particular situations, or from truth procedures to particular truths, then various questions that concern the status of particular situations, or particular truths and the effects that ensue from them inevitably follow. In his small but important book *Ethics*, Badiou observed that a generalized ethics (of human rights or life, for example) 'equates man with a simple mortal animal, it is the symptom of a disturbing conservatism, and—because of its abstract, statistical generality—it prevents us from thinking the singularity of situations'.[5] The statement is startling, not least because it foregrounds a weakness in Badiou's own thought: no one would argue that set theory, a pure multiplicity of nothing, allows one to think particular situations. In fact, Badiou's precise point is that set theory is purely rational—it is ontology irrespective of any applicability to experience. Nor would one expect the singularity of situations to be the starting point for human action, since the event from which subjective action emanates is, as I understand it, perfectly generalizable and transitive to any situation: the inclusion of the void, in fact, follows not from situations but from a set-theoretical axiomatic. And from this perspective, taking the singularity of situations as a starting point for subjective actions is immediately questionable. As I see it, Badiou devises his own protocol for ethical action by replacing one set of general tropes (life, human rights, respect for others) with a mathematical framework that is resolutely indifferent to the singularity of situations altogether.

This is only one particular manifestation of a very general problem for Badiou. How can a philosophy with minimal foundations that are grounded, in effect, *upon nothing*, account for novelty in any effective sense? Badiou's philosophy may provide a cohesive system that is purely foundational for subjective action and the various truths that result from it, but any kind of criteria for speaking about particular situations or—perhaps more importantly—predicting, in the present, the foreseeable change that results from subjective commitment seems altogether absent from the system outlined in *Being and Event*. What makes Badiou's thought what it is results from the fact that it is independent of experience. Certainly, thinkers such as Kant and Hegel depart from purely formal, if not empty, foundations, but these are altogether different from what Badiou proposes, if these formal foundations can provide the possible conditions of experience (as in Kant) or determination as a procedural operation (as in Hegel).

---

5. Alain Badiou, *Ethics: An Essay on the Understanding of Evil*, trans. Peter Hallward, London, Verso, 2001, p. 16.

If there is to be a possible movement in Badiou's philosophy beyond the sterility of the system put forth in *Being and Event,* two supplementary trajectories are required.

On the one hand, there needs to be some sort of possible application of the categories of being and truth to the situations that can be thought in a manner other than subtraction. And secondly, there needs to be some possible phenomenology of subjectivity that could serve as a unifying principle to relate the particularity of situations to the various actions and evaluations (which ultimately are purely mathematical) that define subjective engagement. The first approach would lean towards Foucault's various attempts to define and engage with historically specific situations—with the particular problems that certain situations established for themselves as their transcendental, albeit historical, conditions of possibility. And, as for the latter question of subjectivity, it is Lacan who may provide the framework for speaking of a subject's relation to the inconsistent presentation of an event.

As regards the first problem (the specificity of situations), I will put Foucault aside and instead examine a question internal to Badiou's philosophy. I asked whether there is any way of thinking the relation between being and the situation apart from subtraction. This question was certainly not left unanswered by Badiou, given the centrality of the category of the event. The event, insofar as it is not derived from any given term of the situation, is neither a category of presentation or representation. To put it schematically, it is an unpresentation. The status of this unpresentation rests upon a problematic circularity, since events are events insofar as they are named and put into play in situations, which seems to be the exact same operation that informs presentation. Presentation presents, and this is constitutive of situations, while the naming of events is what is constitutive of truth procedures, but in both cases what is presented or named is purely nothing: what presentation presents is neither more nor less inconsistent than the events that are named. Being, in this instance, is univocal. But this leaves us with a problem. The only manner in which we can distinguish the appearance of inconsistent multiplicity (qua presentation and representation) from the appearance of inconsistent multiplicity (qua event) is through a rather crude recourse to experience. That is, we can assume that presented multiples are more or less recognized by everyone (given a proper paradigmatic framework), whereas events are presented or seen only by those subjects who declare it and recognize it as such. The distinction, then, hinges upon the ability of a select number of human beings to recognize events.

I emphasize this as a problem not simply because it necessarily falls back upon a purely empirical account for distinguishing presentation from events. What I find surprising is the fact that Badiou does not appear to think that the conditions under which events occur require any other foundation than naming and recognition as such. The problem with this is that it is tautological: subjects constitute events at the same time that subjects are miraculously constituted by the naming and recognition of events.[6]

Given that events and subjects are coextensive with one another (insofar as it is impossible to have events without subjects or subjects without events), it is difficult to find a third term to account for their coextensive relation, which is why Badiou grounds the possibilities for each in the possible disjunction between presented multiples and the representative practices of the state: those singular multiples that events name. 'The fundamental ontological characteristic of the event is to inscribe, to name, the situated void of that for which it is an event'.[7]

Here Badiou seems to refer the term 'void' to something that is situated. This is very different from the inherent inconsistency of a situation's latent being that is subtracted from presentation. To be subtracted is to not be situated at all. But the question is what the situated void is, if it is neither a presented multiple among others, subtracted being, nor the event itself (insofar as the event is what inscribes the situated void)? As previously stated, singular multiples are presented but not represented— they provide the site for events at an ontological level. But at the same time, there seems to be the event itself, which names not simply that void, but the *subjective conditions* under which that void will be taken up in a truth procedure. To establish the event both as the inconsistency of the situation and a part of the situation itself, Badiou is forced to divide the event in two: part of it is directed towards that situated void, and part is directed towards that aspect of the event that escapes the situation. If exclusive emphasis is placed on the former part of the event, then it simply becomes another version of the state: it is simply a non-statist way of counting indiscernible elements. In order to avoid doubling the event with the state, another part of the event is needed which exceeds the situation, and in so doing, calls upon nothing other than itself for its own validity. It is this part

---

6. '[. . .] only an interpreting intervention can declare that an event is present in the situation; as the arrival in being of non-being, the arrival amidst the visible of the invisible', Alain Badiou, *Being and Event*, trans. Oliver Feltham, London, Continuum, 2005, p. 181.
7. Badiou, *Ethics*, p. 69.

of the event that instigates subjective action. The event now supplements the situation and it is this, rather than presented or unpresented multiples, that is the true catalyst for subjective action or fidelity. Such principles, along with the definitions of the subject and the event, are supplementary to the rather closed connection between ontology and truth, as Badiou is well aware insofar as he believes that, beyond the static presentation of multiplicity set theory makes available, something must happen in order for there to be a transformation, in order for there to be truth. In ontology, I would argue, nothing happens; things simply are.

By focusing on the set theoretical foundations of Badiou's philosophy, one overlooks the fact that events emerge in an unpredictable manner, and thus require a possible framework outside ontology to explain how they happen. This is not to say of course that events are not engaged with unknown multiplicities that have their grounding in a mathematical ontology: it is to say, rather, that events and their subjects are what force the plastic univocity of being to assume new or unforeseeable trajectories, new truths and modalities of existence. This, at bottom, is novelty in Badiou. But in order to effect a possible movement from ontology to truth, Badiou's system must add an additional step that is extrinsic to ontology. Notably, when Badiou speaks of something that happens, his terms reveal an uncharacteristic display of sentiment. In a personal quote in reference to the events of May of 1968 in Paris, for example, he stated that: 'for what was taking place, yes, we were the genuine actors, but actors absolutely seized by what was happening to them, as by something extraordinary, something properly incalculable'.[8]

What is initially so striking about this quote (and others like it that one finds periodically in Badiou) is that it makes recourse to personal experiences that are otherwise entirely absent in Badiou's philosophy. In particular, here Badiou seems to be appealing to categories of affect that presuppose a subject of experience who is gripped or seized by something incalculable, who becomes a catalyst for all possible action. What seems to be potentially overlooked, then, within the overall sterile, formal framework of the ontology of *Being and Event* is any possible theory of affect that could account for that very act of gripping the subject. This absence is telling when it comes to addressing the manner in which subjects are gripped by events.

If this objection seems to imply a reproach that is entirely at odds with what makes Badiou's philosophy what it is (a minimalist metaphys-

---

8. Badiou, *Ethics*, p. 124.

ics), consider the following two points. First, it seems necessary to fall back upon some category of affect if we are to account for the processes through which subjects and events mutually enable one anther.[9] That is, there may need to be something of a necessary engagement with the possible conditions that seize and grip subjects in the constitution of events, and which may define a political mode of subjectivity. I would be arguing here for fidelity as a certain drive that propels a subject forward in the pursuit of truths.

The second consideration is even more ambitious. In Badiou's thought, there are four conditions under which truth can occur, art being one among others. It seems, however, that a classical philosophical engagement with art is impossible in Badiou's system—there is no possibility for aesthetics for Badiou. Given that the mathematization of ontology entirely strips being of any notion of affect, and given that it is precisely affect or sensation that aesthetics studies, the only possibility for a philosophical engagement with art in Badiou's philosophy is through *inaesthetics*—that is, the means through which philosophy can oversee the possible creation of truths in the arts. Art, in other words, is one instantiation of the void as truth. Now, this is only one instance of what occurs when Badiou subordinates a possible arena of human action and engagement to the foundations that philosophy sets for it through science. In other words, art is philosophically important only insofar as it is capable of producing truths that are subject to various conditions established by mathematics (and, by extension, science). I have argued elsewhere, by looking at Deleuze, that it is possible to have a theory of novelty that is not necessarily subjected to a criterion of truth.[10] One could say that, despite its concessions to science, Deleuze's philosophy is an aesthetic philosophy through and through. By making a move to Lacan, however, one finds a possible vocabulary for speaking of artistic production that is, on the one hand, compatible with Badiou's overall theory of the new, while nonetheless being independent of the criterion of truth.

To summarize the argument so far. I am claiming that Badiou needs a framework through which one can speak of how subjects are gripped by events. Lacan, I suggest, provides such a conception in his relation of the subject to its indiscernible being, its own real. The catalyst for action

9. As Hardt and Negri observe, this could be part of a wider politics of accounting for affect in politics. Michael Hardt and Antonio Negri, *Empire*, Cambridge, Harvard University Press, 2001.

10. Sam Gillespie, *The Mathematics of Novelty: Badiou's Minimalist Metaphysics*, PhD., University of Warwick, Warwick, 2004.

(what Badiou calls fidelity) will be found in Lacan's notion of the drive— the means through which subjects create new modalities of relating to, or experiencing, being. And the drive, my argument will go, can also provide a framework for artistic production that thinks action through an impersonalization of being at the same time that it is independent of the category of truth as such.

This move becomes necessary because it strikes me that the condition of art is the most problematic for Badiou's philosophy in terms of the category of truth. There certainly can be various movements in art that establish formal groupings that resemble Paul Cohen's process of constructing a generic set, but it would seem unnecessarily restrictive to subordinate these formal groupings to generic conditions set to it by this addendum to Cantorian set theory. In other words, one is left with a rather brute minimalism to account for what truth can be in artistic practice. For this reason, there can only be inaesthetics in Badiou's philosophy. What a psychoanalytic notion of the drive—and, by extension, sublimation—might entail is a broadening of the protocol that Badiou uses for subjective action (a response to the indiscernibility of being) that is not necessarily confined to truth. Whether or not such an aesthetics can be philosophical is an altogether different question: it may be that such an aesthetics is a properly psychoanalytic affair. All the same, it may be necessary to explore such an option so as to accomplish two things: one, to think the proper framework that determines subjective action and two, to think through the problematic category of art as a truth condition.

THE VOID: SUBJECT OR BEING?

Lacan's influence upon Badiou is evident. One could compile a book length study on the subject, but perhaps it is more useful here to take the primary differences between the two as our point of departure. Badiou has been prominent in stating that he proposes a different 'localization' of the void than Lacan and that, unlike for Lacan, being for Badiou is separate from the real. The implication of this is that philosophy and psychoanalysis presuppose different points of departure: one departs from being as a foundation, while the other starts with the position of a subject immersed in language. The question that immediately arises, then, is whether the void is localized in being, for which it is an ontological category, or is it the place from which the subject speaks?

If Lacan aligns himself with the latter position, Badiou unhesitatingly opts for the former. It should be clear that Badiou's void is 'inhuman and asubjective', whereas for Lacan, on the contrary, the void is the main core of subjectivity. The barred subject, $, is the void that is marked as a subject of lack, a subject alienated from its own being through the mediation of the signifier. The inscription of such a lack (void) in a linguistic chain of signifiers is what makes the subject's ability to relate to the world through the shifting of signifiers possible.[11] The subject that those signifiers represent, however, is nothing but the mark of an excluded existence inside an inert symbolic framework that is necessary for experience. The subject is that void that emerges dead on arrival in the symbolic register.

One can almost immediately take issue with this distinction. From a Lacanian perspective, it is not entirely certain that the subject is simply a void *tout court*. The subject as void exists only insofar as it is marked and designated by the signifier, and not as some sort of substantial absence that can be uncovered through a procedural stripping away of material signifiers. The void is always stained or tainted by the signifier that designates the subject as lack. The subject, in such a perspective, is as material as it is empty. Judith Butler, among others, has consistently argued that the Lacanian category of the real depends upon some instantiation of a kernel that resists symbolization, and this is what makes it an ahistorical and oppressive category. She asks: 'On the one hand, we are to accept that "the Real" means nothing other than the constitutive limit of the subject; yet on the other hand, why is it that any effort to refer to the constitutive limit of the subject in ways that do not use that nomenclature are considered a failure to understand its proper operation?'[12] Butler's argument extends to argue that conceiving the real as the constitutive limit to the social (which is the place of the subject) amounts to determining the subject as outside the social. This is how Butler qualifies her Hegelianism: the real is simply an empty void of determination. In other words, to use the terms from the Badiou of *Theory of the Subject*, to refer to the subject as void overlooks the fact that lack is more likely the result of a structural law of placement rather than an excess of lack over and above that system. Thus, lack is a thoroughly immanent category.

The crucial point that Butler misses in her argument, however, is that it is precisely the point that the real does not designate something outside the social—it is *nothing* outside language. In other words, Butler's criti-

---

11. The classically psychoanalytic statement 'I feel like a motherless child' is possible on the basis of substituting one signifier, 'I', for another, 'motherless child'.
12. Judith Butler, 'Competing Universalities', in Judith Butler, Ernesto Laclau and Slavoj Žižek, *Contingency, Hegemony, Universality*, London, Verso, 2000, pp. 136-81, p. 152.

cism overlooks the fact that speaking subjects designate their own real in and through the materiality of language and the limits it presupposes, not through some determinate process of exclusion. The Lacanian subject is the place of that nothing outside language, just as Badiou's void is the name for the nothing that exceeds particular instantiations of either thought or being. For the Lacanian subject, then, there is nothing outside the history that the signifier induces and the place of this nothing is the void of the subject. The void of the subject is not something that exists outside the symbolic chain. Rather, the unique position of the subject extends from the fact that there is *nothing* outside the symbolic chain. This is what makes the Lacanian subject a structurally determinate category: the impasses that render the closure of the symbolic impossible would result in a failure to determine the symbolic as a structured system were it not for the fact that a speaking subject fills that empty place of indetermination. In other words, the failure of the symbolic to inscribe itself as a closed totality is constitutive of the failure of the subject to be fully present to itself through the medium of speech.

This has, I believe, direct implications for Badiou's theory of the subject. For it asks how is it that a subject can be propelled to act through something that is manifest only through negation? Whether that negation designates the place of the subject or the place of being is a moot point: the fact of the matter is that it is a question of a determinate nothing. To interrogate the relation between the two thinkers, it will be necessary to retrace certain steps in Badiou's thought. We could start with a primary text of Lacan's theory of the subject. In his seminal essay 'Suture', Lacan's disciple Jacques-Alain Miller produced a comparative reading of Lacanian psychoanalysis with Frege's logic, which functioned as an implicit critique of the logical assumption that one can have existence without a subject.[13] Given that Frege founded his thought of numbers upon the exclusion of any psychological subject of reflection, the subject was excluded from Frege's systematic account of the genesis of numbers through a purely logical necessity. This was a simple assertion that the existence of numbers does not depend upon the existence of a subject who thinks them. According to Miller, however, the subject reemerged in his system at that very point where Frege sought to derive an existence through logic alone. In Frege's system, zero was the primary logical number, insofar as it was the only number that could be attributed to a 'purely logical',

---

13. Jacques-Alain Miller, 'Suture (Elements of the Logic of the Signifier)', *Screen*, vol. 18, no. 4, 1977-8, pp. 24-34.

non-empirical concept. The point, for Miller, is that the assignation of the number zero to the lack of an illogical object is the very relation that defines the subject's relation to the signifying chain. In other words, zero is the marking of the subject as a lacking subject who tries to compensate for its own lack of being through a substitution of one signifier for another (in the same way that the number 1 in Frege marks the number 0 as the number assigned to the concept 'not-equal-to-itself'). What makes Miller's essay more than a simple analogy between Lacan and Frege is that it also aims to be an explicit critique of science itself. Science, which is presumed to exist independently of a subject, must reintroduce a subject in order to sustain the progression of number. We are left to assume, then, that a psychoanalytic theory of the subject is the very sustenance of a logical (or scientific) system.

In an early essay, 'Marque et manque', Badiou took issue with this very assumption insofar as he remained skeptical that science requires a concept of either a subject or of suture.[14] Given the tenets of Gödel's theorem of incompletion, there was no need for a logical system to be closed in upon itself in order to function as a consistent system for producing knowledge. Science, that is, did not need closure in order to function. 'Stratified to infinity, regulating its passages, science is a pure space, without an outside or mark, or place of what is excluded'.[15] This position entails that if there is no need to mark what is excluded from a scientific order—insofar as in science 'the not-substitutable-with itself is foreclosed with neither recourse or mark'[16]—then there is no subject of science. This is, of course, in striking contrast to the position he would develop in *Being and Event* where subjects only exist in and through truth procedures, of which science is one part. But this does not mean that Badiou saw suture as a useless category: it founded a subject's relation to ideology. Departing from a classically Althusserian distinction between science and ideology, Badiou puts forth the theory that psychoanalysis has nothing to say about science, and that this is the negative determination of the desire that is operative in ideology. The negative determination of desire in psychoanalysis is a direct effect of the impossibility of giving a distinctly scientific account of the structural relations that make that desire possible. That is, the psychoanalytic definition of desire as lack is a desire for a scien-

---

14. Alain Badiou, 'Marque et manque: à propos du zero', *Cahiers pour l'analyse*, vol. 10, 1969, pp. 150-73.
15. Badiou, 'Marque et manque', p. 161.
16. Badiou, 'Marque et manque', p. 157.

tific knowledge that can account for a subject's conditions of possibility at the same time that, at the level of that desire, such an account is strictly speaking impossible. The subject who passes from representation (ideology) into knowledge is a subject that would cease to exist at the moment of its gaining scientific knowledge. What we are left with, then, is the notion of a subject that plays a constitutive role in the 'production' of science as truth, even if that role is itself nothing more than a transitory stage towards the gaining of that knowledge.

The shift from this position (where the subject is an ideological, non-scientific category) to the work of the 1970s (where the subject was a dialectical, political subject) to the current position (where there can be both political and scientific subjects) presupposes a potentially broad set of factors that could have influenced the development of Badiou's work. On the one hand, in 1967 he maintained that if there is no subject of science, it is because science is the proper subject of philosophy. But by the work of the 1970s, science had taken a backseat to politics—both as a subject of philosophy and as a condition for subjectivity altogether. In other words, there are only political subjects.

The shift to a set theoretical ontology in *Being and Event* signaled two changes in Badiou's thinking. There was first the possible coexistence of both political and scientific (as well as artistic and amorous) subjects, at the same time that the void became an exclusively ontological category. It is this second move that firmly distinguishes Badiou from Lacan, such that, by the time of *Being and Event*:

> The choice here is between a structural recurrence, which thinks the subject-effect of the empty-set, so exposed in the unified network of experience, and a hypothesis of the rarity of the subject, which defers its occurrence to the event, to the intervention, and to the generic paths of fidelity, referring back and founding the void on the suturing of being for which mathematics exclusively commands knowledge.[17]

The rarity of the subject is what is put in the service of a mathematical determination of the void as non-subject, at the same time that subjective action is rendered possible through both the intervention of an event, as well as the void of local situations that becomes determinate in and through the forcing of truths. The subject, from such a perspective, is defined through its action. In the Lacanian register, in contrast, Badiou posits the void as the 'subject-effect of the empty set', which is nothing other

---

17. Alain Badiou, *L'être et l'événement*, Paris, Seuil, 1988, p. 451.

than the purely empty-place of inequality that allows for the movement from one signifier to the next, and for which the subject is the unified condition of possibility. Ostensibly, this severs the subject from any possibility of transformation or change, given that the void that is the subject works exclusively in the interests of a structural system of determination. Aside from language, there is nothing.

The above distinction is made possible on the basis of a single question: what does the void do differently in philosophy than in psychoanalysis? In departing from the above distinction, Badiou concludes that being is distinct from the Lacanian real insofar as the real is only possible on the basis of a subject, while for philosophy, the void *is* independently of a subject. That is, the void is the primary name for an inhuman and asubjective being that precedes any possible advent of subjectivity. Such a position should hardly surprise: it is entirely consistent with the outlined trajectory of *Being and Event,* and it is concomitant with any philosophy that takes ontology as foundational. It would be absurd to make ontology a subjective category given that many non-human, or non-subjective entities have an ontological validity.

If so, why does Badiou bother to have a subject in his philosophy at all? Why did he move from declaring science to be the subject of philosophy to writing a book on the philosophy of the subject? The reason, I believe, depends on the conditions under which something new can occur. For the new to emerge, something needs to disrupt the structural. In order to account for the supplementary means with which subjects and events appear in Badiou, it becomes necessary to appeal to categories that were central to Lacan. To determine the manner in which they inform Badiou's own position, perhaps more intimately than he realizes, one will have to undo the above distinction that Badiou has drawn between Lacan and himself.

Consider the assumption that the Lacanian subject is a pure void, a barred subject—in short, $. Is it really the case that the subject is nothing other than a void that receives its determination through a linguistic structure that exceeds it, on the one hand, while being nothing but an empty system of structural determination, on the other? This position falls prey to an interpretation of the subject as nothing but its symbolic designation, given that the lack of the subject is, strictly speaking, nothing at all. This would be no different from a rather crude interpretation of psychoanalysis as a variant of constructivist logic—the subject is insofar as it is constructed in language. Such a perspective fundamentally misinterprets the radical nature of Lacan's definition of subjectivity insofar as it reduces the question of the subject as the foundation for the constitution of meaning (insofar as it is from this position of the subject that meaning is constituted) to a definition of the subject as a determinate effect of meaning (that is, the subject as it is posited in language). Is the emphasis here put upon the materiality of language which, in some variant of behaviorist psychology, comes to determine an identity? Or is it rather the case that the exclusion of being that is essential for language as a closed system exerts an influence upon the meaning that the speaking subject produces? In other words, the lack that sutures the subject to the signifying chain, if it is to be something more than an indeterminate nothing that escapes the grip of language, must play a constitutive role in Lacanian psychoanalysis.

The implications of this distinction do not hold exclusively for sorting out the internal coherence of Lacanian psychoanalysis; they are also what found Badiou's entire critique of constructivist mathematical logic—that is, the belief that existence can only be given through the discernibility of language. To counter constructivism is, of course, to maintain that there is an existence that is not exclusively subsumed within the tenets of what can be demonstrated within language. The Lacanian real is one such manifestation of an anti-constructivist tendency, given that it is what remains of being in the aftermath of the failure of meta-language. The real, as a subjective function, is the result of the following paradox. On the one hand, there is no metalanguage—everything is explicitly posited in language; on the other hand, language cannot totalize itself as a closed system for which it can then definitively state that there is nothing outside it.[18]

Thus, while one can maintain that the subject is purely a void, that it receives its only material support through the signifier, this is quite different from arguing that the subject is nothing other than a lack conjoined to a signifier. There is an additional something that fills out this gap between the failure of a meta-language and the impossibility of determining language as a closed system (for which the nothing outside language would be truly nothing). This something is Lacan's famous objet petit (a). The

---

18. As Joan Copjec has put it: 'Whenever the split between being and appearance is denied, you can bet that one particular inscription is being overlooked: that which marks the very failure of metalanguage. Language speaks voluminously in positive statements, but it also copiously speaks of its own lack of self-sufficiency, its inability to speak the whole unvarnished truth directly and without recourse to further, exegetical speech. Some elision or negation of its powers writes itself in language as the lack of meta-language. This negation is no less an inscription for its not being formulated in a statement, and the being it poses presents no less a claim for our consideration'. Joan Copjec, *Read My Desire: Lacan Against the Historicists*, Cambridge, MIT Press, 1994, p. 9.

object (a) is not subsumed within language, and thus does not exist as one signifier among others. At the same time, however, what makes object (a) what it is results directly from the fact that language fails to subsume the totality of being: the object (a) is the emergence, in the symbolic, of that which remains outside its grasp, a positive determination of the negative indeterminate. Like Badiou's event, the object (a) is the appearance of something that is anterior to presentation; at the same time, it is subtracted from what is subtracted. It is neither being-qua-being, nor a consistent presentation, but rather a category of the subject.

Lacan's famous formula for the fantasy is the conjoining of a barred subject to its virtual object: $S \lozenge a$. To the lack in the subject instituted by the signifier corresponds a determination of that lack in the form of a fantasm of presence (say, in a psychoanalytic context, the desire of the analyst). What lies behind that fantasm is precisely nothing, but it is a nothing that gains determinate form in the various desires, repetitions, or sublimations of the psychoanalytic subject that desires presence beyond language. At the risk of making a mere analogy, is this not the very same logic informing Badiou's theory of the event—precisely the fleeting appearance of that which is indiscernible from the position of experience, and which is given determinate form through the activity of a subject? The very problematic status of the event in Badiou hinges upon a paradox: on the one hand, there is an excess of being over presentation; on the other hand, this excess is purely nothing. How can nothing present itself? Precisely insofar as there are events that are given form by those subjects who recognize them. We can only understand the possible correspondence between Badiou's event and Lacan's object (a) if we understand that the former is not a phenomenal event any more than the object (a) is a phenomenal object. Instead, both are what one could call 'supplements' to presentation itself that makes the move from a purely subtractive theory of presentation to a direct determination of the indeterminate possible. That is, the event is what facilitates a movement from a negative ontology (in which the question of inconsistency remains a negative determination of something that is subtracted from presentation) to a positive determination of that subtracted inconsistency qua production of truths. Likewise, in order to move from a purely negative determination of desire (which always hinges upon the immanent failure of some impossible object), the psychoanalytic subject must shift its activity to the drive, where it gives form and determination to the empty ground of its causality in and through the formation of an object (a). A distinctly Lacanian question is, how does the subject give form to its own existence?

One possibility was put forth in Lacan's theory of sublimation. In a rudimentary sense, sublimation is the creation of determinate things in and out of a constitutive lack that is inherent to experience. It emerges out of the constitutive relation of the subject's relation to its own real. In the remainder of this essay, then, I want to examine the potential relations that inhere between Lacan's theory of sublimation and Badiou's theory of truth, while at the same time as looking to Lacan's theory of the drive (which is closely linked to sublimation) for a possible account for the subjective conditions that enable such activity. Doing so will allow me to initially reconsider the supplementary framework that is necessary to account for Badiou's theory of the event, the subject, and fidelity, at the same time as putting us in a position to question the ultimate aims of Badiou's entire project—the knotting of novelty to truth.

Now, in order to adequately assess the possible connections between Lacan's object (a) and Badiou's event, we have to ask after the ontological status of each. The reason I say 'ontological' is because the event, in and of itself, is not exclusively an ontological category: 'with the event, we have the first *exterior* concept to the field of mathematical ontology'.[19] The event supplements presentation and, by extension, ontology. For example, when considering the French revolution, there are states of affairs that are presented in the situation (to name only a few: the bourgeoisie, Jacobins, the guillotine, the massacres, the storming of the Bastille) which, in and of themselves, are a multiplicity of elements that lack a unifying principle without the name 'French Revolution' that creates of these elements an event from which a political procedure can be derived. The event 'French Revolution' is not one multiple among others (insofar as it is not, in itself, presented among the other multiplicities). It is what unifies these disparate multiplicities under the banner of its occurrence. Or, to put it another way, the event takes these elements and adds something more that exceeds direct presentation. But this something more, insofar as it is not presented, cannot be accounted for as something. Insofar as it escapes presentation, it is ontologically undecidable.

Now, in a parallel trajectory, what exactly is Lacan's object (a) if it is neither an object nor a strictly linguistic designation? How can something be said to exist if it is not articulated in language? Consider one of the most basic examples of an object (a), the breast. It would be a mistake to assume that the object simply is the breast on account of its breast-like properties. That is, the breast is not *in itself* an object of satisfaction. An in-

---

19. Badiou, *L'être et l'événement*, p. 205.

fant could presumably be just as satisfied with the warm milk it provides, the pleasure it produces when digested in the body, and the satisfaction that is associated with the act of suckling. The breast, as the object (a), however, is what is imputed to give the coupling of bodies and organs the satisfaction that are proper to them: it represents something more than just one subsidiary object among others. It is the object that acts as a support for the satisfaction proper to these objects. The object (a), then, is not the object of satisfaction but that something more that satisfaction aims at. As Alenka Zupančič puts it:

> After a need is satisfied, and the subject gets the demanded object, desire continues on its own; it is not 'extinguished' by the satisfaction of a need. The moment the subject attains the object she demands, the *objet petit a* appears, as a marker of that which the subject 'has not got', or *does not have*—and this itself constitutes the '*echte*' object of desire.[20]

What Lacan's object (a) represents is a surplus satisfaction that language fails to produce. That is, if a psychoanalytic subject enters language, she does so at a price: there is a necessary acceptance that an unmediated relation to one's being falls out of the equation. What is left in its place is the installation of a lack.[21] This is not to say, however, that this lack is simply left to persist on its own accord: something reemerges to the subject that comes to fill that lack, as it presents itself in the form of an object that embodies the surplus-value of a being anterior to language. Likewise for Badiou, if inconsistent being-qua-being must, by structural necessity, be subtracted from consistent presentation under the law of the count, that subtracted being can nevertheless come to supplement the consistent presentation of a situation in and through the fleeting appearance of an event. Both Badiou's event and Lacan's object (a) are what resist the structural necessity of subtraction of exclusion: they subtract themselves from their initial subtraction as inconsistent being at the same time that their supplementation of a given field provides a unity for disparate phenomena.

---

20. Alenka Zupančič, *Ethics of the Real: Kant, Lacan*, London, Verso, 2000, p. 18.
21. In Lacan's Seminar VII, which led to his eventual conceptualization of object (a), this constitutive lack, or unnamed being, was called *das Ding*. '*Das Ding* is what I will call the beyond-of-the-signified. It is as a function of this beyond-of-the-signified and of an emotional relationship to it that the subject keeps its distance and is constituted in a kind of relationship characterized by primary affect, prior to any repression'. Jacques Lacan, *The Ethics of Psychoanalysis, 1959-1960*, trans. Dennis Porter, New York, Norton, 1992, p. 54.

One immediate objection presents itself with the above analogy. For the purposes of the present discussion, it is questionable whether the object (a) is in any way a catalyst for action. One could argue that the cause of a subject's desire is a determination of the subject as pure passivity whose desire exists in a negative relation to its posited object. In contrast, Badiou's event calls a subject into being in such a way that its residual effects will hinge upon the action and decisions taken by the subject that retroactively give form to it. The event is determined in and though subjective activity. To make an analogy between Badiou and Lacan is problematic if we lack a means of ascribing an active agency to the Lacanian subject. What possible forms can the object (a) assume that directly result from the activity of the Lacanian subject?

We can start with the rudimentary assumption of Lacan's that the subject's relation to the signifier is a structural relation to emptiness, or lack. The question that emerges from this is one of the possible relations the subject can form with that lack. One obvious example of such a relation would be the avoidance, or repression, of that lack that is constitutive of neurosis. Neurotic subjectivity may in fact have some coincidence with situations in which the void is foreclosed from presentation—in either case, normativity or stability depends upon a foreclosure of the void. But there are other possible relations of the subject to its own lack that presuppose the direct activity of the subject in determining that relation, and thus determining the lack. One such possibility was given in Freud's account of sublimation that was subsequently modified by Lacan. Sublimation is conventionally taken to be the desexualization of libido in and through the production of scientific and artistic objects and knowledge. In contrast, the drive is usually taken to be the realization of primal, destructive impulses. The former would be the cultural purification of the latter. Lacan's radical move is to have united the two terms—drive and sublimation—in the very notion of an object (a): in each case, it is the activity of the subject that gives form to the object as satisfaction. This means that the object is the residual effect of subjective action and not the object that determines a subject's desire.[22] Thus, the sexual activity of bodies could be one possible (perhaps convenient) way of producing

---

22. Alenka Zupančič has opposed the drive to sublimation as such: 'if the drive is a "headless" procedure, sublimation is not. Sublimation is a kind of "navigator" of the drives, and this is why it plays such an important role in society'. Sublimation can thus lead to productions of determinate modes of that nothing, whereas the drive is simply the expenditure of that nothing—a drive towards nothing. See Alenka Zupančič, 'The Splendor of Creation: Kant, Lacan, Nietzsche', *Umbr(a): A Journal of the Unconscious*, no. 1, 1999, pp. 35-42, p. 40.

modalities of affect (that is, of aiming at a being beyond language), while the production of objects or knowledge in science, religion and art could exemplify other possibilities of giving determinate form to the negative determinations of the real. Science would entail a quest for the complete symbolization or determination of the real—anything that remains un-symbolizable within it would simply imply a limitation in our own knowledge. Religion attempts to fill out this lack through the imposition of a radically transcendent other, while art, it is argued, is the realization of this lack in and through its representation as something. That is, it renders the impossibility of the real possible in and through the medium of representation (a result of the paradox that the real cannot be represented). Art, it would appear, has a unique relation to the real insofar as it neither fully excludes it from experience (as in the case of religion) nor fully incorporates it within knowledge (as in science). And this may have implications for Badiou's theory of art as a truth procedure, given that, for Badiou, truth is determined through mathematics.

Badiou, no less than Lacan, defines art as an instantiation of the void: the artists he designates as exemplary producers of truth can all be noted for their minimalist tendencies: Beckett, Mallarmé, Pessoa, Schoenberg. 'Art is [...] mobilized, not because it has worth in and of itself, or with an imitative and cathartic aim, but to raise the void of Truth up to the point at which dialectical sequential linking is suspended'.[23] This notion of a purification of being is, of course, not altogether dissimilar to the commonplace notion of sublimation in Freud, who saw the sublimation of an instinct or drive as the purification of crude, and potentially destructive, instincts, into higher aims that could be met with social approval.[24] It is a telling sign of Freud's conservative, and under-theorized, take on the matter of sublimation that his aesthetics tended, more often than not, to focus on the classical or conventional: Michelangelo, Leonardo, Shakespeare. In 1930, at the time of *Civilization and its Discontents*, where he put forward his theory of the cultural value of arts, the work of Picasso, Lissitzky, Duchamp, and others, was left unmentioned. Freud's theory of sublimation

23. Alain Badiou, *Manifesto for Philosophy*, trans. Norman Madarasz, Albany, State University of New York Press, 1999, p. 125.
24. 'A satisfaction of this kind, such as an artist's joy in creating, in giving his phantasies body, or a scientist's in solving problems or discovering truths, has a special quality which we shall certainly one day be able to characterize in metapsychological terms'. Sigmund Freud, 'Civilization and its Discontents', in Albert Dickson (ed.), *Civilization, Society and Religion*, trans. James Strachey, vol. XII Penguin Freud Library, London, Penguin, 1991, pp. 243-340, p. 267.

not only ran the risk of subscribing to a conservative sexual morality (an accusation commonly leveled against psychoanalysis regardless); it fell prey, to put it mildly, to a conventional aesthetics that denied art its potential for innovation.

Freud's notion of sublimation, then, was articulated as a function of the superego, insofar as it sought a way for the satisfaction of instincts in means that were subject to cultural approval. Lacan's response, although quite contrary to Freud's, did not lead to a rejection of the notion of sublimation. Sublimation for Lacan did result in the purification of affect, but these emotions were precisely those that were instigated by the cultural demands of the superego—fear and pity. Lacan's theory aims to subvert the very cultural authority that Freud's theory of sublimation put to work. To unravel the possible conflict between the two great psychoanalysts, we will have to consider the initial mockery that Lacan made of Freud's own views. In 1964, Lacan proposed the following Freudian interpretation of sublimation and its correlate in the drive:

> In other words—for the moment, I am not fucking, I am talking to you. Well! I can have exactly the same satisfaction as if I were fucking. That's what it means. Indeed, it raises the question of whether in fact I am not fucking at this moment. Between these two terms—drive and satisfaction—there is set up an extreme antinomy that reminds us that the use of the function of the drive has for me no other purpose than to put in question what is meant by satisfaction.[25]

The end of the above quote proposes the following contrast: if the drive is opposed to satisfaction, it is contradictory to speak of the satisfaction of a drive. Taken further, it is clear that satisfaction itself is a contradictory notion, insofar as there are individuals who are clearly capable of producing a certain stability in their lives in and through the manifestation of their symptoms (say, compulsive hand-washing)—this stability, while forever frustrated and dissatisfied, is what satisfaction aims at. To borrow the famous term of Slavoj Žižek, the command to 'enjoy your symptom' does not result in a possible attainment of an aim, but in a prolongation of frustrated desire that typifies neurosis. But it is just as clear that individuals who manifest neurotic symptoms are nonetheless discontented despite their attainment of satisfaction: just as, we could assume, the act of speaking does not result in the same sort of jouissance that can

---

25. Jacques Lacan, *The Four Fundamental Concepts of Psychoanalysis*, trans. Alan Sheridan, New York, Norton, 1981, pp. 165-66.

be enjoyed in sexual intercourse. This is what Lacan means when he opposes drive to satisfaction. The question then is what exactly the drive or
sublimation aims at if not satisfaction. How exactly does the drive play out
a trajectory of impossibility?

This question brings us to the centrality of the Lacanian real. From
most of the cultural literature that has come out in the past fifteen years
on the topic, it should be evident that the real is the impossible. The
impossibility, that is, of having an ontology from within the parameters
of psychoanalysis. Or, yet again: the impossibility of the real results from
the paradoxical conclusion that there is no meta-language at the same
time that language cannot foreclose the possibility of an existence that
escapes language. For the speaking subject, there is no meta-discursive
position from which one can state with certainty that there is nothing
outside language. The real is thus the minimal ontological framework
that results from the fact that, within language, being is excluded at the
same time that no definitive limits for that exclusion can be demarcated.
We have already established that the subject occupies the limit point from
which language proceeds, but there is also the question of the excess of
being that is not exhausted by the presentative capacity of language. The
minimal ontological form this being takes is that of the object (a), or, in
Badiou's case, the event. The question that intimately links Lacan's object
(a) to Badiou's event properly concerns the activity of the subject: how
does the subject give form to being beyond simply leaving it as an empty,
indeterminate excess?

For Badiou, it is evident that the indiscernible is granted form through
the forcing of truths. And it is unquestionably just as true that the conditions under which forcing can occur depend upon a generic, and thus
universalizable, framework put into place. Truth is universal, for all.[26] The
contrast with Lacan should be obvious: if the drive is itself an attainment
of Lacanian jouissance, should not jouissance be universalizable, had by
all?[27] Moreover, the drive itself, as an answer of sorts to the problems that

---

26. And this is not simply a formal mathematical counterpart to Badiou's ontology: a suf-
ficient account of universalizability was given in Badiou's account of Saint Paul. See Alain
Badiou, *Saint Paul: The Foundation of Universalism*, trans. Ray Brassier, Stanford, Stanford
University Press, 2003.

27. This is a bit of a lengthy argument in itself. The basic premise behind it is that no matter how much one enjoys, there will always be others who enjoy more. This would appear
to be the driving impetus behind Lacan's writing of 'Kant avec Sade', trans. James Swenson, *October*, vol. 51, 1989, pp. 55-104, as well as Slavoj Žižek's recent writings on enjoyment
as a political factor, see Slavoj Žižek, *For They Know Not What They Do: Enjoyment as a Political
Factor*, 2nd ed., London, Verso, 2002.

irrational forms of enjoyment may represent to the subject, remains an ultimately individual notion: there can be no collective solution to the problem of jouissance precisely because, from the perspective of psychoanalysis, only individuals can be treated on the couch. There cannot be a collective jouissance of the community.[28] As such, psychoanalysis would be an ultimately individual notion that carried very little truth. By extension, its usefulness for speaking about Badiou's notion of subjective fidelity would appear quite limited.

My response to the above objection is twofold. First, while there is certainly a connection between what happens at the level of a subject being gripped by an event and the universal truth that may follow from such an account, the universalizability of a truth cannot in any way serve as a criterion for what happens at the level of a subject being gripped by an event. A subject declares its fidelity to the event as a pure matter of faith. This is because, in a position Badiou may since have retracted, the truthfulness of an event cannot be decided at the time of its occurrence. And from this perspective, it is just as true that subjects gripped by events can form reactionary—and hence untrue—tendencies in response to events (say, collective unities who oppose political revolution, people who regarded Schoenberg's music as noise, etc.). Nothing at the level of universalizability can define the trajectory of the subject in response to something that has the power to form collective subjects out of individuals. A theory of what creates those subjective formations is what I am looking for in psychoanalysis.

Second, Badiou has, on at least two occasions, made concessions to the Lacanian cure as a potential truth procedure, insofar as the subject on the couch can, over the course of analysis, give form to the unconscious (or indiscernible) mechanisms that compel it to act.[29] At an immediate level, the answer is clearly that certain individuals make decisions to change their 'situations' (their individual lives) in order to form new relations to the being (the *jouissance*) they have to bear in everyday life. The hard work

---

28. Ultimately, this is what Lacan meant with his maxim 'do not cede your desire!' That is, do not let an other dictate to you what your desire should be.

29. In *Theory of the Subject*, Badiou wrote that: 'We won't pay any attention to those who argue that a couch is not as serious as a concentration camp. To them we say without hesitation that this remains to be seen. The axiom of the nouveaux philosophes—"a camp is a camp"—is just as false as what the Chicago therapists wanted to promote through the excommunication of Lacan: "a couch is a couch". The fact is that the psychoanalytic cure has no other real aim than that of the readjustment of the subject to its own repetition'. See Alain Badiou, *Théorie du sujet*, Paris, Seuil, 1982.

of analysis, then, could be regarded as a truth procedure among others that allows subjects (individual human subjects, say) to form new, hopefully more rational, means of existing. The manner in which we move from psychoanalysis, a specialist field that concerns individuals on couches, to arguing for its significance for philosophy will require something else: this is what I am looking for through the theory of sublimation. Sublimation can allow for the creation of something new in art, in a manner that will be applicable, if not useful, for Badiou's own writings on the topic.

I will thus attempt to go through these two points so as to assess what they may have to offer Badiou's theory of the event, the subject and fidelity. It is ultimately a question of affect as a principle of the subject, over and above the structural relations that make subjectivization possible. It may seem odd to appeal to Lacan for these purposes, given that he has often been accused of stripping psychoanalysis of *any* notion of affect. From such a perspective, it offers a cold and sterile framework for speaking about human behavior. Philosophically, however, the psychoanalytic notion of the drive remains tainted by an irrationality that, more often than not, assumes morbid or abject vicissitudes (for example, Žižek's comparison of an encounter with the 'monstrous real' with Badiou's truth procedures). This psychoanalytic approach, for Žižek, constitutes an irrationality that underlies every philosophical approach to fill out the void of the indiscernible through the forcing of truths: in a Truth-Event, the void of the death drive, of radical negativity, a gap that momentarily suspends the Order of Being, continues to resonate'.[30]

In many ways, Žižek is entirely correct. In the first place, truth is indeed an empty category: behind any particular or local instantiation of it, there is nothing other than the void, just as ontology and thinking are nothing apart from their particular presentations or instantiations. But there is a surreptitious jump that Žižek makes from the emptiness of truth as a category to the fact that the truth procedures become nothing more than a way of regulating primordial psychic drives (whereby love is nothing other than the ability of human beings to rationalize an unbridled jouissance, politics becomes a means of modulating the non-universalizability of enjoyment as a political factor, art is a means of sublimating the abject horror of the real into beautiful objects, etc). Žižek's move is to ground *all* subjective action in impulses and interests that are applicable only to a psychoanalytic subject. In other words, at the bottom of Badiou's

---

30. Slavoj Žižek, *The Ticklish Subject: The Absent Centre of Political Ontology*, New York, Verso, 1999, pp. 162-3.

truth procedures lie libidinal impulses. What he has done, then, is oppose Lacan to Badiou without acknowledging that this distinction is possible on the basis of what distinguishes psychoanalysis from philosophy. And secondly, is it not the very point that sublimation, in supposing the de-sexualization of libido, makes categories such as 'unbridled' jouissance secondary to the ultimate aims of its activity? The applicability of the drive for Badiou's philosophy will hold only insofar as the drive ceases to be a purely individual notion and admits of a capacity for universaliz-ability. In other words, I am in no way arguing for a correlation between Badiou and Lacan on the ground that subjective action presupposes a libidinal interest (in the same way that sublimation presupposes a drive), but rather that the elementary relation of a subject to its enjoyment (that is, a speaking subject to its unsaid being) is constitutive of the relation between Badiou's subject and the event. What is required, then, is not a sexualized content, but rather a minimal condition of affect that defines that relation.

AFFECT DEFINED

Lacan's major writing on the topic of affect occurs in his tenth semi-nar, on Anxiety. Anxiety, he says, is the only thing we can be sure of. I take this to mean that the other emotions that regulate human experience are always capable of deceiving. I have already mentioned fear and pity: clearly, with respect to contemporary events, there is no doubt that we live in a world where feared enemies and pitied victims proliferate. And their invocation in politics can often serve contradictory aims. For example, in relation to contemporary events, the same Muslim population we fear in the name of potential terrorist attacks is the same we pity in the name of the humanitarian interventions of 'just wars'.[31] Fear and pity, in either case, arouses the need for a resolution, just as readily as their transgression can find form in other, more threatening, extremes. Anxiety is something different, because it is instituted on an entirely different basis. What we fear or pity is conventionally what is other to us: in contrast, what arouses our anxiety is altogether intimate to us. It's hardly surprising that ethical indignation is often aroused with respect to people at a distance from ourselves (in Bosnia, Palestine, Iraq), rather than with regard to people

---

31. See Jacqueline Rose's admirable editorial, 'We are all afraid, but of what exactly?', *The Guardian*, 20 March 2003, ‹http://www.guardian.co.uk/comment/story/0,3604,917712,00. html›, accessed July 6, 2004.

we encounter in our everyday lives (UK and American citizens who live in poverty or are incarcerated).

What gives structure to anxiety is not a lack (a constitutive wound at the heart of experience), but rather, in Lacan's terms, a *lack of lack*. 'Anxiety is not the signal of a lack, but of something that you must manage to conceive of at this redoubled level of being the absence of this support of lack' (5.12.62). Subjective lack, which makes the emergence of the speaking subject in language possible, is also that which guarantees that the object (a), qua cause of desire, will always remain at a distance from that subject. It is always excluded, and thus open to various irrational vicissitudes. As an object of desire, the object (a) remains an impossible object which the subject relates to by virtue of some kind of constitutive failure. But in the absence of that lack, the object no longer remains at a distance; it emerges full-circle to the subject as the constitutive core of its grounding in being. And this being that is revealed to the subject as its own ground is precisely that empty place, that nothing that is the subject's own being. The confrontation of the subject with this being is the proper catalyst for action. The arousal of anxiety is thus unlike other psychological notions of affect that are constitutive of a subject's relation to the stability of their symbolic order. While fear and pity, among other affects, could be said to determine the manner in which subjects hold irrational relations to their jouissance and its various vicissitudes, it is anxiety, the encounter with the empty ground of being, that prompts an individual to go into analysis with the hope of forming other, preferably more rational, relations to their jouissance. Anxiety is the cause of subjective change precisely because it lacks a support in representation.

I will present this in the simplest form to provide a way into Badiou. In 'normal' situations, there may be certain elements that are subtracted. As we saw in the case of immigrant workers, some may be represented as excluded in the contemporary political situation of France, and this subtractive representation may arouse various feelings of disgust, pity or resentment. The arousal of these feelings depends upon their status as subtracted, as lacking what French citizens have (work permits, legal status, recognition by the state, etc). The movement that would facilitate the shift to an event would be to consider them not as subtracted elements of the situation 'France', but rather as human beings that, like French citizens, occupy the same place. If an event, or a political sequence, is to be established in their name, what is required is a recognition of the common being that is shared with French citizens, from which various prescriptions against the French state can be made on behalf of their ontological validity.

It is one thing to say that the example of the *sans-papiers* can provide one such example of a situation's recognition of its own subtracted being. It is another thing, however, to say that such a recognition arouses anxiety, or that such anxiety is the sole catalyst for subjective action, or fidelity. And, of course, anxiety is not an exclusively Lacanian notion, given that his work on the topic has been preceded by Kierkegaard, Heidegger and Freud, among others. If anything could be said to unite these latter three interpretations, it is the belief that anxiety is a subject's own confrontation with possibility: the possibility of moral obligation through the acknowledgement of guilt (Kierkegaard), or the possibility of one's own freedom to exist in the world (Heidegger). The indeterminateness of anxiety, then, is not anxiety about something in particular, but about being in general. And this revelation of being in general, the fact that it is not something that can be represented as excluded, and hence managed, is constitutive of a subject's relation to indeterminate being.

Taking this as our point of departure, we must then ask what it is that anxiety may provoke in psychoanalytic theory and what its counterpart may be in Badiou's truth procedure? The answer to the first part of the problem is simple enough: in contrast to emotions like fear and pity, anxiety is distinct from ordinary passionate attachments that define a subject's relation to the world. In other words, a person is compelled to go into analysis less on the basis of a compulsive need or desire for something (however much that can serve as a prop for their wish for analysis) as because of an underlying anxiety that makes ordinary life unbearable. The subject is seized by something it doesn't have a name for, and this is what could be said to prompt the series of investigations that ensue in the course of analysis. So far, this is quite concomitant with how Badiou sees a truth procedure. 'To speak brutally, I do not think that analysis is an interpretation, because it is regulated not by sense, but by truth. This is certainly not an uncovering of truth, of which we know that it is vain to think it could be uncovered, because it is generic'.[32] Analysis does not uncover a preexisting truth, but is rather a means through which a subject gives form and shape to the indiscernible being that grounds its anxiety.

This final point is the pretext for the conclusion of this discussion. If analysis is ultimately something that individuals, as opposed to collective subjects, undergo, why should it then be seen as universal or generic? Isn't

---

32. Alain Badiou, *Conditions*, Paris, Seuil, 1992, p. 208.

the whole point of Lacan's enterprise that jouissance cannot be universalized, had by all? Lacan's famous utilitarian analogy of jouissance as a white sheet illustrates this logic perfectly: if you cut enough holes in the sheet for everyone to stick their head through, you end up destroying the sheet in turn. The universalization of jouissance is its own abnegation. And if we conceive the ultimate goal of analysis to be new, more rational, relations subjects form with their jouissance, we are left with something that is fundamentally incompatible with Badiou's truth procedure. The crux of this problematic takes us to the difference between being and the real. I mentioned before that the real is a category of the subject. What is implied by this is that the being of a truth that comes to be instituted in the situation traverses the individuality of the subject who chose to recognize it over others who did not. Badiou's subjects are unique subjects to the extent that they recognize events that others don't; however, if truth is for all, the particularity of the subject is abnegated. The move from psychoanalysis to philosophy, and from the real to being requires that truth must pass over from being a subjective principle of fidelity to become a truth that exists for all qua forcing. The real, as I see it, names that part of a truth that the subject operates in the service of, at the same time that the subject's actions traverse the individuality of the real.

I previously distinguished satisfaction from jouissance on the grounds that the former attains a certain stability that is rooted within language, whereas the latter is an explicit excess of being over language. Jouissance, at bottom, is Lacan's name for being. And the object (a), that bit of jouissance that supports subjective activity, is the correlate for Badiou's event. What the object (a) and the event both provide is a minimal framework through which a subject confronts being. Given that neither the event nor the object (a) have proper supports in representation, there is never a guarantee that disaster might not ensue from the subjective relations they establish. Perhaps their indeterminacy is what allows them to, quite often, assume irrational forms, as witnessed in the example of false truth procedures in Badiou, or in the obscure attachments that subjects form with obscure forms of enjoyment, in Lacan. The conditions of possibility of change and novelty in both Badiou or Lacan are just as readily the possible conditions for evil.

When Badiou remarks that analysis is not interpretation, he means that there is a point in the analytic situation that cannot be reduced to the dimension of language, which guides the subject forth in his or her pursuit of a truth. In the absence of a metalanguage, jouissance is that excess of the subject to itself, that part of the subject that is more than simply the sum total of its activity. When coupled with the object (a), then, the subject is driven in pursuit of something that is not reducible to its experience. And conversely, to see the real as a category of the subject is to put the subject in tandem with something that exceeds its structural configuration in a linguistic network: it is that part of the subject that exceeds its own activity. What distinguishes Badiou's subject from Lacan's, then, is the process through which that subjective excess passes over from being a purely subjective principle (qua the real of jouissance) into something that holds for a collective human situation in its totality (qua generic being of a truth). Forcing is what makes that shift possible. But it would be difficult to see how forcing would be possible were it not for the activity of a militant subject who is put in the service of something that exceeds all positive or representative value in the situation. Lacan, I have argued, provides the framework for Badiou's subjectivity.

The final question, then, concerns what we are to make of sublimation in Lacan. Is it a notion that is concomitant with art as a truth procedure in Badiou? The question returns us to Badiou's comment that truth in analysis cannot be uncovered because it is generic. Is there a generic, higher faculty of jouissance? Sublimation, I have suggested, offers one such possibility in and through the production of aesthetic objects that instantiate the empty ground of being that is annulled in and through the advent of language. And artistic sublimation may do this in a manner that is altogether different from the realizations that occur in religion or science.

When Badiou remarked that jouissance cannot be reduced to interpretation, he meant that it was that limit point of the situation which refuses closure. It becomes quite easy, then, to see that jouissance cannot be universalized: it cannot be given as a totality that can then be cut up and dived equally among all inhabitants of the situation. Like Russell's paradox, this is a direct effect of the inherent incompletion of being itself. What needs to be asked is whether it is possible for art to instantiate that incompletion. The artists that Badiou champions seem to share a tendency to strip away detail to uncover, or localize, the purity of the void. When Lacan describes sublimation as the 'elevation of an object into the dignity of a Thing',[33] I take him to mean that a Thing remains irreducible to the exchange or distribution of goods that typify stability in a social situation. This Thing, this object (a), that embodies our jouissance maintains its generic or universal value insofar as it is not reduced to the dominant

---

33. Lacan, *The Ethics of Psychoanalysis*, p. 112.

logic of the situation, whether that be the baseness of fear or pity, or the customary circulation of goods in a capitalist society.

What sorts out the disparity of terms (jouissance, drive, sublimation, object (a), anxiety) with regard to the terms of Badiou's philosophy? For readers less familiar with Lacan, the following shortcut can provide an axiomatic framework with which to digest the preceding remarks:

1. The subject's declaration of an event defines a rudimentary means of relating to being. If the event is object (a), the affect that defines the subject's relation to that object (or event) is anxiety.

2. Being is distinct from the real insofar as the real is a category of a speaking subject's relation to its own (impossible) being. The real presupposes a subject, while only the appearance of an event presupposes a subject. Events cannot be deduced from an asubjective, impersonal ontology.

3. If the drive can typify a subject's fidelity to an event (insofar as the psychoanalytic theory of the drive is a subject's instantiation of its object (a)), sublimation is a means of instantiating the forms of indiscernible being that can be met with recognition from other subjects. It provides a productive form in which a drive can achieve satisfaction irrespective of its object. Thus, the value we impute to the artistic object depends less upon its usefulness or ability to satisfy human wants or interests, but rather upon the fact that it gives form to a being that eludes the speech of the speaking subject.

8

Conditional Notes on a New *Republic*

A. J. Bartlett

'Could anything show a more shameful lack of [education] than to have so little justice in oneself that one must get it from others, who thus become masters and judges over us?'[1]

'The sole remit for thought is to the school of decision'.[2]

'...whence arises the obstacle to every valid account of the effects of education, since what brought about the results cannot be admitted to in discussing the intention'.[3]

Alain Badiou says that what he admires most about Pascal is his effort to 'invent the modern forms of an ancient conviction, rather than follow the way of the world' (BE 222).[4] That education *is* good is an ancient

---

1. Plato, *The Republic of Plato*, trans. F.M. Cornford, London, Oxford University Press, 1941, p. 95, 405a. Or, in Desmond Lee's translation, 'It is the sign of a bad education if one seeks justice at the hands of others', London, Penguin Books, 1974, p. 168. See also *Apology*, 24b-27b esp. in Plato, *The Last Days of Socrates*, trans. & intro. Hugh Tredennick, London, Penguin, 1954, pp. 56-59.
2. Alain Badiou, *Being and Event*, trans. Oliver Feltham, London, Continuum, 2006, p. 149 (henceforth BE).
3. Jacques Lacan, 'Kant with Sade', in *Ecrits*, trans. Bruce Fink with Heloise Fink and Russell Grigg, New York, W.W. Norton & Company, 2006, pp. 665/787. First published in English in *October*, trans. James B. Swenson Jr., vol. 51, 1989, pp. 55-75.
4. It is obvious that this says as much about Badiou as Pascal.

conviction. That the good it is needs to be given 'modern form', which is to say, something other than a state form is the underlying wager of this paper. We take our direction from Badiou's axiomatic and singular declaration that 'the only education is an education *by truths*'.[5] Truths make 'holes in knowledge'—that encyclopaedia of the state. This encyclopaedia provides the predicative order of judgements such that a multiple 'finds itself belonging to a set of multiples, that is, to a part' (BE 328). In other words, to paraphrase from Lacan it is the state which 'know[s] what you will do'.[6] For Badiou, a truth, constituted as a generic procedure and subject to its event, necessarily entails a type of indifferent and 'logical revolt' against the *state* of the situation. Badiou's claim in regard to an 'education by truths' suggests therefore something like an operation of immanent rivalry, 'within justice', to an education by the state.[7] Of course, today, at the level of the (state) system, the knotting of the state and education is tighter than ever. This knot binds a complex historicity of ideology, economy, desire and demand. This historicity is itself well worth tracing in light of Badiou's 'ethic of truths' insofar as the state today incorporates and reconfigures many of the radical, emancipatory and authentic demands associated with education since the French Revolution. However, we will not be investigating the particulars of this situation here. Rather, we will attempt to discern what Badiou's system provides for thinking of education in a form which separates the ancient conviction as to its virtue from its contemporary representation in the state. These notes will, nevertheless, set Badiou's 'education by truths' against the education of the state in the hope of discerning the possibilities for a 'modern form that does not follow the way of the world'.

We will work through three linked variations on the pedagogical theme. First we will address the significance and function of the term

---

5. Alain Badiou, 'Art and Philosophy', in *Handbook of Inaesthetics*, trans. Alberto Toscano, Stanford, Stanford University Press, 2005, p. 13 (henceforth HI).

6. And, 'to know what your partner will do is not proof of love'. Jacques Lacan. *Seminar XX: On Feminine Sexuality, The Limits of Love and Knowledge, 1972-1973*, ed. Jacques-Alain Miller, trans. Bruce Fink New York, W.W. Norton, 1999, p. 146, (p. 133 in the French). If the state does not love, how then does it educate? One should recall that in articulating the argument that 'deductive fidelity' is the 'equivocal *paradigm* of all fidelity', Badiou claims that one such example of this is the 'proofs of love'. See BE, p. 254.

7. Alain Badiou, 'Philosophy and Politics', in *Infinite Thought: Truth and the Return to Philosophy*, ed. and trans. Oliver Feltham and Justin Clemens, London, Continuum Press, 2003, pp. 69-78. Also translated under the same name by Thelma Sowley, *Radical Philosophy* 96, July/August 1999, p. 30 and as 'Truths and Justice', in *Metapolitics*, trans. Jason Barker, London, Verso, 2006, pp. 96-106 (henceforth M).

'conditions'. Secondly we will address Badiou's essay 'Art and Philosophy' from *Handbook of Inaesthetics*, the only essay in fact where Badiou addresses education in a specific manner,[8] and in which Badiou discusses the link between art and philosophy in terms of the 'pedagogical theme': A theme, he says, that has been brought to collapse. Thirdly we will attempt to discern what might make up what Badiou refers to as the 'fourth modality' of the link between philosophy and its conditions through a somewhat speculative discussion of the dual 'militant' praxis known in Badiou's work as 'subtraction' and 'forcing'.

AXIOMATIC CONDITIONS

One of the more well known features of Badiou's philosophical system is that philosophy does not produce truths itself but 'has begun' as a discourse under 'conditions'.[9] The four conditions are Badiou says, 'uniform... recognisable from afar, whose relation to thought is relatively invariant. The name of this invariance is clear: it is the name truth'.[10] It is through a tripartite relation with the 'wholly empty' yet invariant category of truth that these four truth—or generic—procedures condition philosophy. Philosophy as such, will come to be as the thinking of their compossibility through the categories of being, event and subject. Although this certainly causes some debate we are not concerned in this paper with why he opts for these four procedures alone.[11] Our concern ultimately is only for the 'modality' of the relation this term implies be-

---

8. In the collection *Conditions,* Badiou does devote a short article to the question '*Qu'est-ce qu'une institution philosophique?*' See *Conditions,* Paris, Seuil, 1992, pp. 83-90. See ch. 2 of this volmue. He discusses it in passing in an interview with Bruno Bosteels published in Gabriel Riera (ed.), *Alain Badiou: Philosophy and its Conditions,* New York, Suny, 2005. And there are vague references in *Logiques des mondes,* Paris, Seuil, 2006, i.e. see the table on p. 87.

9. Alain Badiou, *Manifesto for Philosophy,* trans. Norman Madarasz, New York, Suny Press, 1999, p. 33. Hereafter, MP.

10. Badiou, MP, p. 33.

11. For arguments concerning this issue see Slavoj Žižek. *The Ticklish Subject: the absent centre of political ontology,* U.K, Verso, 2000, esp. Ch 3, 'The politics of truth, or, Alain Badiou as a reader of St Paul'. pp. 127-170. Here, Žižek argues for religion as a condition. As does Simon Critchley in 'Demanding Approval: On the ethics of Alain Badiou', *Radical Philosophy* 100, March/April 2000, pp. 16-27. Ray Brassier argues Capital itself might 'think' and therefore qualify as a condition in, 'Nihil Unbound: Remarks on the Subtractive Ontology and Thinking Capitalism', in *Think Again* ed. Peter Hallward London, Continuum, 2004, pp. 50-58. Justin Clemens sees in the 'letter' a 'condition of conditions' in 'Letters as the Condition of Conditions for Alain Badiou', *Communication & Cognition,* Vol. 36, Nr. 1-2, 2003, pp. 73-102.

tween the four procedures, truth and philosophy. This is because Badiou institutes the notion of the configuration of the four conditions—as a *set* of generic procedures—precisely as the condition of the freedom of philosophy.[12] And so the form of the modality of the link, what he names in *Handbook of Inaesthetics* as the 'pedagogical form', as that which, suitably reconfigured, prevents philosophy's suture to, and saturation by, one of these procedures, and yet maintains each as a condition, must be a pedagogy of freedom in some sense.

From the ontology of love to the partitioning proofs of Ramsey cardinals, Mao's expression 'one divides into two' has an axiomatic status in Badiou's work. Metapolitically speaking, an axiom is that which is thrown up within the antagonism and contingency of a situational sequence. It is that immanent principle which a collective act not so much marches behind as pushes forward—*liberté, egalité, fraternité*—as itself.[13] But, as Badiou argues, this equality (the political form of justice) is not objective or part of the putative ends of a state program, but subjective; an expression *in actu* of the equal capacity for thought. He says, it is 'not what we want or plan but what we declare under fire of the event, here and now as what is and not what should be'.[14] An axiom functions as a declaration in language of the immanent singularity of what *happens* in a situation. It authorizes an operational decision drawn from its conditioning event, which it is the labour of thought to render consistent. Oliver Feltham, deploying the term Badiou himself 'steals' from Deleuze, names this operation the 'disjunctive synthesis' saying the 'synthesis' is what 'allows such an interruption to endure'.[15] This division, at any stage, is not in the form of a subjective, objective split. It is instead a wholly operative, subjective and situational division, 'singular and immanent', and as such, this is what authorizes Badiou's deployment of Deleuze's terminology.[16] However, we must insist here that this borrowing of a name is not the same as borrowing that which it names. Although it marks for both a conceptual form for thinking the (non)relation between being and thought, for Badiou it is

12. Badiou, MP, p. 35.
13. On what has become of these today under conditions of a contemporary Thermidor see, Alain Badiou, *Le Siècle*, Paris, Seuil, 2005, pp. 145-6. See also, Badiou, 'What is a Thermidorean', in M, pp. 124-140.
14. Badiou, 'Philosophy and Politics', p. 72.
15. Oliver Feltham, 'And Being and Event and…: Philosophy and its Nominations', *Polygraph*, no. 17, 2005, p. 37.
16. Alain Badiou, *Deleuze: The Clamor of Being*, trans. Louise Burchill, Minneapolis, University of Minnesota Press, 1999, p. 79.

through the event as (rare) irruption or, surrection, and not as 'univocal issue' that this 'relation' is form[ed]: events mark 'absolute beginnings'… 'and singularities of thought incomparable in their constitutive gestures'; whereas for Deleuze, according to Badiou at least, this 'non-relation is still thought in relation to the One, which founds it by radically separating the terms involved'.[17] For Badiou 'disjunctive synthesis' entails a non-conceptual, operational deployment and as such a procedure of inseparation as enduring fidelity to this immanent division.

This does not mean that philosophy (nor the philosopher) provides resolution or totalization of this division, between the event *and* its consequences, *in the concept* or anywhere else for that matter. Philosophy draws the consequences of this constitutive division in thought, faithfully maintaining the real of the disjunction within the resultant synthesis or consistency, demanded by the subjective creation of the concept—or, the thinking of its thought. This fidelity to Mao's axiom has consequences all the way through Badiou's work.[18] Philosophy itself, on his terms, is the consequence or rather, the consequences drawn, of the decisive splitting of philosophy and ontology. The latter declared by Badiou to *be* mathematics. And mathematics provides the model of an 'infinite thought' or, a thought capable of thinking infinities.[19]

When Badiou claims that philosophy is subject to conditions we are to hear this term functioning in two ways: It is the generic name for the four procedures as procedures, that is, 'conditions' is the nominal form given to mark these procedures in their 'compossible' singularity. At the same time these autonomously operating procedures 'condition'—as in form or shape—that which is or will be the discourse of philosophy. They are the

---

17. Badiou, *Deleuze*, pp. 90-91 and p. 22 respectively.

18. It is worth noting that in his essay on justice and politics Badiou cites Mao's dictum from the sixteen point decision: 'Let the masses educate themselves in this great revolutionary movement, let them determine by themselves the distinction between what is just and what is not'. 'Philosophy and Politics', p. 29. (*Radical Philosophy* version for this translation). See for the full text Mao Tse-Tung, 'The sixteen point decision', Point 4. Appendix to Jean Daubier, *History of the Chinese Cultural Revolution,* trans. Richard Sever, New York, Vintage Books, 1974, p. 300.

19. Bruno Besana argues that it is in regard to 'a model' that Badiou's thought of the be-ing *and the* event can be most strictly demarcated from Deleuze's thought of being *as an* event. The argument involves 'two readings of Plato' and is beyond this essay. See Bruno Besana, 'One or Several Events? The Knot Between Event and Subject in the Work of Alain Badiou and Gilles Deleuze', trans. Justin Clemens, in *Polygraph*, no. 17, pp. 245-266. See also Ray Brassier, 'Badiou's Materialist Epistemology of Mathematics', *Angelaki*, vol. 10, no. 2, August, 2005.

disciplinary operations by which these four procedures act upon the discourse that will be philosophy. And it is thus only within this constituted discourse that the 'truths' produced by the four conditions are one-ified or become compossible, or can be thought together: the ontological disjunction 'synthesized' through the thinking of their truths in a retroactive syntax which affirms the 'being *there*' (or *there are*) of truths. In this sense the conditions prescribe, and absolutely so, the possibilities of a philosophy's form.[20]

In this way the 'wholly empty' category of Truth acquires the tools necessary for it to become operational. Both 'condition' and 'condition*s*', as two instances of the singular (non)relation between a procedure and the philosophy it convokes, name, but again in two ways, this split between the finite *conditions*, the works of the procedures, and the infinite *condition*, the (immanent) idea, or the thought of these works that philosophy comes to think *together*.[21] Philosophy is what will have been conditioned by its conditions. Badiou renders the structure of this effect, which is evidently pedagogical—though not as we might ordinarily understand it—as 'what a thought declares to be a thought, on condition of which it thinks that which is a thought'.[22]

The singular importance for philosophy of these conditions—the work of the procedures—is that in their various operations they are capable of creating a sequence (of works), a consistent multiple, subject to an event (of its situation), such that it will be possible to say, something new, some truth, has come to be. It is important to remember however, that that which Badiou calls a truth is not incarnate, substantial or adequate by correspondence. In the final section we will elaborate on this further but it is important in light of what a condition is for Badiou to remark that in relation to these 'truths' philosophy proceeds 'in its history' under these conditions, as the 'desubstantialization of Truth, which is also the self-liberation of its act'.[23] Thus it is incorrect to say, for example, a revolution *is* True or a poem *is* an event or to conflate the two. These may mark or inscribe a finite point in a process of truth but the process itself can never be totalized. A process does not belong to being as being but is precisely a

---

20. On the importance of this point see Justin Clemens, 'Had We But Worlds Enough, and Time, this Absolute, Philosopher...' in this volume .

21. Alain Badiou, 'Definition of Philosophy', in MP, p. 141.

22. Alain Badiou, 'The Political as a Procedure of Truth', trans. Barbara P. Faulks, *lacanian ink 19*, Fall 2001, p. 81 and in M, as 'Politics as a Truth Procedure', pp. 141-152.

23. Badiou, 'Définition de la philosophie' in *Conditions*, p. 82. I cite the original because I have modified the English translation from 'Definition of Philosophy', p. 144.

subtraction from being that forces the logic of its appearing. Its trajectory cannot be circumscribed by any predicative or finite expression because it is founded in the void, and as such is without representation and therefore without knowledge in the state. If this trajectory could be discerned or, in other words, predicated by a curricular process, it would merely belong to the existing regime of knowledge. Its process would belong to the order of what was readily verifiable.

Thus these four procedures, art, mathematics, politics and love, are conditions for philosophy precisely because of their 'extraordinary' ability to formalize by the processes unique to their functioning the 'truth(s)' of the situation in which they operate; truths that are singular to their field, irreducible to any other and immanent to the situation in which these procedures appear. That is, the truths produced are singular to the work and thought of the procedure itself. There is no external surveillance in this regard and at the same time, nor does any single procedure organize the whole of truth within itself. No procedure can say that it alone constitutes all that Truth is on pain of 'disaster'.[24] Thus, these procedures provide the 'conditions' for philosophy by their singular and immanent production of truths. In the dictionary definition wholly appropriate here, these conditions are 'an indispensable requirement'. At the same time, in the modality of their operation, these procedures are a qualification, a limit and a restriction. They are a discipline. Here, 'condition' takes on its more directly pedagogical sense of forming, shaping (*éduque*), even prescribing. What they prescribe is precisely the form and shape of the trajectory of the enquiries made in the production of the generic, and by which the thought produced within this procedure is seized under the name of philosophy. We can get a sense of how this works if we think of it in the manner in which a coach is said to 'condition' an athlete. In effect without the condition-*ing* the 'athlete' would not, as the athletic subject, 'have begun'.

It is worth looking at an example here of how a condition 'works'. To do this I will move quickly across Badiou's description of the importance of the mathematical conditioning of philosophy initiated by the Platonic decision to enquire into the consequences of the 'mathematical rupture'. As one move in what amounts to a series of moves against the Heideggerian influence on contemporary thought, Badiou claims that philosophy begins with Plato. This beginning is due to the Platonic attention to math-

---

24. Alain Badiou, *Ethics: An essay on the understanding of evil*, trans. Peter Hallward, London, Verso, 2000, p. 71.

ematics as a form of thought which, as atemporal and ideal constitutes a break with doxa.[25] This break is both once and for all, in the sense that mathematics *is* a break with doxa, and discontinuous in the sense that it will continue to be that thought which will have to break with doxa again and again.[26] Certainly, time and again in Plato's work Socrates establishes as his starting point that there in fact is such a break with doxa. That is, that doxa, established circulating knowledge, already includes within its delimitations of knowledge a site 'at the edge of the void' which it represents as nothing. For Plato/Socrates it is this nothing, this knowledge *of nothing* which can be thought under the condition of mathematics. Such a thought will be a break with knowledge. As such, void to knowledge, it founds a thought whose intelligibility owes nothing to the regime of already existing knowledge. This intelligibility exists as that which will have been established. Effectively, it is established that mathematics is a form of thought, one that thinks that which is intelligible against the perceptually immediate.[27] This break, with what is for Badiou effectively opinion—mathematically speaking there are no opinions—demands a further break or intervention. This is because this first break is obscure insofar as its consequences for thought are concerned. What does it mean that mathematics proceeds as it does? In one sense this is perfectly amenable to doxa, knowledge or the state, insofar as mathematics proceeds to follow a trajectory whose discoveries remain within mathematics. Such discoveries remain, so Badiou says, 'obscure and forced' in the sense that mathematics is not free to break with opinion, or not, but working from hypothesis and making use of 'axioms it cannot legitimate' it is thus forced 'under constraint of its own deductive chains [...] themselves dependent upon a fixed point', axiomatically or prescriptively stipulated, to rupture with opinion. Thus it is this dual constraint of being forced and obscure that at once makes mathematics an essential thought due to its singular ability to affect the entirely necessary break with opinion, to instate discontinuity into thought, *and* makes necessary a second break. And this precisely because the significance of this break must itself be thought. What consequences does the existence of a form of thought which breaks with doxa, with the knowledge that repeats as the way of knowing, that establishes discontinuity within thought, have for the freedom of thought?

---

25. Badiou, 'Philosophy and Mathematics', in *Theoretical Writings*, ed. and trans. Ray Brassier and Alberto Toscano, London, Continuum Books, 2004, p. 24.
26. Badiou, 'Philosophy and Mathematics', p. 29.
27. Badiou, 'Platonism and Mathematical Ontology', *Theoretical Writings*, p. 50. Whether mathematics 'thinks' is a thorny issue (for some) still.

Philosophy must begin here. It is the discourse of the second break. As such the dialectic (in Plato) is the procedure by which this deductively present discontinuity is placed within thought. Its obscurity is (or must be) rendered consistent outside itself. But this is not to be understood in the form of a subsumption; rather, in Badiou's words 'mathematics amounts to an in between (*metaxu*) of thinking as such: that it intimates a gap which lies even beyond the break with opinion'.[28] What Badiou is moving toward here is the claim that mathematics is ontology. What he wants to establish and precisely what links the notion of conditions and the notion of the 'pedagogical theme' is that mathematics is that which presents nothing. This nothing is the gap between knowledge as opinion or doxa and being. Being, being precisely what knowledge, in its sophistic state sense, claims to be knowledge of. What Badiou insists on and what he finds so essential in the thought of Plato for example, is that Plato himself, in a sense forced by his fidelity to mathematics, elaborates a discourse named philosophy which 'establishe[s] the illumination of the continuous at the moment of discontinuity'. And he does so precisely at that point where mathematics has to offer only its 'blind, stubborn inability to propose anything other than the intelligible and the break'.[29] Philosophy as a particular conditioned operation comes to elaborate within a space of freedom this truth which is the demonstrated break with opinion. Philosophy thinks the consequences of a thought that is other than opinion (or in Badiou's terms, knowledge) on condition of the conditioned break with that knowledge. We have no room here to do so but as is well known each of Badiou's four conditions can be similarly explicated as to their particular and irreducible role in conditioning philosophy; which is to say, of establishing the effect of an encounter as a transformation.

So 'condition', or to condition, one could almost say belongs to the register of the *future anterior* in that to argue that the conditions as we have described them also condition philosophy is, in a way, to subject philosophy to an exam as to its performance regarding what it does with these truths produced by the four procedures.[30] This might suggest, to take up the terminology of a thesis developed by Bruno Bosteels, that we are dealing with a dialectical materialism, of a sort (perhaps, indeed, a 'materialist dialectic'), in which neither the finite (subject) nor the infinite (of the procedure it supports) provide the substance of which the other is 'merely'

---

28. Badiou, 'Philosophy and Mathematics', p. 31.
29. Badiou, 'Philosophy and Mathematics', p. 32.
30. Badiou, 'A Philosophical Task: To Be Contemporaries of Pessoa', in HI, p. 37.

the idea.[31] Such a suggestion, on the one hand, would then invert what Badiou calls the didactic schema, whereby it is philosophy that authorizes the truths of art and, on the other, it would authorize a step beyond what he calls the romantic schema whereby philosophy drags along in the wake of art (or logic) as a fawning servant come journalist in thrall to art's immanent ability to reveal absolute truth.[32] We now turn to the artistic condition.

ART, PHILOSOPHY AND THE PEDAGOGICAL THEME

For Badiou ultimately, it is under the condition that *there are truths* that philosophy functions (HI 15). The pedagogical theme he suggests is that which enables the encounter between these truths that are produced within the process of these conditions, and the thought which thinks them. It is in the essay 'Art and Philosophy' that Badiou makes several explicit claims regarding education. As stated above, to my knowledge, this is the only text in which Badiou addresses education qua education. Indeed the term is (symptomatically?) absent from his work. So for anyone looking for some sort of master methodology or hoping to draw some instances from these claims that might be adapted to the contemporary scene of a state education, the following will (hopefully) be singularly unhelpful. What the several claims in this essay signify is an inherent pedagogical operation, operating within Badiou's project for philosophy which teaches the immanent power of what is (and is) not, as against the ruthless repetition of what must be. Such is the project of all philosophy, Badiou contends, which is nothing less than discerning 'the possible modalities of a single statement: "The Same is at once thinking and being"'.[33] Obviously the interconnection between pedagogy and philosophy is embedded in

---

31. Bruno Bosteels, 'Alain Badiou's Theory of the Subject: The Recommencement of Dialectical Materialism', Part 1. *Pli* 12, 2001, pp. 200-229 and Part 2, *Pli* 13, 2002, pp. 173-208.

32. Badiou, HI, p. 5. In regard to mathematics Badiou names the three schemata which organize the link between philosophy and mathematics, the *ontological*, the *epistemological*, and the *critical*. There is some scope for mapping the first three schemata from the realm of art and philosophy onto the latter from mathematics and philosophy but such an attempt must proceed with caution. And in any case Romanticism is for Badiou the central concern, as for him it is our subjection to Romanticism post-Hegel that constitutes the 'time of our time'. See, 'Philosophy and Mathematics: Infinity and the end of Romanticism', *Theoretical Writings*, p. 22.

33. Badiou, *Deleuze*, p. 79. The statement is of course from Parmenides. See translator's note (p. 137; note 1) for an explanation of this translation.

the tradition of the discipline itself. However, in the same way that Badiou determines one aspect of the relation between art and philosophy to have been characterized, the relation between education and the state has itself been one determined by a form of philo-sophistical surveillance. Despite the plaintive cries lamenting the state's attack on the academy, the university persists in being that institution which sets and determines the standard and form of the curriculum for the final years of high-school, as for itself.[34] It also, at the behest of and as an immanent function of the state, persists in being that nexus of knowledge and training which reigns down upon both the secondary and the primary schools, upon itself, and upon the social realm in general its methods, its economic, social, cultural and psychological insights (such as they are) and its graduates. All this and so much more, operate as the education system. And today of course, as Althusser and Lenin before him (and many others in various less radical ways) have pointed out, this is inextricably linked to the capitalist form of the state.[35] Concerned as we are with an education which serves as a mo-

---

34. Consider that the highest degree available in any discipline is still called Doctor of Philosophy (PhD). It is thus that we here conflate the university, as an institution of the state and philosophy as the (master) discourse of this institution. Apologies to Lacan(ians) and, of course, to Plato(nists).

35. 'The revolution that the bourgeois class has brought into the conception of law, and hence into the function of the state, consists especially in the will to conform (hence ethicity of the law and of the state). The previous ruling classes were essentially conservative in the sense that they did not tend to construct an organic passage from the other classes into their own, i.e. to enlarge their class sphere 'technically' and ideologically: their conception was that of a closed state. The bourgeois class poses itself as an organism in continuous movement, capable of absorbing the entire society, assimilating it to its own cultural and economic level. The entire function of the state has been transformed: the state has become an "educator"'. Antonio Gramsci, *Selections from the Prison Notebook*, trans. Quentin Hoare and Geoffrey Nowell-Smith, New York, International Publishers, 1971, p. 260. One should note here that in the U.K. (as elsewhere) prior to the installation of the state-school many worker groups maintained a distance from this 'good' on offer by the state. Prophetically, or rather because they were very well aware of their relation to the state, they were concerned that it was merely a vehicle for further co-option. Of course it is neither *wholly* one nor the other. Precisely this is Badiou's reason for a move away from a traditional dialectics. This because it is in the sphere of representation that the void is seen to be included in the situation. This void, what immanently escapes significant representation, is the foundation for the new. One must be careful here though to not slip into liberalism which happily grants that in and through 'education for all' in its state sense, new relations emerge in the social. Liberalism forecloses the void precisely under operations of reform. Reform or reaction, if you like, is a veil of the void. It incorporates any and all interruptions within itself as its virtue. In liberalism the individual under education may change his place in the social relation; the social relations themselves are maintained by just this move. See Mao Tse-Tung, *Combat Liberalism*, Peking, Foreign Languages Press, 1954.

dality of a procedure of truth, a modality subject to the encounter of being and thought, then we are engaged with Badiou in thinking the thought *that is*, against such surveillance, and is 'nothing other than the desire to finish with the exorbitant excess of the state'.[36]

In the essay 'Art and Philosophy' which serves to introduce a 'series of variations' on the theme *Inaesthetics*,[37] Badiou distinguishes three primary schemata which he maintains have governed the thinking of the modality of the link between art and philosophy. He links these schemata to what he calls the three 'massive tendencies of thought' in the 20th century. In the 20th century these tendencies have become saturated by particular schemata which are in themselves 'out of time' due to the fact that they themselves are not the product of these 20th century tendencies. As such, in regard to the 'thinking of art' Marxism (dialectical materialism) is didactic, hermeneutics (after Heidegger) is romantic, and psychoanalysis (in relation to Art, vis-a-vis Aristotle) is classical (HI 5). Each 'massive tendency of thought' is thus saturated by being deployed in the form of a particular schema that either utilized or identified with them.[38] Badiou contends that the thinking of the relation between art and philosophy has thus become saturated by the predominance of one of these three tendencies or, by a '*simultaneously conservative and eclectic*' combination thereof (HI 5 emphasis added).[39] Badiou argues that these tendencies saturated by their schemata are thus incapable of offering anything new in regards to thinking (the thinking of) art.

Along with the production of a disentanglement between art and philosophy, something he restates in different ways in regard to philosophy and all its 'conditions'[40], this saturation has also produced 'the pure and simple collapse of what had circulated between them; the pedagogical theme' (HI 7). The difficulty assumed in this essay, 'Art and Philoso-

---

36. Badiou, BE, p. 282. See also Peter Hallward, 'Generic Sovereignty', *Angelaki*, Vol 3, 1998, p. 92.

37. Which he describes thus; 'By inaesthetics I understand a relation of philosophy to art that, maintaining that art is itself a producer of truths, makes no claim to turn art into an object for philosophy. Against aesthetic speculation, inaesthetics describes the strictly intraphilosophical effects produced by the independent existence of some works of art'. Badiou, HI.

38. See, on these 20th Century tendencies, or 'passion(s) for the real', Badiou's *Le Siècle*.

39. 'Though it is considered to be the century [20th] of endings, breaks and catastrophes, when it comes to the link that concerns us here, I see it instead as a century that was simultaneously conservative and eclectic', HI, p. 5.

40. See for example Badiou, 'Philosophy and Mathematics: Infinity and the End of Romanticism', in *Theoretical Writings*, esp. pp. 21-22.

phy'—as in many others—is to account for the dis-relation that this link
(a link he determines to 're-found'),[41] signifies 'between' two entirely distinct, yet intimately (non)related operations of thought. In other words,
what is the method, in reality the non-method produced within the singular, situational praxis of these four 'conditions'?[42] Badiou proposes a
'new schema, a fourth modality of [this] link', thus proposing a formal
trajectory, between art and philosophy (HI 8). And one which at the same
time 'subverts' the sophistic 'subterfuge' that an artistic apprenticeship is
the way to an education (HI 1).

While it is not the place of this essay to provide a critique of the veracity of Badiou's diagnoses of those 'schemata' and their attendant saturation of the 'massive tendencies' (schemata, by the way, that can definitely
be found to be operating 'conservatively and eclectically' (HI 5)[43] within
the theory, policy and practice of the contemporary education system),

---

41. See Badiou, HI, where this link has 'collapsed' and must therefore also be re-founded
in the fourth modality; see also MP, where this re-founding is more accurately a return [of
philosophy] {to} itself. See, 'The Return of Philosophy to *Itself*', pp. 113-138.

42. It is interesting on this point to compare with Badiou what Jacques Rancière describes
as the 'non-method' of intellectual emancipation 'stumbled' upon by Joseph Jacotot,
whereby one may 'teach what one doesn't know'. This method, as with Badiou, begins
with an axiomatic statement. Rancière declares an 'equality of intelligence'. Thus: 'Let's
affirm then that universal teaching *will not take*, it will not be established in society. But *it
will not perish* because it is the natural method of the human mind, that of all people who
look for their path themselves. What the disciples can do is to announce to all individuals,
to all mothers and fathers, the way to teach what one doesn't know on the principle of
the equality of intelligence'. See Jacques Rancière, *The Ignorant Schoolmaster: Five lessons in
intellectual emancipation*, trans. Kristin Ross, Stanford: Stanford University Press 1991, p. 105.
cf. Badiou, 'Philosophy and Politics', p. 71. 'What does equality mean? Equality means that
the political actor is represented under the sole sign of his specifically human capacity…
[t]his specifically human capacity is precisely thought, and thought is nothing other than
that by which the path of a truth seizes and traverses the human animal'.

43. This at once 'conservative and eclectic' tendency is ruthlessly at work in the theoretico-
policy work of the contemporary state system—at least here in Australia and especially
noticeable within the 'New Basics' regime of Education QLD. It is also very to the fore
in educational theory. This summary paragraph is all too exemplary: 'Each child, as a
unique human being, can be enlarged and enlivened in the inclusive, enactive environment of the transactional curriculum. In such classrooms the lived experience of students
and teacher co-exist, learning and knowledge co-emerge, the multiplicity of curricula
converge, nature and nurture co-originate as product and process; and, the cognitive and
non-cognitive learning of each as Other are brought forth through pedagogical love into
a new world of knowledge, acceptance and understanding. Truly, in such classroom set-
tings… "the light gets in", and heart in becomes heart of teaching'. Blaine E. Hatt, (Assist-
ant Professor, Faculty of Education) 'Heart In is Heart Of Teaching', in (funnily enough)
Ecclectica, December, 2000, http://www.ecclectica.ca/issues/2002/4/hatt.asp

nevertheless it is necessary to follow closely the trajectory of Badiou's diagnoses because it is against the 'saturation' of these schemata that he introduces his (un-explicated) and quite extraordinary notion that 'the only education is an education by truths' (HI 14). What we will do is explore the 'pedagogy of conditions' in Badiou's essay in order to understand how that which Badiou proposes as a 'fourth modality' of the pedagogical link between art and philosophy (HI 11), or of the re-entanglement of mathematics and philosophy,[44] or the subjective role of justice that philosophy will come to seize from politics[45] or the exact condition of the 'immanent two' that constitutes philosophy as a thought of love,[46] might offer a return of the pedagogical theme to itself, as an instance of overcoming its 'collapse' (HI 7).

Against the thesis that art is the being-there of truth, Badiou contends that the didactic schema treats art as mimesis. This, Badiou insists, accounts for art's singularity as a process (HI 9). Art functions as the charm of a truth. Its power, derived from its immediacy, consists in charming us away from the necessary 'dialectical labour' of reasoned argument that leads to principle (HI 2). Art is imitation, in regard to a certain effect of a truth extrinsic to art as a process. Art is true only insofar as it is a verifiable re-presentation of the Truth. This capitalized, substantialized Truth properly belongs to the regime of philosophy or at least to its police function. And as such truth is not a procedure immanent to art. In this sense there is no art other than what philosophy authorizes. As Badiou puts it, '[t]his position upholds a didactics of the senses whose aim cannot be abandoned to immanence. The norm of art must be education; the norm of education is philosophy' (HI 3). Here philosophy operates much as master to a pupil, verifying the truth of a work or, it's the same thing, its *good*, by the effect it has in its display (HI 3). In this schema, philosophy 'graduates' a work as art, subject to it effectively achieving a response in the spectator (the marker?) that the master, in accordance with the master's knowledge of the Truth, can verify as correct. The process of the work itself achieves only, and at best, the status of (the act of) re-presentation. Didacticism as a pedagogy places all power in the hands of the master and the master's knowledge. As Badiou argues in discussing the power of Brecht's didactic art, 'the philosopher is in charge of the latent supposition of a dialectical

---

44. Badiou, 'Mathematics and Philosophy', p. 37.
45. Badiou, 'Philosophy and Politics', p. 71.
46. Alain Badiou, 'The Scene of the Two', trans. Barbara P. Fulks, *Lacanian Ink*, no. 21, 2003, p. 55.

truth' (HI 6). It becomes essentially a question of sovereignty; a sovereignty retained by knowledge as truth over the mimesis achieved by mere practice; or, in another register; the intellectual over the manual. As we see in *The Republic* (at the point where it over-reaches itself—perhaps—in its desire to have done with 'sophistry') a strict protocol of surveillance is maintained between these two forms. An alienation is activated as all that proceeds in the city as the work of the day to day is only a semblance (or a semblance of a semblance) of the state. The truth of the state remains extrinsic to the functioning state. The 'obvious' gap opened by the 'protocol' of surveillance between the quotidian, working city-state and the sovereign truth of the state affirms the didactic demand of the 'extrinsic objectivity of the true' (HI 6).

Romanticism, essentially in total opposition to the educative surveillance of this schema, understands truth to be that of which art alone is capable. In Badiou's words regarding this schema, 'Philosophy might very well be the withdrawn and impenetrable Father—art is the suffering Son who saves and redeems' (HI 6) The relation between art and truth here is indeed one of immanence. The romantic schema proposes an education by its com-plex of pure subjective example. It is an example of a practice which in itself is one of truth absolutely, because it 'teaches of the power of infinity held within the tormented cohesion of a form' (HI 9). Thus, only what the artist unveils of the infinite through the finitude of the work is True. Philosophy (as hermeneutics) bears this as the fundamental ground of its relation to art. Badiou says, 'it is *the same truth that circulates between them*' (emphasis in original). The philosopher thinker is held in thrall to the artist poet for it is the poet alone who 'preserve[s], not Being itself …but the *question* of Being' (MP 50). Pedagogically speaking, romanticism, under this analysis, has something in common with pastoralism as its concerns are with the shepherding of that authenticity which (it supposes) inhabits the individual qua subject and which through the process invoked as its process alone, this Truth of the individual (literally, *of the individual*) might come to be revealed as the very speaking of Being. In this way the thinker (or teacher) is merely the reversal of the artist/poet/(true) subject, as they both approach the same truth. The truth reveals itself as Janus-like. Janus as shepherd of salvation from, *pace* Heidegger, the 'annihilation that Being, in the terminal technical figure of its destiny, has as its being to *will*' and pastorally, from the evil wrought by a certain ignorance (of God and all his shadows)[47] and towards a 'resacralisation…' (MP 52).

---

47. See Louis Althusser, 'Ideology and the State', In *Lenin and Philosophy and Other Essays,*

Contrary to Mao's dictum the two is here revealed as an effect of the one which is not at all a mere obverse of 'one divides into two'.[48] It is at this point that romanticism, despite itself, might be implicated in terms of the state. Ideologically—and therefore educationally—speaking, to locate the very agency that provides the ballast of the subject within each individual uniquely, serves at the same time to structure the alienation of one subject from another as an inherent law of Being, or nature. Thus the extrinsic, self-authorized truth of the state as the site of freedom is exhibited precisely through the authentic expression of alienation as effect. That is, the expression of this romantic alienation as the mark of the truth of being is not at all, at least under contemporary democratic state ideology, that of a radical separation but is precisely the kind of subjectivity authorized by that very state and (re)produced in its institutions.[49]

The third schema, classicism, removes the question of truth from art altogether. Badiou proposes that Aristotle employed this schema to defuse, albeit in an unsatisfactory manner, the quarrel between art and philosophy, As Badiou puts it, fusing Lacan and Aristotle, the classical

---

trans. Ben Brewster, New York, Monthly Review Press, 2000, where he says education as the dominant Ideological State Apparatus is 'as natural indispensable-useful and even beneficial to our contemporaries as the church was… for our ancestors a few centuries ago', p. 106.

48. Alain Badiou, 'One Divides into Two', trans. Alberto Toscano http://culturemachine. tees.ac.uk/frmf1.htm. In this essay, discussing revolutionary China in the 1960's, Badiou articulates the conflict of these two positions. The latter is considered leftist because its partisans hold that, from the perspective of the revolution, there is no view of the one as synthesis in sight. So it is a maxim of division and struggle, of, if you like, continuing to draw the consequences of a central antagonism. The former, in this essay 'two fuses into one' is considered rightist, reactionary, a plea for a return to the '*old one* under cover of syntheses'. It is a conflict that occurs in a different form, to give it a nominal mark, between Lenin and Kautsky. In both cases the reactionary form is the mark of a retreat, a throwing up of one's hands, a declaring of 'only a God can save us now'. This essay is translated from *Le Siècle*, Ch 6.

49. Badiou, BE, pp. 164-5. First published in English as 'Hegel', trans. Marcus Coelen & Sam Gillespie *Umbr(a)*, no. 1, 1996, p. 30. Badiou defines 'bad infinity' as the 'repetition of the alternative between one and another under the law of "ought to be"'. See also Alain Badiou, 'A speculative disquisition', *in Metapolitics*, p. 78. First published in English as 'Highly Speculative Reasoning on the Concept of Democracy', trans. Jorge Jauregui in *lacanian ink*, No. 16, 2001, at www.lacan.com, p. 1. 'Actually the word "democracy" is inferred from what I term "authoritarian opinion." It is somehow prohibited not to be a democrat. Accordingly, it furthers that the human kind longs for democracy, and all subjectivity suspected of not being democratic is deemed pathological'. We suggest that with certain grammatical changes in place the term 'education' can take the place of 'democracy' in these sentences and be understood in much the same way.

schema '*dehystericizes* art' (HI 6). It declares art innocent of either hysteri-
cally submitting its always already there-ness to the master's surveillance
or of incarnating, in the simultaneity of the declaration and its act, the
Truth—self-identity as profound alienation. Instead under Aristotle's classical prescription, which a certain 'applied *psychoanalysis*' (HI 7) carries
into the contemporary situation, art is subordinated not to knowledge, but
to its performance of an ethical function of therapy. It provides a space of
'catharsis' whereby art is that which 'makes it so that the object of desire
which is beyond symbolisation, can subtractively emerge at the very peak
of an act of symbolisation' (HI 7). It provokes an affirmative, captivating
and ultimately therapeutic effectiveness upon the passions. This effect is
rendered upon the passions through a process of 'liking', or *verisimilitude*,
in which the work of art within the regime of semblance provides that
likeness which 'calls to mind' *what is true* and arranges an identification
which is always ex-centred and yet at the same time does not command
the determination of the work itself (HI 4). Or, in more psychoanalytic
language, according to Badiou it 'links up to a transference because it exhibits, in a singular and contorted configuration, the blockage of the symbolic by the Real, the extimacy of the *objet petit a* (the cause of desire) to
the Other (the treasure of the symbolic)' (HI 7). The passions are relieved,
desire is pacified, merely having 'imagined' this ex-centred truth (or, *objet
petit a*) through the work of art.[50] Such a work, of itself, does not aim at this

---

50. It is interesting to note here what Lacan himself said about desire in the context of
state educators. In Seminar VII he says that desire—that desire one should never give up
on—has been 'domesticated by educators' and 'the academies', he says, 'betray it'. If we
recall Badiou's claim that 'a thought is nothing other than the desire to have done with
the exorbitant excesses of the state', we come across a suggestive link between thought and
desire. Further, Lacan says, and Alain Badiou takes this up, 'what I call "giving ground
relative to one's desire" is always accompanied in the destiny of the subject by some betrayal'. Lacan goes on to say that either the subject betrays himself in some way or that
someone with whom he is involved betrays that to which they were jointly committed and
this commitment is to some good. This betrayal sends the subject back to the service of
goods but he is forever out of joint there. So my contention is overall that education functions today as a betrayal. What does it betray? It betrays the good. That it betrays some
good rather than any individual in particular is both what allows this process of betrayal to
be 'tolerated' as Lacan says, (and one should hear this word especially in its contemporary
context) and also illustrates the essential disinterest of the state in individuals as such. This
good, as Lacan sees it, is that which 'serves to pay the price for access to desire' and desire
is, he says, a 'desire for both what we are and what we are not'. Betrayal thereby is an act,
rather a process that forecloses the possibility which inheres in the desire for the 'what we
are not'. Surely that desire or rather that we are desiring, is precisely that aspect of being
which sustains that side of the subjective disjunction that we, at any given time are not,
that which in fact we 'will have been'. This desire then is like a wager on the future, or on

Truth but renders its likeness 'constrain[able] within the imaginary', an effect recognizable by the 'catharsis' achieved by the spectator. 'Art', as Badiou says in relation to the classical schema, 'captures desire and shapes
[*éduque*] its transference by proposing a semblance of its object' (HI 5).
Such a state of affairs signals for Badiou, for whom truth and thought are
intimately identified, that art, innocent of truth is therefore not a form of
thought. It is, he says, little more than a 'public service' (HI 5). Under the
rule of patronage in the absolutist state so under the rule of 'arts councils'
then in contemporary capitalist bureaucracy (or democracy), the therapy
or, ethical catharsis that art will render must first be approved before any
funding is forthcoming. To Badiou, the state, in relation to the thinking of
art, is 'essentially' classical (HI 5).[51]

As I have suggested an effect issues in the contemporary state of these
three schema under the saturation of these tendencies.[52] So, to reiterate
and reduce: The didactic schema operates a pedagogy of surveillance, the
romantic, a pedagogy of authentic identity as alienation, and the classical,
a pedagogy of public service or state ethics. Thus, we can say, subtracting
from Badiou's otherwise occupied assessment, that surveillance, identity,
and ethics make up, the pedagogical forms inherent to the 'saturated'
20th century. According to Badiou, what these schemata have in common is the negative fact that all three propose a modality of this relation
that we 'must rid ourselves of' (HI 7). For Badiou, this commonality is

---

the very being of an encounter; a future other than that which it has always already been.
State education works its magic on the 'what we always already are' —the animal with
interests inscribed in the signifying chain, interests expressed materially by our activities
within the service of goods. How does a state education function in this way? Precisely
because it prescribes, through its errant power to deploy its knowledge, 'what we will do'
and what we *will do* subject to its demand is enter some-how, some-way—with a school
certificate or with a PhD—into the service of goods. And the more we enter into it as Lacan says, the more it demands. Thus what this demand must prevent is '...the least surge
of desire'. See Jacques Lacan, *Seminar VII The Ethics of Psychoanalyses*, Jacques-Alain Miller
(ed.), trans. Dennis Porter, London, W.W. Norton, 1997, pp. 311-325. One should also
juxtapose here Marx's analysis of the July days in his *18th Brumaire of Louis Bonaparte*, where
he says something remarkably similar in form regarding the betrayal of the proletariat by
the bourgeois-democratic party.
51. '[E]except for the socialist states which were "rather didactic"', HI, p. 5
52. I have shown elsewhere how actual policy prescription from the state in regard to the
everyday functioning of education can be seen to operate under the injunction of similar
schemata; whereby it operates a series of surveillance, alienation and an ethics thoroughly
conducive to the perpetuation of the state form. All of these are shown to be 'without
truth' in Badiou's sense. See my 'The Pedagogical Theme: Alain Badiou and an Eventless
Education', *anti-THESIS*, vol 16, 2006, pp. 129-147.

constituted by the fact that none of these schemata operate a pedagogical form that is both singular and immanent. It is because of this that they have offered nothing new. Concerned as we are with this link, with the 'pedagogical theme', we must insist on two points: One, that effectively the reduction of these three schema through their negative commonality allows us to claim that what has effected this collapse as its own, is a 'state' pedagogy. Second, that in regard to this state pedagogy it becomes possible to say that this collapse is a functional collapse.[53] The pedagogical theme under the saturation of the state schema functions as a collapse that at the same time maintains an impasse. The operational function here is nothing other than the perpetuation of the state or, the knowledge of the state—which in Badiou's words is the 'profit of statification, calculable interest and placement'.[54] And the impasse, as the effect of this operation, functions to preclude a subject from effecting the extent of its enquiries which is to say, 'a truth from coming to be'.

Under the condition of singularity (irreducible taking place of truth) and immanence (whereby the condition is 'rigorously co-extensive with the truth that it generates'), the 'pedagogical theme' is granted a specific task within the infinite procedure of a truth. It must be that which 'arrange[s] the forms of knowledge in such a way that some truth may come to pierce a hole in them' (HI 9).[55] Lest the philosophical act—the thoughtful composition of these disparate truths—be 'nothing but an academic quibble',

---

53. It is instructive to compare this tripartite schema with Badiou's own in 'What is a Thermidorean', where he analyses that which is constitutive of a sequence of Thermidor. Such a sequence is objective in its conception of the country, conservative in its conception of law and obsessed with security. Thus a triple alliance -objectivism, status quo and security. Under Thermidor—and Badiou is certainly explicit that Thermidor is now—a disarticulation is active. What it does is render a political sequence 'unintelligible'. It produces the unthinkable. This is what we claim a 'state' education involves. See, Badiou, M, p. 129.

54. Badiou, M, p. 136. For example, a pervasive slogan of education in Australia—one that enlists a wide and stupefying consensus—is that it functions to make one 'job-ready' or employ-able. One should above all *know* or rather, *be*, what the bosses want. Thus the good of education equates nicely with the 'profit' of these three. Badiou conceptualizes this nicely: 'Today, it seems that 'modernisation', as our masters like to call it, amounts to being a good little dad, a good little mum, a good little son, to becoming an efficient employee, enriching oneself as much as possible, and playing at the responsible citizen. This is the new motto: 'Money, Family, Elections'. See Badiou, *Le Siècle*, p. 100. Many thanks to Alberto Toscano for the use of his forthcoming translation. I cite the page number of the French edition.

55. Badiou borrows this from Lacan who is nothing less for Badiou than 'the educator for every philosophy to come'. See, Badiou, 'Truth: Forcing and the Unnamable', in *Theoretical Writings*, p. 119.

there must 'be truths'. '[To] make truths manifest... [is] to distinguish truths from opinion'. To decide therefore that there is 'something besides opinion' or, as Badiou 'provocatively' puts it, 'something besides our "democracies"' (HI 15). On Badiou's terms, education is that which makes the necessary arrangements for the manifestation of truths which are not opinions and which signify therefore the possibility for some other, new (political etc.) configuration. In fact using Badiou's analysis it is not going to far to claim that as our democracies are manifestations of the organized rule of opinion then the state system of education for which our democracies are responsible is without truth, without thought, and thus cannot operate other than as either 'oppressive or perverted' or indeed as both (HI 9).[56]

What is significant concerning an education which arranges the forms of knowledge in a way that can make truths appear therein is that this education can have no predication *in* those forms of knowledge. The process *is* immanent to the situation and it does proceed to work through the knowledge of the situation but that knowledge qua knowledge of the state (encyclopaedia) can have no determinative role over what is in essence a process of *fidelity to what happens* and not to *what is*. And this, as we know, because knowledge is a result; and as such, it never *encounters* anything. Knowledge is not that which is subject to the encounter but such an encounter is the very presupposition whose conditions of possibility it works to foreclose (BE 395).[57] This is why education, in Badiou's sense, is a (permanent?) revolutionary process, an auto (but not individualistic) education whose only predicate is the axiomatic form. An axiom being, as we have said, the immanently produced principle of the event; the formalizing, within a linguistic address capable of transmission, of that which has effectively disappeared. As such the subject, this finite support of the truth of this address, is in fact he/she/we/it which educates and is educated in the faithful process of this arrangement. Subject then to the inherent declaration of the political event, the equal capacity of all

---

56. What is perverted, we could say, is fidelity, what is oppressed is the (possibility of a) subject. Althusser's contention in regard to state education being the leading ISA in our epoch should be recalled here.

57. cf. Rancière. *The Ignorant Schoolmaster*, pp. 6-7. Rancière says this; 'before being the act of a pedagogue explication is the myth of pedagogy, the parable of a world divided into knowing minds and ignorant ones, ripe minds and immature ones, the capable and the incapable, the intelligent and the stupid'. Jacotot calls the method of the master 'enforced stultification'. The trick of the pedagogue in this sense is two. On the one hand the pedagogue decrees when learning is to begin; on the other he presents all that is to be learned as veiled and the pedagogue of course is the only one who can lift this veil.

for thought, the arrangements carried out by this subject of the forms of knowledge—or the enquiry of enquiries within the situation—will constitute a 'generically educative set', as each enquiry whose trajectory is regulated by chance, whose ethic amounts to the courage to continue, reveals elements of the initial set that confirm the justice (i.e. belonging) of the eventual declaration. The generic is not an act of representation but a regathering of presented terms—singularities—subject to their belonging (BE 396). And belonging is a relation whose intercourse with inclusion, or representation by the state, is not mutually reciprocal. The latter, being what the state in its excess must assume. Given then, that the pedagogical theme is effectively 'caught' in the non-space between what presents of truth subject to an event, and the state of that situation which is the procedure of annulment of the extensive consequences of these truths, this theme then must perform something of a dual operation of subtraction and forcing which in turn is the very constitution of itself. As such it becomes legitimate to say that education amounts to nothing more and nothing less than *establishing the effect of an encounter as a transformation.* And this is said of course under illegitimate conditions.[58]

SPECULATIVE REMARKS ON THE COMPLEX PROCEDURE: SUBTRACTION AND FORCING

'Transformation', in the work of Badiou, 'goes under the name of 'generic truth procedure'.[59] As we know, the generic truth procedures or, the conditions in relation to philosophy, produce these truths in the singular labour they perform. To put it bluntly they render an existence; an existence precisely, 'wrested from all founded inclusion', from that is, the knowledge that represents it as nothing. And 'nothing', as Badiou claims, 'can be granted existence… without undergoing the trial of its subtrac-

---

58. In passing, this authorizes us to turn the Socratic problem of the teaching of virtue (and despite the vicissitudes of 'interpretation' in regard to this term and the utilitarian disavowals, this *is* the ongoing question of education especially at a time when the state represents virtue) from a question into an axiom. Rather than consider virtue from the *perspective* of knowledge and then consider the mode of its transmission as such, we can instead now begin with the declaration 'virtue teaches'. Here we have the form of a truth whose veracity is wholly suspended in the procedure it authorizes. From this point the deductive process of subjecting this declaration to the real of the situation defines 'an education'. As Lacan put it, 'to be on the side of virtue is not to change under an effect of law'. 'Kant with Sade', *Ecrits.*
59. Oliver Feltham, 'And Being and Event and…: Philosophy and its Nominations', in *Polygraph*, no. 17, p. 27.

tion'.[60] To put it somewhat schematically the pedagogical theme in this process articulates the affirmative core of a taking away. The state form of education so long concerned with that which supports its addition—what the Brazilian Educator Paulo Friere once described not inappropriately, as a '*banking* education'—functions in thrall to a logic of quantitative repetition. As we have mentioned, it cannot conceive of itself as split or divided in any affirmative way and so its adding is always that which serves to repeat what it is under the law, as Badiou says, of 'what must be'. Thus to proffer truth as revolt against the state it is logically necessary to locate that which is negated by the state. And further in order to avoid transcendence or the appeal to any form of theology it is doubly necessary to affirm that 'void-site', affirmed through a process of 'taking away', as wholly within the situation ordered by the state. One, in fact, divides into two. Eschewing the explicative equations, we know, via the axioms of foundation and separation that any situation represented as a one is at some point constituted by a division, a point where the consistency, or the well ordered-ness, or constructability of the set or situation cannot hold. It is from this point that subtraction proceeds to render an existence, which is nothing more than the operations necessary to make being appear.

Subtraction essentially names four operations which Badiou says are irreducible to one another. They are: the undecidable, which philosophically is linked to the event; the indiscernible, linked to the subject; the generic to truth; and the unnameable to an ethics of truths.[61] Essentially, subtraction works by 'voiding' all predication. As an operation of thought it asserts the primacy of being over language. However, Badiou cautions, it is not a process of extraction, of 'drawing out of' but it is one which 'draws under'.[62] For Badiou, there is no position from which to operate upon a situation other than from within that very situation. As is the case in all Badiou's analyses however, there can be no clearing of the ground *before* something takes place.[63] So this removal of predication is a part of the very process initiated by the act of irruption or surrection within the situation. What marks the difference between an event as an interruption within the situation and say a strike for wages and conditions,

60. Badiou, 'On Subtraction', p. 103.
61. Badiou, 'On Subtraction', p. 111. The latter term has disappeared in recent times. We will maintain it here as it nevertheless has an ethical truth to it which continues in Badiou's work under new names, perhaps.
62. Badiou, 'On Subtraction', p. 111.
63. 'Destruction was my Beatrice', Badiou says, quoting Mallarmé, comparing his *Théorie du sujet* to *L'être et l'événement*. *Le Siècle*, p. 85.

is precisely that in the latter the state is immediately able to include such an interruption within its order of operations. It may instigate negotiations, declaim the strikers in the press or send in its police but in any case such a strike 'fits' within the logic and knowledge of the state.[64] The logic of subtraction pertains to the event in an intrinsic form. The event so to speak undoes or will have undone, through its sheer novelty, the order of this knowledge of inclusion and thus, subtracting from the state of the situation its formal process of evaluation, it opens a space which marks the immanent separation of the truth of the state from its knowledge.[65]

However, as we know, it is of the very 'empirical character' of the event to disappear. And as Badiou says, 'this is why it will always be necessary to say... the event has taken place'.[66] This statement in effect constitutes a decision for the undecidable. Effectively it is a decision which intervenes in the indices between the event and its naming as an event. The decision decides for the event, itself subject to pure contingency. It is constitutively an act of fidelity which is ontologically prior to any 'formal announcement'. It is a pure 'yes' saying, to use a Nietzschean formula, but within the confines of a wager. The decision says nothing more than that which happened, happened. The decision founds a declaration; to the effect that what has disappeared has being and it is to this declaration that the subject is faithful. The subject, being that which crosses any temporal conditions by declaring a fidelity to a sequence that 'will have been true' and at the same time pursues the consequences of this 'evental occurring' within the situation as the finite being that it (also) is. The pursuit of the consequences has no predicative order, no established law by which the subject guides itself in its enquiries. As Badiou puts it, such a subject is 'a hazardous trajectory without a concept' one who can find no verifiable comfort in the representations of the object of his enquiry or from the principle of objectivity more generally.[67] What then is the logic of this subject's progress given that it is faced at every turn with the necessity

---

64. Indeed most strikes today in the rich 'west' seem to a priori fit themselves to the demands of the state. At a recent teachers' 'rally' in Melbourne the police were accorded an ovation for their efforts at securing the march. In their clamour to 'professionalize', many teacher organisations have adopted the term 'pedagogy' to describe their 'praxis'. There is a naive accuracy to this as all too often we see these 'pedagogues' acting toward the state in the manner of slavish petitioners desirous only of being well thought of by their master. Althusser reminds us to account for the militant exceptions: 'They are a kind of hero'. These 'exceptions' are active today in Latin America in particular.

65. Badiou, 'On Subtraction', p. 111.

66. Badiou, 'On Subtraction', p. 111.

67. Badiou, 'On Subtraction', p. 111, also BE, p. 394.

to choose and yet due to its fidelity to a disappearing and devoid of a law of operation, it has no way to distinguish between terms? Given this situation, whatever terms present to the subject for choosing, present as properly indiscernible. We must first backtrack somewhat for it appears we have two subjects; one which decides for the undecidable and one which is 'co-ordinated by the indiscernible'.[68] We must recall that we are tracking the trajectory of a truth as it makes its way across a situation. We could say the four figures of subtraction mark the stations of its progress. In regard to a temporal schema it is not the case that one station follows the other in a graduated stage of becoming. There is no particular time frame or objective determination which either verifies the time of a truth nor determines the instances of the subject within a chronological form. The schema of the truth procedure is operationally structural and it is true to say that a truth after circuiting the trajectory of the structure under the logic of subtraction, will only be seen or be 'known' to have been true once it has effectively returned as the 'knowledge of the subject'. This subject, Badiou says, in relation to its procedure is 'ruled in its effects, but entirely aleatory in its trajectory' (BE 394). Thus to decide for the undecidable is to immediately be situated between the event and the void; two indiscernible terms. And in terms of Badiou's schema, this place is 'at the edge of the void'.[69] The subject then is structurally situated between— or is founded as the split of—the disappearance which it has decided for and the void, or nothing, from which the order of its trajectory must be drawn. It is not that the subject so situated has to choose between nothing and nothing. Rather, it is that the subject faithful to this constitution as the fragment of a disappearance and the order of the void proceeds to make enquires from the perspective of a truth that *will have been 'true'* and not from that of the knowledge of the state. Thus, as the logic of truth is such that it addresses itself to all indifferent to differences—circumcized or uncircumcized, Greek or Jew—the subject proceeds as that which does the work of indiscernibility, effectively subtracting the mark of difference.[70] The subject proceeds with what Badiou calls confidence, a 'knowing belief' (BE 397). Belief being, Badiou says, the 'what is to come under the *name* of truth' (BE 397), such that, pedagogically speaking, the

---

68. Badiou, 'On Subtraction', p. 113.

69. We could posit that it is precisely at this point that mathematical inscription and poetic inscription 'meet'. See, Alain Badiou, 'Lacan and the pre-Socratics', in Slavoj Žižek (ed.), *Lacan: The Silent Partners*, London, Verso, 2006, p. 11.

70. Alain Badiou, *St Paul: The foundation of universalism*, trans. Ray Brassier, Stanford University Press, Stanford, 2003, p. 26.

knowledge the subject has recourse to, is essentially this confidence. This confidence equates with the belief that what is discernible is subject to an order of thought whose trajectory, is indiscernible. The subject has confidence that the truth to come will have been true for the very situation within which the subject proceeds to conduct its enquiries (BE 397). Such confidence, we can say, owes its modal power to that procedure Badiou names 'forcing'; '*a fundamental law of the subject*' (BE 401).

The complex ontological exposition of 'forcing' (the term taken from Paul Cohen) is beyond the scope of this essay. Instead, in order to situate the subject as that which performs this act and as that which constitutes itself in this act, we will sketch its topology in a speculative interlacing of Badiou's concept with the notion of the pedagogical theme. Let's preface what we are here faced with: an understanding or rather a declaiming of education as contingent, risky, without predicate, opposed to knowledge, subject to fidelity, to courage, to a certain ruthlessness in regard to continuing. Education in essence is founded on the chance encounter between a site and its inconsistency, that sets forth subtractively to maintain this irruptive demand from pure multiplicity by a forcing of its truth through the terms already known to the situation. With such effect that a transformation literally *takes place*. To go to school, sit up straight, attend, repeat with a certain facility and graduate well behaved, which includes of course suitable acts of rebellion, certainly appears the simpler form.

To educate is certainly to transform. To have been educated is no doubt to have been transformed. Thus education amounts to either 'being' or, 'to have been' transformed. The questions, of course, are: by what, from what, to what? Is it by the state whose goal is perpetuation and whose method thereby is predicated on meiosistic repetition or, in Althusser's more 'structural' terms reproduction (of the relations of production)? Or is it by truths and thus to be transformed without predicate, educated without curriculum, subject to the 'what will have been' by grace of the event? A procedure which is at once immanent and thus without surveillance and singular in that it universally presents singularities without representation (BE 401). But what is this thing that is being or has been transformed? Certainly contemporary democratic educational logic, as we have seen above, performs a process of subjectivisation whose goal is the creation of a certain individual(s) fit for the state. This state mode of transformation apprehends the collective as a generically amorphous mass, both empty of what it is that makes them fit for the state and possessed of nothing but this. This mass is then that which, via the processes of the state, will be operated on in such a way that it will render to the state individuals capable of performing pursuant to the norms, laws and procedures of the state. The subjectivizing process of the state as transformation from equality of ignorance to equitable redistribution as heterogenous entities conforming to its 'count' renders a re-presentation of ideologically self-identifying individuals. It achieves a sort of one to one correspondence in which each, libidinally invested in the other, considers an 'objective' interest to be theirs in common.[71] That is, the state guarantees the suitably educated subject access to his/her interests. As suitably educated, the interests of this subject will correspond, more or less, to the interest of the state.[72] And of course in its excess the state terrifies this subject through its retaining the imminent threat of withdrawal. Its excessive count *for* one, that operation by which a state is the state of the situation, collecting one-multiples into one-parts constitutively threatens un-representation. Its subjects are thus those whose very representation as 'a' subject is subject to their desire for representation. Such a desire is the very constitution of their subjectivity. Such is why theories of recognition are so attractive in social theory today. And such is why notions like adaptability, flexibility and 'availability for learning across the life-span' proves so intensive in educational discourse. These are of course pure subordinate responses to the state as excess provided by the state itself for the subject: A balm for permanently open sores and they remind us of nothing less—and this is entirely appropriate in this context—of Lacan's description, 'from a philosophical perspective', of the truth of human

---

71. In this 'new and risky future' the *New Basics* will deliver a student who is 'flexible', 'adaptable', capable of a form of 'self-analysis that copes with this flexibility' and possesses an 'educability'—for 'retraining across the life-span through a range of media'. The student will be capable of 'designing him/herself a 'social future', be proficient in the 'care *and maintenance of the self*' and practice an 'active citizenship'—*within* our 'democracy'. It should come as no surprise that the theoretical parameters of the three year longitudinal research of which the 'New Basics' is both a result and an experiment were coordinated by a constructivist and reconceptualist paradigm. See, *New Basics Research Paper*. No. 2. 'Synthesis and Research'. p. 6 http://education.qld.gov.au/corporate/newbasics/ and *New Basics Technical Paper*, pp. 85-6 Lacan's remark in relation to Sade's treatise on the education of young girls should be recalled here: 'The victim is bored to death by the preaching and the teacher is full of himself', Lacan, 'Kant with Sade', *Ecrits*, p. 664/787.
72. A subject capable of making their way within a 'globalized information environment' Such a subject [will help] '...gain access to the benefits (sic) of the knowledge economy of the future...'[a]nd 'will improve our [QLD's] economic performance'. Non-performance' of this 'role', this document says, has 'dire consequences for the individual'. See, Education QLD 2010, 'New Basics Research Program', 2003, pp. 3-10. Available through http://education.qld.gov.au/corporate/newbasics/. The use of the term 'role' is somewhat fascinating, but we leave it to 'sit' here.

rights as 'the freedom to desire in vain'.[73] Opposed to this is the subjectivizing process of the generic truth procedure whose initiation in the event
as disruption of the state—of precisely its excess—convokes a collective
as *subject* (in the case of a political situation). Its address, so to speak, is
carried by the practice of its thought; by that of which 'we are equally
capable'. For Badiou, no subject at all precedes this subject. Subject to the
axiomatic declaration of an equal capacity for thought any one (multiple)
might be/could be/can be transformed from public alienation into the
collective subject alienated *from* the public. This is a subject at once *of* and
to truth. Of this we can say that a subject is that which at each stage 'will
have been educated'. So there are two readings of what it is to be transformed. On the one hand, the 'thing' is transformed into an individual
issuing as and within the states permanent reordering of its parts. Representation here makes void the possibility of 'generic extension'. That is
to say, the site of the generic is represented as nothing. And on the other,
from the egalitarian multiple is subtracted, subject to the disappearance
that is the empirical mark of an event, the generic set whose trajectory
as infinite collection proceeds by subtracting itself at every step from the
logic of the situation in which it labours.

What then makes this anything but some form of anarchic wandering? What makes this education by truths distinct from no education at
all or mere reaction? The state is after all (and this is a symptom we must
be very attentive to, I suggest, such is the basis for this exploration) de-
terminedly focussed on an 'education for all'. Publicly, this is seen as its
chief credit or virtue (just think of the dialectic of election time rhetoric
and publicity where education is demanded by the state and equally by
its petitioners) and again we must be attentive to this as a symptom. What
serves to differentiate here are two things: One, as we have seen, is the
event itself. It establishes the possibility for the new in being. A subject
is convoked who, under the discipline of a fidelity to that which is disappeared, itself becomes a rising of that which was not. Secondly, in regard
to the subject we must ask the question, what does this subject hold to?
The subject is that which is caught in a procedure between what has gone
and what is to come. We know that truths interrupt knowledge, that they
are in fact an a-voidance of (the determinants of) knowledge and so on.
But what of the subject split by the 'two'? How can it avoid knowledge?
The question in relation to forcing is two-fold. On the one hand there is
some knowledge, while on the other, by fidelity, this subject is faithful to

---

73. Lacan, 'Kant with Sade', *Ecrits*, p. 661, 783.

that knowledge which is sustained in its veracity *as knowledge* by the future anterior and as such, it is knowledge that is itself the *effect* of a 'rearrangement'. It is in this space that education by truths is enacted. Between the event and its forcing, or rather, *as its forcing*, a subject is educated. To quote Badiou:

> What one must be able to require of oneself, at the right time, is rather that capacity for adventure to which ontology testifies, in the heart of its transparent rationality, by its recourse to the procedure of the absurd; a detour in which the extension of their solidity may be restituted to the equivalences: 'He shatters his own happiness, his excess of happiness, and to the Element which magnified it, he rends, but purer, what he possessed' (BE 254).

Badiou's claim that 'the only education is an education by truths' demands in fact that this equation result. Thus we can say that, as the finite carrier of an infinite procedure, a truth, it is only a subject who is *educated*.

It has been argued elsewhere that forcing constitutes the real praxis of the subject and I can only concur with this.[74] By extension, I am suggesting that it is entirely within a praxis of this type that an education takes place, whereas in the state situation 'nothing takes place but the place' which is to say the 'positive' production of impasse. So rather than force a subject to be educated, in this idea, forcing, as that complex of the subject, is what educates. As part of the complex of forcing we can say that it is by non-knowledge that the subject proceeds. As we have seen, the subject follows no curriculum, no pre-established method in its enquiries. That it makes inquiries at all is, as Badiou says, subject to chance: On the one hand, the chance of an event occurring and, on the other, the decision for its occurring qua event. But with no 'method', how does the subject proceed?

For any 'obscure occurrence' to be an event it must produce its name in the subject. The name given by the subject, as an act of its very subjectivity, under condition of the event, belongs in the first instance to the subject-language. It is the singleton of the occurrence in Badiou's terms. This name is the minimal condition of the subject qua enquiries, or for us, of the subject qua education. How then to 'remake' the name, a name already included by state knowledge, into a name belonging to the occurrence? That is, how does the name make eventable that which is 'obscure'? In this first instance the subject supports the transitory status of the name

---

74. Oliver Feltham, *As Fire Burns: Of Ontology, Praxis, and Functional Work*, unpublished PhD diss., Deakin University, 2000.

which is at once attached to an obscurity and an encyclopaedia. In a sense this is a first instance of 'tearing holes in knowledge'. The name is subtracted from the encyclopaedia of the state for which language is the 'medium of commensurability between itself and the situation it represents' (BE 288). The void, by which the name as supernumery is founded as exposed, is mobilized in the subjective procedure of forcing. Precisely through this immanent gap—between the presentation of inconsistency marked by the event and its consistent presentation marked by the (void) name of this event—a truth procedure authorizes itself. Forcing hereby names the procedure of tearing the name from encyclopaedic inclusion and remaking it as belonging to the event.[75] Similarly to the dual nominalism of 'condition', 'forcing' also names the arduous process of this becoming-true, of which fidelity is the ethic of a militant operation and subtraction the mode of deployment. By its series of enquiries the subject establishes, in the first instance, the connection or non-connection of this name to the multiples of that situation through which it works (BE 330). This is the procedure which establishes (or does not) the grounds for the universality inherent to the disappeared event by organizing via connections the 'belonging to' the 'generic set'. Thus these enquiries follow a militant trajectory of connection—multiples subtracted from the laws of presentation—and a subsequent decided deployment rather than a 'scholarly' process which by (institutional) instinct and not by thought, seeks to mediate and not commit.[76] Structurally speaking, we could say that the scholar marks the 'place of announcement'.

'Education for all', that common refrain of the representative state, thus takes on a very different and critically particular meaning in this process than that which is meant by this state. To put it schematically, we might say that the latter is concerned with what to do with its subject within the confines of a state, and the former with the extension 'for all' of that which a subject is capable.[77] At every step, forcing articulates the

---

75. Thus, Badiou calls the statement of the subject-language in regard to names 'bricolés'. See Alain Badiou, *L'être et l'événement*, Paris, Éditions du Seuil, 1988, p. 441. Barker translates this as 'makeshift' (p. 107), and Feltham as 'cobbled-together', BE, p. 403. The point is that this name is brought about by a forced relation between the language of the situation and the subject-language. The latter itself is a part of the former but is co-coordinated by a different 'logic'. See Jason Barker, *Alain Badiou: A Critical Introduction*, London, Pluto Press, 2002.

76. Hallward, *Badiou*, p. 126.

77. In relation to Badiou's newer work in which the faithful subject opens a space within which the 'reactive subject' and the 'obscure subject' can also come to exist, we can argue that what education today educates for is a 'reactive subject'. This is a subject who

crucial aspect of this minimal difference by its imposition of its positive connections. The name of the event thus holds as that single term by which the infinite of the truth of the event may become veridical over and above its declaration.[78] But as was mentioned above, this is not, as some have intimated, simply the coming of a truth back to knowledge. Or rather; it is and it is not.[79] The whole point of Badiou's enterprise is of course that the situation as it is is transformed in truth. Thus the statement 'for every situation there is a truth' is, as we can see, the complex of a disjunction and its synthesis or, the 'junction of a disjunction' (BE 239). This is because this statement contains two temporal schemas. First, the schema marked by the claim 'for any situation there *will be* a truth' and by the statement, 'for any situation there will *have been* a truth' and thus the knowledge that 'returns' is precisely not the knowledge that was. And further this knowledge does not by necessity merely reprise the structural form of the previous knowledge for that situation. As Andrew Gibson has made a point of, what are forced are generic extensions to the situation and not the constructions of 'new' situations entirely.[80] As Cohen showed

---

is constituted by an education which tells that an event is unnecessary, that attempts at establishing 'justice' are not worth it, that truths are relative (or belong to 'fact' alone), and that opinion and consensus decide the political and so on. What is of interest is that the 'obscure subject' and the 'reactive subject' seem to have an investment in each other.

78. One should recall here Badiou's text on Nietzsche where he singles out Nietzsche's conflation of the declaration and the event as the form of an archi-politics. See, 'Who is Nietzsche?' *Pli: Warwick Journal of Philosophy*, no. 11: Nietzsche: Revenge and Praise, 2001.

79. In relation to what we are calling the pedagogical theme—that truths mobilize a desire for the end of the state—what we mark here is that Socrates' crime is all that it is made out to be. Socrates does not bring knowledge but rather he submits all to the singular procedure of subtracting truth from knowledge. Plato describes this in the *Sophist* as that of 'follow[ing] our statements step by step and, in criticizing the assertion that a different thing is the same or the same thing is different in a certain sense, to take account of the precise sense and the precise respect in which they are said to be one or the other'. Having hereby affirmed the procedure affirmed in the Socratic practice he then goes onto impute to the sophist a method 'like' but ultimately unlike, due to its proximity to the sensual and the immediate. He says, 'merely to show that in some unspecified way the same is different or the different is the same, the great small, the like unlike, and to take pleasure in perpetually parading such contradictions in argument—that is not genuine criticism, but may be recognized as the callow offspring of a too recent contact with reality'. Plato, 'Sophist', in *Plato's Theory of Knowledge: The Theaetetus and the Sophist*, trans. F. M. Cornford, Mineola, Dover Publications, 2003, 259b-d, pp. 297-8. See also Plato, 'Parmenides', in *Plato and Parmenides: Parmenides' Way of Truth and Plato's Parmenides*, trans. F.M. Cornford, London, Routledge & Kegan Paul, 1939, p. 113.

80. Andrew Gibson, 'Repetition and Event: Badiou and Beckett', *Communication and Cognition*, vol 37, no. 3-4, 2004, p. 271.

ontologically and Badiou here translates philosophically in relation to being and truth, a generic set is situated precisely in the space 'normally' occupied by the state. And this space is the immeasurable excess of inclusion
over belonging: An excess for which, in Badiou's metaontology, the event
provides the first measure.[81] The price for the avoidance of transcendence, as for holding fast to the axiom 'the one is not', is that of extension.
Extension, however, is in no way reform. The latter, as we know, is almost
constitutive of the contemporary state. It exists only to reform and this reform is of course in order to better capture whatever threatens to escape.
And nowhere it seems as much as in education (and this is consensual) is
this type of reform regarded as imperative.[82] Extension of course is the
extension by evental rupture of that which was represented as nothing—
precisely the 'truth of the situation'. Somewhat paradoxically but logically,
representation exposes the unique singularity immanent to the situation
it represents —that of the void, the very possibility of extension, of same/
other. The subject is again this figure of, or rather *in*, extension. To put it
somewhat enigmatically we can say that extension is what 'sames in truth'
what was 'other in knowledge'. Thus the modality of extension is forcing
and thus the subjective trajectory is that which is forced on two sides. The
two relate to Cohen in particular. On the one hand the subject comes to
be under the axiom of choice. It decides itself into being as it decides for
the undecidable; that an obscure occurrence is an event subtracted from
all knowledge; or as Badiou puts it, *'knowledge knows nothing of this'* (BE 332,
Badiou's italics). On the other 'side' the subject is forced by that which
continues. It continues faithful to the undecidability which it has decided
for.[83] It has decided that there will have been a something (rather than
nothing) to decide for. Structured in this way it can hold fast to the name
subtracted from (thus independent of) the state encyclopaedia but *known*

---

81. Hallward, *Badiou*, p. 131.

82. Again this should be read as symptomatic and not as evidence of the state's good intent.
It has two forms. On the on hand the state must of course organize the worker/consumer
in such a way as to be readily available in the right way for subjection to the dominant
relations of production. But it must also do this under the ideological cloak that it thereby
reflects the 'non-ideological authentic longing'—to quote from Žižek—of the population
for precisely what is perceived of education, as being that which is more than just such a
'job readiness'. The idea that education is not just utilitarian training is that idea, prevalent
in the community at large, which enables the capture of all under the education system. A
system dear to the state for reasons already outlined.

83. Cohen, of course, proved the independence of CH from the axioms of set theory. CH
is thus 'undecidable'.

to the subject by its *belonging* to the 'makeshift' subject language.[84] The real force of the subject then is precisely the maintenance of this 'complex of forcing'.

The subject, as we have seen, has nothing, purely nothing, as its curricular instruction; no method, no syllabus, no state. The trajectory of the educated subject is a-voidance, of the state and of knowledge. It is separated from the state by its non-knowledge and from the truth that will have been by an 'infinite series of aleatory encounters' (BE 399). What it has is pure structure or rather pure axioms of operation by which it regards every step of its enquiries. Such is why fidelity for Badiou is drawn from mathematical procedures of deduction and not from its theological variant.[85] And we propose that this fidelity, under the complex of forcing, extends into the situation itself. Should such a truth procedure be 'forced' into the situation, should a truth come to be that which it was, fidelity to that fidelity which extended and sustained the procedure does not end. Should there be an end, then decidedly we have had reform but not revolution, not transformation.[86] Even though Badiou reminds us that knowledge in its constructivist orientation with its 'moderated rule, its policed immanence to situation and its transmissibility' is unavoidable, he at the same time reminds us that this is the 'ordinary regime of the relation to being under circumstances in which it is not time for a new temporal foundation, and in which the diagonals of fidelity have somewhat deteriorated for lack of complete belief in the event they prophesise'. Then again, Badiou claims that even for those 'who wander on the borders of evental sites staking their lives' on events, 'it is, after all, appropriate to be knowledgeable' (BE 294). But even as it is in the process of enquiries that a faithful subject approximates a procedure of knowledge, such enquiries are nevertheless first and foremost a matter of a militant fidelity. Such a fidelity demands that the void constitutive of every situation not be foreclosed or veiled or counted as no-thing but be rigorously marked

---

84. To the state what the 'subject knows' is precisely nothing at all. In Platonic terms the subject is that which can claim only that it 'knows nothing'. This claim 'places the void' within the situation. Non-knowledge as void of knowledge is that name of the void which is the very mark of *their* knowledge. The subject sets their enquiries by this mark in order not to fall back into the knowing comforts of the state—such as they are.

85. A variant still very prominent in the methods of the state through the pastoral-welfare complex it runs as an ideological 'soul supplement' to the material 'syllabus of the market'.

86. Ultimately this is why Badiou talks of exhaustion not ends. A procedure can become exhausted, subjects may be lacking, but the truth for which a subject is a subject has not, by this, come to an end. And nor are we finished with truths.

as such: Which is to say that this, at a certain point, necessary coincidence with knowledge must not itself be coincident with a taming by the state (BE 294). Only in this way is 'justice done' and subjects appear in their belonging as constituted by this very fidelity to their belonging, and not as the mere consequence of an 'inclusive education'.[87] That is to say that ontology, which presents beings in the singularity of belonging, links with truth as that which is true for all or not at all and with justice which is the philosophical name for equality whose very being is the presentation of a 'communism of singularities'. Ultimately the invariance that pertains to education, to the name education in the generic phrase 'education for all', is that which today must be forcefully subtracted from the state; which is to say the one multiple that it is must be found to be 'indiscernible and unclassifiable for the encyclopaedia' of the state (BE 333). Plato's *Republic* was one attempt at this, being as it was an ideal non-state articulated on the basis of a certain event within the state (of the situation).[88] As Badiou has said, we need a 'new Republic' for it is quite obvious that today the educated-subject—a being struck by the desire to think the truth that it also is, and thereby produce a generic present—is precisely that which cannot be tolerated. As Badiou says, such a subject, linked as it is to the infinity of a truth and its generic indiscernibility, is 'without qualification' (BE 408) and fundamentally irreducible to 'the pedagogy of the world as it goes'. [89]

---

87. As is well known, 'inclusion' is the concept of the age. It and 'recognition' form the crux of a weak leftism—taken up by the 'democracies' as their rhetoric of choice—which still sees a state education, a state program, as the way to (social) justice. Or, to use the timid and defeated contemporary form, 'equality of opportunity'.

88. Like Plato, what we object to is the claim that this state education *is* an education. For if the only education is an education by truths then this cannot be an education at all unless the state can in some way be equated with truth. This is precisely what Plato seeks to found, this knot of truth and the state in his 'thought institution' named the *Republic*. This designation of the *Republic* as 'not a state' goes against the very language Plato uses to describe his republic but, so I would argue, not against his thought. That Plato deemed it necessary to invent an entirely new form by which to support this truth in its transmission is what legitimates this notion that the *Republic* is not the repetition of 'the state'. And neither is it an ideal state; it is rather the *idea of a non-state*: precisely a utopia.

89. Alain Badiou, *Théorie du sujet*, Paris, Seuil, 1982, p. 318.

art

9

An Explosive Genealogy:
Theatre, Philosophy and the Art of Presentation

Oliver Feltham

> 'Il n'y a la peste,
> le choléra,
> la variole noire
> que parce que la danse
> et par conséquent le théâtre
> n'ont pas encore commencé à exister'
> —Antonin Artaud, 'Le Théâtre de la cruauté', 1947[1]

It is not only in the conceptual reconstruction but in the straightforward application of Badiou's thought that its problems and tensions come to light. When things are no longer quite so straightforward perhaps we can start to think. The purpose of this paper is thus to identify a generic truth procedure in the domain of art; specifically within theatre. It turns out that in doing so one ends up sketching an explosive genealogy whose effects cannot be easily contained.

I. THE HISTORICAL SITUATION

Where to start? The question of origins is tricky in Badiou's thought and not only because the temporality of a truth procedure is that of the future anterior. For the sake of the argument let's start where Badiou's theory of praxis appears to start: with the existence of a historical situa-

---

1. Antonin Artaud, *Oeuvres Complètes*, vol. XIII, Paris, Gallimard, 1974, p. 105-118.

tion in one of the four conditions of philosophy.[2] For us: the situation of theatre at the turn of the twentieth century. Given Badiou's ontology, we know that this situation is an infinite multiplicity, and that any attempt to circumscribe it linguistically presupposes the excess of its being over any specification of its properties. Thus we should not be embarrassed by our historical situation traversing national and European cultural spheres to include that of Russia which itself includes elements of India (the influence of Hindi philosophy and yoga on Stanislavski).

II. THE EVENT

It is evident that what goes under the name of 'theatre' today is far more varied than what went under that name in the late nineteenth century; thus a certain transformation must have taken place. The problem is where to situate *an* event that marks the beginning of that transformation. I hold that it is the Meyerhold-event—the *dual* advent of Meyerhold's scandalous and innovative productions *and* his writings, which occurred at the beginning of the transformation of the situation called 'theatre'. There are four reasons for this:[3]

     1.   In Meyerhold's work the plasticity of the acting body is liberated from the constraints of mimesis via the exploratory system of exercises called 'biomechanics'.

---

2. It actually starts with the axioms of set-theory ontology; to be specific the axiom of infinity is fundamental because a *finite* truth procedure would be indistinguishable from the unfolding of state knowledge. For the vexed question of the interdependence of Badiou's set theory ontology and his theory of praxis see Ray Brassier, 'Presentation as Anti-Phenomenon in Alain Badiou's *Being and Event*', *Continental Philosophy Review*, 2006.

3. Why not call Stanislavski's Moscow Art Theatre's productions, especially the 1898 production of the *Seagull* an event? It does seem to be an event insofar as Stanislavski imports Eastern techniques such as yoga to transform his actor training. Of course, one could argue that these techniques are appropriated and employed in the service of mimetic naturalism which was not a new orientation in Western art. On the other hand, the effects of such importation were not necessarily predictable or containable; once these exercises and techniques of corporeal exploration are introduced, they inevitably break the bounds of naturalistic acting. I think Stanislavski's fundamental innovation, and this is obvious in the work of his disciples Eugene Vakhtangov and Michael Chekhov, is the introduction of the laboratory model of rehearsal. The final objection, however, to there being a Stanislavski-event in Badiou's sense is that he installs and reinforces the very fourth wall between the actors and spectators which so many twentieth century directors attempted to dismantle.

2. Meyerhold consciously worked to liberate theatrical space from the box-set with its illusional painted scenery and pro-scenium arch.[4]

3. Meyerhold named the fourth wall as an obstacle to be dis-mantled insofar as the spectator was to be transformed into a co-creator.

4. The mask is reintroduced as essential to theatre along with clowning, mime and play-acting.[5]

All of these elements were present in Meyerhold's work from 1907 onwards, over a decade before he attempted to create a proletarian thea-tre in line with the October revolution.[6] In Meyerhold's essays he names his own productions as evental, claiming that his work along with that of a few other directors constituted 'the stylized theatre' that answers the demands of the age. Thus the Meyerhold-event—which is fragile, note, *not just ontologically* but in its very mode of appearance; the ephemeral-ity of performance—is named in polemical writings which then circulate amongst theatre practitioners.

III. THE OPERATOR OF FIDELITY

But for a truth procedure to ensue from an event not just a name but an operator of fidelity must emerge, and this is where things get tricky. In the four constituent elements of the Meyerhold-event identified above there is a common phrase which could be taken as the operator of fidelity; the phrase 'liberate theatre from the constraints of X'. Any innovation in twentieth century theatre could thus be taken as faithful to the Meyer-hold-event and as part of the truth procedure *if* it liberates theatre from a constraint. But then what do we end up with? A story of progressive liberation that looks suspiciously like Clement Greenberg's classic history

---

4. 'Meyerhold fut sur le point de réaliser un théâtre conçu sur ce principe: forme ovulaire, double aire de jeu, amphithéâtre enveloppant un plateau d'ailleurs relié à la salle par des passerelles… le projet manqua de justesse'. In Mikhail Barkhine and Serge Vakhtangov 'Le batiment théâtral moderne vu par Meyerhold', *Revue d'Histoire du Théâtre*, 1967-4, p. 350.

5. Meyerhold attempts to reintegrate *commedia dell'arte* into high theatre. In his seminal essay 'The Fairground Booth' Meyerhold rehabilitates the following terms as key to his conception of theatre: *mummery*—ridiculous ceremonial, religious ritual which is silly or hypocritical, performance by mummers; *mummers*—actors in a traditional masked mime or dumbshow, poor actors, play actors; *cabotin*—strolling player, third rate ham.

6. See Meyerhold, *Meyerhold on Theatre*, trans. E. Braun, London, Metheun, 1969, p. 159-67.

of modernism as a teleological sequence of increasingly radical breaks. If all we can do after Badiou's conceptual fireworks is replicate Greenberg then we're wasting our time. In the introduction to *Being and Event* Badiou exhorts the philosopher to circulate through the referential of the four conditions. If one circulates through art nowadays, even just a little bit, one soon realizes that Greenberg's account is obsolete. The trick is to identify another operator of fidelity—in fact, the *re*introduction of masks and mummery already does not fit this schema of liberation. Evidently the operator has to be material, it has to figure within the situation to be transformed. It also has to be transmissible and it has to be general insofar as it can be used to judge the connection or non-connection of distant multiples to the Meyerhold-event. At present I hold the operator of fidelity to be the following sentence and in particular its last three words—found in a 1907 essay: 'We intend the audience not merely to observe, but to participate in a *corporate creative act*.'[7] The operator of fidelity is actually a concept which does a lot of work in Badiou's theory of praxis, perhaps too much work; it alone determines the consistency of a truth procedure. Before going into this we need to determine where this truth procedure starts: what is the evental-site for the Meyerhold event?

IV. THE EVENTAL SITE

If a site, strictly speaking, is evental only insofar as an event occurs, then we can retrospectively read the site off the event. Given that I defined the event in four ways, its site can thus be identified in four different ways. Two of these turn out to be promising. On the one hand, the evental site for Meyerhold is the material space of the auditorium. The latter is definitely present in the situation of theatre, and its expressive capacities were inexistent according to established canons of theatrical practice. On the other hand, inasmuch as the Meyerhold-event also consists of his proletarian theatre, the evental site is social differentiation or class: again, necessarily an element of the situation of theatre, but one whose implications for theatrical practice remained entirely foreign to pre-WWI theatre.

How can these two different identifications of the evental site be reconciled?[8] The operator of fidelity is—'does this multiple make for a *cor-*

---

7. Meyerhold, 'The Stylized Theatre', in *Meyerhold on Theatre*, p. 60.
8. The identification of evental-sites is one of the most difficult challenges Badiou's philosophy lays down to those who would work on it. Without the evental-site his ontology is merely a competitor to other formalist ontologies whose most striking applications are in database and intranet design. The evental-site is how Badiou anchors the possibility of

porate creative act'? Hence, what the Meyerhold-event does is transform *not just* the stage and its objects, but the *entire material space* of the auditorium *including* the audience members *into* the work. To backtrack, what marked Stanislavski's reforms within realist theatre was that he sought to transfer the sovereign singularity of the art work—using the terms of classical aesthetics—from the play to the actor's performance. Through the actor's attainment of a 'creative state of mind' during their naturalistic performance, they intuitively add or modify tiny details such that each performance will be singular. The obvious trap with this 'reform' is that it leads directly to the star system: the play *A Streetcar Named Desire* remains the same but people say the star, Marlon Brando, shone on a particular night. What the Meyerhold-event does—or starts off, because it is an infinite task—is far more profound: it seeks to transfer this singularity *from* the literary work or the actor *to the performance as a material whole* including the participant-audience members. In other words, the task is to create a 'corporate creative act', to integrate, however momentarily, an acting collective body that cannot be repeated. The evental site for the Meyerhold event is thus all the material elements in the auditorium inasmuch as they could become part—however briefly—of a transindividual act.[9] A confirmation of this identification of the evental site is found in the tale that, in one production, Meyerhold wanted to extend a flight of stairs across a picture box stage, have it sweep towards the footlights, pass them and continue down to the level of the audience. The producers vetoed this design and allowed the stairs to come as far as the footlights and no further. The material space of the auditorium was absent from the state of theatre at Meyerhold's time. The veto is a sign of this lack. In another paper I argue that one *can* identify a site without an event actually occurring due to the

---

change in being. Moreover, the identification of such sites counters the tendency of academic institutions to encourage eclectic individualism and specialization: thinking evental sites gives a tactical orientation to research, it connects it to spaces of potential praxis: spaces where thought as such is likely to emerge.

9. Finally, one last way of identifying the site of the Meyerhold event is to say that it was Stanislavski's rehearsal processes. Meyerhold started his theatrical career by spending four years acting in the Moscow Art Theatre. Stanislavski's rehearsal techniques involved continual experimentation and a proliferation of exercises that were unpublicized and restricted to him and his disciples. What was at stake in these rehearsals was the creation of signifying bodies and non verbal communication between actors and audience. Again the crucial difference between Stanislavski and Meyerhold was that Stanislavski did not consider the potential creativity of the audience and the emergence of a collective which included it.

signs of lack and excess that emerge at the level of the state with reference to the site.[10]

V. ONE OR MORE INTERVENTIONS?

According to Badiou, for a truth procedure to occur not only must an event occurring at an evental site be named and turned towards the situation via the emergence of an operator of fidelity, but enquiries must be conducted into the multiples of the situation, determining whether or not they are connected to the event. Both the direction and the results of these enquiries cannot be predetermined: otherwise one would be dealing with the practical unfolding of state knowledge and not with a generic truth procedure.

What happens to theatre after Meyerhold? A whole number of different enquiries and explorations take place, some of them more or less simultaneously. I am going to focus on two names which crystallize innovation in the situation of theatre: Artaud and Brecht. These two figures respond to the Meyerhold-event—to its echoes—but in different manners.

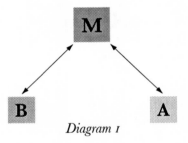

Diagram 1

How does Brecht work in theatre in fidelity to the Meyerhold-event? Brecht knew of Meyerhold's work—notably he saw one of Meyerhold's productions in Berlin in 1926 and cites Meyerhold in his writings- but this is not the point.[11] Brecht was faithful not to Meyerhold's directing style or productions, but to the 'Meyerhold event'. His fidelity lies in his investigation of what he calls 'the social function of theatre'; an interested investi-

---

10. See O. Feltham, 'Singularity Happening in Politics: the Aboriginal Tent Embassy, Canberra 1972', *Communication and Cognition*, vol. 37, no. 1, 2004, 225-245.

11. Brecht refers to Meyerhold in relation to Stanislavski and Vakhtangov and as part of a complex of Russian directors, and also with reference to choreographic work in Brecht, *Brecht on Theatre*, ed. and trans. J. Willett, London, Methuen, 1964, pp. 130, 134. Piscator refers to Meyerhold's *La Dame aux camelias* in April 1935 conversation with Brecht (see *Brecht on Theatre*, p. 76).

gation in that he seeks to dislodge theatre from what he calls its 'culinary function' of providing an evening's pleasure in the form of merchandise.[12] This displacement is carried out by exploring theatre's capacity to expose the existence of social classes. The idea was to interrupt and frustrate the audience's habit of identifying with characters and empathizing with their inability to change their fate—such, for Brecht, was the essential operation of what he called 'Aristotelian drama'; his name for that theatre which was not connected to the Meyerhold-event.[13] Rather, the audience was to be encouraged to think about how characters choose to act in so-cial situations. The horizon or promise of these interruptions and stimuli to thought was a possible politicization of the audience. Brecht's explora-tion lead to a proliferation of new names, as Badiou remarks of all truth procedures: 'epic theatre', 'alienation or distanciation-effect', 'theatre of a scientific age', 'theatre for instruction'. Insofar as such names were and are picked up and reworked by other theatre practitioners they form part of what Badiou terms 'a subject idiom'. Insofar as the names can be used to regroup multiples encountered in the situation of theatre, they become part of the truth procedure's 'counter-state'.[14]

But Brecht is faithful to the Meyerhold-event in yet another man-ner: in line with Meyerhold's embrace of masks and mummery Brecht incorporates into the language of theatre complicated stage machinery, marionettes, and the projection of titles and pictures onto screens. For Brecht these devices, in particular the projections, were not mere aids but, 'organic parts of the work of art'.[15] The third and perhaps the most important element of Brecht's fidelity is his critical interrogation of mass media which were rising in prominence in his time. It is this interrogation that generates a classic example of forcing for us.

What is forcing exactly? It is a relation between a statement concern-ing the situation-to-come—the situation supplemented with its generic subset—and a particular multiple which, *if* it turns out to belong to the

---

12. Brecht, 'The Modern Theatre is the Epic Theatre' (1930), in *Brecht on Theatre*, p. 36.

13. 'We are free to discuss any innovation that does not threaten the stage-apparatus' social function—that of providing an evening's entertainment. We are not free to discuss those which threaten to change its function, possibly by fusing it with the educational system or with the organs of mass communication'. Brecht, 'The Modern Theatre is the Epic Theatre', p. 34.

14. New York performance artist Dan Graham used Brecht's alienation-effect to think his own work in the 1970s. See Rosa Lee Goldberg, *Performance Art: From Futurism to the Present*, revised ed., London, Thames and Hudson, 1988, p. 162.

15. Brecht, 'Notes to Die Mütter: the Indirect Impact of Epic Theatre' (1933), in *Brecht on Theatre*, p. 58.

generic subset, renders the statement true in the situation to come. In Badiou's metaontology—not in Cohen's maths—what determines whether a multiple belongs to the generic multiple is whether or not it is connected to the event. Therefore the concept of forcing provides a more complicated account of what happens in an enquiry. In an 1932 essay Brecht claims that one way of changing the social function of theatre would be to fuse it with the organs of mass communication; he considers the case of radio. At this point we already should note that the generic truth procedure of 'new theatre' has proceeded *beyond* the bounds of the situation of 'theatre'—by encountering the mass media. In this essay Brecht argues that radio as it stands has no 'social object' because it is unidirectional and the listeners cannot supply content. The public occasions it reports upon are not genuinely public because listeners cannot communicate themselves, only receive. The statement 'the social function of theatre would be changed by fusing it with the organs of mass communication' is thus not forced by the element 'radio', insofar as the latter does not belong to the generic multiple of 'new theatre'. Why? Because it does not lend to the generation of a 'corporate collective act'. However, Brecht then makes another statement that *could* be forced: if the radio apparatus were 'changed over from distribution to communication (it) would be the finest communication apparatus in public life, a vast network of pipes. That is to say, it would be as if it knew how to receive as well as to transmit, how to let the listener speak as well as hear, how to bring him into a relationship as well as isolating him'.[16] What clearer anticipation could one want of contemporary debates around uses of the internet and grass-roots democracy.

However this example of forcing appears quite problematic. Given the statement, what is the related element which if it turned out to belong to the generic multiple would force the statement? Wouldn't it simply be the existence of an interactive radio technology and the institutional means to put it in place? Surely such a multiple has turned out to exist: the internet. Then forcing would be no more than an avatar of Aristotle's concept of actualization; an empirical fleshing out, an incarnation of an idea. Such a conclusion would be too hasty: what has to be decided is *what part* of the internet and its use is an element of the generic multiple; how is the internet—not all of it, perhaps very little of it—connected to the Meyerhold-event?[17] But we are way ahead of ourselves here; on the outer limit

---

16. Brecht, 'The Radio as an Apparatus of Communication', in *Brecht on Theatre*, p. 52.
17. What actually decides whether a multiple belongs to the generic subset? Obviously in the case of the 'new theatre' it is not a particular production style being validated by its

of an explosion that we have just began to map. Indeed, to decide such a question by applying the operator of fidelity we would need to identify many more forced statements on the part of other practitioners which flesh out and qualify the sense of a 'corporate creative act'. As Badiou says, an activist or an artist works according to truth as a process rather than the categories of knowledge, but they cannot afford not to know their situation and thus, here, the preceding enquiries.

Let's turn to Antonin Artaud. Although Artaud's primary references are to Appia, Craig and Copeau, he explicitly cites Meyerhold and other Russian directors with admiration for their combat—which he also sees as his own—against 'psychological' or 'literary theatre': he sees in their work a 'theatre of action and of the masses'.[18] He saw Meyerhold's productions in Berlin in 1932 and scholars wager that he was aware of the latter's Parisian tour in 1930. Artaud's thought responds in three ways to the event of new theatre. First he continues the enquiry into the plasticity of theatrical space towards a dissolution of the actors-audience distinction. At the age of twenty he already planned a 'spontaneous theatre' which would perform in the middle of factories.[19] In *The Theatre and its Double* he speaks of using granges or hangars for theatres and developing a turning spectacle with the spectators in the middle.[20] Not only that but he also follows Meyerhold's reintroduction of masks and mummery by seeking to develop a unique concrete language of theatre that would include 'everything which can be materially manifested and expressed on stage' such as 'music, dance, plasticity, mime, gesticulation, intonations, architecture, lighting, décor', later adding masks and mannequins.[21] Artaud understood the construction of this plural yet unique language as both a purification and an enrichment of theatrical practice. It was to be achieved by recourse to non-Occidental theatrical traditions—for example, the Balinese—, and directed against the hegemony of the text or of 'articulated language' in European theatre.

'success' in commercial terms or even in terms of publicity. The Dadaists and the Futurists were criticized by art critics for seeking notoriety for the sake of notoriety. Evidently notoriety is available without art. I hold that the only viable criterion for belonging to a generic multiple is whether or not the multiple in question repeats and transforms in an unpredictable unsettling manner certain decisions and innovations made by other artists in other contexts.

18. In a 1931 text in Artaud, *Oeuvres Complètes*, vol. III, Paris, Gallimard, 1961, p. 216.
19. Alain Virmaux, *Antonin Artaud et le théâtre*, Paris, Seghers, 1970, p. 29.
20. Artaud, 'Le Théâtre de la Cruauté (Premier Manifeste)', *Oeuvres Complètes IV*, Paris, Gallimard, 1964, p. 115.
21. Artaud, 'Le Théâtre de la Cruauté', pp. 58, 47, 111.

Finally, and most importantly, underneath the names of the 'theatre of cruelty' or 'Balinese theatre' or 'metaphysical theatre', Artaud thinks theatre as an immediate act of communication which directly affects the spectator's sensibilities, a transfiguration of their state of nerves akin to a disaster in its intensity. Hence his long exploration of the metaphor of the plague, itself drawn from St. Augustine who deplored theatre as a form of mental infection.[22] It so turns out that it is none other than Meyerhold who lamented in 1907 that theatre was losing its power of *infectious transformation*.[23]

However, at a certain point in his thought Artaud distances his conception of theatre—a magical metaphysical event—from the 'Russian' conception:

> I consider as vain all those attempts made in Russia to place the theatre at the service of immediate political or social ends. This is the case however new the staging procedures employed. These procedures, insofar as they wish to subordinate themselves to the strictest givens of dialectical materialism, turn their back on the metaphysics that they scorn, and remain scenic staging following the most vulgar sense of the word.[24]

The distance that Artaud thus places between himself and Meyerhold is commutative insofar as it is the same distance which is normally understood to exist between Artaud and Brecht's political theatre.[25]

Nevertheless, Artaud's thinking of theatre did remain faithful to the Meyerhold-event: witness this extract from his last letter on theatre, written in 1948, two weeks before his death. He reflects on what he saw as the complete failure of his censored radio programme 'To have done with the judgement of God':

> …I will never touch Radio again
> and from now on I will consecrate myself exclusively to the
> theatre

---

22. Artaud, 'Le Théâtre de la Cruauté', p. 32.

23. Meyerhold, 'The Stylized Theatre' in *Meyerhold on Theatre*, p. 60.

24. Virmaux, *Antonin Artaud*, p. 138.

25. 'Schéma banal et simpliste: Artaud représenterait un théâtre de participation, de frénésie, d'irréalisme; Brecht, un théâtre de 'distanciation', le didacticisme, d'insertion dans l'histoire. Bref, deux pôles, deux univers inconciliables. En fait, les position ne sont pas si tranchées et les passarelles ne manquent pas d'un univers à l'autre, même si la tentative du 'Living Theatre', jouant l'*Antigone* de Brecht, paraît décidément insuffisante à combler la fossé. Qu'on relise plutôt le livret *d'Il n'y a plus de firmament* (II, 9): dans l'animation des foules, dans la montée de la révolte contre les possédants, on trouve des procédés et des accents qui semblent repris des grandes oeuvres de Brecht'. Virmaux, *Antonin Artaud*, p. 139.

such as I conceive it
a theatre of blood
a theatre that, in every performance will have caused to gain
corporeally
something as much the one who performs
as the one who comes to see performing
besides
one doesn't perform
one acts
theatre is in reality the genesis of creation...[26]

Here Artaud's fidelity to the idea of theatre as a 'corporate creative act' is evident.

'Artaud' and 'Brecht' thus name diverging exploratory transformations of the situation of theatre, both of which are faithful to the Meyerhold-event. It is already clear that Badiou's theory of praxis does not lead to a uni-linear account of modernism: we already have two diverging lines with independent chronologies.[27] Moreover, not only do these particular lines continue and fork in the work of other theatre practitioners, but these are not the only lines that emerge from the Meyerhold event.

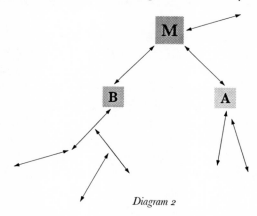

Diagram 2

Explosion: the truth procedure proceeds multi-directionally into different domains via forcings

What is at stake here is the mapping of a generic truth procedure. No doubt this is an oxymoronic if not moronic activity: the generic does

---

26. Virmaux, *Antonin Artaud*, p. 279.

27. In any case, to criticize a theory of change for being 'linear' and reductionist in contrast to the virtues of the 'non-linear' is to betray an impoverished understanding of the nature of line, especially in the field of art (the line outlines strata and opens up universes).

not let itself be diagrammed, only written mathematically. For the sake of communication, let's say this is a rough sketch, not a map. To sketch a generic procedure one can either identify a sequence of enquiries via a proper name or indicate forcings to which proper names may be attached. At least six general statements can be identified which force the 'new theatre'.

1. *The space of performance, including the audience, is totally mobile and plastic.* This forcing may be traced from Meyerhold to the 1918 outdoor reconstruction of the October revolution with 8000 actors, to Brecht's stage machinery, to Grotowski's complete integration of stage and auditorium and it evidently includes street theatre and happenings but not all of them and perhaps very few.

2. *Actions which make up a theatrical work may be non-intentional and subject to chance.* See the function of improvization in Artaud's early thought, the work of John Cage and Allan Kaprow's happenings.[28] However, not all collective events involving chance and presentation belong to the new theatre; chance is staged in commercialized sport.

3. *In the age of machines, theatrical movement—whether of puppets or humans—must be mechanized to the point of blurring the organic-mechanic distinction.* In 1908 Edward Gordon Craig calls for abolition of the performer and his or her replacement by an uber-marionette. The Futurist Prampolini repeats this call in 1915 but actually builds and uses marionettes.[29] Marinelli writes of the metallic mechanic Dance of the Aviatrix. Meyerhold developed a biomechanical theory of actor training. Erwin Piscator, Brecht's early partner, used marionettes in Berlin, Artaud calls for them in his 1932 'Theatre of Cruelty' text. Again, the use of marionettes does not per se guarantee that a work belongs to the 'new theatre'.

4. *Actors do not have to present well-rounded characters or roles, but functions.* In 1934 Brecht says, 'the people were just cyphers serving a cause'.[30] In the late 1950s, Jerzy Grotowski abandons

28. I owe the reference to Allan Kaprow's work to Barbara Formis who is a specialist in the area of fluxus, happenings, contemporary dance and the Judson Dance Group.
29. Goldberg, *Performance Art*, p. 22.
30. Brecht, *Brecht on Theatre*, p. 66.

characters and coherent roles. Nevertheless, *not all* collective presentations in which people do not present individuality belong to the new theatre (Nuremberg rallies).

5. *A theatrical and musical language incorporates the noise of the modern world.* See the Futurist Russolo's 1913 manifesto *The Art of Noises*; Dada's use of 'bruitist' poetry in the Cabaret Voltaire in 1916;[31] Artaud's call for the use of cries and intonations in his 'Balinese Theatre' and 'Staging and Metaphysics' in 1932; and John Cage's 1937 manifesto entitled 'The Future of Music'. The new theatre thus includes the enquiries of contemporary music.

6. *The mass media can be appropriated and diverted to critical ends.* See Brecht on radio as mentioned above but also on film in 1931.[32] Brecht met Eisenstein in 1929. Thus the exploration-transformations of the 'new theatre' could then include certain enquiries of film, and more recently, as I suggested earlier, parts of mass media movements such as open-source and creative-commons on the internet—but not all of them, perhaps even very few.

Note that none of these statements *per se* identifies a subset of the generic multiple 'the new theatre': the deciding factor is whether particular multiples related to these statements—performances, works, schools—turn out to be connected to the Meyerhold event or not. Hence not all and perhaps very few uses of chance and noise will turn out to belong to the 'new theatre'.

With this caveat, each of these statements can be said to serve as a synecdoche for a trajectory of enquiry which can be traced to the Meyerhold event. The problem, however—and this is only a problem for the strict application of Badiou's philosophy of change—is that these enquiries take the 'new theatre' truth procedure into other domains than the original situation. Many of the artists I attached to these statements appear to belong to other situations, if not other truth procedures such as 'Performance art', 'visual art', or 'dance'. Indeed, once one identifies these forcings it is evident that the exploration-transformation of the new theatre passes as much through Futurism and Dadaism as it does through Bre-

31. Goldberg, *Performance Art*, p. 67.
32. See also as a line of enquiry the function of masks in Meyerhold, 'The Fairground Booth', 1912, Cabaret Voltaire, 1916, and Edward Gordon Craig's influential magazine on theatre called *The Mask*.

cht's theatre. The genealogy—and genealogies are usually selective—thus explodes from original situation of theatre out into different realms.

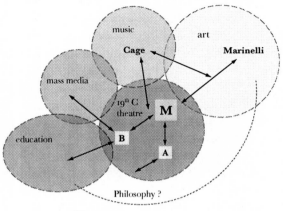

Diagram 3

We could blame such multiplicity on our choice of artform; unlike Badiou's favourite examples of artistic truth procedures, music, poetry and painting, theatre is already a *hybrid* art, combining painting, sculpture, literature, and music. But this is not enough. We could divide the 'new-theatre' up into political theatre, avant-garde theatre and art-theatre, but this would be mere academic convenience. If the 'new-theatre' invades spheres of art, performance art and even cinema, then the obvious question is raised of whether the Meyerhold-event is its unique source of fidelity. What is usually called 'performance art' is usually traced back to *Marinelli*, not Meyerhold, if not back to commedia dell'arte and Roman circuses. Via forcings the explosion thus rushes outwards and then chronologically backwards to secure new sources of fidelity. For example, Dario Fo—whose work is definitely part of the 'new theatre'—explicitly rejects avant-garde theatre in order to return to the popular theatre of scandalous Medieval mystery plays.

According to Badiou's philosophy of change *a* generic truth procedure proceeds within *a* historical situation. It separates out, in fidelity to *an* event, *its* generic submultiple and then adds it to the former situation. The schema in diagram 3 is a twist on Badiou's set-up. Not only do we have multiple historical situations—art, music, cinema, etc.—but we may even have multiple events.[33]

---

33. The irreducible multiplicity of the arts is precisely Jean-Luc Nancy's question in *Les Muses*, Paris, Gallimard, 2001. What we have is Meyerhold-event not as absolute source

It is here that Badiou's theory of generic truth procedures can be supplemented. What is required is a more complicated account of forcing and of the development of a counter state. I hold that within the domains of art and politics one can think a counter-state as a collective assemblage of enunciation which reinforces and unfolds the truth procedure by a number of typical operations. It is these operations which allow for the multiplication of the procedure's situations and for its possible *convergence* with *other* truth procedures, in the realm of dance or music for example. One of these typical operations is *the renaming of the whole*. It occurs frequently in the 'new theatre' truth procedure: Meyerhold attempted to name the new theatre as 'stylized theatre'; Brecht as 'epic theatre' or 'theatre for a scientific age' and these names can be used to multiply the domains of the truth procedure. Brecht speaks of cinema as an ideal vehicle for epic theatre. In other words, if a historical situation—theatre—is slowly transformed by a truth procedure, then evidently its name and its boundaries have to change. The philosophical question of what distinguishes one artform—such as theatre—from another artform—such as sculpture or performance or dance is in fact an *immediate practical question* insofar as the reworking of these boundaries is precisely what the truth procedure does in its renaming of the whole.

In my work on the Jacobin assemblage of enunciation in the French Revolution I identify three typical operations: catachrestic metonymy (the renaming of a whole by a part); centrifugal translation (Jacobin spokesmen travelling to outlying villages and translating the law passed by the Assemblée nationale into local dialects for the resolution of disputes) and centripetal incarnation (Robespierre's attempt to let the people speak through him). I mention this to indicate the kinds of operation—which are not just rhetorical but also technical and physical—which could be active in the new theatre truth procedure. To round off this preliminary investigation let's mark some unexpected effects of this explosive genealogy on both theatre and Badiou's philosophy.

VI. THE EMERGENCE OF A GENERIC ART OF PRESENTATION

As for theatre, the multi-directionality of the truth procedure means whatever the setbacks of, say, political theatre, the 'new theatre' continues

---

but as an early knot/conjuncture/transistor which concentrated and then exploded out lines of energy. We also have a series of event-knots in Futurism, Dada and post-Schoenbergian music that lead to converging truth procedures.

its exploration-transformations in other directions. Its inclusion of certain enquiries in the realm of mass communication enables it to expand beyond the trap called the 'death of theatre'. Its inclusion of work which abandons aesthetic autonomy and seeks to integrate itself into ordinary practice means that it doesn't so much surpass the 'end of art' trap as envelop and enfold it. Ultimately what is at stake in these multiple enquiries is not so much a new *theatre* but the unfolding of a *generic art of presentation*: *generic* insofar as it links up all of these arts—time-based, visual, sonorous, tactile or odorous—which appear to be distinct to theatre; *indiscernible* insofar as *not all* of the work in these fields (perhaps *very little* of it) belongs to it.[34]

But then how does this generic art of presentation carve out what belongs to it? Earlier I suggested that the operator of fidelity—that which decides whether a multiple is connected to the Meyerhold-event of not—was the idea of a 'corporate creative act'. Yet isn't this, at least in the realms of art and politics, another name for any generic truth procedure: a 'corporate creative act'? Perhaps Badiou's philosophy itself has been conditioned by the 'new theatre' truth procedure.

Before exploring this possibility, let's step back in history for a moment. Long before Badiou's work, philosophy had already been conditioned by theatre as a truth procedure. If we look at the intraphilosophical effects of Greek tragedy in Plato's work we see that in fact it is precisely there that philosophy comes closest to thinking the generic *avant la lettre*, before Cohen, and before Meyerhold. In Book 10 of *The Republic* Plato thinks the being of the mimetic actor-poet as that presentation which both appears to occupy *every (professional) place*, and which, insofar as it does not maintain a proper relation to knowledge and the Idea, *does not occupy any place whatsoever*. The other moment in which Greek philosophy comes *close* to thinking the generic is in its examination of matter and change. Not to mention the *chora* in Plato's *Timaeus*, if we turn to Aristotle's *Metaphysics*, we can see that he is led to think being, *ousia* (substance), not only as definable form and as composite substance—form plus matter—but also as *hypokeimenon*, the material substrate *that underlies change* in his consideration of production (which is none other than the economic constituent of the

---

34. These exclusions mark the difference between the idea of a generic art of presentation and the German romantic program of turning life into a work of art, which I hold to be an illusory temptation and trap necessarily generated by the ambition of a truth procedure: Marinetti mistakenly imagined at one point: 'Thanks to us the time will come when life will no longer be a simple matter of bread and labour, nor a life of idleness either, but a *work of art*'.

polis).[35] The substrate has no properties in itself since it is the bearer of any property whatsoever and this is why it is not a definable 'this' (*tode ti*).[36]

The result of this conditioning is that the Greek dispensation of the rapport between philosophy and theatre triangulates them by means of a third term, the *polis*. This is so not just for philosophy but also from the perspective of theatre—think of Aristophanes in *The Clouds* or *The Frogs*—insofar as both seek to monopolize the relation to the *polis* which they name *not* as mimesis but as education. However, education, in both cases, is thought under the rubric of presentation.

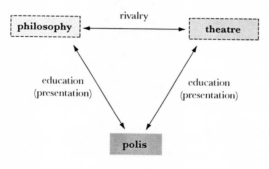

Diagram 4

If we return to the twentieth century it is obvious that certain enquiries of the 'new theatre' are not indifferent to this Greek dispensation: in fact, Brecht's work transforms it. Already for Plato, thus from this viewpoint of philosophy the (pseudo) function of theatre is the presentation of society to itself via simulacra. The Brechtian twist is to argue that in doing so the only way can theatre avoid presenting simulacra is by not presenting society as a stable unity. That is, under Brecht's directives theatrical presentation necessarily involves an identification of the social body but at the same time an exposure of its disjunctions *even if* only at the place of the gap between the subject of enunciation of the social identity and the enunciated of that social identity. Brecht thus thinks theatrical practice *as* the true installation of the reflexive moment within society.

---

35. For Aristotle, nothing can come from nothing. Moreover, a form is generated through the process of production—such as a table—which is different to the original form—separate pieces of wood—therefore there must be something which persists throughout the change of form but which is separate to form: this something is the material substrate.
36. See Badiou, *Logiques des mondes*, p. 377 on being suffering neither generation nor corruption and on the inconsistent multiple as substrate.

This Brechtian dispensation immediately reveals the *intraphilosophical effects* of the 'new theatre' truth procedure: the explosion has reached philosophy and it has definitely conditioned the very model of change that we have been using to sketch it. These effects can be seen in three places:

1.   First, for Badiou, the slow outlining of a generic subset involves traversing all of the properties of the historical situation—the situation is thus *identified* in its totality.

2.   Second, the truth procedure is said to decide upon and measure the immeasurable gap between the situation and its state—thus the practice of reflexivity exposes and bridges the principle disjunction of the situation.

3.   Third the structure of the event itself involves reflexivity inasmuch as it is a multiple whose name belongs to itself—thus a reflexive moment is at the origin of change.

The investigation of a 'new theatre' truth procedure via the strict application of Badiou's philosophy of change thus bears strange fruit: the very *least* we can say, now, is that Badiou's model of change is eminently theatrical, but in a completely reworked sense of 'theatrical'. If Badiou's concept of the event as appearing-disappearing is a result of his philosophy being conditioned by Mallarme's poem *Un coup de dès...* then the construction of a generic body can be understood as the intraphilosophical effect not only of Cohen's mathematical inventions, but also of the art-of-presentation truth procedure.

But the consequences go further still: *if* it is the very nature of truth procedures to cross and redraw boundaries, *then* Badiou's *philosophical* concept of a generic truth procedure could be understood as a *part of* the art-of-presentation truth procedure. Of course, Badiou, dealing with the spectre of fusion between philosophy and its conditions, calls for a strict distinction between philosophy and truth-procedures. I am no longer sure that this is the best way of thinking the real of an explosive genealogy. Insofar as Aristophanes, the Greek playwright, feels it necessary to *combat* the rival discipline of philosophy in the education of the city's youth, philosophy itself could already be understood as an emergent *collective assemblage of enunciation* which *interferes with* if not *conditions* if not *takes part in* theatre. Then—and here the explosive genealogy carries right back out of the twentieth century and into the fifth and fourth century B.C.— the Greek philosophy machine itself could be thought to be part of the generic art of presentation; not all of it, perhaps very little of it, but definitely some of it.

10

Ontology and Appearing: Documentary Realism as a Mathematical Thought

Lindsey Hair

From its very inception, cinema has grappled with the question of presentation, or being-there, versus representation. The Lumière brothers' early shorts or actuality films appeared, in the eyes of the first 'naïve' filmgoers, to present 'life as it is', Dziga Vertov's experimentation with the 'Kino-eye' and montage claimed to construct a more penetrating window on reality via the harnessing of technology; neo-realism's framing of the Real broadened the conception of the field of presentation, and the (post)-modern filmmakers' reflexive techniques challenged the very possibility of documenting reality. Thus, it would seem that documentary plays in the fringes of the ontico-ontological division, in the interstices between being as pure presentation, and being as appearing, the area that Badiou's latest work in category theory seeks to explore.

If documentary can be said to produce a world, it is because the film-maker undertakes an artistic procedure following a decision on existence. Each different orientation raises the question of being as the director undertakes a commitment to present a reality or 'truth' that the actual situation obscures. Analogous to the case of foundational mathematical orientations, being as such is established following a particular axiomatic decision that shapes the presented universe in the light of certain artistic convictions, or thought protocols. Badiou defines an artistic world as a 'relation between the chaotic disposition of sensibility and form.'[1] Thus, the infinity of the material situation is given an order, or form, as a result of the artistic conviction, or vision, which can be understood as an onto-logical decision that orients the production of a truth that structures the particular being-there of the world produced by the documentary.

To be effective, art must take as its starting point that which Empire does not recognize—its void—and build a truth process from its imma-nent distribution within its context such that its 'in-existence' is rendered visible, a de-structuring process that sheds particularity, returning to the 'elemental' level prior to the overlay of representation. This paradigm places Empire in the position of knowledge, and figures the artistic truth procedure as radically disjunct. The purity of art stems from its ascetic separation, however: its purported aim, to 'render visible to everyone that which, for Empire (and so by extension for everyone, though from a different point of view) doesn't exist',[2] distinguishes between the state of the situation, and people's inevitable captivation by the symbolic order. This is at the heart of Badiou's injunction against the unthinking material re-production of existent (countable) elements of the state: '(w)hat there already is, the situation of knowledge as such, only gives us repetition. For a truth to affirm its newness, there must be a *supplement*.'[3] The criterion of 'novelty' demands that *each* work must initiate a new mode of enquiry. If an artistic creation is not surprising, incalculable, unanticipatible, it mere-ly reiterates knowledge, rather than exposing a truth. Repetition is the mechanism by which the state regenerates, whereas art is charged with the production of a generic singularity.

Documentary is engaged in the struggle to overcome mere repetition of the pro-filmic or material world in front of the camera. Its mandate is to produce a work of art that brings to appearance those elements of a situation that were previously foreclosed by current modes of representa-tions as legislated by the State of the Situation. Thus, while we would seem to be dealing with re-presentation (in so far as documentary gains its special status via its manipulation of indexical traces), since its inception as a genre it has defined itself in terms of what it *adds*—a supplement, the space for a new appearance. John Grierson, in his canonical *First Prin-*

---

1. Alain Badiou, 'The Subject of Art', *The Symptom*, no. 6, Spring 2005, http://www.lacan.com/symptom6_articles/badiou.html

2. Alain Badiou, 'Fifteen Theses on Contemporary Art', *Lacanian Ink*, no. 23, 2004, pp. 100-19, p. 2.

3. Alain Badiou, 'The Ethic of Truths: Construction and Potency', trans. Selma Sowley, *Pli: Warwick Journal of Philosophy*, no. 12, 2001, pp. 245-55, p. 250.

ciples of Documentary, deliberately excluded the 'actuality film' as one of the 'lower forms' because it was constructed largely of 'natural materials', arguing that 'the only world in which documentary can hope to achieve the ordinary virtues of an art [is when] we pass from the plain (or fancy) descriptions of natural material, to arrangements, rearrangements, and creative shapings of it'.[4] From this has grown a wide diversity of creative output and critical discussion, each hotly contesting the relation between reality, truth, objectivity and textuality. I am not presently concerned in establishing the validity of one particular stance in this complex debate; rather I would like to relate this whole discourse to Badiou's elaboration of the different mathematical orientations that I see as similarly contesting the nature of ontology, and the appropriate means of approaching the formalization or construction of its objects. Mathematicians and documentarists alike start from a foundational decision that orients the nature of the universe they set out to explore and determines the appearance of objects (mathematical or human) within the context of the delineated world. Just as Badiou argues for a *single* field of mathematics, wherein the different orientations (Platonic, constructivist, generic etc.) bring various aspects of this infinite field into being as a result of the institution of protocols of thought, we can see how the documentary also forms particular instances of being-there which are similarly shaped by an orientation that derives from an artistic decision regarding *what Is*.

Traditional ontological approaches to the question of 'being as being', either take what Desanti identifies as a maximalist approach, associated with empirical or logical readings whereby 'being' is adequate to its extensional concept, *or*, like Badiou, undertake a minimalist reading and set out to think being in its being, without external reference to an extension[5]—the question of the '*There is*' (il y a), or pure presentation. If being is to be treated within its own, proper framework, the logical, or analytic approach that seeks to delineate an conceptual extension is excluded because it sets up an analogical relation that mediates between instances of being and pure being, while the contemporary linguistic turn in philosophy attempts to redress this problem by maintaining the impossibility of re-presenting being or presence, and instead seeks the trace of being in

---

4. John Grierson, *First Principles of Documentary* quoted in Philip Rosen, *Change Mummified: Cinema, Historicity, Theory*, Minneapolis, University of Minnesota Press, 2001, p. 233.

5. I am grateful to Jean-Toussaint Desanti's elaboration of this point in Jean-Toussaint Desanti, 'Some Remarks on the Intrinsic Ontology of Alain Badiou', in Peter Hallward (ed.), *Think Again: Alain Badiou and the Future of Philosophy*, London, Continuum Books, 2004, pp. 59-66.

poetry which retains a unique opening to presence without subjecting it to the violence of linguistic determinacy. The desire to think being 'intrinsically' leads Badiou to reformulate the question within mathematical (or set-theoretical) terms, which means that to approach the thinking of being, we must also understand mathematics as a thought. Badiou turns to (ZF)[6] set theory because it makes no existential claims, nor adds any extension, or predicate to its bare inscription of being.

Re-reading Leibniz's maxim 'What is not *a* being is not a *being*' Badiou suggests that rather than this necessitating a Onenness of Being, and hence entailing predication, the singularization of a specific entity or multiple is always the result of an operation performed upon pure (inconsistent) multiplicity, and it is the operation of the count that structures it as one, or as *a* thing.

> In sum: the multiple is the regime of presentation; the one, in respect to presentation, is an operational result; being is what presents (itself). On this basis, being is neither one (because only presentation itself is pertinent to the count-as-one), nor multiple because the multiple is *solely* the regime of presentation.[7]

At the level of pure presentation all elements are simply registered on the level of 'belonging' to the multiple/set, or are counted, such that 'what is' appears as presented consistency. If Being as pure inconsistent multiplicity is subtractive (there is no Whole, no One) and existence, or *being-there* is the result of an onto-logical ordering that falls within a different level, there is no way of substantiating ontological claims. It follows that any statements about Being must be founded upon pure decision, given its fundamental inaccessibility to presence as inconsistent (uncountable) multiplicity. Badiou's interest in category theory lies in its ability to map the consequences of any decision regarding the nature of being and the conditions that structure its particular mathematical universe, allowing the logic of different orientations to be directly compared within a framework that is intrinsic to the ontological structures they describe. In particular, the absence of a meta-language is a strength of category theory

---

6. Zermelo-Fraenkel set theory offers a first-order system built up from the primitive notion of belonging ($\in$), and which constructs its axiomatic framework from the void, or empty set $\{\varnothing\}$. It makes no existential claims about the nature of sets, or their elements; in effect the system provides a means of describing the generation and organization of multiples, or sets, from nothing. It does not legislate over existential quantifiers (being specifically formulated to by-pass Russell's paradox).

7. Alain Badiou, *Being and Event*, trans. Oliver Feltham, London, Continuum, 2005, p. 24 (henceforth BE).

that makes it compatible with the minimalist approach to Being that Badiou adopts—all logical relations are intrinsically generated specific to the various mathematical worlds, mapping their potential existence, in terms of the different logics that structure the 'being there' or appearing of elements, within each world.

Thus, although there are different orientations, there is but a single mathematics whose domain is the inconsistent multiplicity, the very stuff of Being, that is able to be brought to presentation in various different ways, depending upon whether one upholds the constructivist conviction that all mathematical entities must be capable of being generated from a consistent, demonstrable axiomatic framework, whether the mathematician accepts unlimitable cardinality that is regulated by a separate axiomatic framework, or whether s/he allows generic sets, and therefore a subtractive notion of Being. Badiou turns to the significant impasses that have formed mathematical thought, such as the paradoxes of set theory or generic sets, to support his insight that these blind spots function as the Real of mathematical thought, and the decisions arise from these areas of undecidability demonstrate the manner in which thought produces orientations that shape the various conceptions of existence: each decision on Being underwrites the foundations of the mathematical universe whose existence it declares.

In each case, it is a conflict in the thinking of Being, but on the level of *existence*, which Badiou glosses as that which 'thought declares and whose consistency is guaranteed by Being'[8], is grasped differently in each case. Since thought alone supports the foundational decision regarding an undecidable impasse, existence itself is the meeting point between 'decision and encounter', 'act and discovery', in other words, existence is produced by its particular thought: each decision axiomatically founds being via its initial inscription thereby determining the logic of its construction. The peculiar nature of such a decision entails both the positing of what is, and the paradoxical discovery of the structure of that existence, on the basis of this initial intuition/conviction. Since this inaugural decision can have no grounding—being qua being is radically inaccessible—it is open to be thought in a range of orientations, but the conviction that is upheld in each orientation leads to the formulation of a potential being via its 'fictive activation': 'Existence is precisely Being itself in as much as thought

8. Alain Badiou, *Briefings On Existence: A Short Treatise on Transitory Ontology*, trans. Norman Madarasz, Albany, State University of New York Press, 2006, pp. 45-58, p. 54 (henceforth TO).

decides it. And decision orients thought essentially' (TO 55)· The Parmenidian insight 'Thinking and Being are One' is demonstrated through the retroactive consistency that each orientation endows upon the mathematical universe declared to exist as a result of its particular thought. As Badiou notes: '... a position has to be taken. For we stand actually as an act (*au pied de l'âct*), if I dare say, upon the very norm of the decision the act accomplishes. // At any rate, what is referred to in this obligation to decide is Being' (TO 52).

Badiou's latest work explores the process whereby mathematical decision on how the inconsistent stuff of Being can be brought to presentation, ordered, or numbered *produces* a framework of possible entities, or that forms being according to certain conceptual convictions. If, as Badiou suggests, the divergent mathematical decision to attribute existence can be metaphorically mapped with the three different political orientations that dominate contemporary society (TO 55-6), it would seem plausible to extend this analogy to the field of art which, broadly speaking, is similarly oriented relative to the three modes of thinking Being: constructivist, transcendent and generic.

The constructivist/intuitionist approach limits mathematical thinking of Being to a 'logical grammar' (BE 287) with origins that are traceable back to the Aristotelian rebuttal of Platonic ideality. Aristotle's proposal that mathematics is ultimately a branch of aesthetics rests on his conviction that mathematical thought consists of a 'fictive activation' of objects that have only potential existence in the realm of the sensible and thus deals with questions of order and symmetry, governed by a norm of the beautiful. This power to 'inseparate the inseparable' (TO 47) Badiou equates with language, and the various inscriptions of Being that dominate the thinking of mathematics today. For example, the aesthetic principle underpins the conviction that mathematics 'tells us nothing of real-being, but it forges a fiction of intelligible consistency from the standpoint of the latter, whose rules are explicit' (TO 48). Thus, mathematics is reduced to a consistent set of rules and structures rather than being the science of Being qua Being: 'thought subsumes the relation to being *within the dimension of knowledge*' (BE 293). The constructivist limits the set universe within which operations can be carried out to the class model of 'Constructible Sets'. This is characterized as a 'thin' set universe, in that it is generated from a spine of ordinals from which all the counting operations which are concretely constructible are appended. Such a model produces a universe that is as 'tall' as any potential universe, in that it contains the ordinals up to infinity, but it does not fully utilize the power set axiom, which would theoretically generate all potential subsets of a given ordinal, and so exhaust the combinatorial abilities inherent within the system. In the thin set universe, these denumerable subsets are not included, only those which can be directly counted are added on to the spine of ordinals. Such an omission is acceptable in that the continuum hypothesis is unprovable within ZF which remains consistent with and without its addition.

However, this opens the question as to the nature of the resulting set universe 'L' (known as the 'class of constructible sets') relative to the infinity of sub-sets capable of generation under the power set axiom, giving rise to the complete universe of sets 'V', designated as the 'real world'. One would intuitively assume that the latter is much larger than the thin set universe (L), however, the Axiom of Constructability states $V = L$, and has been shown to be consistent. From $V = L$ the existence of a minimal model can be consistently assumed, however, this in effect conditions the boundaries of the set universe relative to the language in which it is accessible. At this juncture, mathematics is encountering the Wittgensteinian dictum 'whereof one cannot speak, thereof one must be silent'.[9]

Badiou links this approach to Being with the neo-classical norms in art, that privilege continuity: 'The neo-classicist fulfils the precious function of the guardianship of sense on a global scale. He testifies that there *must* be sense' (BE 292). In terms of documentary, if we think the condition of existence being determined by constructibility, or conditioned by language, textuality, we can include those directors that privileged the structuring of the film as the means of producing a consistent construction of existence. We can relate this to Pudovkin and Kuleshov's conception of montage as an unfolding sequence built out of separate filmic elements that were placed together, piece by piece, to depict a specific narrative sequence.[10] This approach can be seen as a forerunner of what Bazin identified as the 'transparent' technique of classical Hollywood cinema in the 40's. Film theorist Philip Rosen has remarked the joint emergence of the classical fiction film along side the new documentary genre, suggesting that many of the conventions of sequencing and narratorial regulation of the latter resulted from this newly established viewing practice. This is

---

9. Ludwig Wittgenstein, *Tractatus Logico-Philosophicus*, trans. C.K. Ogden, London, Routledge and Kegan Paul, 1922.

10. Dziga Vertov's 'Kino-pravda' uses montage in an entirely different manner: the use of split screen, superimpositions and rapid montage to produce a 'truth' that only the superior technological resources of film could capture, distances him from the more conventional constructivist stance. A full discussion of Vertov's contribution the development of the documentary genre is beyond the scope of this present article.

most closely realized in Robert Flaherty's *Nanook of the North* (widely accepted as founding the genre) which was structured along classical narrative lines. The daily existence of the Inuits captured on film was a reality produced especially for and by the film. Most scenes were staged, and the dramatic structure collaboratively predetermined between Flaherty and Nanook. Broadly speaking, the thought that underwrites the treatment of appearing within this orientation aims to deal with that which can be shown—to close off aporia, making the diegetic world seamless. At this point, constructivism can be equated with textuality—there is no 'Real' to which the film/mathematical proposition refers, only the manipulation of signification within a conventionally governed framework that allows the production of meaning. As Badiou comments: 'the constructible universe is [...] the ontological symbol of knowledge. The ambition which animates this genre of thought is to maintain the multiple within the grasp of what can be written and verified. Being is only admitted to being within the transparency of signs which bind together its derivation on the basis of what we have already been able to inscribe' (BE 309). That construction is commensurate with knowledge is a dangerous proposal, as evidenced in the colonialist overtones of early anthropological documentary. For instance, Fatimah Tobing Rony has critiqued Flaherty's *Nanook* for its 'romantic preservationism', viewing its appropriation of the Inuit lifestyle as a fetishization of Otherness ('ethnographic taxidermy') and the deliberate production of a nostalgic fiction.[11] The contemporary rejection of the traditional omniscience of the documentarist/ethnographer nevertheless retains a self-conscious constructivist approach. As Cool and Lutkenhaus suggest, 'Although these enthnographies take a number of different forms, they share a self-conscious effort to portray the socially *constructed* nature of ethnographic knowledge'[12] (my italics). This overtly ethical stance nevertheless foregrounds the textuality implicit in its ideological orientation, reflecting what Badiou has termed the 'ethic of knowledge': 'act and speak such that everything be clearly decidable' (BE 314).

For Badiou, art enters into an antagonistic relation to the dominant cultural regime which he terms 'Empire', and he frames the goal of art as the production of abstract, non-imperial works that achieve the generic universality common to each of the truth processes. In this context,

---

11. Fatimah Tobing Rony, *The Third Eye: Race: Cinema and the Ethnographic Spectacle*, Durham, Duke University Press, 1996, p. 102.

12. Nancy Lutkehaus and Jenny Cool, 'Paradigms Lost and Found', in Jane Gaines and Michael Renov (eds.), *Collecting Visible Evidence*, Minneapolis, University of Minnesota Press, 1999, p. 118.

knowledge is equated directly with the generalized meta-structure, and Badiou writes: 'Since it is sure of its ability to control the entire domain of the visible and the audible via the laws governing commercial circulation and democratic communication, Empire no longer censures anything'.[13] This means that the drawback of any constructivist stance is its limitation to the realm of knowledge, which is governed by the State of the Situation/Empire. While any post-modern documentary that interrogates the repression and appropriation at play in any construction of social/racial/gender within its own framework as an artistic artefact, as well as the wider social context with which it engages is foregrounding the play of signification and its incommensurability with knowledge, its paradoxical reliance upon the properties of language to do so is nevertheless, from Badiou's perspective, a limitation. It precludes the possibility of an event, and denies the possibility of a (subtractive) truth, in favour of an endlessly disseminating relativity.

The attraction of such an approach is nevertheless appealing, and, within discussions of documentary practice, the insight that the work is a 'text' rather than a slice of reality has been extremely influential. Badiou accounts for this 'linguistic turn' by noting that the totalizing force of Empire is not manifestly repressive: rather than imposing an openly dogmatic program against which an artist might strive to retrieve the light of truth, the contemporary situation is unremittingly permissive, urging its subjects to 'consume, to communicate and to enjoy'[14], in effect fusing with the super-egoic injunction to 'enjoy!' such that one is bound by the duty to indulge. The granting of absolute licence binds the subject more tightly within the transparent operations of its regime. The meta-Statist stranglehold currently saturates the situation to the extent that it is always already in excess of any new artistic configurations that might be formed—the structure is capable of anticipating all potential developments within the elements it regulates.

Against a regime that performs a perversely Foucauldian discipline of surveillance, that exercises absolute control over the domain of the visible and the audible such that nothing is censured simply because nothing can be produced that is outside the parameters of its control, Badiou turns to the force of the subtractive as the only space that is outside governance. To this end, his theses on contemporary art focus on the process of the generic, and the technique of purification. Art becomes possible at the

---

13. Badiou, 'Fifteen Theses on Contemporary Art'.
14. Badiou, 'Fifteen Theses on Contemporary Art'.

point which the individual resists the imperative to enjoy (and hence participate), and practices a rigorous asceticism both in the personal realm, becoming 'the pitiless censors of ourselves', and in the refusal to (re-)produce in the service of the state. Indeed, '[i]t is better to do nothing than to contribute to the invention of formal ways of rendering visible that which Empire already recognizes as existent'.[15] In a constructivist orientation, all sets are always already constructible, hence there is no space for the 'new' to emerge: nothing to challenge the prevailing regime. A self-conscious or post-modern incorporation of this maxim does not destabilize this state of affairs as it is simply a reflexive re-configuration of that which is already counted, or controlled. Whatever can be (ac)counted for is by definition always already within the governance of Empire, and is indeed sanctioned as yet another means of proliferating its meta-structural control.

Badiou identifies a second mathematical orientation, which he terms prodigal or transcendent. The finitude of the constructivist orientation is superseded in set theoretical terms by the introduction of inaccessible cardinals, which he claims serve to introduce a 'theological' transcendence that breaks down the maxim of constructability via the positing of ordinals that cannot be reached from within the limits of the constructible universe. In this orientation $V \neq L$. Rather than work from the finite set universe towards its potential limit, the transcendent orientation works from the unquantifiable cardinals towards the constructible universe. This orientation revives Cantor's original theological insight, maintaining the undecidability of such cardinals from within ZF. Badiou discusses this in terms of different 'species' of multiple being—the successor ordinal, that has a local status and is identifiable within V, whereas the limit ordinal 'ex-sists from the sequence whose limit it is' (BE 155), and has a global status. The existence of large cardinals rests on a decision of thought, which produces a divergent mathematical orientation that conceives of the mathematical universe as far exceeding the part that has currently been formalized by its theorists. Although the positing of an 'indiscernible' breaks the tyranny of the language/knowledge dyad, Badiou remarks its negative connotations, such that it indicates the inability of exact nomination, whereas the generic positively designates the truth of a situation that is incommensurable with knowledge.

We can compare this thinking of being with the neo-realist movement, which proposes a similarly transcendent 'Wholeness' of reality that the totalizing gaze of the camera brings to appearance. The unflinching

---

15. Badiou, 'Fifteen Theses on Contemporary Art'.

recording of the detail of the everyday brings to presentation a deeper understanding of the local, producing a 'description of reality conceived as a whole by a consciousness disposed to see things as a whole',[16] a consciousness that Andre Bazin, has described as properly 'ontological'. The crucial difference is that meaning is constructed *a posteriori*, from the cumulative effect of the fragments of reality it juxtaposes, rather than aiming to construct a particular argument from the fragments by their deliberate arrangement. While such films are nevertheless crafted artefacts, and as such prey to the same dictates of textuality, Bazin suggested that neorealism presented 'documentary reality *plus* something else, this something else being the plastic beauty of the images, the social sense, or the poetry, the comedy and so on'.[17] Badiou links this valorization of transcendence with Heidegger's notion of the Open, and indeed Bazin's appeal to the intangible evocation of the Real via 'poetry' certainly speaks to this desire to locate a trace of being as such.

Neorealism's belief in the truth inherent in uncontrolled events countered the earlier use of documentary to produce a subjective, personal truth whereby random, unpredictable happenings were retroactively reframed within a larger structure of governance, by editing and voice over narrative. Knowledge/language is exceeded by the intervention of the Real, here indicated by the poetic trace that lends a teleological transcendence to the artistic world of the film. Badiou dismisses the Heideggerian appeal to poetry as the conduit to access the withdrawal of Being, equating it with the chimera of the inconsistent multiple that becomes retroactively thinkable as a result of the operation that brought the consistent multiple to presentation. There is no ineffable 'Whole' of being.

This same appeal to totality can be seen in the French *cinéma vécu*, where the documentarists' immersion in a particular way of life and the subsequent recording of testimonies claimed to produce an excess of truth. Likewise, Direct Cinema, and *Cinéma Vérité* were influenced by neorealism's drive to present a more 'complete' reality, introducing such diverse techniques such as the hidden camera, the provocative onscreen interview, or a narrowed focus on the 'crisis' structure, in a bid to capture the full 'event' as it unfolded. This belief in the camera's ability to capture the 'real nature of the world' soon came to be widely challenged by theo-

---

16. Andre Bazin, 'In Defence of Rossellini: A letter to Guido Aristarco, editor-in-chief of Cinema Nuovo', *What is Cinema?*, trans. Hugh Gray, Berkeley, University of California Press, 1971, p. 97.
17. Bazin, 'In Defence of Rossellini', p. 100.

rists and film makers alike. As documentarist James Lipscome notes: 'we cannot assume as c-v seems to, that there is a universal or absolute truth about objects and events—and thus we must face up to the fact that, to paraphrase Euclid on mathematics, there is no royal road to the real nitty-gritty'.[18] Which brings us to Badiou's third mathematical orientation, that of the generic.

The construction of a generic extension entails a positive mapping of an indiscernible part of a situation—an excrescence—via an infinite truth procedure that verifies, element by element, those aspects which can be said to have a positive connection to the event and those which do not. The crux of this procedure is that the elements of this indiscernible part are all named within the prevailing knowledge of the situation, but the generic set that results forms a diagonal to the current representational norms, including at least one element that does not share an identifiable property with the rest of the infinite set to which it belongs, making the generic set indiscernible from within the situation insofar as it evades nomination. This indiscernibility is precisely that which characterizes the set as generic since its property is solely the fact of its *being* in the situation, and does not refer to its classification within language, as per the other constructible sets. It is this that allows the construction of the 'being-multiple' of a truth, insofar as the enquiry focuses on being, and its suture to the void, rather than on veridical determinations: what 'we are looking for is an ontological differentiation between the true and the veridical, that is between truth and knowledge' (BE 333).

The generic art-idea is not included in the *presented* work, simply because the parameters of space and time within which it is produced constrain the material artefact to finitude. Badiou's emphatic insistence that: '[…] the work of art is in fact the only finite thing that exists—that art creates finitude'[19] derives its justification from the Greek aesthetic principle of completion, in which perfection and completion are co-determinate. Thus the single work of art cannot be coextensive with a truth procedure as this would repeat the romantic error of seeing art as the privileged site of the incarnation of the infinite within the finite. Badiou's inaesthetic schema figures the relation between art and truth as being both singular and immanent:

---

18. James. Lipscome, 'Correspondence and Controversy: Cinéma Vérité', *Film Quarterly*, vol. 18, 1964, pp. 62-3.

19. Alain Badiou, *Handbook of Inaesthetics*, trans. Alberto Toscano, Stanford, Stanford University Press, 2005, p. 11 (henforth HI).

> Art *itself* is a truth procedure. Or again: The philosophical
> identification of art falls under the category of truth. Art is a thought
> in which artworks are the Real (and not the effect). (HI 9)

An artistic truth is immanent to the work of art and is constructed from the unlocatable point of the void: we are dealing with a subtraction that bears witness to the reductive exigency of the structuring regime of the count-for-one. The first axiom of Badiou's 'Fifteen theses on contemporary art' states: 'Art [...] is the production of an infinite subjective series, through the finite means of a material subtraction.'[20] Parsing this in terms of its mathematical context, we can understand each point, or element, as the site of an enquiry as to whether it can be said to be a member of the generic sub-set, given that there is no unifying predicate that determines membership (since the generic set/truth is infinite it remains untotalizable). As such, the modality of any particular truth lies in the future anterior—*what will have been true*— a wager that founds the undertaking of the process and so brings the possibility of that truth into being as the 'infinite result of a risky supplementation'.[21]

The truth of any single presented multiple is that which 'from inside the presented, as *part* of this presented, makes the inconsistency—which buttresses in the last instance the constancy of the presentation—come into the light of day' (MP 106). Thus, the truth of a work of art is an immanent, but anonymous aspect of its material presentation, retrospectively readable as the operation that *formed* its finite consistency: a constitutive aspect that is not strictly commensurate within its spatio-temporal context, but is a rem(a)inder of the creative process itself.

The generic orientation, then, 'explore[s] how, from a given situation, one can construct another situation by means of the 'addition' of an indiscernible multiple of the initial situation'. This approach can be metaphorically linked to the documentary style of Alain Resnais, whose landmark documentary, *Night and Fog*, undertakes the bringing-to-'appearance' of those aspects of the holocaust that continue to be 'invisible' (or 'indiscernible') from the perspective of the state, creating a form that is adequate to the investigation of that which is most properly formless. What I am identifying as a 'generic truth procedure' is the painstaking manner in which the elements of the situation are 'counted', both according to the prevailing regime of knowledge and, simultaneously, as being included

20. Badiou, 'Fifteen Theses on Contemporary Art'.
21. Alain Badiou, *Manifesto for Philosophy*, trans. Norman Madarasz, Albany, State University of New York Press, 1999, pp. 106-7 (henceforth MP).

within a separate (what Badiou would call 'excrescent') part of that same situation that is indiscernible from within the governing norms of representation. Thus, Resnais' documentary can be said to construct a generic set that cuts a diagonal across the veridical truth of the situation, initiating an on going interrogation of the foreclosed aspects of an immanent truth. Much as the generic set cannot be totalized and therefore is resistant to being simply added to the constructible set universe (since such nomination would destroy its being *as* generic), Resnais' work does not set out to present the Truth of the holocaust. However, by his serial interrogation of the material traces, he seeks to extract immanent fragments from which he constructs his truth procedure. This leads us to suggest that Resnais' orientation, or manner of 'thinking of being' avoids the pitfalls of constructivism: since the localized truth of the holocaust is precisely the unthought of the situation, it cannot simply be brought to representation, since it ex-ists as its Real. In other words, it exceeds V=L. It is equally apparent that Resnais' work does not seek to evoke a transcendent Truth of the holocaust—a temptation to which many contemporary ethical theorists fall prey,[22] rather, he departs from a formalization which allows him to interrogate the excess of the Real over the governance of representation. It is this subtractive approach that makes Resnais' work analogous to Badiou's mathematical orientation. We shall return to Resnais' film shortly, as I undertake an exploration of the capacity of category theory to offer a more nuanced reading of localized being-there within the diegetic world(s) of the documentary.

While set theory remains the proper means of inscribing being as being, it does not offer any insight into *how* particular beings interact within a particular context, thus Badiou's latest work turns to category theory to provide a means of mapping the structure of any localized section of being—or a way of thinking the 'appearing' of a world. In particular, topos theory affords the means of explicating the *plurality* of 'worlds', since it models the structural determination of all potential situations, or topoi, rather than providing a global regulatory framework that accounts for a single, totalized Being. In terms of mathematics/ontology, this means it can map the set universe that holds for the different thought orientations or 'decisions' taken by the working mathematician, providing a consist-

---

22. Badiou distances himself from the contemporary 'ethical' stance in philosophical thinking that valorizes the victim, and seeks to make suffering sacred. Resnais' documentary avoids this stance, framing a political challenge to think the truth of the holocaust in order to prevent its recurrence.

ent map of the relations that structure the universe following certain axiomatic presuppositions.

Traditionally, we have approached the question of world from the point of view of a being and their degree of consciousness of, or relation to it. Category theory by-passes this binary subject/object relation, placing the emphasis on the relation itself as the active component that effectively gives the being its capacity for appearing, legislating its mode of *being there*—the donation of place. A 'world' is a topos delineated by a finite series of identifications and operations. The anchor for all relations stems from the Void, as the only multiple-being that has no elements as is thus immediately determined.[23] All other multiples are made up of elements, which means that the multiple itself is determined according to its elements.[24]

> [...] one calls 'world' (for those operations) a multiple-being such that, if a being belongs to it, every being whose being is assured on the basis of the first—in accordance with the aforementioned operations—belongs to it equally.
>
> Thus, a world is a multiple-being closed for certain derivations of being.[25]

'World' in this sense, is properly speaking, the situation, or localized context within which the operation that allows a being to appear-there is performed. This formal condition of 'appearing' or becoming locally situated is extrinsic to the proper Being of an essent, but which allows an aspect of its Being to appear a certain way, as conditioned by its contingent network of (multiple) relations.[26] Something can only be said to 'appear' in

---

23. Alain Badiou, 'The Transcendental', *Theoretical Writings*, trans. Ray Brassier and Alberto Toscano, London, Continuum Books, 2004, pp. 189-220, p. 191.

24. Since all of these operations are contingent on the void as the only immediately determined being, it is theoretically possible to produce an ontological rank, relative to the multiple's distance from its origin, or the number of operations performed in its composition. However, since there is no whole of Being, there can be no single scale upon which multiple being can be ordered—there are multiples whose construction does not intersect with other multiples outside the single shared foundational set of the void. This cancels the possibility of any global uniformity, or categorization of beings: identifications and relations are always local. It is this property that Badiou exploits in his definition of 'world'.

25. Badiou, 'The Transcendental', p. 192.

26. It is important to note that the operation is dependent upon the place: without an ontologically presented multiple, there is nothing which can be located via the onto-logical operation. As we have seen, a world is constituted by a sequence of operations that map relations from an already existent being to a second being that is thinkable with respect to

a world if it participates in a relation with another being within the same localized context. Thus an object x can be expressed on an ontological level as a pure multiple, using a set theoretical framework, but this makes no existential claims. As Badiou notes '[w]hen x is said mathematically the possible and real become indiscernible'.[27] If we want to claim that x exists, it has to be situated (x belongs to S). Thus, existence is not an attribute of x alone, but is a function of its relation to S, hence what Badiou terms 'appearance' is 'what is thinkable about x in so far as it belongs to S'.

It is important to note that the being-ness of an existent is always thinkable relative to the situation within which it is embedded. Since being itself is not-all, then '[b]eing is only exposed to thought as a local site of its untotalizable unfolding' (TO 153-68, 161) Indeed, determination itself can only be understood in a relative sense, since the essent must be situated in order to show its 'beingness'. The morphisms of a situation form the objects that make up its map, thus any instance of 'being there' does not derive its attributes from the ontological manifold, but relative to the onto-logic of its context. Hence Badiou's focus on 'appearing', which he argues is an intrinsic determination of Being:

> Appearing is the site, the 'there' (*là*) of the multiple-existent insofar as it is thought in its being. Appearing in no way depends on space or time, or more generally on a transcendental field. It does not depend on a Subject whose constitution would be presupposed. The manifold-being does not appear *for* a Subject. Instead, it is more in line with the essence of the existent to appear. (TO 162)

This leads to the paradoxical overturning of the Platonic binary of appearance and ideality, since the immediate or given world is a world that is intimately structured, a web of relations and intensities, that stabilize the inconsistency of multiple-being within a determinate, situated logic. In contrast, the world of idealities—as inscribed by set theory—is a space

---

the first. The operation itself does not 'exist', but is inferred relative to the new point that is nameable as a result of its action. Thus: '[w]e call "situation of being", for a singular being, the world in which it inscribes a local procedure of access to its being on the basis of other beings'. The onto-logical operation actualizes possible formations within the different multiples of presentation and allows them to appear within a localized context. The being of these elements insists prior to their actualization; the operation one-ifies them, by linking them in a network of relations that establish degrees of difference and identity within the presented situation. These values are not absolute, i.e. they are not ontological, thus the 'same' element can be appear concurrently (and therefore differently) in a variety of worlds.

27. Alain Badiou, 'Notes Toward Thinking Appearance', *Theoretical Writings*, trans. Ray Brassier and Alberto Toscano, London, Continuum Books, 2004, p. 181.

of disjunction and absolute differentiation, a 'sense-deprived' rationality that lays down the composition of manifolds in an axiomatic austerity. The practical applications of categorical analysis remain to be established. In terms of film studies it affords the possibility of mapping the appearing of elements within a given diegetic world, and in particular, the 'in-appearing' of those elements that would (potentially) be included within the construction of a generic extension.

Alain Resnais' documentary, *Night and Fog*, can be approached as a meditation on 'appearing', explored through the disjunctive worlds of the Jews in the concentration camps, the Germanic 'Volk', and the present day world of the viewer. While the potency of Blanchot's writings on the disaster remain unparalleled in providing a nuanced insight into the destitution of subjectivity and the peculiar timelessness of the event, Badiou's framework adds an invaluable commentary on the logic of the situation—the lack of mediating phenomenological consciousness[28] in the categorical framework paradoxically enables one to think the relational complexity of the different worlds, without inflicting the violence of determining the being of any of those who suffered this inapprehensible experience. Badiou's onto-logic describes the being-there, or the degrees of intensity of appearance of any single being within a given situation—it does not make judgement regarding their actual Being, since each essent has the potential to appear in a variety of ways, and in multiple situations. It remains important to underline that the holocaust itself does not figure as an 'event' for Badiou, primarily because it is a product of the Nazi's *political* agenda. The ideology of the Third Reich is identified as a simulacrum of an event, and as such serves as a paradigm of evil.

The opening shots of *Night and Fog* introduce the antagonistic multiples, or 'envelopes'[29] of a world, that will structure the film. The present

---

28. Badiou stresses that his own demonstrations of the applicability of categorical logic are largely allegorical, retaining a 'vulgar' phenomenological slant, whereas in fact '[t]his entire arrangement can do without my gaze, without my consciousness, without my shifting attention...' (Alain Badiou, *Theoretical Writings*, ed. and trans. Ray Brassier and Alberto Toscano, London, Continuum Books, 2004, p. 208.). My own analysis follows Badiou's mapping of the terrain. To take full advantage of category theory's departure from the privileging of consciousness it remains necessary to theorize the construction of worlds within the diegetic framework, and concurrently map their relation to the world(s) of the spectator. In the case of *Night and Fog*, the film addresses an audience on the tenth anniversary of WWII, which has to be factored in alongside the viewing present of each particular screening. I am particularly interested in how category theory might lead us to re-think specularity and appearance outside traditional matrixes of spectatorship.

29. The highest value of the synthesis of the total network of relations that form the

day site of what will be revealed as the former concentration camp, shot
in colour and accompanied by the light-hearted flute music (scored especially for the film by Hans Eisler) is introduced as a 'tranquil landscape'.
The camera then pans down to include the stark outline of an electric
fence that cuts across the harmony of the landscape, dividing the screen
with a gesture which seems to signal a rupture, or a 'disjunctive' conjunction between this element and the rest, since they are situated within a
single world (they each appear within the film frame) yet the common
element of their respective intensities of appearance is nil—it approaches
the minimum value of appearance within a part of being. While the film
would seem to be setting up an emblematically disjunctive relation between what it identifies as the 'closed world' of the camp, and the 'tranquil landscape' surrounding it, topos theory allows us to approach this
differently: despite the effective (and deliberate) lack of appearance of the
camp from the situation of the free world, it nevertheless is demonstrably
present as an element of that world, but one that in-appears. It is precisely
this paradox of effacement and inclusion that we will be exploring.

The operation that regulates the appearing of beings does not guarantee that every element of a multiple be granted a place according to
the governing transcendental.[30] As we have seen, since there is no Whole
of Being, the very fact of localization means that the placement of beings
is similarly 'not-all'. Thus, we need to account for this 'zero degree' of

---

consistency of a section of being-there is termed its 'envelope': 'The regional stability of
a world comes down to this: if you take a random fragment of a given world, the beings
that are there in this fragment possess—both with respect to themselves and relative to
one another—differential degrees of appearance which are indexed to the transcendental
order within this world. [...] *Consequently, we call 'envelope' of a part of the world, that being
whose differential value of appearance is the synthetic value appropriate to that part*. (Badiou, 'The
Transcendental', p. 208.). In other words, the envelope is the value of the composite
intensities of appearances within a given segment of a world, and as such it provides a
global stability to this section that underpins all appearances, even those with zero-value,
as this lack of appearance is still a ration that maintains its relation to the envelope itself,
and hence is included as a non-appearance.

30. The transcendental provides a basic ordering of a situation, stemming from a series of
measures that determine the relations between the elements that comprise the situation.
It is important to note that the transcendental is itself a multiple that orders and self-
regulates: the situation itself *is not ordered*. The transcendental determines the conditions
under which its elements operate within the specific, localized appearance. In moving
from the potential real to the actual, we are tracing a reconfiguration of identity from
a formal, singular mode, to a contingent, relational mode. The same set, and the same
elements could appear as or in a wide context of situations, and as such their governing
transcendental would vary according to the different constitution of worlds.

appearance, one which falls within the operating logic that structures a given situation without actually designating a place of 'being-there'. Badiou speaks of a logical mark, or index of non-appearance, an inscription of absence. Moreover, this being that lacks a situation of appearing is fundamental as the lower limit against which all other appearances in the transcendental envelope are to be measured, providing a stable scale against which the variations, or degree of beings draw their meaning. It is important to bear in mind that situational difference between elements is simply a question of the intensity with which they appear *in relation* to all the other elements within that world: there is no absolute measure of appearance, or appearance 'in itself'. This being given, an element with 'zero degree' appearance within a world is one with the least degree of relation with all other elements, thus, from the perspective of that particular world, it is not 'there': it is an element in the multiple being on the ontological level, but from the onto-logical perspective of the situation itself, it is not present.[31]

While the wire fence does not seem to appear within the envelope of the rural world, their juxtaposition entails a re-configuring of the topos. The widening of the context allows a re-calibration of the network of relations, and what Badiou calls the 'global unity' of the section of the world is reconstituted to allow for its conjunction with the totality of its elements. This degree of relation, then, is calculated in terms of the value of the conjunction between the wire fence and the synthesis of the value of its relations to all of the apparents within the envelope of the tranquil landscape, considered case by case. In our current example, the train tracks that appeared with a LM degree of intensity within the initial rural configuration, when taken in conjunction with the wire fence immediately take

---

31. To bring out this crucial distinction, Badiou offers an example of natural numbers, which we have already established consist of transitive ordinals and contain their own logic of succession—thus their ontological status is given. However, when we turn to an instance of their use within an empirical situation, such as the numbering of the pages of a book, whilst their intrinsic being remains unaltered, it becomes possible to make claims about their varying degrees of appearance. Any page number participates in the situation of the book, and is governed by a transcendental logic that relates each number to the rest in terms of their sequencing. Within this, it is evident that some numbers appear more intensely than others—for example the chapter numbers that are singled out in the index and form a separate sub-set of extra-significant numbers, a difference that gives them a higher value of appearance since these are the ones to which all the other numbers in that respective chapter are related. Similarly, numbers that do not correspond to a given page (say, 37777) can be said to have zero-appearance within this situation—whilst ontologically they share the same being as other ordinals, or natural numbers, within this finite situation of appearing their relation is minimal (Badiou, 'The Transcendental', p. 217).

on a maximal degree of appearance, since they change from being part of a sleepy rural railroad, to being implicated in the deportation of the Jews—the path that anticipates the link between the two different worlds of the camps and the free world. This gesture is to be repeated throughout the film, as the routine of the present which initially seems removed from the inarticulable horrors of the camps, is re-connected to this unquantifiable multiple, demonstrating over and again the logical *relation* that binds the two as a single world. The documentary foregrounds the formal difficulty of being present-to that which remains subtracted from nomination, or representation, while paradoxically underlining the insistence of that which 'in-appears' within the current situation.

Certainly, the documentary foregrounds the intercalary relation between the 'tranquil landscape' and the camp site: grass has overgrown the tell-tale tracks, and the literal sites of the atrocities seem softened by the summer sunshine, the crumbling buildings ironically becoming almost picturesque such that, the narrator informs us, the crematorium has become the subject of postcards and snapshots. The buildings that housed the subjugated now appear bland, neutral, baldly refusing any appearance of extraordinariness that one feels events ought to have inscribed upon their surface. This aura of specious normality is taken up by the narration that details the production, planning and construction of the camps, undertaken as pragmatically as if they were any 'hostel or stadium', with 'estimates, bids, bribes'. The black and white documentary footage that accompanies this section again fails to bring-to-appearance any of the horror that the re-visiting of these images now invokes. It is only in the incongruous listing of the various architectural styles chosen for the camps, presented almost as though it were a lesson in real estate 'alpine style, garage style, Japanese style, no style', that we begin to understand that the failure to form a consistent envelope proper-to the appearing of the camps is not simply due to a current disjunction of worlds. Rather, it signals an operating logic which deliberately sought to efface that appearance, building facades, semblances that present a transcendental that mimics that of its rural context, an act that testifies to the 'imagination' of the designers, who indeed had the ability to envisage 'gates to be passed through only once', and the callous foresight to design them as part of the 'tranquil landscape', such that the atrocity remained screened, having a nil value of appearance within the larger world of the German people. To put this differently, the very fact that the various styles of the camps are all included within the larger matrix of representation that constitutes the German state of the situation, enabled the prevention of the 'appearing' of the camps as such: at the time, they ex-sisted as an undetermined generic set without a unifying predicate to make them identifiable.

The documentary's meditation on the destitution of subjectivity maps the descent from singularity to the de-humanized dissemination of parts, devoid of particularity: the deliberate attempt to erase the being-there, or appearing of a whole section of humanity. To trace this, we must first review the identity laws, which consist of three categorical prescriptions for stabilizing a universe. For every object '*a*' there is an identical arrow *id(a)* associated with it, i.e. a map in which the domain and codomain are the same set *A*, *and* for each *a* in A, *f (a)* = *a* is called an identity map, written I_A.[32] Badiou remarks that the identity arrow is a 'neutral element' in the operation of an arrow composition. The identity map is also known as an 'endomap', as its compositional map is internal, leading Badiou to equate it with the 'null action of the One's minimal power' (TO 143-52, 146), or the inertia of reflexive relations that function as a stopping point.

The tautological composition of the identity map is contrasted with the expression of 'the same' *extrinsically*, or isomorphically. Unlike in set theory (on the ontological level) in which we determine two sets (or multiples) to be identical if they have the same elements, otherwise they are absolutely distinct, category theory admits degrees of relation. Two objects are said to be categorically indiscernible if there is a reversible (or isomorphic) arrow connecting them. This means that logically the same set of relations hold for each object. However, there remains the possibility of cancelling an inversion, which in itself identifies each object as literally distinct, although within the map they are identical—a formal, relational judgement.

This definition is added to the laws of composition and association[33] to generate the definition of a group within category theory: 'A group is a

---

32. F. W. Lawvere and S. H. Schanuel, *Conceptual Mathematics: A First Introduction to Categories*, Cambridge, Cambridge University Press, 1997, p. 15.

33. 1) Two arrows following one another make up a composition, or to put this differently, if we have an arrow 'f' that links a to its codomain b, and a second arrow 'g' that has b as its domain, and c as its codomain, then we can state that object a is linked to c (by g o f—expressed as 'g following f'). The two maps represented by the arrow and its respective domain and codomain produce a composite map written:

$$A \xrightarrow{f} B \xrightarrow{g} C.$$

2) the associative law, which shows that

f o (g o h) = (f o g) o h

(and thereby allows us to leave out the parentheses and just write ' *h o g o f*, or 'h following g following f'). cf. Lawvere and Schanuel, *Conceptual Mathematics: A First Introduction to*

category that has a single object in which every arrow is an isomorphism' (TO 148) Thus, a group comprises an object that is identified purely by the anonymity of a letter and the set of morphisms that are associated with it, or 'the set of the different ways in which object-letter G is identical to itself' (TO 149). Where set-theory looks at the ordering of elements to determine identity between sets, in category theory the 'elements' are arrows, the operations mapping a composition, not the objects upon which it operates—indeed the object is the point of inertia, or neutral element that offers zero information, other than tautological self-evidence. We are clearly offered a different perspective on 'identity'—rather than the repetition of the same, we have a plurality of active ways of producing the same, the configurations via which it isomorphically manifests itself *as* the same. Badiou theorizes this via reference to the Platonic dialectical relation between the Same and the Other: whereas the identity endomap conforms to a mimetic relation, the activity of the isomorphisms perform a 'specular' relation as the reversibility of each arrow that claims two literally distinct elements as logically the same performs a doubling, a pair of symmetrical identifications that, when taken simultaneously, collapse back into the inertia of the endomap.

In rethinking identity in this categorical manner, we see how the being-there of an essent is determined not by the composition of its fixed properties (i.e. the ordering of its elements, which comprise its ontological being) but through to its active self-production which 'gives' its identity via the combination of relations it entails. Difference is not absolute, since the identity arrows are caught up within a network of Same/Other relations, but a question of degree—and here we are close to Deleuze's notion of intensities. These areas of convergence between same/other are not simply points of mimetic similarity between distinct essents (shared elements, such as the null set that is common to all constructed sets) but active relations that *produce* the identities of the two domains that are joined by the isomorphic arrows. Since these relations are not derived from fixed attributes but comprise active links that produce connections of sameness and difference, we can see how a situation is fluid, and yet rigorously structured.

Relating this back to the operational logic of the camps as portrayed in Resnais' documentary, we can note the deliberate attempt to erase the differential of appearances, as each inmate is stripped of any external marker that might distinguish them. This descent from ontological singu-

---

Categories, p. 15.

larity, to the erasure of onto-logic appearing, is portrayed in the film as a passage from family groups, lingering close-ups of individual faces prior to their boarding the trains, to the sealing off of carriages as prelude to the ultimate concealment of appearance in the camp. Within the confines of the camp we no longer see images of 'whole' people, the fragmentation of identity is signalled by the de-subjectivized close-ups of the different body parts that are regulated, disciplined, upon arrival —naked, tattooed, numbered, and shaved—operations that do not seem to happen to some*one*. All inmates appear with a similar, minimum degree of intensity, or lack of appearance, since differentiation itself is systematically effaced.

The effacement of identity can be thought of as severing, or restricting, the multiple relations via which an individual constitutes the identity. In being reduced to just one more name, or number, meticulously recorded in a register, identity ceases to be interrelational, and is restricted to the minimal tautological relation that Badiou equates with the inertia of the One, the pure inscription that opens the place for an essent to appear, without allowing any dialectic between self/other to modulate the relational intensity with which an ontological singularity manifests the diversity and variety of its situated appearing. This inertia in effect is the minimum degree of self-relation that produces a limited identity, or fixes the being-there within a localized world as merely 'countable'.

This minimal inscription of presence/absence is emphasized in the film by the many ways in which the prisoners are systematically 'erased' from the registers. The 'closed universe' of the camp enters into relation with a simulacrum of the Germanic world beyond its gates, having a hospital, but one in which all illness is reduced to a single ailment, the 'same ointment for every disease', or 'treatment' is in fact 'death by syringe'. Suffering is homogenized 'in the end each inmate resembles the next, a body of indeterminate age that dies with its eyes open'—even death, that which gives beings their singularity, is reduced to a process in which there remains no 'I' to die, only the endless dying of 'someone'; again, the degree of visibility of all apparents is negated such that even death fails to register as a singularizing event. Counter to this hospital in which all patients receive the same degree of inattention, we have the surgical block where the patients receive an inordinate degree of surveillance, becoming guinea pigs for pointless, grotesque operations, testing grounds for drugs, or simply a focus for idle experimentation. The well equipped surgeries here are not to heal the body, but produce deviant variations, new modes of appearing that violate the laws of nature and the humanity of the victim.

Once identity is reduced to the minimum inscription of place, number, one would imagine that no further destitution were possible. However, the imperative of the Final Solution provoked Nazi ingenuity to take the mania for dismantlement even further: the total effacement of the appearing of the Jewish prisoners is undertaken via the methodical dissemination into parts. That all elements that combined to produce the singularity of an individual were methodically stripped away we have already established, however, the perverse extent of this process that demanded the cataloguing and storing of all these dismembered attributes speaks to a desire to mutilate the identity of the prisoner beyond any possible recognition or recuperation. Footage from the Nazi warehouses depicts vast piles of confiscated property—the corollary of the 'properties' of each individual that were shed. Piles of clothes, dusty and moth eaten; mountains of odd shoes, spectacles, carelessly piled up, indifferent to scratches; combs, shaving equipment, the intimate debris of particular lives, separated out into their disparate elements and formed into a new, amorphous multiple, constructed of a single element that is reiterated to the nth degree, a magnitude of such scale that their original value, or use becomes lost, their specific features blurred in the sheer incomprehensible volume of which they are an indiscernible element —who is to re-use these mouldy shaving brushes, or pick out a particular cracked pair of reading glasses? Surely the point is not the thrifty cataloguing and recycling of resources, but the dismantlement of a section of humanity to its minimum parts, an operation Badiou terms 'immanent dissemination' whereby the elements that comprise an element are further broken down into their sub-elements, an extrapolation of relation, to its limit point—to the point at which the original being loses all particularity, being denuded of property, and the sub-elements themselves are re-configured to form infinitely large multiplicities that extend beyond any imaginable capacity to think their individual use. Each item is placed in a context where there is no possibility of it retaining its intrinsic personal value, as operated in relation to its original context. Thus, even the smallest elements are reduced in their appearing to an absolute minimum.

In category theory, the logical operation of negation derives from the relation of dependence. As we saw with the zero-value of a being that does not appear within a world, this lack of relation is not understood as a simple negation, but is linked to the envelope or the synthesizing transcendental, such that it has a value in the world—it inappears—rather than functioning as a hole, or break in the fabric of its continuity. This insight is generalized to produce a logic of negation. Rather than restricting our operation to a single element that accords to the minimum degree of appearance, we can deduce whole sections, or envelopes that belong to a world, but are unrelated to other envelopes. Thus, if we construct the envelope that centres around the initial being-there of an apparent we are also able to construct a set, or envelope of those beings, or elements, with which it has zero (or minimum) relation, and within this set we can again extract the measure that synthesizes this collective being-there for this separate part of the world. This provides a measure of the reverse of our former situation.

> We shall call 'reverse' of the degree of appearance of a being-there in a world, the envelope of that region of the world comprising all the beings-there whose conjunction with the first has a value of zero (the minimum).[34]

Badiou stresses that it is of particular significance that the logical operation of negation occurs as a *result* of the transcendental parameters (minimality, conjunction and the envelope) and is not a meta-structural condition imposed from without.

This mania of effacement and control reaches its zenith in the Nazi hoarding of the hair of the shaved camp women. Here we have the material link between property as possession and property as attribute. Not only are the women made anonymous, sexless via the humiliating act of being shorn, but the markers of their individuality and freedom is retained and amassed, forming an shapeless billowing mass of curls and tangles, impossible to take in as the camera pans across the expanse of the warehouse showing acres of hair, a quantity so expansive that there is no other contextualizing feature within the frame to help the viewer to comprehend what they are seeing. Here surely is the height of redundancy, a dismantling that exceeds sense.

But no, the documentary transitions to its final phase, where it traces the logic of in-appearing from the attempt to deny visibility, difference, to its actual transformation—its appearing-as-other. The shapeless hair becomes neat bales of cloth, stacked ready for the practical German Hausfrau, the recalcitrant skeletons that withstood the fires of the crematorium are re-cycled as fertilizer, bodies yield up fat to produce soap, and even skin is re-used as paper: one of the fluttering scraps that testify to this has, ironically, a beautiful female face drawn upon it—a grotesque inscription of lack at the very site of the inexistent whose absence it attests. In focusing on this literal inappearance of the Jews within the German situ-

---

34. Badiou, 'The Transcendental', p. 214.

ation, Resnais seeks to discuss the wider problem of thinking the Real of the holocaust. While the very use of document, of historical footage, to construct his argument might suggest that, on the contrary, the reality is all to evident, the closing sequence of the film underlines its continuing resistance to being thought. The universal denial of responsibility extends beyond the depicted post-war trials, ironically implicating the work of art itself, as its release for distribution (so Resnais tells us[35]) was contingent upon the erasure of a French soldier's cap, shown supervising the deportation of the Jews. In answer to the closing question 'Who is responsible?' even ten years later, the answer continued to be no one. In submitting to the change *and* remarking it, Resnais remains faithful to his artistic conviction which demands that he inscribe the impossibility of the bringing-to-appearance of the inexistent within the current state of the situation—ontological impossibility proper, but in parallel with the onto-logic (as here, the crassly political) level.

So long as we consider 'appearing' within a traditional ('vulgar') phenomenological framework, we can leverage only indirectly, through allegory, category theory's ability to map the logic of appearing within the diegetic frame. The real strength of category theory is its independence from phenomenology, from the centering consciousness of the subject, from the parameters of space and time. This makes category theory a particularly attractive tool for mapping the site of subtractive truth(s) in the field of art, for discussing works of art purely in terms of their 'in-appearing', and in terms of their relation with truth, and the character of that truth. In closing, we may consider some words of Chris Marker, another thinker of the generic, that 'truth is not the destination, but perhaps it is the path'[36]—and where documentary truth is at stake, it is perhaps even more explicitly the procedure, rather than the constructed artefact.

---

35. Interview at the time of the film's release, now included with the distribution of the film on video.
36. Chris Marker, quoted in Mark Shivas, 'New Approach', *Movie 8*, no. 13, April 1963.

11

Can Cinema Be Thought?:
Alain Badiou and the Artistic Condition

Alex Ling

I. THE ART OF THE MATERIALIST DIALECTIC

In his recent *Logiques des mondes: l'être et l'événement, 2*, Alain Badiou names the tension integral to his philosophy—namely the one which runs between being and event, knowledge and truth—a 'materialist dialectic'. It is on the basis of this peculiar dialectic that he opposes his own philosophical project to the contemporary 'democratic materialism' which more and more defines our epoch (prescribed as it is by the master signifiers 'relativism', 'democracy', 'terror' and the like). In contrast to the apparent sophistry of this democratic materialism—whose principal assertion is that 'there are only bodies and languages'[1]—Badiou's materialist dialectic proclaims 'there are only bodies and languages, *except that there are truths*' (LM 12). Or again: there are only worlds in which beings appear (of which the pure multiple figures being qua being) *except that there are truths which can come to supplement these worlds (and which are universalizable)*. Such is Badiou's philosophical axiom, within which we find the three principal strata comprising his thought, namely, the ontological (the thinking of the pure multiple, of being qua being), the logical (the thinking of appearance, of being-in-a-world) and the subject-ive (the thinking of truths, of *thought* itself). Yet these three terms alone are meaningless without an (albeit subtracted) fourth, which is of course the 'abolished flash' that is the event (LM 156). Already we can discern here a clear conditional divide between

---

1. Alain Badiou, *Logiques des mondes: l'être et l'événement, 2*, Paris, Seuil, 2006, p. 9 (henceforth LM).

the first three terms (ontology, logic, thought) and the fourth (event), insofar as whilst the former are themselves thought mathematically by virtue of three distinct scientific events—respectively the Cantor-event (set theory), the Grothendieck-event (category theory), and the Cohen-event (genericity or forcing)—mathematics can say nothing of the event itself. On this point Badiou is unequivocal, for

> if real ontology is set up as mathematics by evading the norm of
> the One, unless this norm is reestablished globally there also ought
> to be a point wherein the ontological, hence mathematical field,
> is de-totalized or remains at a dead end. I have named this point
> the '*event*'.[2]

Simply, mathematics can think the event only to the extent that it can think its own real qua impasse. Or again, mathematics thinks the event insofar as it axiomatizes its own aporetic structure (as we see for example in Gödel's theory of incompletion or in the axiom of foundation). Contrarily, the event, of which science must remain silent, and on which the concept of truth relies absolutely, is thought solely under condition of art.

Given then the evental importance of art (coupled with the fact that Badiou is an accomplished novelist and playwright in his own right) it is surprising to observe the relative scarcity of critical reflection on Badiou's conception of art (when compared to, say, the abundance of works considering Badiou's understanding of politics).[3] Indeed it follows that—insofar as it is art and art alone that thinks the event—the real nexus of Badiou's dialectic lies with the artistic condition, or, to be more precise, with the 'subtractive' poetry of Stéphane Mallarmé.[4] Thus Badiou notes immediately after introducing his dialectic that in its principal assertion ('there are only bodies and languages, except that there are truths') 'one will recognize here the style of my master Mallarmé: nothing will have taken

---

2. Alain Badiou, *Briefings on Existence: A Short Treatise on Transitory Ontology*, trans. Norman Maderasz, New York, SUNY, 2006, p. 60 (henceforth TO).

3. This is further compounded if we consider Badiou's own efforts to tie the question of art to that of political emancipation. For example, in his 'Fifteen Theses on Contemporary Art' Badiou states that 'the question of art today is a question of political emancipation, there is something political in art itself. There is not only a question of art's political orientation, like it was the case yesterday, today it is a question in itself. Because art is a real possibility to create something new against the abstract universality that is globalisation', *Lacanian Inc*, vol. 23, 2004, p. 107.

4. Badiou says as much on numerous occasions. To pick but a single example: 'Mallarmé is a thinker of the event-drama, in the double sense of its appearance-disappearance … and of its interpretation which gives it the status of an "acquisition for ever," Alain Badiou, *Being and Event*, trans. Oliver Feltham, London, Continuum, 2005, p. 191 (henceforth BE).

place but the place, except, on high, perhaps, a constellation' (LM 12).[5] So the sequence of scientific events (Cantor-Grothendieck-Cohen) principally conditioning Badiou's philosophy is supplemented by the Mallarmé-event, exceptional in its singular, non-mathematical and axial status. Of course this separation—of poetry and mathematics—is far from innocent, being on the contrary illustrative of a fundamental antagonism lying at the (voided) interval of art and science.[6] Accordingly within Badiou's artistic system or his 'inaesthetics'—inaesthetics being namely his approach to art which restricts its considerations to 'the strictly intraphilosophical effects produced by the existence of some works of art' (LM 12)[7]—the 'imperial poem' takes pride of place. Indeed, it is the expressly *literal* arts—those arts of the letter: of poetry as much as theatre and the novel—which command Badiou's closest attention, to the extent that, as Jacques Rancière has remarked, 'ultimately only two arts are required in Badiou's system of the arts: the poem as affirmation, as inscription of a disappearance, and theatre as the site wherein this affirmation turns into mobilization'.[8] In point of fact, beyond these expressly literal arts art becomes for Badiou both decidedly less artistic and less amenable to inaesthetic consideration. Hence in Badiou's eyes dance for example falls short—undeservedly, one hastens to add—of artistic status, serving instead as its metaphor (or rather as the metaphor of real thought). Painting, on the other hand—though clearly itself an art (in *Logique des mondes*, for example, painting exemplifies artistic truth)—by virtue of its decidedly non-literal form, proves itself (as we shall see) somewhat difficult to justify artistically (to say nothing of sculpture or architecture, let alone the myriad other 'illiterate' arts).

---

5. cf. Stéphane Mallarmé, *Collected Poems*, trans. Henry Weinfield, Berkeley, University of California Press, 1994, pp. 142-144.

6. Indeed, Badiou notes that in their subjective (true) dimension 'science proves to be the opposite of art, which explains the spectacular isomorphism of their evental traces', LM, p. 84.

7. Alain Badiou, *Handbook of Inaesthetics*, trans. Alberto Toscano, Stanford, California, Stanford UP, 2005, p. xiv (henceforth HI).

8. Jacques Rancière, 'Aesthetics, Inaesthetics, Anti-Aesthetics', in Peter Hallward (ed.) *Think Again: Alain Badiou and the Future of Philosophy*, London, Continuum, 2004, p. 235. I am of course aware that in describing theatre as a 'literal' art I am essentially ignoring its fundamentally performative nature. It should be noted however that whilst Badiou clearly recognizes performativity to be vital to theatre's artistry, his writings on the subject (or at least those which have been translated into English) tend to focus on the texts themselves (outside of the singularity of their performances).

II. CINEMA DECONDITIONED

In considering Badiou's inaesthetics this paper will however take as its focal point the case of cinema, insofar as Badiou's typically polemical writings on the subject appear symptomatic—and arguably serve as the most extreme example—of the decreased amenability to inaesthetic discourse presented by the illiterate arts. Indeed, Badiou's writings on the subject of cinema are distinguished foremost by their deep ambivalence: in his eyes film rests somewhat precariously on the border of art and non-art (although one's immediate impression is that it leans somewhat toward the latter). Simply, cinema is for Badiou an art 'both parasitic and inconsistent' defined first and foremost by its own impurity (HI 83). This impurity hinges as much on cinema's inherent bastardry (film being the product of an unsanctioned union between theatre, photography, music, literature, painting, vaudeville, and so on) and compromised nature (cinema being a collaborative medium governed for the most part by capitalistic concerns), as on its artistically 'porus' nature, that is, its peculiar status as a 'place of intrinsic indiscernibility between art and non-art'.[9] Indeed according to Badiou

> no film strictly speaking is controlled by artistic thinking from beginning to end. It always bears absolutely impure elements within it, drawn from ambient imagery, from the detritus of other arts, and from conventions with a limited shelf life.[10]

Insofar as cinema figures as something of a grey area between art and non-art Badiou contends that artistic activity can be discerned in cinema only as a 'process of purification of its own immanent non-artistic character'.[11] Yet at the same time he consents to the fact that such a process can never be completed (as such cinematic 'purity' might be at best approached only asymptotically). Badiou's overall position regarding the artistic status of cinema would then appear to be the following: the impurity proper to cinema forecloses from the start any possibility of its attaining true (pure) artistic status.

And yet Badiou clearly recognizes cinema to have been an art, his frequent citing of the 'thinking cinema' of Griffith, Welles, Murnau and Eisenstein (as much as Godard, Kiarostami, Visconti, Oliveira and the

---

9. Alain Badiou, 'Philosophy and Cinema', in *Infinite Thought: Truth and the Return to Philosophy*, ed. and trans. Oliver Feltham and Justin Clemens, London, Continuum, 2004, p. 111.

10. Badiou, 'Philosophy and Cinema', p. 111.

11. Badiou, 'Philosophy and Cinema', p. 111.

like) amply attesting this fact. Indeed, cinema's artistic status would seem to have been confirmed far in advance of Badiou's own inaesthetic incursions, insofar as it has served to condition philosophy, most notably that of Gilles Deleuze. As Badiou explains,

> film buffs have always found it difficult to make use of [Deleuze's] two hefty volumes on the cinema, for, however supple the individual film descriptions may be in their own right, this malleability seems nevertheless to function in philosophy's favour, rather than to fashion, in any way whatsoever, a simple critical judgement that film enthusiasts could draw on to enhance the authority of their opinions.[12]

Deleuze's apprehension of film's intraphilosophical effects would thus seem at first glance an absolutely inaesthetic operation (this being accordingly incongruous to any aphilosophical thinking of cinema—namely any other consideration of cinema whatsoever—which simply fall into the thoughtless and self-interested realm of opiniatry). And yet Badiou proceeds to isolate Deleuze's conceptual understanding of cinema as an example—or rather, as *the* example—of Deleuze's 'monotonous' production of concepts insofar as his cinema books propose in the end 'a creative repetition of concepts and not an apprehension of the cinematic art as such':

> let us understand that, under the constraint of the case of cinema, it is once again, and always, (Deleuze's) philosophy that begins anew and that causes cinema to be there *where it cannot, of itself, be.* (D 16)

Which is to say that those concepts found in cinema are in fact not so much found as re-found.[13] Thus the Deleuzian screen—mediated as it is through the thought of Badiou—is stripped of its genitive powers, revealing a space through which Deleuze deploys concepts which, whilst certainly immanent to cinema, are fundamentally anterior in nature.[14]

---

12. Alain Badiou, *Deleuze: The Clamor of Being*, trans. Louise Burchill, Minneapolis, University of Minnesota Press, 2000, pp. 15-16 (henceforth D).

13. One can judge for oneself whether this conception jars with Deleuze's explicit assertion—cited by Badiou—that 'a theory of cinema is not a theory 'about' cinema, but about the concepts that cinema gives rise to', Gilles Deleuze, *Cinema 2: The Time-Image*, trans. Hugh Tomlinsom and Robert Galeta, London, Continuum, 2005, pp. 268-269.

14. In his 'One, Multiple, Multiplicities' Badiou is much more direct: 'I cannot register any kind of caesura between *Difference and Repetition* and the more detailed philosophical texts to be found in the two volumes on cinema', in *Theoretical Writings*, ed. and trans. Ray Brassier and Alberto Toscano, London, Continuum, 2004, p. 70.

By thus attesting to the (conceptually as much as manifestly) re-pre-
sentative nature of cinema Badiou implicitly determines film to not in
fact condition Deleuze's philosophy: the concept is not borne of cinema,
rather, it endures as a passage through the works themselves. Hence as
Badiou, as Badiou explains, in Deleuze's philosophy

> concepts, which are never 'concepts-of', are only attached to the
> initial concrete case in their movement and not in what they give
> to be thought. This is why, in the volumes on the cinema, what one
> learns concerns the Deleuzian theory of movement and time, and
> the cinema gradually becomes neutralized and forgotten. (D 16)

Can we not discern a certain structural (as much as conceptual) homology
between this assertion and Badiou's own inaesthetic conception of cinema
as 'the passage of the idea, perhaps even of its phantom'? (HI 77) As with
the idea, the concept merely passes through the concrete case, meaning
that, insofar as it evinces not 'the sensible creation of the Idea' (LM 27) but
rather serves only to signify its ephemerality, cinema once again falls short
of its artistic aspirations. In fact, we might (provisionally) say that cinema
remains for the most part in Badiou's writings a fundamentally Deleuzian edifice, the peculiar twist or torsion here being that this 'Deleuze' is
a distinctly Badiouian 'Deleuze' (and indeed Badiou's writings on cinema
clearly constitute an implicit dialogue with Deleuze, as can be seen for
example in Badiou's thesis regarding the 'false movements of cinema').[15]

III. IDEAL IMMOBILE MOVEMENT

As we have seen, Badiou's materialist dialectic hinges on the question
of the event which is thought solely by art (and which finds its immediate
coordinates in the poetic thought of Mallarmé). Further, his inaesthetic
conception of art accordingly allows room principally for the literal arts,
making it difficult to properly grasp those arts which fall outside of this category. Having seen then how Badiou grants cinema an artistic *past* (which
paradoxically take the form of 'presents', that is, as specific artistic configurations) whilst ultimately undercutting its conditional status we might
wonder whether—insofar as it fails to produce any 'intraphilosophical effects'—cinema can truly occupy a place in Badiou's inaesthetic system.
Indeed, can concrete cinematic art be identified at all? The opening lines

---

15. cf. HI, pp. 78-88. To take a simple example Deleuze asserts that as a consequence of
the supersession of the movement-image by the time-image 'time ceases to be derived
from the movement; it appears in itself and itself gives rise to *false movements*', *Cinema 2*, pp.
xi-xii.

of Badiou's essay on 'Philosophy and Cinema'—in which he asserts 'there is no 'objective' situation of cinema'[16]—would seem to suggest not. Here Badiou appears to deny from the first the very possibility of there being any truth to (contemporary) cinema for the simple reason that in Badiou's philosophy truth, by virtue of its generic nature, must affect the entirety of the situation: if there is no coherent situation there can be no truth *of* the situation. Nonetheless Badiou acknowledges that select cinematic situations (plural) might be derived on the basis of previous identifiable artistic configurations (or subjects), which he does not shy from cataloguing: 'the films of Oliveira, of Kiarostami, of Straub, of the early Wenders, of a certain Pollet, of some Godards, etc'.[17] Yet even though we can identify multiple cinematic situations in which truth is thinkable—where the 'new new' (the contemporary subjects of cinema) can come into a dialectic with the 'old new' (as delineated by the Oliveiras, the Kiarostamis and the like)[18]—cinema's ineradicable impurity would seem nonetheless to ensure its position as properly antithetical to truth. Badiou's stance is after all that a filmic work is both contemporary and universalizable (that is to say, capable of truth) inasmuch as it purifies its own intrinsic non-artistry (plus all the 'visible and audible materials of everything which binds them to the domination of representation, identification and realism', as much as 'spectacle' and its various operators),[19] which is of course, as he readily admits, an ultimately impossible task. Clearly then a novel cinematic thought—an 'artistic' cinema (or rather one recognized as such by Badiou)—should appear as a sequence of subtractive or dissociative gestures built upon—and recognizable as entering into a dialectic with—those prescriptive works of Straub, of Godard, of Pollet and so forth. That is, cinematic thought would appear, like any other artistic procedure, as a body of works which constitute themselves as finite points of an infinite, albeit anterior, truth (for unlike truth one cannot force an event).[20]

---

16. Badiou, 'Philosophy and Cinema', p. 109.

17. Badiou, 'Philosophy and Cinema', p. 110.

18. 'The new does not enter into a dialectic with the old, but rather with the old new, or the new of the preceding sequence', Badiou, 'Philosophy and Cinema', p. 110

19. Badiou, 'Philosophy and Cinema', p. 114.

20. Badiou thus implicitly argues that an artistic cinema would constitute a fundamentally anti-statist cinema (statist cinema being all cinema in the service of representation, identification, spectacle and the like). We might then infer that, insofar as statist cinema is clearly the dominant filmic guise (qualitatively as much as quantitatively), any artistic cinema would necessarily present itself paradoxically as an anti-cinema. On this point Badiou would be in clear agreement with another of his favoured artistic exemplars Kazimir Malevich and his contention that 'cinema ... must realize that art can exist without the

However cinema's impurity presents a further difficulty, one which concerns any speaking of film qua film, insofar as 'when the film really does organize the visitation of an Idea ... it is always in a subtractive (or defective) relation to one or several among the other arts' (HI 86). Which is to say when an idea 'visits' us cinematically, it is necessarily brought forth by way of an intrafilmic complication of the other arts (for example an ostensibly cinematic idea might be indebted to a certain musical evocation, an actor's peculiar theatricality, and so forth). On this point Badiou concedes nothing to romantic notions of an essence peculiar to cinema: for Badiou there is nothing artistically singular in film per se; 'cinema is nothing but takes and editing. There is nothing else' (HI 86). Which is why cinema is for Badiou nothing other than a sequence of (false) *movements*, meaning that any truth specific to the cinema must relate this movement or passage of the image to the idea itself (or more specifically, to the timeless *immobility* of the idea thus brought forth). Indeed, Badiou goes so far as to state that such ideal immobile movement constitutes the imperative proper to cinema:

> by means of the possibility that is proper to it—of amalgamating the other arts, through takes and montage, without presenting them— cinema can, and must, organise the passage of the immobile. But cinema must also organise the immobility of a passage. (HI 87)

Which is to say that if cinema is in any way to facilitate the passage of an idea it must concurrently ensure that the idea thus brought forth does not itself pass. Thus in other words the unenviable task Badiou demands of any properly artistic cinema would appear to be nothing short of the presentation of immobility *in* movement. However this formulation itself raises a number of questions (to which Badiou offers little by way of answer). For example, how exactly might this peculiar immobility be realized? Badiou's own example taken from Jacques Tati's *Playtime* (1967)—of the dialectic established 'between the movement of a crowd and the vacuity of what could be termed its atomic composition' (HI 87) as spatially accounting for the passage of the immobile—achieves little by way of clarification: how precisely does Tati's sequence effect the immobility of a passage (to say nothing of the precise status of the dialectic established

image, without everyday life, and without the idea's visage', Kazimir Malevich, 'And Visages Are Victorious on the Screen', in Oksana Bulgakowa (ed.) *Kazimir Malevich: The White Rectangle; Writings on Film*, trans. Oksana Bulgakowa, San Francisco, Potemkin Press, 2002, p. 43. One does tend to wonder however exactly how Badiou can resolve such a thinking of artistic cinema with his realization that '"pure cinema" does not exist, except in the dead-end vision of avant-garde formalism'. Badiou, 'Philosophy and Cinema', p111.

therein)? Furthermore, what exactly is the idea that Tati is mobilizing (and if the idea is that of the immobile itself how does Tati's sequence differentiate itself from other seemingly equally re-presentational cases, such as are found in the contemporary cinemas of Terrence Malick or David Lynch)? In addition, if as Badiou states cinema is itself 'nothing but takes and editing' we might wonder what the ultimate result of a purging of its non-artistic content might be? Lastly we might question whether the very concept of immobile movement is itself consistent with the remainder of Badiou's thoughts on cinema, which is to say, can Badiou's conception of cinema as both a potential passage (of the idea) and an inexorable passing (of the image) be reconciled with the idea of immobility itself?

IV. ILLITERATE CINEMA AND THE REMAINDER OF ART

In considering these questions let us first restate the difficulties encountered in Badiou's writings on cinema are to a large extent symptomatic of its imagistic nature, insofar as it is plainly more conducive for philosophy (which is, after all, a fundamentally literal medium) to consider those arts which themselves find concrete support in the letter. The fact of the matter is that, outside of formal exegesis and the subjective fleetingness of affect, the image does not lend itself well to the letter. This is of course not to say that that artistic inscription itself is directly at issue—on the contrary it is inscription (of the inexistent of a world) which serves as the overriding imperative of art qua generic procedure—but rather to highlight the problem of transmissibility, which might be formulated as follows: how might the non-literal be transmitted by way of the letter?[21] Take for example Badiou's recent words on Claude Monet's *Nymphéas*:

> the goal of Monet is to directly inscribe on the artificial surface of the painting the light and colours as the process of division of light. But light and its division does not exist at the surface of water ... So Monet has to force the painting to express the inexistent, the inexistent which is not things in light, but light as a thing ... and finally when we see the painting we understand that it's not really light as a thing, it's the impossibility of something like that. But this failure is the victory of painting. This failure is the glory of painting as such.[22]

21. On this point we cannot help but think both of the Lacanian concept of the 'pass' and of the ultimate aim of the analytic cure, which is to render 'a knowledge that is wholly transmissible, without remainder', Alain Badiou, 'The Formulas of *l'Etourdit*, *Lacanian Inc*, vol. 27, 2006, p. 81.

22. Badiou, 'Arts Imperative: Speaking the Unspeakable' *Lacan.com*, vol. 26, 2006, http://

We can clearly observe here the difficulty—faced by artist and philosopher alike—of articulating the image through the letter in Monet's expressing 'light as a thing' (indeed, it is the necessary failure of such an inscription—pictorially as much as literally—that designates for Badiou its true artistry). This difficulty is one Badiou does not shy from acknowledging. On the contrary, Badiou is refreshingly forthcoming about the problem the visual arts present philosophy, admitting

> of all the arts, it's the one that intimidates me the most. Its intellectual charge is the greatest … So turning to visual art philosophically has always been rather difficult for me. It's not a feeling of ignorance at all, but a feeling that the mode in which intellectuality proceeds irreducibly into complex and powerful sensory forms . . . really, painting intimidates me … What's more, I've never been very satisfied by the attempts of my predecessors to place themselves under the condition of painting. Nor have I ever found a regime of prose adequate to talk about painting.[23]

Returning then to the case of cinema it is clear that we encounter in fact not one but two complicated passages: of the idea through the image (the artistic or aesthetic passage), and of the image through the letter (the philosophic or inaesthetic passage). This in mind we might conclude the apparent hegemony of the letter in Badiou's inaesthetics to be ultimately one of convenience, resulting as it does from the simple fact that the non-literal consistently fails to render a wholly—or even partially—transmissible knowledge. Yet, however problematic it may be to express literally, as we have seen painting is for Badiou clearly an art whereas cinema remains artistically unclear (a fact which appears all the more strange given that Deleuze's two cinema books spend a great deal of time addressing this very problem).[24]

There is of course another basis for the hegemony of the letter in Badiou's inaesthetics. Simply, given the fundamental role played by subtraction and the void in his philosophy—and given that it is art and art alone that thinks the event (which itself issues forth from the void)—we might

www.lacan.com/issue26.htm.

23. Alain Badiou & Lauren Sedofsky, 'Being by Numbers', *Artforum*, Oct, 1994, http://www.highbeam.com/library/docFree.asp?DOCID=1G1:16315394.

24. In Deleuze's words 'cinema is not a universal or primitive language system … It consists of movements and thought-processes (pre-linguistic images), and of points of view on these movements and processes (pre-signifying signs)', Deleuze, *Cinema 2*, p. 251. Hence, for Deleuze, 'if … a semiotics based on linguistics worries me, it's because it does away with both the image and the notion of the sign,' Deleuze, *Negotiations: 1972-1990*, trans. Martin Joughin, New York, Columbia University Press, 1995, p. 57-58.

conclude that the more artistic a work is then the more intimate its relation to the letter qua matheme (this being again an asymptotic approach:
art, be it literal or otherwise, can of course never be properly reduced
to the mark of the void). Which is to say that Badiou's inaesthetic conceptions are themselves profoundly affected by—and indeed are symptomatic of—his mathematical leanings: if art thinks the event (at the precise
point at which mathematics itself falters) it does so only by virtue of its
relation—or rather, non-relation—to the matheme. Thus for Badiou the
artistic work would seem to be ultimately inseparable from its mathematization. And yet, as we saw above, Badiou contends that in their subjective
dimension 'science proves to be the opposite of art' (LM 84). Indeed, the
fact that mathematics and poetry in particular admit a strained relation
is, according to Badiou, of maximal importance for philosophy in general.
Badiou stating 'let us struggle for this flash of conflict, we philosophers,
always torn between the mathematical norm of literal transparency and
the poetic norm of singularity and presence'.[25] Which is to say that art has
a more ambivalent relationship to the question of transmissibility—whose
ideal form is of course the matheme—than first assumed. Indeed, we
might go so far as to rewrite the imperative of art—namely, the (decidedly political) need to 'to inscribe the inexistent'—as the necessity to, via
the process of subtraction, *approach* the purity of the matheme.[26] We say
'approach' rather than encounter because as we have seen the mark of
real artistic 'success' according to Badiou paradoxically coincides with the
very failure of inscribing the inexistent or voided content of a particular
world (a failure that would itself fail were the work in question were to purify itself to the level of the matheme).[27] Clearly then in its (non)relation to
the matheme art proves itself a fundamentally subtractive—as opposed to
purificatory or purely destructive—programme, insofar as its aim is 'the
staging of a minimal, albeit absolute, difference; the difference between
the place and what takes place in the place, the difference between place

25. Alain Badiou, 'Language, Thought, Poetry', in *Theoretical Writings*, ed. and trans. Ray
Brassier & Alberto Toscano, London, Continuum, 2004, p. 241.

26. We might of course further contrast the apparent literality of art to Badiou's assertion
that 'what, amongst the processes of truth, singularizes art, is that the subject of truth is
drawn from the sensible ... [whilst] the subject of truth in science is drawn from the power
of the letter', Alain Badiou, *Circonstances, 2: Irak, foulard, Allemagne/France*, Paris, Léo
Scheer, 2004, p. 98.

27. Whereas true art inscribes what is voided (and is thus, while universal, necessarily situated), the matheme marks the ab-sense of the void itself (and is thus both universal and
unsituated).

and taking-place'.[28] Which is to say, the point of the artistic endeavour is nothing less than to yield a *real remainder* which would ultimately mark the 'minimal difference between [the] void and an element which functions as its stand in'.[29] And indeed on this point we can perhaps understand why in Badiou's writings poetry holds pride of place while cinema remains inaesthetically questionable: of all the (literate as much as illiterate) arts cinema would surely appear the least capable of such a task.

However, returning to the problematic of those in/aesthetic passages specific to cinema—of the idea through the image; of the image through the letter—might we not just as easily argue the contrary, affirming cinema to be instead, by virtue of its very form, eminently capable of realising this passage toward the ideal of the matheme? Indeed cinema, which is after all as Badiou states 'nothing but takes and editing', is a fundamentally subtractive medium, being one whose (imaginary) presence is in truth (real) absence, and whose essence is accordingly void.[30] Film theoreticians have in fact spent a great deal of time establishing this precise point (to take but one example, what does Metz's famous 'imaginary signifier' mark if not the void itself?).[31] This is of course not to suggest that cinema finds any (real or otherwise) relation to the matheme but rather simply to say that cinema exhibits an intrinsic *formal* affinity with the concept of the mathem(e)atical concept. Such a correspondence remains, however, unacknowledged in Badiou's writings for the simple fact that he understands cinema to be 'an art of the perpetual past, in the sense that it institutes the past of the pass' (HI 78). Or again, film's formal relation to the matheme breaks down for Badiou insofar as he understands cinema, in its movement, takes and editing—and in decided opposition to his attestations regarding cinema's immobilization of the idea (and vice versa)— to be an art of *loss*: cinema is for Badiou an art not of subtraction but of *purification*, and hence of destruction (or again, an art not of the void nor the voided, but rather of *voiding*). Simply, if cinema is ultimately a mechanistic process of loss—as opposed to a subtractive passage issuing a remainder—it

---

28. Badiou, *Le Siècle*, Paris, Seuil, 2005, p. 86.

29. Slavoj Žižek, 'From Purification to Subtraction: Badiou and the Real', in Peter Hallward (ed.), *Think Again: Alain Badiou and the Future of Philosophy*, London, Continuum, 2004, p. 165.

30. This is a fact Badiou clearly recognizes, as each of the three 'false movements' Badiou identifies (the global, the local, and the impure) which together allow for the passage of the idea operate by way of subtraction (the image is subtracted from itself, etc.).

31. cf. Christian Metz, *Psychoanalysis and Cinema: The Imaginary Signifier*, trans. Celia Britton, Annwyl Williams, Ben Brewster and Alfred Guzzetti, London, Macmillan Pres, 1983.

can in no way hope to facilitate so much as the passage of the idea, let alone inscribe the inexistent, for the simple reason that everything which appears in its field only does so only in order to immediately disappear: cinema is for Badiou ultimately an art of dis-appearance. And such a dis-appearing cinema can of course yield no remainder, for what finally 'remains' *is* void (hence Badiou's differentiation between subtraction and purification). Thus Badiou's contention regarding the immobility of the idea (that if cinema is to facilitate the passage of an idea it must concurrently ensure that the idea thus brought forth does not itself pass) would seem ultimately inconsistent with his overall conception of the filmic art: in Badiou's cinema, everything passes.

The entirety of Badiou's considerations on film are then governed in the final analysis not by his attestations to its inherent impurity (a necessary factor), nor by its incoherent situatedness (a contingent factor), but rather by his presupposition that 'cinema is visitation' (HI 78) (the immediate upshot of which is that—in the case of cinema—the idea can have nothing other than an equally transitory existence). Indeed, the peculiar understanding of cinema mobilized through the use of the term 'visitation' (as much as 'passage', 'past', 'pass' and the like) would seem to constitute not only Badiou's real point of departure from Deleuze's writings on cinema—whose concept of the crystal alone stands in direct opposition to such an insistently linear chronology (to say nothing of duration or experience)[32]—but also from all hope of establishing any thought proper to cinema. Accordingly, if any cinematic truths are to be registered whatsoever Badiou's understanding of cinema as an art of dis-appearance—which is itself a contention arguably grounded less in philosophy than in subjectivity—must be rejected as being in all senses of the word fundamentally anachronistic.[33] Film is neither a mechanism of dis-appearance nor a process of becoming. Cinema is not a passive art; it does not simply *pass*. Nor however is it an accumulative process of coming-into-being.[34] Rather,

---

32. Of course, the concept of the crystal itself does not bear on Badiou's philosophy insofar as he has himself no recourse to the virtual.

33. We might even go so far as to suggest his position remains ultimately untenable unless he were to concede that *all* art—painting as much as poetry, literature as much as theatre—are themselves (to varying degrees) finally nothing but visitation, insofar as all subjects of art invariably pass (the novel is finished, the play concludes, the poem is put down). Indeed, is this not the precise characteristic separating the subject of art from the truth it enters into: whereas the subject is finite, local and passing, truth is infinite and spatially unlocalizable (hence of truth and the subject only the former is properly immanent).

34. Of course we might discern here a certain (albeit limited) homology with Deleuze's argument that 'the chain of connections in cinema ... cannot be reduced to the simple

real cinema is in both form and content a subtractive procedure insofar as, like all art, its aim is to yield a remainder (which would of course present the minimal difference between the void and its stand-in). Or again, real cinema must be, contra Badiou, nothing other than an artistic process whose aim is to inscribe the voided or inexistent elements of a world, to realize 'the difference between place and taking-place'. Perhaps then it is in this precise sense that we should reinterpret Badiou's two principal demands of cinema, that is, that it purify (or rather subtract) itself of all non-artistic content (as much as its incidental artistic content, or its internal complication with the other arts) and that it concurrently organize the immobility of a passage: to risk a Freudian analogy, with respect to its manifest content the impossibility of cinema's becoming wholly artistic would ultimately constitute the formal mark of its remainder (that is, its 'artistic kernel', or the element which keeps cinema from degenerating into the pure abstraction of 'takes and editing'), while in terms of its latent content the remainder would be finally nothing other than the very immobility of the passage itself (indeed, how else could the 'immobility of the idea' be conceived outside such an ideal remainder?).

Doubtless numerous complications arise with such a conception of cinema.[35] And yet, ultimately, whether such a conception is or is not in fact legitimate is in many ways incidental. Rather, given the fundamental importance placed on the artistic condition in Badiou's philosophy (insofar as it constitutes—in its thinking of the event—the nexal point of his materialist dialectic), the purpose of this paper has been less to establish the conditions of cinematic thought per se than to critically examine Badiou's inaesthetic programme by way of cinema. Thus we have seen how, whilst he in no way reduces the entirety of art to that of the letter, Badiou's cogent inaesthetic writings are nonetheless essentially prescribed by the relative literality—and hence mathematicality—of the arts (there are of course obvious exceptions to this rule, although these examples invariably relate to specifically formal ruptures such as those found in the

---

association of images. There is always something left over', Gilles Deleuze, 'The Brain is the Screen', in David Lapoujade (ed.), *Two Regimes of Madness: Texts and Interviews 1975-1995*, trans. Ames Hodges & Mike Taormina, New York, MIT Press, 2006, p. 284.

35. The most immediate problem being knotted to the question of time, insofar as in Badiou's philosophy 'time—if not coextensive with structure, if not the *sensible form of the Law*—is intervention itself, thought as the gap between two events' (which is to say Badiou conceives of time solely in evental terms). BE, p. 210. Here the problem would reside in the discerning of what precisely would constitute cinematic time (be it evental, purificatory or otherwise).

cases of Malevitch or Schoenberg). This concurrently means that Badiou's philosophy, in being conditioned first and foremost by those literal arts, regrettably neglects by and large those manifold illiterate arts which might otherwise serve to augment his thought. Furthermore, we have seen how Badiou's conception of cinema falters at the point of irreconcilability between the relentless movement of the image and the idea of immobility itself. Which is to say that whilst Badiou may think cinema his considerations do not themselves allow finally for cinema to be thought. Furthermore it is at the same time clear that Badiou has as yet not engaged properly with Deleuze's writings on the cinema, choosing instead to short-circuit the filmic question through recourse to the 'monotony' of Deleuze's conceptual production (and to a lesser—albeit otherwise welcome—extent through an outright rejection of the virtual). Ultimately however it would seem that if Badiou is to maintain a certain coherency to his inaesthetic programme he needs either dispense with the idea of a 'thinking cinema' altogether (meaning film would be intrinsically incapable of presenting so much as the passage of the idea, let alone inscribe the inexistent) or otherwise reconsider his position on the inexorability of cinematic movement (meaning film cannot be a solely purificatory—or contrarily associative—edifice). In the event of the former, his inaesthetic programme would certainly become more hermetic (if more 'literally' curbed). In the event of the latter however Badiou might begin to allow for new illiterate thoughts to condition his at present decidedly literal philosophy.

politics

12

Towards an Anthropology of Infinitude: Badiou and the Political Subject

Nina Power

INTRODUCTION

Against the evacuation of any positive use of the term in Althusser's work and its reduction to mere ideological effect, it is clear that Badiou wants to retain a post-Sartrean conception of the 'subject', and that this has been the case from his earlier, more heavily political, works (*Théorie du sujet* from 1982), to his later exercises in meta-ontology and a theory of truth (*Being and Event*, 1988 and *Logiques des mondes*, 2006).

However, we can immediately complicate this claim by further stating that the later Badiou does take on board one aspect of the Althusserian claim that there are no extant 'subjects' qua autonomous agents *alongside* the seemingly opposed Sartrean idea that subjectivation is possible and, indeed, desirable. Badiou's relationship to the claims and vicissitudes of the so-called humanism-antihumanism debate play out over the question of how and why he retains and defines, not just a question of who or what the collective political subject might be, but also what the significance of the 'subject' might be for philosophy *in toto*. His work is an attempt to merge and go beyond the two terms of the debate, in which structuralism 'opposes' humanism, by entering into a topological discourse that nevertheless permits the continued possible existence of the subject (indeed, we could say that Badiou's preservation of the 'subject' is the most consistent element of his work). Whilst Badiou seeks to align himself with the antihumanism of Foucault, Lacan and Althusser, against both a 'return to Kant' in human rights discourse and the 'bad Darwinism' of a contemporary conception of man as finite animal, there are hints, both explicit and implicit, of his belonging to a longer trajectory of 'political humanism'. Indeed, we will see this in particular in Badiou's mathematico-political deployment of terms such as 'generic', and its political correlate 'generic humanity'. It will not be argued that Badiou's 'mathematical turn' is necessarily over-determined by his politics, as some have suggested, but rather that the mathematics and politics co-implicate each other in ways that entail that when Badiou uses terms like 'revolution' the resonances are intended to be heard at both levels, scientific and historico-political.

The major claim made here is that Badiou's use of the term 'humanism' is, however, evidence of a political struggle whose vicissitudes have leant the philosophical implications of the word a different sense at different points between the original 'debate' of the 1960s and the contemporary era: the story here with regard to Badiou's work is how the impossibility of using the term in the era of Stalin ('a "Soviet humanism" through which we can glimpse the well-heeled dachas and the black Mercedes'.[1]) has been transformed into the possibility of equating the quasi-Feuerbachian term 'generic humanity' with the politics of an egalitarian communism ('Equality means that the political actor is represented under the sole sign of the uniquely human capacity'[2]).

Also at stake in this article is an attempt to confront some of the early English-language reception of Badiou's philosophy of the subject as a contemporary continuation of the Cartesian project. This is a reading primarily promulgated by Žižek in his *The Ticklish Subject*, where he is explicit in his attempt to 'reassert' the Cartesian subject, and enlists Badiou in this endeavour by aligning him on his side in the war against those who would oppose 'the *hubris* of so-called Cartesian subjectivity'.[3] This article, on the other hand, will take seriously Badiou's claim in Meditation Thirty-Seven of *Being and Event* where he writes: 'The "there is" of the subject is the coming-to-being of the event, via the ideal occurrence of a truth, in its finite modalities. By consequence, what must always be grasped is that there is no subject, that there are no longer some subjects. What Lacan still owed to Descartes, a debt whose account must be closed, was the idea that there were always some subjects'.[4] What Žižek downplays in Badiou

1. Alain Badiou, *Théorie du Sujet* , Paris, Seuil, 1982, p. 201 (henceforth TS). All translations are my own with the kind help of Alberto Toscano.
2. Alain Badiou, *Metapolitics*, trans. Jason Barker, London, Verso, 2005, p. 97 (henceforth M).
3. Slavoj Žižek, *The Ticklish Subject*, London, Verso, 1999, p. 132.
4. Alain Badiou, *Being and Event*, trans. Oliver Feltham, London, NY, Continuum, 2005, p. 434 (henceforth BE).

is the fact that it is precisely not a question of the psychoanalytic subject
(as it surely must remain the case for Žižek in his project to rehabilitate
Lacan), which is why the latter must preserve the idea that Badiou remains in some sense Cartesian, or post-Cartesian in a nevertheless strictly
indebted manner, and thus partly Lacanian in the way that Žižek desires:
'The subject is strictly correlative with the ontological gap between the
universal and the particular'.[5] Whilst Žižek does recognize a split between
Badiou and Lacan on the question of the identification of the subject with
the void (imperative for psychoanalysis, but an illegitimate 'ontologiza-
tion' for Badiou), he nevertheless aligns Badiou with a philosophy of subjective decisionism, on the model of a psychoanalytic 'act': 'For Badiou
… the subject is cosubstantial with a contingent act of Decision'.[6] The
problem with this conflation is that, whilst it represents a common criticism of Badiou, it makes Badiou's position a kind of voluntarism (see the
section on Badiou and Schmitt below), which has indeed been one of the
charges levelled against Badiou in his initial English language-reception.
Contra Žižek, I seek here to unpack Badiou's own definition of a subject,
in particular, his notion of a political subject, which pays attention to and
defends its collective, procedural and organized nature.

But what, to begin with, of Badiou's *own* philosophical concessions
to Cartesianism? In his monograph on Deleuze, Badiou himself analyses
the reasons why the latter cannot uphold any kind of Cartesianism, even
though Descartes does not appear to have any ostensible recourse to 'the
transcendence of principles', a position to which Deleuze would otherwise
appear committed. Badiou presents a series of reasons why Deleuze cannot be aligned with a 'philosophy of the subject': that the principle of the
univocity of being precludes the primacy of the subject, which can only
reverberate within the confines of equivocity, body-soul, being-nothing-
ness, extension-thought (and here Deleuze is close to Heidegger's opposition to the metaphysics of the subject); that the subject is predicated on a
certain reflexive negativity that is again precluded by a prioritization of
the univocity of Being, which cannot abide negativity; that philosophies
of the subject place the operator 'subject' within a scientific paradigm
(the relationship between the cogito and Galileanism); that a certain reactionary tendency towards the capitalist-parliamentary model of politics
generally brings with it a commitment to a moral and humanitarian sub-

---

5. Žižek, *The Ticklish Subject*, p. 158.
6. Žižek, *The Ticklish Subject*, p. 159.

ject.[7] In place of these four criticisms of the subject, Badiou argues that Deleuze replaces their starting-points with a different model: that of the fold, the 'auto-affection of the outside' where thinking coincides with Being: 'It is remarkable that one can name this identity "subject" without having conceded anything to the Cartesian filiation. For to be a subject is "to think the outside as time, on the condition of the fold"' (D 90). The problem for Badiou with this 'escape-route' from subjectivity is its identification of thought with the One of being, the aestheticization of 'folding', and its consequent political and philosophical inadequacy: for Deleuze in the end 'what always matters is folding, unfolding, refolding',[8] the mere performance of the expression of univocal Being. Whilst Badiou will of course retain the language of subject and subjectivation, it is imperative that this subject not be understood as an individuated thinking or doubting entity, i.e. as classically 'Cartesian'. For Badiou, it is clear that some subjects are not conscious (the subject of a truth in art is an artwork, for example), some are collective (the political subject) and some are dyadic (the truth of the amorous couple is their separate two-ness, not the romantic 'fusion' itself).

As a prelude to a more detailed exploration of Badiou's theories of the subject, however, it is important to set out a certain non-philosophical thread—in essence, a positive, active, usually Marxist 'subject'—as it is this notion, which in part takes its cue from one particular element of Descartes (namely the activity of the thinking thing) that underpins Badiou's own conceptions and the political history of his thought. This takes us from a certain line of thought stretching from Rousseau to Dunayevskaya, before we turn to Badiou's own *Théorie du sujet* and *Being and Event*.

Ultimately it will be argued that Badiou's theory of the subject, whilst beginning from a primarily political problematic and broadening out into a conception that will also include such processes as art works (in the domain of art), mathematical innovations (in the domain of science) and couples (in the domain of love), nevertheless demonstrates certain conceptual continuities at the level both of its formalized character and procedure. As Vainqueur puts it, for Badiou: 'The subject is neither conceived as the existential place of a set of representations, nor apprehended as the transcendental system of the constitution of objects of possible experience, similarly, truth can no longer be envisaged as the adequation of subject

---

7. All these points are taken from Badiou's *Deleuze: The Clamor of Being*, trans. Louise Burchill, Minneapolis, London, University of Minnesota Press, 2000, pp. 80-81 (henceforth D).
8. Gilles Deleuze, *The Fold*, trans. Tom Conley, London, Continuum, 2001, p. 137.

and object'.[9] It is this evacuated subject that persists in Badiou's thought as the primary basis of all the truth procedures, including politics.

THE ACTIVE POLITICAL SUBJECT

Prima facie, we know that the category 'political subject' has, at different historical points, operated in completely antonymic ways: from the passive subservience of a subject (*subjectum*, 'that which is kept down'—literally 'that which is thrown underneath'), to the active subject, and its seizure of politics itself. This active subject, we can say, is largely a 'collectivizing' of an idea of the Cartesian 'self-subject' in the realm of politics, rather than a reversal of the substantive passive qualities of an older Aristotelian notion. However, it also bears a relation to the history of the term *subjectus*, namely the being submitted to an authority (sovereign, monarchical). When Dunayevskaya writes in 1971 that '[n]o word is more important than Subject ... Whether we mean the workers or a single revolutionary; whether we mean women's liberation, Blacks, Indians, "organization," it is clear that "Subject" is the one responsible for both theory and practice',[10] there is no doubt that 'subject' is here understood as the propulsive, active, revolutionary force manifested by *both* individuals and collectives in the fusion of theory and practice. It retains absolutely none of its traditional passive senses. How did the term 'political subject' become mediated by these two senses of the subject (the Cartesian active subject and the political *subjectus*)?

It is clear that this is not merely a theoretical question, but one that engages the historical invention of certain mediating terms, such as 'people' (*peuple*) and citizen (*citoyen/ne*), and certain events (the French Revolution, the Paris Commune). Balibar argues, for instance, that it was only by way of the citizen 'that universality could come to the subject'.[11] Linguistically, there is evidence in the term of a move from adjective to noun, from individuals who are subjected to the power of another, to the representation or active force of a people or a community as a set of 'subjects'. We

---

9. Bernard Vainqueur, 'De quoi "sujet" est-il le nom pour Alain Badiou?', *Penser le Multiple*, Paris, L'Harmattan, 2002, pp. 313-38, p. 314.

10. Raya Dunayevskaya, 'Marxist-Humanism's concept of "Subject"', letter to young members of News and Letters Committees, *The Raya Dunayevskaya Collection, Supplement*, 1971, pp. 14110-11. Available at http://www.marxists.org/archive/dunayevskaya/works/1971/subject.htm.

11. Etienne Balibar, 'Citizen Subject', *Who Comes After the Subject?*, Eduardo Cadava, Peter Connor, Jean-Luc Nancy (eds.), London, Routledge, 1991, p. 45.

can contrast this 'political fusion' of the Cartesian subject and the *subjectus* with the recent Hegelian and psychoanalytic attempt to trace another history of the subject as a prelude for a discussion of radical politics, such as we find in Žižek: 'the standard notion of the gradual becoming-subject of the substance (of the "active" subject leaving its "imprint" on the substance, moulding it, mediating it, expressing in it his subjective content) is ... doubly misleading ... [it] is always the remainder of substance which eludes grasp of "subjective mediation"'. [12] Žižek thus turns the question of the subject into something like a haunting remainder to be psychoanalytically traversed, rather than addressing the activity of a collective political subject in all its potential historical force.

It is in Rousseau's 1762 text, *The Social Contract*, above all, that we explicitly witness the metamorphosis of subject in the old sense (obedience) into a new kind of subject, the subject of law which is, nevertheless, also the final arbiter of legal pronouncements and is thus active and passive to the same degree, although not yet the wholly active revolutionary subject of Dunayevskaya's theory and practice:[13]

> The public person thus formed by the union of all other persons was once called the *city*, and is now known as the *republic* or the *body politic*. It its passive role it is called the *state*, when it plays an active role it is the *sovereign*; and when it is compared to others of its own kind, it is a *power*. Those who are associated in it take collectively the name of *a people*, and call themselves individually *citizens*, in that they share in the sovereign power, and *subjects*, in that they put themselves under the laws of the state. [14]

This collective of associating beings who are *simultaneously* people, citizens and subjects, operates at the level of the law, and is neither subject to it in the more classical sense, nor does it impose laws from above (for it would be merely imposing them upon itself): 'There must be an exact correspondence between the absolute activity of the citizen (legislation) and his absolute passivity (obedience to the law). But it is essential that this activity and this passivity be *exactly* correlative'.[15] The inhabitant of such a republic splits himself or herself between general and particular interests, and thus

---

12. Slavoj Žižek, *Tarrying with the Negative: Kant, Hegel and the Critique of Ideology*, Durham, Duke University Press, 1993, p. 21.

13. Historically, the first recorded use of the term 'citizen' to mean 'bearer of rights' was in 1751. See *Trésor de la Langue Française*. Available at http://atilf.atilf.fr/tlf.htm.

14. Jean-Jacques Rousseau, *The Social Contract*, trans. Maurice Cranston, London, Penguin, 1968, pp. 61-62.

15. Balibar, 'Citizen Subject', p. 49.

inaugurates a new subject, as Balibar demonstrates, the citizen-subject ('[t]he citizen properly speaking is *neither* the individual *nor* the collective, just as he is *neither* an exclusively public being *nor* a private citizen').[16] In this historical turn, there is a certain move towards informality with regard to the state. The term 'citizen', from a 12th century term meaning 'inhabitant of a city', carries with it an actual attempt to reinvent certain public forms of address—after the French Revolution, a bill was issued to replace 'Monsieur' and 'Madame' with 'citizen' (qua non-deferential, urbanized, generic term).[17] We could perhaps call this the 'Republicanization of thought', which finds its rapid historical culmination in the Declaration of the Rights of Man and of the Citizen (26th August 1789): 'Article 6: Legislation expresses the overall will'.

But what is this overall (so-called sovereign) will? In Rousseau, we are presented with a concept of the subject mid-way between the passivity of the sovereign-subject and the activity of the revolutionary subject: this subject is mediated not only via the citizen, but also by a new conception of sovereignty. When Rousseau asks 'what then is correctly to be called an act of sovereignty? It is not a covenant between a superior and an inferior, but a covenant of the body with each of its members',[18] there is another circularity, not just of subject and law, but also of subject and sovereign. But how is this circularity determined?

It is via the conception of the 'general will' that the laws decided upon by subjects will operate equally for all: 'since each man gives himself to all, he gives himself to no one; and since there is no associate over whom he does not gain the same rights as others gain over him, each man recovers the equivalent of everything he loses, and in the bargain he acquires more power to preserve what he has'.[19] How does the suppressed subject of sovereignty come to be collective? By associating in such a way as that to assume one's being subjected to the law is simultaneously one's giving oneself to 'no one' *and* the recovery of one's rights in the equal and simultaneous agreement of all. The social pact or contract expresses this generic, empty will, which functions by subtracting the sum of individual differences (the pluses and minuses of interest) in the name of a common

---

16. Balibar, 'Citizen Subject', p. 51.

17. The question of the term 'citizen' is also tied up with the question of tutoiement (the informal use of 'you' in French): 'Times that one would [use the informal form of 'you'] and one would say: citizen' (as in Victor Hugo's *Les Misérables* from 1862).

18. Rousseau, *The Social Contract*, p. 77.

19. Rousseau, *The Social Contract*, p. 61.

claim. But why does Rousseau maintain the classical link between subject and sovereign at all? Merely because of the traditional connotations of the concept? If the subject and sovereignty coincide in the legislating power of the subject as general will, why not dispense with the formal framework of a hierarchical political, theological and monarchical system by replacing the term 'subject' with a completely new term?

It is perversely enlightening in this regard to turn to one of Rousseau's most reactionary critics for a summary of this problem, Joseph de Maistre who, in his *Study on Sovereignty* (1821), defends classical sovereignty in the following way:

> It is said that the people are sovereign; but over whom?—over themselves, apparently. The people are thus subject. There is surely something equivocal if not erroneous here, for the people who *command* are not the people which *obey* ... If a democracy in its theoretical purity were to exist, there would be no sovereignty within this state: for it is impossible to understand by this word anything other than a repressive power that acts on the *subject* and that is external to him. It follows that this word *subject*, which is a relative term, is alien to republics, because there is no sovereign, properly speaking, in a republic and because there cannot be a *subject* without a *sovereign*, just as there cannot be a *son* without a *father*.[20]

De Maistre points out a certain linguistic and structural irony in Rousseau's idea that 'the sovereign, which is simply a collective being, cannot be represented by anyone but itself'.[21] Whilst De Maistre's own conception of sovereignty is without doubt anti-philosophical, theological, elitist and nationalist (a clutch of sentiments handily summarized in the following quote: 'whoever says that man is born for liberty is speaking nonsense'), this depiction of the 'circularity' of subject and sovereignty in Rousseau's 'republicanization of thought' is important: It means that the political subject, as egalitarian and as generic, is perilously close, etymologically and in practice, to tipping back into forms of despotism. Rousseau himself recognizes this possibility very clearly: 'if the danger is such that the apparatus of law is itself an obstacle to safety, then a supreme head must be nominated with power to silence all the laws and temporarily suspend

---

20. Joseph de Maistre, *The Works of Joseph de Maistre*, trans. and with an introduction by Jack Lively, London, Allen and Unwin, 1965, p. 120.
21. Maistre, *The Works*, p. 69.

the sovereign authority'.²² We are thus left with an odd formula that at any moment potentially replaces the old sovereign (i.e. the will of the people expressed through law and subject to those laws) with a new 'supreme head'. The moment the subject and law slip out of alignment with each other is the moment a novel, perhaps even more despotic, form of authority could fill the breach. This scenario is reflected in this retort to Rousseau, again from De Maistre: 'People complain of the despotism of princes; they ought to complain of the despotism of *man*'.²³ Whilst De Maistre promulgates a form of naturalized politics, which emphasizes tradition and divine purpose: 'all sovereignty derives from God; whatever form it takes, it is not the work of man',²⁴ De Maistre's criticisms of Rousseau nevertheless point to the fundamental difficulty of reversing the meaning of the term subject from a politically submissive entity (either collective or singular) to an active self-regulating collective noun, namely the 'people', the 'citizens' (we could call this the question of a subject-predicate reversal within the term subject itself). This difficulty remains in so far as the political subject is mediated by the concept of the sovereign, since the sovereign structures the entire space and placing of that which is contained in the political framework, namely the subjects therein. It is the destruction of what he will call this 'space of placements' that Badiou is concerned to explicate in *Théorie du sujet*.

The same theo-political hierarchization that remained in Descartes in his conception of man engenders difficulties for a more explicitly political project with egalitarian aims. When Balibar, in an explicit attempt to justify some of the egalitarian elements apparent in Rousseau (and compare his own project of *egaliberté*, where the coextensivity of equality and freedom immediately concerns the universality of individuals), argues the following: '[a]fter the subject comes the citizen ... and whose constitution and recognition put an end (in principle) to the subjection of the subject', there is a sense in which he overlooks the inherent limitations of a such a positive conception of the political subject and its inscription within constitutions. While it is clear, as he suggests, that one cannot think a modern concept of the political subject without taking into account its *mediated*

---

22. Rousseau, *The Social Contract*, p. 171.
23. Maistre, 'Study on Sovereignty', in *The Works*, p. 118
24. Maistre, 'Study on Sovereignty', in *The Works*, p. 114. Compare Rousseau's incidentally pre-emptive response: 'all power comes from God ... but so does every disease, and no one forbids us to summon a physician'. *The Social Contract*, p. 53.

role through the terms 'citizen' and 'people',[25] there remains an inherent
danger that the retention of the term 'subject' will leave it open to recuperation by whatever force desires to subordinate it. By transforming the
discourse on the political subject from that of representation in a certain
political space to a reformulation of the very question of 'placement' in
politics, Badiou attempts to overcome the circular logic that would always
leave a subject (however 'active') prey to recapture by the logic of the
(sovereign) state.

BADIOU, BALIBAR AND ROUSSEAU

It is revealing, with regard to the analysis of the terms subject, citizen
and politics, to briefly compare Balibar and Badiou's readings of Rousseau, composed around the same time (and indeed published in the same
year, 1988), but rather different in emphasis and conclusion.[26] Whilst acknowledging, at the outset, with Balibar, that for Rousseau 'the words
subject and *sovereign* are identical correlatives', Badiou will subsume this dyadic relationship (what we could call the 'republican democratization' of
power) under what he names, and will call in his own work, 'the generic
becoming of politics'. Why? Because what he wants to unveil in Rousseau
is an instance of a conception of politics that manifests certain key features
present in Badiou's own theory: a demand for generic equality, an 'event'
in politics (in this instance, the social contract), and, above all, the idea
that politics 'is a *creation*, local and fragile, of collective humanity'. This is,
in the end, the form of 'political subjectivity' that Badiou wishes to extract
from Rousseau, rather than remaining within the historical-conceptual
locus of questions concerning the citizen *per se*, as Balibar does. Instead
of focussing on the more classically bourgeois elements of Rousseau's proposals (the defence of property, security and the 'rights' of the state qua
state), Badiou sees in the general will an almost pure form of 'fidelity' to
egalitarian aims ('[t]he general will is the operator of fidelity which directs
a generic procedure'). The citizen, in this account, becomes translated
as a 'militant' of a political cause, faithful (albeit precariously) to the rare
emergence of an 'event' in politics, the social contract (or rather to its

---

25. Very much more could be said of this latter term 'people', of course: in its very origins
it is ambiguous; it could potentially refer to ethnicity, inhabitants of a nation, a territory,
etc.

26. See Balibar's 'Citizen Subject'; *Being and Event* was originally published 1988.

generic demands).[27] Later, Badiou will speak of the 'militant identification' of politics: 'which, for me, is ... the *only* identification which can ally
politics and thought' (M 13).

However, there are two problems here, aside from the question of
whether Badiou's reading of Rousseau is something of a theoretical imposition. One is the instability of the political event itself, whereby there is an
'inherent and inevitable vice which relentlessly tends to destroy the body
politic from the moment of its birth' (BE 345). In essence, this represents
the acknowledgement that the egalitarian impulse behind the social contract will inevitably be corrupted. Badiou's point here is again extremely
close (and will remain so in his own work) to Sartre's argument in the
Critique of Dialectical Reason, namely that there is a kind of constitutive failure, an inevitable ossification or falling-off of the demands behind every
revolutionary impulse and any collective project.

The second major difficulty here is the distance between what Badiou
wants to valorize in Rousseau (the generic nature of the will, the 'event'
of the social contract, the precarious creation of a 'collective humanity')
and the way Rousseau sees this in which the generic or general will manifested, namely through voting, the counting of each representation: 'this
act of association creates an artificial and corporate body composed of as
many members as there are voters in the assembly' and 'for the will to be
general, it does not have to be unanimous; but all the votes must be counted'.[28] Badiou admits that Rousseau submits the general will to the 'law of
number' and thus turns a generic, egalitarian political programme into a
majoritarian one. (In France, the major historical definition of whether
one was technically an active or passive citizen was determined by whether the person voted or not.) If the critical question for both Badiou and
Rousseau is ultimately 'how can the generic character of politics subsist
when unanimity fails?' (BE 349), with the emphasis on the genericity of
politics, then Rousseau clearly finds the answer in a form of electoral systems and majority agreement. Badiou, on the other hand, will turn to the
concept of fidelity (and, etymologically at least, introduces a new version
of the theological 'faithful subject'). Ultimately Badiou criticizes Rousseau for eliding politics with legitimation (and the electoral) and not with
truth. It is politics as a 'truth procedure', and the separation of truth from
knowledge that grounds Badiou's own presentation of politics. Clearly, if
the 'general will is infallible, due to being subtracted from any particular

---

27. The Badiou quotes are from Meditation 32 of BE, pp. 344-54.
28. Rousseau, *Social Contract*, p. 61, 70.

knowledge, and due to it relating solely to the generic existence of people'
then ballot boxes and the counting of representations would seem to be *a
priori* superfluous, or at least something that wouldn't touch the 'correctness' of the will.[29] Carl Schmitt has a quite different criticism of Rousseau,
which nevertheless chastises him for something very similar to Badiou,
albeit from the *other side* of sovereignty, as it were: this critique (famously)
circles around the need to maintain a purer concept of 'decision'. Schmitt
argues the following:

> The general will of Rousseau became identical with the will of the
> sovereign; but simultaneously the concept of the general will also
> contained a quantitative determination with regard to its subject,
> which means that the people become sovereign. The decisionistic
> and personalistic element in the concept of sovereignty was thus
> lost.[30]

For Schmitt, as we saw in the previous section for De Maistre too, it is the
becoming-anonymous of the arbitrary and idiosyncratic element of the
sovereign that is at fault in Rousseau, because it deprives the Sovereign of
his fundamental characteristic, namely, to intervene in the name of an exception ('Sovereign is he who decides on the exception').[31] Similarly, again
following De Maistre, Schmitt points out the peculiarity of retaining the
(originally) theologically-structured term 'subject' in a political context if
the concept of sovereignty is, according to Rousseau, to be dissolved into
its antonym ('The politicization of theological concepts [in Rousseau] is
so striking that it has not escaped any true expert on his writings'[32]). For
Schmitt, it is a question of the 'systematic structure' of these secularized
theological concepts which renders their new 'democratic' use suspect.

---

29. A clear indication of Badiou's opinion of voting can be found in *Metapolitics*: 'If our
knowledge of planetary motion relied solely on suffrage as its protocol of legitimation, we
would still inhabit a geometrical universe' (M 15).
30. Carl Schmitt, *Political Theology: Four Chapters on the Concept of Sovereignty*, trans. George
Schwab, Cambridge, The MIT Press, 1985, p. 48.
31. Schmitt, *Political Theology*, p. 5.
32. Schmitt, *Political Theology*, p. 46. See also p. 36 'All significant concepts of the modern
theory of the state are secularized theological concepts not only because of their historical
development...but also because of their systematic structure, the recognition of which is
necessary for a sociological consideration of these concepts'. And also Atger: 'The prince
develops all the inherent characteristics of the state by a sort of continual creation. The
prince is the Cartesian god transposed to the political world'. (*Essai sur l'histoire du contrat
social*, 1906).

With reference to the idea of decision, whilst Badiou will separate his notion from the idea of the personal, arbitrary decision and fix it instead to a kind of collective experience of the egalitarian and generic demand of politics itself, it is clear that Rousseau's ultimate subsumption of the faithful and decisional character of the general will to representation via the electoral system *also* strips it of a certain purity for Badiou: 'As a procedure faithful to the event-contract, politics cannot tolerate delegation or representation' (BE 347). It is also intriguing to note a certain similarity in the tone of both Schmitt and Badiou's disgust with what Schmitt calls 'technical-organization' and what Badiou names 'capital-parliamentarianism' (and its corollary, 'opinionism'): The core of the political idea, 'the exacting moral decision' is evaded in both the economic or 'technical-organization' and the political dissolves into 'the everlasting discussion of cultural and philosophical-historical commonplaces'[33] (Schmitt); 'The essence of politics is not the plurality of opinions' and his description of 'the State ... the normative threefold arrangement of economic management, national assessment and democracy' (Badiou) (M 84). Obviously there is no sense in which Badiou and Schmitt share the same political aims—Badiou's concept of politics consistently opposes any statist, arbitrary or personalist arguments, and the *decisional* nature of Badiou's faithful subject is predicated on a certain undecidability, not sheer arbitrary will. Bosteels, for one, points to some of the problems with understanding Badiou's faithful subject simply as a 'decisionist' conception, emphasizing instead the centrality of process and not merely the act of decision: 'The impure and equivocal nature of all truth processes is ... inseparable from any topological understanding of the subject'.[34]

BADIOU'S POLITICAL SUBJECTS: FROM *THÉORIE DU SUJET* TO *BEING AND EVENT*

It is important to set out the relation between Badiou's conceptions of force and destruction in the earlier work of *Théorie du sujet* (which consists of seminars presented from 1975-79 with a preface from 1981) to his later (*Being and Event* and *Metapolitics*). Badiou is politically at his most Leninist in the earlier text, both terminologically and rhetorically. The book is without doubt, at least in part, an attempt to come to terms with certain

---

33. Schmitt, *Political Theology*, p. 65.
34. Bruno Bosteels, 'Alain Badiou's Theory of the Subject: The Recommencement of Dialectical Materialism? Part II', *Pli*, vol. 13, 2002, p. 205.

responses to the explosion and rapid recapture of the events of May '68, as well as a certain reactionary moment in French political life ('the bitter period of betrayal' as he later describes it) (M xxxiv). It is also an attempt to demonstrate his distance (as well as his debt) to Althusser in the wake of the 'Humanist controversy'.

The question of why Badiou wants to maintain a concept of the subject in the first place is a crucial one. Whilst it is clear that he is heavily indebted both to Lacan and to Althusser for their structural analyses and their anti-humanism, he sees a danger in the way in which they handle the question of the subject. He writes: 'the essence of an activist materialism requires … the production of a theory of the subject, which it once had the task of foreclosing' (TS 202). So whilst the 'materialism' of Althusser and Lacan usefully criticized certain classical, humanist conceptions of subjectivity and the subject *at one critical juncture*, there is a sense in which Badiou is unwilling to give up on the term in the context in which he now writes. Indeed, he speaks instead of a kind of 'subjective deficiency':

> More deeply, I know that what has happened to us which is essential, in force as in humiliation, bears the mark of a *long-term* lack, whence derives the fact that, however sudden, the irruption is also light, whilst, as could be predicted long in advance, moral disarray is no less ineluctable. This lack is essentially subjective. It relates to the way in which potential forces, at the heart of the people, have been kept apart from their own concept. (TS 13)[35]

As Callinicos puts it, Badiou seeks 'a conceptual black sheep—a materialism centred on a theory of the subject'.[36] Not only, but a materialism that allegedly takes its cue from Hegel, as summarized by Badiou in the ironic statement: 'We must conceive imperialist society not only as substance but also as subject' (TS 60).

Badiou sets out two political temptations, or 'deviations', that he argues followed the events of 1968: on the one side, the left deviation, a fetishism of the 'pure' political act that would have done with everything that belongs to the original situation and, on the other, the right deviation, the

---

35. In an interview from 2001, Badiou makes the following claim, with reference to his own work in the late 1960s and 70s: 'I found in Sartre's theory of practical freedom, and particularly in the subjectivized Marxism that he was trying to produce, something with which to engage myself politically, in spite of everything, in the situation', 'Can Change be Thought?', 2001 interview with Bruno Bosteels, in *Alain Badiou: Philosophy and its Conditions*, ed. and with an introduction by Gabriel Riera, New York, SUNY, 2005, p. 242.
36. Alex Callinicos, *The Resources of Critique*, Cambridge, Polity, 2006, p. 93. This is one of the chapter headings in Badiou's TS.

cynical denial that nothing had in fact taken place, that all was perfectly 'normal'. Both of these temptations he argues, were inadequate to explain the singularity of the events, and also inadequate for an understanding of political subjectivity more generally. Badiou, instead, revisits Hegel and introduces a notion of 'scission' in order to refute both these deviations. In *Théorie du sujet* Badiou argues that there are two 'dialectical matrices' in Hegel's *Logic*. The former is covered by the term alienation, 'the idea of a simple term that deploys itself in its becoming-other, to return into itself as a completed concept' and the latter, a matrix whose operator is 'scission', 'and whose theme is that the only unity is a divided one' (TS 22). It is this second matrix that Badiou will use as the basis of an attempt to found a distinction between 'something' and 'another thing' (*Etwas und Anderes*). The repetition of the same thing posed twice, which Badiou will refer to as A (A as such) and Ap (A at another place) introduces a discussion of 'placement' (where p is place). Whilst he explicitly denies that p is to be understood spatially or geometrically ('A doubling can be temporal, or even fictional') (TS 24-5), it is this split that he depends upon for his positing of a 'constitutive scission', which he formulates as A=(AAp) (A is A, but also its placement as A). This 'minimal difference', he states, can also be understood as the relationship between theory and practice, the letter and the site in which it is marked. The dialectic is first and foremost a process, not of negation and the negation of the negation, but of internal division. Every force must be split into itself and that part of it is placed, or determined by the structure of assigned places.[37] Every force thus stands in a relation of 'internal exclusion' as to its determining place: 'As the history of the twentieth century shows in excruciating detail, what happens actually is the constant struggle of the working class against its determination by the bourgeois capitalist order, an order that divides the proletariat from within'.[38] Bosteels repeatedly stresses the dialectical thread of Badiou's work as a whole, refusing to understand the title of *Being and Event*, for example, as the presentation of two disjunct areas, rather, 'Badiou's later thought remains dialectical, despite the mathematical turn, in rejecting such stark opposition between being and event, in favour of the specific site through which an event is anchored in the ontological deadlock of a situation that only a rare subjective intervention can unlock'.[39] It is the process of 'internal division', as set out in Badiou's heavily politicized read-

---

37. See Bruno Bosteels, 'Alain Badiou's Theory of the Subject', p. 176.
38. Bruno Bosteels, 'Alain Badiou's Theory of the Subject', p. 176.
39. Bruno Bosteels, 'Alain Badiou's Theory of the Subject', p. 206.

ing of Hegel's *Logic*, that founds his claims about the subject: his analysis falls somewhere between a structural presentation and a more classically Marxist one (such as Dunayevskaya or Lukács) that would always stress the importance of retaining a post-Hegelian notion of the subject. In retaining a notion of the subject, however, Badiou nevertheless does not take up a notion of history, as Sartre would do, as a way of *placing* this subject. In fact, Badiou aligns 'history' on the side of the objective, structural, reactionary drive *to place* in the negative sense: 'it is always in the interests of the powerful that history is mistaken for politics—that is, that the objective is taken for the subjective' (TS 60). His position on this, at least, does not radically alter in the later work: 'There are only plural instances of politics, irreducible to one another, and which do not comprise any homogeneous history' (M 23).

In *Théorie du sujet* Badiou goes further in these paradoxical non-spatial, anti-historical claims regarding place. When he states that 'the true contrary of the proletariat is not the bourgeoisie. It is the bourgeois world ... the project of the proletarian, its internal being, is not to contradict the bourgeois ... Its project is communism and nothing else. That is to say, the abolition of all place in which one could deploy something like a proletariat. The political project of the proletariat is the disappearance of the space of placement of classes' (TS 25-6), there is a clear sense in which the (non)space of politics is what is at stake, the complete overturning of the subjective alignment of class positions, of the very opposition proletariat-bourgeoisie. There is a double play on the terms subjective and objective in *Théorie du sujet*: not only must political subjectivity be posited as an active force in the face of the seemingly static nature of the existing order, but 'subjective' is also opposed to the apparently 'objective' basis of placement, in the sense of an understanding of class as a social 'object'—the total number of people who would 'count' as 'the working class', for example. Turning to Badiou's claim that 'there is only one subject, so there is only one force, whose existence always produces the event' (TS 160), we must ask: why only one? In this early conception of politics, it is a question, not of a conception of politics as a battle, taking place in history (as in late Sartre), but, again, of place. The proletariat is not opposed to the bourgeoisie in a battle over who owns the means of production (the bourgeoisie is thus not a 'subject' in the same way as the proletariat; there is a fundamental dissymmetry between the two classes), but, as Badiou puts it we must reject 'a vision of politics as subjective duel ... There is one place, one subject' (TS 148). Furthermore, as a counterweight to certain of the discourses surrounding May '68, in which running battles with the police summed up the oppositional structure of active politics: '[t]here is not only the law of Capital, or only the cops. To miss this point means not to see the unity of the order of assigned places, its consistency' (TS 60).

Ultimately it is a question of the separation between what Badiou calls *l'esplace* ('splace' or 'splacement'—the neologistic combination of 'space' and 'place') and *horlieu* ('outplace'—another neologism fusing 'outside' and 'place'). 'The dialectic is the *horlieu* against the *esplace*' (TS 148). What does this mean? For Badiou, the working class cannot be synonymous with the proletariat—the former is the object of a well-defined social and economic placement, with a set of identifiable roles and positions.[40] The proletariat is instead the 'active', destructive, purifying force of the undoing of all object-placement (hence its primarily subjectivized nature):'the proletariat exists wherever a political *horlieu* is created. It is thus in purging itself that it exists. It has no existence anterior to its organization of political survival' (TS 204-5). The question for Badiou here is one of destroying (intended quite literally) a certain structural distribution of place. In his later works he will openly regret this rather violent presentation: 'I was, I admit, a little misguided in *Théorie du sujet* concerning the theme of destruction. I still maintained, back then, the idea of an essential link between destruction and novelty. Empirically, novelty (for example, political novelty) is accompanied by destruction. But it must be clear that this accompaniment is not linked to intrinsic novelty; on the contrary, the latter is always a supplementation by a truth' (BE 407). It is critical to note that the introduction of 'truth' as a category in Badiou's later works is conceptually bound to the attempt to separate out his political project from the violence historically perpetrated in the name of communism and instead links to a different theoretical lineage, that of Plato and, indeed, to an older concept, that of 'justice': 'We shall call "justice" that through which a philosophy designates the possible truth of a politics' (M 97). This self-placement in the political trajectory of justice and truth is also reflected in his turn from the term Proletariat to more generic conceptions of man, thought and humanity, as we shall see.

Aside from the terms *horlieu* and *esplace*, in *Théorie du sujet* Badiou more broadly opposes the terms 'force' and 'place', such that the *horlieu* (outplace) is not to be understood as another other than a *force*, rather than a

---

40. As Hallward puts it: 'In the early work, this distinction obtains above all in the (still dialectical) movement from the working class (as object) to the proletariat (as subject)...Insofar as they are conditioned by their well-defined social and economic *place*, the working classes are the mere object of history, not its subject or motor'. Peter Hallward, *Badiou: A Subject to Truth*, Minneapolis, London, University of Minnesota Press, 2003, p. 34.

set location: 'the double articulation of force and place', whereby 'the one is the loss of the other ... this is Marx's great discovery' (TS 188). Badiou goes on to say that: 'We will call *subjective* those processes relative to the qualitative concentration of force' (TS 59). There is a point of comparison to be made here with regards to the earlier and later work on this question of force, or as it is later termed, forcing: in *Being and Event* Badiou will define forcing (a 'fundamental law of the subject') in the following way: 'the belonging of [the] term of the situation to come is equivalent to the belonging of this term to the indiscernible part which results from the generic procedure' (BE 403). What does this entail? That the indiscernible part of a situation, that which cannot be captured by knowledge (and Badiou will always oppose knowledge to truth in the later works) cannot be known to a subject, yet the 'subject of truth' 'forces veracity at the point of the indiscernible' (BE 411), in other words, it realizes an indiscernible by deciding on a truth even whilst not being certain that it belongs to the situation in which it is found: 'The subject, which is the forcing production of an indiscernible included in the situation, cannot ruin the situation. What it can do is generate veridical statements that were previously undecidable' (BE 417). The move from the indiscernible to the undecidable is what characterizes a faithful subject for the Badiou of *Being and Event*, and precludes any illegitimate forcing of the naming of the event, precisely because it is based on the indiscernible elements within a specific situation, not the imposition of a name from a pre-existing sum of knowledges. In the terminology of the later work, Badiou will put this claim with regard to knowledges in the following way: 'Any subset, even that cemented by the most real of interests, is a-political, given that it can be named in an encyclopaedia. It is a matter of knowledge, and not of truth' (BE 347). Furthermore, '[a] truth is that indiscernible multiple whose finite approximation is supported by a subject, such that its ideality to-come, nameless correlate of the naming of an event, is that on the basis of which one can legitimately designate as subject the aleatory figure which, without the indiscernible, would be no more than an incoherent sequence of encyclopaedic determinants' (BE 433). It is on the basis of this indiscernible, not the force of a pre-named collective, that a political truth rests. In *Théorie du sujet*, Badiou claims, however, that 'every subject is political'[41], and it is not unfair to ask whether this is still the case to some extent, or at least whether the structure of subjectivation in Badiou is primarily conditioned

---

41. cf. Peter Hallward's claim that 'In Badiou's early work, the mechanism of this subjectivation is exclusively political'., *A Subject to Truth*, p. 35.

by his analysis of the 'rare' political processes he repeatedly returns to (TS 46). In *Conditions* (1992), Badiou does in fact criticize his earlier position in *Théorie du sujet*: 'Today, I would no longer say 'every subject is political', which is still a maxim of suturing. I would rather say: 'Every subject is induced by a generic procedure, and thus depends on an event. Which is why the subject is rare'.[42] It is not clear, however, whether this amounts to a retraction of the *form* of subjectivation which was originally understood solely politically—subjects were already 'rare' in *Théorie du sujet*, for example.

However, in the earlier work, Badiou's thought itself does precisely circulate around a certain collection of names and knowledges: Marxism, Badiou argues, 'is the discourse that supports the proletariat as subject. This is a principle we must never abandon'. Despite his separation of proletariat from the working class, the fact that Badiou sets up a name as a 'principle' can be retroactively criticized from the standpoint of his later work as overdetermining that which is left undecided and unseen in the later formulation of a political event. The political question in the early work is 'what is the organic link between the masses in revolt—the decisive historical actor—and the Party, as constituted political subject?'[43] It is this notion of an 'organic link' that marks Badiou out as essentially vanguardist in his conception of the political subject at this point, albeit a vanguardism that oscillates with regards to who the 'subject' is: there is an inherent ambiguity about who is the true subject in this situation—the party or the proletariat? Or a fusion of the two? As Hallward puts it: '[t]he subjective, or historical, "topology" of partisan antagonism explodes the static algebra of class ... Whereas every object stays in its place, every subject violates its place, inasmuch as its essential virtue is to be disoriented. Subjectivism operates in the element of force whereby place ... finds itself altered'.[44] Yet it is not an unmediated proletariat that seeks to abolish the 'space of placement' of classes. On the contrary, 'It is only through the party that the (objectively) working class becomes revolutionary Subject ... the masses make history, but as vanishing or ephemeral; the party makes this very vanishing *consist* and endure'.[45] As well as a response to Sartre's problems of the 'fleetingness' of the group-in-fusion, as outlined in *The Critique of Dialectical Reason*, there is a presentiment of Badiou's later

---

42. Alain Badiou, *Conditions*, Paris, Seuil, 1992, p. 234, n. 41.
43. Alain Badiou, 'Jean-Paul Sartre' (pamphlet), Paris, Potemkine, 1980, p. 7.
44. Hallward, *A Subject to Truth*, p. 35.
45. Hallward, *A Subject to Truth*, p. 36

'faithful subjects' in the role he assigns to the Party in this earlier work: 'the initial univocal act, which is always localized, inaugurates a fidelity, i.e. an invention of consequences, that will prove to be as infinite as the situation itself'.[46] In this sense, we could say that Badiou's attempt to make fidelity an on-going process, rather than a simple declaration mutates from donating to the party a vanguardist role to a retention of this same form in later non-political and more generically political conceptions of the subject. Badiou's criticism in *Théorie du sujet* of mass movements without a party is furthermore extremely close to Lenin's criticisms of 'spontaneity' and his centralizing of the party in *What is to be Done?*: '*We* must take upon ourselves the task of organizing ... an all-sided political struggle under the leadership of *our* party that all and sundry oppositional strata could ... give assistance to this struggle and this party according to their capacities'.[47] Indeed, Badiou is adamant in his defence of Lenin's affirmation of the subjective aspect of politics, and in fact argues against the common claim that Lenin delegates too much strength to the party: 'For Lenin, the party is nothing but the ... mandatory focal point for a politics. The party is the active purification of politics, the system of possibility practiced through the assessment of the Commune. It is inferred from politics (from the subjective aspect of force)' (TS 64). Later Badiou could not be more explicit in his turn away from the logic of the party, however: 'the question worth highlighting is one of a politics *without party*, which in no sense means unorganized, but rather one organized through the intellectual discipline of political processes, and not according to a form correlated with that of the State'. (M 122).

This earlier recourse to the party is Badiou's response to the problem shared by Rousseau and Sartre, as noted above, namely, how to preserve over time the initial moment of the subjective realization of revolution (for Sartre it is in some sense hopeless; for Rousseau, politics becomes a question of legitimation). Indeed, Badiou makes it clear in *Théorie du sujet* that his conceptualization of the party is precisely the 'subject' (however unclear its relation to the proletariat whose struggle it carries) that preserves the initial moment of force: 'The party is something subjective, taken in its historical emergence, the network of its actions, the novelty it concentrates. The institution is nothing but a husk' (TS 59). Again, Badiou is

---

46. Alain Badiou, 'Eight Theses on the Universal', *Theoretical Writings*, ed. and trans. Ray Brassier and Alberto Toscano, London, NY, Continuum, 2004, p. 150.
47. V. I. Lenin, *What is to be Done?*, trans. S.V. and Patricia Utechin, Oxford, Oxford University Press, 1963, p. 128.

very close to Sartre on this point (although for Sartre there is no question of 'the party' preserving the initial moment of revolt)—the ossification of force into institutions is not the framework that preserves the initial moment of novelty: here we see why Badiou must maintain the centrality of the 'subjective'—structures and organization are not enough if their participants are not gripped by the motive force that catalysed their initial movement. Placing, institutionalizing, is always on the side of the objective: 'every force is … a subjective force, and inasmuch as it is assigned to its place, structured, splaced, it is an objective force' (TS 59).

In later Badiou, this question will mutate into a more historically reflexive, again more Sartrean, and, we should say, less rhetorically Leninist, one: 'Why do the most heroic popular uprisings, the most persistent wars of liberation, the most indisputable mobilisations in the name of justice and liberty end … in opaque statist constructions wherein none of the factors that gave meaning and possibility to their historical genesis is decipherable?' (M 70) As Hallward puts it:

> What has happened in Badiou's subsequent work is that he has slowly adopted, while struggling to maintain his strictly political principles, a perspective similar to Sartre's historical-ephemeral pessimism. … but whereas Sartre was able to move beyond the ephemeral only by equating an ultimate historical coherence with a global political coordination—which accounts for the failure of the second volume of his *Critique* to move beyond Stalin as the apparent end of history—Badiou's determination to avoid this alternative has driven him ever further toward the radical subtraction of politics from history altogether.[48]

The rhetoric of the party leads Badiou in the earlier work to preserve a 'pure' aspect of the proletariat amidst its 'contradictory unity' as the 'practical' working class (in the historical context, to differentiate the Marxist-Leninist and Maoist movements from the PCF). If *Théorie du sujet* considers the party the only effective organizational structure, later Badiou will, on the contrary, turn his back completely on the necessity of the proletariat-party movement: 'the balance of the twentieth century is the withering away of the party-form, which knows only the form of the party-State'.[49] We can again note this move as the shift from a conception of party as subject to the idea of 'politics without a party' (the latter in fact being the maxim behind Badiou's work with *l'Organisation politique*).

---

48. Hallward, *A Subject to Truth*, p. 43.
49. *La Distance Politique*, no 35, 2001.

Badiou's later conception of the subject uncouples its relation to the proletariat in favour of a more generic conception of humanity, what he calls 'polyvalent man': 'the real characteristic of the party is not its firmness, but rather its porosity to the event ... what needs to come about is nothing but the affirmative multiplicity of capacities, whose emblem is polyvalent man, who undoes even those secular connections that bring together intellectual workers on the one hand, and manual workers on the other'. (M 75). This radical lack of political specification indicates a perhaps surprising turn to pre-Marxist considerations, at least partly on the basis of real historical failures, and aligns Badiou more with a Feuerbachian lineage than a strictly politically Marxist-Leninist one. This is particularly the case with Badiou's transition from the rhetoric of 'destruction' to the axiomatic assertion that 'people think ... politics is a thought' (TS 46). The rationalist philosophical universality of Badiou's newer conception of politics removes the antagonism of the earlier work between the proletariat and the bourgeois world, but precisely at the expense of a Marxist analysis of the structure of capitalism. The later theory of the subject is ahistorically affixed to the notion of event, and less to the topology of the proletariat/bourgeois relation: 'If one were to identify a cause of the subject, one would have to return, not so much to truth, which is rather its stuff, nor to the infinity whose finitude it is, but rather to the event' (BE 433). The 'event' of politics will, however, subtract Badiou's subject from a structured analysis, not only of capitalism, but also from 'worldy' politics altogether. This later subject (political and otherwise) is ultimately characterized more by what it is not than by what it is—neither the existential place of a set of representations, nor the transcendental system of the constitution of objects of possible experience. It is a subtractive entity, a 'fragment' of 'collective humanity' that arguably remains wedded, because of Badiou's later theoretically pre-Marxist turn, to the problem of sustaining the original political impulse behind mass movements, and thus again to the Sartrean problem of the depressing ossification of the group-in-fusion. The subject's exemption from a philosophy of history perhaps avoids some of the problems of Sartre's progressive-regressive method, which ultimately sees the totality of history refracted in the life of a single individual, but brings with it its own problems, namely, how we are to understand the *relation* between the structure of the political subject/collective and the state of affairs more broadly, not to mention historical forces and tendencies.

It was briefly noted above that Badiou's later 'theory of the subject' uncouples the term from a strictly political affiliation and broadens its possible points of reference to other 'conditions', namely art, science and love, as well as politics. Nevertheless, the structure of the political subject in the later works (*Being and Event* and the collection of essays uniquely devoted to his more recent position on politics, *Metapolitics* from 1998) has its own specificity that Badiou is clear to delineate: 'every situation is ontologically infinite. But only politics summons this infinity immediately, as subjective universality' (M 143). If Badiou has delinked this newer conception of the political subject from questions of antagonism and terms such as Proletariat, as it seems clear he has, what is the status of this 'subjective universality'? In a sense, Badiou is deliberately vague, perhaps in part to atone for the overly polemical thrust of his earlier work. For example when he claims the following: 'In collective situations—in which the collective becomes interested in itself—politics (if it exists *as generic politics*: what was called, for a long time, revolutionary politics, and for which another word must be found today) is also a procedure of fidelity ... its infinite productions are indiscernible (in particular, they do not coincide with *any part nameable according to the State*), being nothing more than "changes" of political subjectivity within the situation'. (BE 340). The admission that 'another word must be found today' indicates the difficulty Badiou has in trying differentiate his own project both from that of Marxist-Leninism and from that of the lineage of political humanism (Feuerbach and the early Marx, as well as parts of the later Sartre) that has characterized much of twentieth-century political thought. Despite stressing Badiou's relationship to the trajectory of thought that concerns itself with the generic in politics, we must be a little wary of trying neatly to fit Badiou back into a lineage of humanism which he seems to ignore or repudiate, or of neglecting the historical and political circumstances of the impossibility of an unproblematic usage of the term 'humanism' in a period when its invocation implied devastating inhumanity in practice (Stalinism). As further noted in the introduction, a key component of Badiou's contemporary criticisms of the discourses of 'human rights' and his attack on the inherent 'victimization' of man in contemporary ethical discourse in the *Ethics* is the defence of those French thinkers that we would typically characterize as 'anti-humanist'—Althusser, Foucault and Lacan. For Badiou, in what is only seemingly a paradox, these attempts to think beyond 'man' and 'without' man remain among the most politically emancipatory available to us. However, it seems clear that whilst Badiou is faithful to Foucault in some sense, and to the explicit problematic of Foucault's *The Order of Things*, i.e. that the historical emergence of the very posing of 'man' as a problem and the empirico-transcendental overcodings that inevitably follow is due for surpassing, nevertheless this argument is not taken up in the same way for Foucault as for Badiou. *Pace* Foucault, it seems that for Badiou there is a different way of both asking and answering the question of what man is that manages to obviate the temptation of post-Kantian (transcendental or naturalist) answers. So, despite having gone through the filter of theoretical anti-humanism, the question itself—'What is man?'—remains in place for him in the political context. Politics, however, becomes something of an autonomous region, tied to the situation, but oddly distanced from larger tendencies and geopolitical processes: 'Politics is, for itself, its own proper end; in the mode of what is being produced as true statements—though forever unknown—by the capacity of a collective will' (BE 354). If philosophy's task vis-à-vis politics (as with the other truth conditions) is to gather together the 'truths' revealed in situations, we can in fact retroactively use the early Badiou to criticize the later. When in *Théorie du sujet* he states that '[a] sum of rebellions does not make a subject, regardless of how much you may want to "coordinate" them' (TS 62), do we not see a kind of pre-emptive self-critique of the later work? If philosophy's task is to 'compossibilize', to hold together, the truths emergent under the four different conditions (whilst possessing none of its own), then what distinguishes philosophy's capture of these episodes of non-antagonistic, non-historical, generic manifestations of politics precisely from this 'sum of rebellions'?

In the later writings on metapolitics, we confront the possibility that that dependency on 'thought' to found the possibility of politics may cause problems from within the system. Badiou makes use of two axioms, in particular, that ultimately seem to occupy a floating role between the set-theoretical ontology, on the one hand, and the discussion of events and truth procedures, on the other. These are, first, the axiom of equality, namely that: 'equality is not an objective for action, it is an axiom of action'.[50] Second, the generic axiom that 'man thinks' or 'people think', namely that: 'philosophy addresses all humans as thinking beings since it supposes that all humans think'.[51] Whilst these seem at minimal or almost banal assertions, without them Badiou could not preserve his commitment to what he calls a modern politics of emancipation. The connection

---

50. Here Badiou shares a similar conception with Rancière, for whom equality is not an outcome to be desired, but an axiomatic supposition.
51. Alain Badiou, 'Philosophy and Desire', *Infinite Thought*, trans. and ed. Oliver Feltham and Justin Clemens, London, Continuum, 2003, p. 40.

between the genericity, equality and politics is basically outlined in the following claim:

> Some political orientations, throughout history, have had or will have a connection with a truth. A truth of the collective as such. They are rare attempts, often brief, but they are the only ones under condition philosophy can think about. These political sequences are singularities, they trace no destiny, they construct no monumental history. Philosophy can, however, distinguish in them a common feature. This feature is that these orientations require of the people they engage only their strict generic humanity. They give no preference, for the principles of action, to the particularity of interests. These political orientations induce a representation of the collective capacity which refers its agents to the strictest equality. What does 'equality' mean? Equality means that the political actor is represented under the sole sign of his specifically human capacity. Interest is not a specifically human capacity. All living beings have as an imperative for survival the protection of their interests. The specifically human capacity is precisely thought, and thought is nothing other than that by which the path of a truth seizes and traverses the human animal.[52]

The following question is important here: Is an anti-humanist fidelity to thought *per se* possible in Badiou, such that it can avoid any question of a specifically human capacity from the outset? Perhaps in the case of mathematics (i.e. Badiou's set theoretical ontology) we can respond in the affirmative. However, when it comes to politics, this seems unlikely. The related question that needs to be posed here is the following: Can Badiou ever truly sever 'thought' from a baseline, axiomatic notion of the human as equal and generic? Badiou's entire project is founded on a commitment to political subjectivation—but subjectivation and generic humanity are not ontological facts, and nothing guarantees their possibility. Indeed, events are strictly speaking impossible, or extra-ontological, given the logic of the situation (which is why Badiou refers to them as 'ultra-ones'). What, then, is the relation between what Badiou calls 'generic humanity', the axiom that 'man thinks', and man's capacity for immortality and infinity as a collective political subject? We could perhaps say that at least one 'meta-event' conditions the very existence of these two non-mathematical axioms—not the existence of philosophy, but rather the existence of *politics*, of events that once contained political 'truths' (Badiou repeatedly refers to the French and Russian Revolutions). Furthermore, *without* the two

---

52. Alain Badiou, 'Philosophy and Politics', *Radical Philosophy*, 96, July/August 1999, p. 29.

floating axioms of equality and generic thought, politics would not even be thinkable, and certainly not the egalitarian forms of politics which Badiou in his later works tries to defend.[53]

If the capacity that is specifically human is that of thought, and, as Badiou argues, 'thought is nothing other than that by which the path of a truth seizes and traverses the human animal',[54] we may wish to ask what the status of this traversing is. The answer seems to be that the path of a truth enables that which is *inhuman* to be borne by the generic thinking of man. But this thought in some sense *pre-exists* the traversing, via the axiom that 'man thinks', and that man has the capacity to think disinterestedly. Why disinterestedly? For Badiou, interest is not a specifically human capacity, since all living beings protect their interests as imperative for survival. Thought as traversed by truth—this peculiarly human capacity—must be capable of being absolutely disinterested. Badiou writes: 'Any truth procedure distinguishes a properly immortal disinterest from an abject properly "animal" assemblage of particular interests'. Furthermore, thought and disinterest coincide in the overcoming of all that is finite in man: 'Thought is the specific mode by which a human animal is traversed and overcome by a truth' (E 16). The relationship of philosophy to politics that comes to take a central role in Badiou's later work takes a historical and theoretical step *backwards* by replacing the question of political practice with this more general conception of thought: 'By "metapolitics" I mean whatever consequences a philosophy is capable of drawing … from real instances of politics as thought' (inscription from M xxxix). There is a potential problem here, aside from the obscured yet apparently necessary philosophical anthropology, if politics is reduced to something like noology, a mere examination of its rational qualities.

Paradoxically, then, it has to be the case that for the later Badiou, it is the generic human capacity for thought that minimally founds a universal inhumanism—and this is the key role of both politics and mathematics. But in order to link this back to the condition of politics we should ask the following question: Does our capacity for mathematics in any sense relate to the fact that we can be seized by specifically political truths? Whilst this might sound like an impossible question from Badiou's point

---

53. Rather than try and force Badiou's mathematical analysis of the generic onto levels of thinking to which it cannot apply, it should be pointed out that it is he himself who uses the language of the generic, outside of its specifically technical role, in order to found the very possibility of politics (separate from philosophy), as well as in his discussions of generic humanity *tout court*.

54. Badiou, *Infinite Thought*, p. 71.

of view, a mixture of two distinct conditions, it directly interrogates the role of infinity in Badiou's philosophy. If it is mathematics that teaches us that there is no reason whatsoever to confine thinking within the ambit of finitude, and yet it is man's capacity to be traversed by the infinite that is immediately relevant to any thinking of politics, rather than mathematics, then it seems that we cannot avoid posing what at first appears to be an illegitimate question.[55]

If every politics of emancipation rejects finitude, rejects 'being-to-wards-death' on the basis of the *immediate* subjective universality of the infinite, then it seems clear that, paradoxically, infinity is just as, if not more, important for a politics of emancipation than it is for mathematics. But what is the relation between infinity and immortality? In the *Ethics* we are told that every human being is capable of being *this* immortal, that 'in each case, subjectivation is immortal, and makes Man' (E 12). This is why there is no ethics in general, and no politics in general. All humanity has its root in the identification in thought [*en pensée*] of singular situations. If infinity is actually only the most general form of multiple-being, then human capacity for infinity is perhaps the most banal of starting points. Nevertheless it plays the founding role for politics more than for any other condition, including mathematics itself. In 'Politics as Truth Procedure', Badiou writes the following: 'The infinite comes into play in every truth procedure, but only in politics does it take the first place. This is because only in politics is the deliberation about the possible (and hence about the infinity of the situation) constitutive of the process itself … politics treats the infinite as such according to the principle of the same, the egalitarian principle. We will say that the numericality of the political procedure has the infinite as its first term; whereas for love this first term is the one; for science the void; and for art a finite number'.[56]

Let us digress slightly here, and look briefly at Feuerbach, in order to go over the role that the generic plays in his thought, and to make sense of its relation to politics in Badiou. In a section of *The Essence of Christianity* entitled 'The Essential Nature of Man', Feuerbach tells us that 'conscious-

---

55. cf. Badiou's 'On the Truth-Process: An open lecture', where he argues that: 'the modern politics of emancipation freed from the dialectic scheme of classes and parties has as its aim something like a generic democracy, a promotion of the commonplace, of a quality abstracted from any predicate—so it's possible to speak of a generic politics, and a warfield of prose such as Samuel Beckett's, which tried by successive subtraction to designate the naked existence of generic humanity' (August 2002, http://www.egs.edu/faculty/badiou/badiou-truth-process-2002.htm).

56. Badiou, *Theoretical Writings*.

ness in the strictest sense is present only in a being to whom his species, his essential nature, is an object of thought'.[57] In the 'strictest sense' here excludes 'brutes' who can only conceive of themselves as individuals and not in a generic sense. There is seemingly nothing unusual in Feuerbach's definition of consciousness; we are familiar with the argument that because man is by nature in possession of both inner and outer life, we can differentiate ourselves from other animals that apparently lack this separation. However, Feuerbach dislocates the role nature usually plays in this equation (as that relating to the outer life, outside of consciousness), and states instead that: 'the inner life of man is the life which has relation to his species, to his general, as distinguished from his individual, nature'. So, to be 'individual' is to be an external, natural being, like the brute who can 'exercise no function which has relation to its species without another individual external to itself'. To be conscious in the 'strictest sense', on the other hand, is to be universal, by virtue of the very fact that man can 'perform the functions of thought and speech, which strictly imply such a relation, apart from another individual'. Thus man's very essence, his *Gattungswesen*, depends on his capacity for universal, abstractive, activity, even (especially) in his isolation (his inner life).

Paradoxically, Man's capacity for 'asceticism' (understood here as the reflection of thought upon thought, or upon the very capacity for thought) is that which most indicates his universality. Feuerbach, in his thinking of man's 'inner life' as *Gattungswesen*, inaugurates a strand of philosophical anthropology that has nothing to do with the equation of interiority with finitude, by which thought comes to reflect upon its own limits, and ultimately the possibility of its own absolute impossibility (as in Heidegger's explicitly anti-anthropological formulation). On the contrary, thought *qua* thought is always based on a demonstration of the *infinity* of thought, and thus simultaneously of man's 'generic essence'. Here are two quotes from Feuerbach that demonstrate this point a little further, the first from the preface to on *the Essence of Christianity*, and the second from 'Towards a Critique of Hegel's Philosophy':

> Consciousness, in the strict or proper sense, is identical with consciousness of the infinite; a limited consciousness is no consciousness; consciousness is essentially infinite in its nature. The consciousness of the infinite is nothing else than the consciousness of the infinity of the consciousness; or, in the consciousness of the

---

57. Ludwig Feuerbach, *The Essence of Christianity*, trans. George Eliot, New York, London, Harper and Row, 1957, p. 1.

infinite, the conscious subject has for its object the infinity of his own nature.[58]

The human form is ... the genus of the manifold animal species; it no longer exists as man but as genus. The being of man is no longer particular and subjective, but a universal being, for man has the whole universe as the object of his drive for knowledge.[59]

Returning to Badiou, we must of course point out the quite distinct roles that universality and consciousness play for him—such that universality can in no way precede an event, and that consciousness plays no part in his radically anti-phenomenological formulations. But what is clear in Feuerbach is that maintaining a generic thinking of infinity as a constitutively human capacity is the *only* way to escape the over-determination of man by his finitude. Hence Feuerbach's philosophical anthropology has nothing to do with limiting thought, and in fact, precisely points to a radically de-individualized generic ability to think the infinite which looks to be very close to the claims Badiou makes in his later conception of politics.

However, Badiou differs from Feuerbach here in more complex ways. First, by having a singular, and not a general, conception of the universal (which also separates him on this specific point from Kant and the transcendental tradition). Thus, when it comes to ethics there can be no general principle of *human* rights, 'for the simple reason that what is *universally* human is always rooted in particular truths, particular configurations of active thought'. Similarly, 'Politics as thinking has no other objective than the transformation of unrepeatable situations' (E 16). To become a subject (and not remain a simple 'human animal'), is to participate in the coming into being of a universal novelty. The subject here will be singular because it will always be an event that constitutes the subject as a truth. However, to return to the axiom of equality, it is important that equality does not refer to anything objective. Equality is subjective, or revealed through subjectivity, and it is this key claim that links both Badiou and Feuerbach, aside from the question of the generic.

Politics, as we have seen, is impossible without the idea that people, taken indistinctly, are capable of the thought that also constitutes the post-evental political subject. But at what point are people capable of this thought? It is my claim that, in the case of politics, Badiou needs to

---

58. Ludwig Feuerbach, *The Fiery Brook: Selected Writings of Ludwig Feuerbach*, ed. and trans. Zawar Hanfi, New York, Anchor Books, 1972, p. 99.
59. Feuerbach, *The Fiery Brook*, p. 93.

found, at an absolutely minimal level, a kind of pre-evental philosophical anthropology of a quasi-Feuerbachian kind. This is something of a problematic position, cutting directly against arguments made elsewhere by others, including Badiou himself, and Peter Hallward, who states explicitly that 'there is no distinct place in Badiou's work for a philosophical anthropology of any kind'.[60] Certainly, there is no room in Badiou for any philosophical anthropology of finitude. The question here is whether one can have a philosophical anthropology of infinitude, as Badiou seems to require for his discussion of politics. That is why asking this question returned us to Feuerbach. The anthropological aspect of the answer to this question would have to be empty, generic, unlimited. In other words, that claim that we are 'subtractively infinite' means that what we do as subjects, without any reference to an object, has infinity as its dimension. That we are infinite because we think infinitely, or in Feuerbachian terms, because we think infinity *as such*.

The reason for this incursion into the (mostly uncharted) territory of an infinite philosophical anthropology is that, without some kind of discussion of a pre-evental generic capacity, or an empty axiomatic regarding the thought of all, it seems that Badiou would be incapable of claiming that the events which set off the truth procedure of politics have any reason to be more or less egalitarian. It could be the case that there are no subjects until an event and its nomination, but without the generic axioms of universal thought underlying the very possibility of subjectivation, there would be no positive content to Badiou's defense of emancipatory, egalitarian politics.

---

60. Hallward, *Badiou: A Subject to Truth*, p. 53.

13

The Bourgeois and the Islamist, or, The Other Subjects of Politics

Alberto Toscano

SUBJECTS OF UNTRUTH

Among the less fortunate by-products of the recent resurgence in emancipatory theories of political subjectivity is the tendency to depict the subject in an exclusively militant or, at the very least, 'progressive' light. Bracketing the contradictions of social class, or the pathologies of ideology, the political subject seems endowed, by fiat, with the steadfast virtues of universalism. While, confronted with a proliferation of noxious political 'agents' and ideas, such a stance may possess an attractive if minimalist rectitude, reserving the term 'subject' solely for the kind of collective egalitarian figure that could divert our baleful course might mean depriving ourselves of a potent instrument to intervene in the present. If we relegate the reactionary, or at best ambiguous, figures that loom large on our political horizon to the rank of structural epiphenomena, fleeting phantoms or mindless tendencies, we run the risk of producing political theories that differ little from plain wishful thinking or self-satisfied sectarianism. Even within the generally optimistic politico-philosophical paradigm which, by way of shorthand, we could call 'the theory of the multitude', some have begun to foreground the deep *ambivalence* of contemporary forms of political subjectivity.[1] But can there be any concessions to such an ambiguity, to the presence of 'untruthful' subjects, in Alain Badiou's affirmative, and avowedly 'Promethean' theory of the subject?

---

1. Paolo Virno, *A Grammar of the Multitude*, New York, Semiotext(e), 2004.

Badiou's decades-long preoccupation with political subjectivity does indeed seem marked by an increasingly trenchant and 'internalist' treatment of the subject as both rare and aloof from the vicissitudes of social mediation. What's more, Badiou makes 'subject' inseparable from the novelty of an exception and the arduous trajectory of a truth which is always in the world, but in many ways not of it (or rather, a truth which, by forcefully including itself in the world makes sure that the world will never be the same). He does this by advocating a strenuously 'post-Cartesian' thinking of the subject in which the latter is only figured as an *effect*, an aleatory trajectory or point of arrival, and not as a pre-existing source. After Marx and Freud, the subject is not a starting-point, it must be 'found'.[2] All signs point to a stance which is wholly refractory to any analysis of the subject's particularistic attachments, violent and violating impulses, repressive desires, and so on. Badiou's explicit decision not to treat the subject by way of a theory of ideology, and—despite his grounding allegiance to Lacan—not to delve into its Freudian unconscious, also militate for a purified, formal theory of the subject that would shun the subject's unsavoury, pathological side. And yet, as I would like to examine in these pages, within the strictures of an asocial, non-ideological and uncompromisingly universalistic theory of the subject Badiou has proposed a number of ways to think and formalize the existence of other subjects, ones which are not the bearers but the enemies or obfuscators of truth.

AMBIVALENCE OF THE BOURGEOISIE

Given Badiou's roots in revolutionary theory one cannot but expect some traces in his work of the numerous contributions to the theory of anti- or semi-universalist subjectivity within Marxism—from Marx's own paean to bourgeois destruction in *The Communist Manifesto*, to the wrestling with the rise of fascist politics in the writings of Trotsky and many others. It is evident, for instance, that a reckoning with the figure of *reaction* has been a constant in Badiou's work. But perhaps one of the more interesting points of entry into Badiou's theory of 'untrue' subjects concerns the status of the bourgeoisie. To begin with, Badiou intends to dislocate the apparently frontal confrontation, the class struggle, between proletariat and bourgeoisie. For the proletariat as a *force* (a crucial concept in Badiou's dialectical writings of the 1970s) does not seem to be pitted against the bourgeoisie as another force. In some of the early seminars that make

---

2. Alain Badiou, *Théorie du sujet*, Paris, Seuil, 1982, p. 295 (henceforth TS).

up Badiou's *Théorie du sujet*, the bourgeoisie is depicted as a mere agent of a system of places, of a Whole which the proletariat seeks to destroy by what Badiou calls a 'torsion', whereby an included but suppressed element comes to limit, then destroy, the totality of which it is a part: 'To say proletariat and bourgeoisie is to remain with the Hegelian artifice: something and something else. And why? Because the project of the proletariat, its internal being, is not to contradict the bourgeoisie, or to cut its legs off. Its project is communism, and nothing else. That is to say the abolition of any place wherein something like a proletariat could be situated' (TS 25). And, *a fortiori*, anything like a bourgeoisie. In this sense, whilst the confrontation with the bourgeoisie might be the 'motor' of history, the proletariat's target is really the social Whole, i.e. 'imperialist society'.

Moving further in the series of seminars that make up Badiou's first major theoretical work, however, we encounter, in the midst of an analysis of the subjective weakness of May '68, a portrait of the bourgeois as subject and force. Indeed, Badiou stresses that revolutionaries have always made the mistake of thinking themselves to be 'the only subject, and represent the antagonistic class to themselves as an objective mechanism of oppression led by a handful of profiteers'. On the contrary, one of the lessons of the Chinese Cultural Revolution, according to Badiou, is that the bourgeoisie too engages in politics, and not simply by means of exploitation or coercion. Asking himself *where* this politics takes place, Badiou answers, with rare Gramscian overtones: 'Exactly as with the proletariat: in the people, working class included, and I would even say, since we're dealing with the new bureaucratic State bourgeoisie, working class *especially* included'. The reason for thus foregrounding the 'subjective force of the adversary' is to counter the feeble-minded and objectivist 'anti-repressive logorrhoea', for which the only enemy would be a Moloch-like State. Contrary to this anarchistic 'leftism', Badiou proposes the following assertion: 'Of course, they are a handful, the bourgeois imperialists, but the subjective effect of their force lies in the divided people. There is not just the law of Capital, or the cops. To miss this is not to see the unity of the space of placements [*esplace*], its consistency'. The suggestion here is that the social space wherein the latent force of the proletariat is captured, placed and instrumentalized cannot be envisaged in a purely structural manner, as an impersonal given, but must instead be conceived in terms of that counter-revolutionary or reactionary subjectivity which carries its own project into the pre-subjective mass of the people. Or, as Badiou summarizes in a Hegelian pastiche: 'We must conceive of imperialist society not only as substance, but also as subject' (TS 60). This, at least, is the position put forward in the seminar dated '15 April 1975', which appears to rectify the earlier understanding of the proletariat as the sole political and subjective force.

In the seminar dated '14 February 1977', Badiou approaches the question of the proletariat/bourgeoisie relation from a topological angle. If we follow an economistic tradition, which sunders Marx's *Capital* from the concrete (strategic) analysis of concrete (political) situations, bourgeoisie and proletariat appear topologically exterior to one another—the first defined in terms of its ownership of the means of production, the second in terms of its separation (alienation) from them. The result of this purely external topology, is paradoxically to render the proletariat functionally interior or immanent to the bourgeoisie. Reduced to alienated labour-power, the proletariat is nothing but a piece in the apparatus of exploitation, whose identity is entirely heteronomous, dictated by the laws of capital. Briefly, 'capital is the place of the proletariat'. Badiou deduces from this the possibility of Soviet state-capitalism, since it is perfectly possible, given this arrangement, to 'suppress capitalists, all the while maintaining the law of capital'. To depart from the compulsion to repeat and the allergy to novelty that characterize the economistic framework, Badiou enjoins us to think the 'interiority of the bourgeoisie to the working class' (TS 147).

Making reference to Marx's analysis of the series of uprisings ('social hysterias' in his Lacanese) of the eighteen-thirties, forties and fifties, Badiou sees the emergence of a proletarian figure not as a functional cog in the machinery of capital, but as an internal 'torsion', an 'exceptional disorder' within the political trajectory of the democratic bourgeois movement. The proletarian subject is born out of its bourgeois impurity, its being indexed to a heteronomous capitalist order, and only emerges by the 'expulsion, the purging ... of the internal infection that, to begin with, constitutes it'. The proletariat is thus depicted, through these somewhat unsettling medical metaphors, as perpetually in the process of healing from the malady of the bourgeoisie. Insisting with the topological vocabulary, Badiou writes that 'the politics of the proletariat is in a situation of internal exclusion with regard to bourgeois politics, that is, with regard to its object'. The proletariat is thus both within and against the bourgeoisie, constantly 'purging' its intimate bourgeois determination. Its 'topology of destruction' means that it is enduringly engaged in an effort to dislocate and ultimately destroy the site of its existence (without this destruction, it might just be a mask or ruse of the bourgeoisie, as Badiou deems to be the case for the USSR); but it can only do so, because of its originary impurity, in an immanent, dialectical combat with the bourgeoisie that internally excludes it. This topological vision transforms the standing of the bourgeoisie within Badiou's theory of the subject yet again:

> Does the bourgeoisie make a subject (*fait sujet*)? I said so in this very place, in April 1975. Let us contradict ourselves, it is just a trick of *par-être*. The bourgeois has not made a subject for a long while, it makes a place (*lieu*). There is only one political subject, for a given historicization. This is a very important remark. To ignore it is to become confused by a vision of politics as a subjective duel, which it is not. There is one place and one subject. The dissymmetry is structural (TS 148).[3]

Class struggle, if the term still applies, is thus not between two separate *forces*, two subjects indexed to different places within the apparatus of capital. It is an effect of the proletariat (that 'surviving body, born from the rot') expelling itself from bourgeois politics, and thus gaining its existence through that very process of organized destruction. The theory of subjectivation as destruction thus appears to require the exclusivity of the term 'subject', and the relegation of the bourgeoisie, and any subjects other than the proletariat, to a phantasmagorical structural semblance.

This oscillation in the appraisal of the bourgeoisie, and the dialectical arguments that motivate it, indicate the thorny problem posed to Badiou's project by the existence of other, non-emancipatory subjects: if the bourgeoisie is not a subject, the theory of the proletariat risks a 'leftist' solution, a repressive hypothesis which singles out an impersonal State or Capital as its only enemy; if the bourgeoisie is a subject, antagonism seems to absorb Badiou's theory of torsion-destruction, and the historicity of politics appears doomed to ambivalence with the introduction of multiple forms of universality into the situation. As we will see further on, this antinomy of the other subject continues to haunt Badiou's work.

JUSTICE AND TERROR, NIHILISTS AND RENEGADES

Abiding within the rich confines of the *Théorie du sujet*, we witness the return, in a very different guise, of the problem of the 'other subject' in Badiou's attempt to formulate an *ethics*. Insisting with the metaphors of location and the topological arsenal that dominates the recasting of dialectics in the *Théorie*, Badiou proposes to rethink the question of ethics in terms of a 'topics' [*topique*]: 'There is no major Marxist text that is not

---

3. The untranslatable notion of '*par-être*', a play on '*paraître*' (to appear) is taken by Badiou from Lacan's seminars of the 1970s.

driven by the question: Where is the proletariat? That is why politics is the unity of opposites of a topics (the current situation) and an ethics (our tasks)' (TS 297).[4] But this topics also acquires a more precise meaning, referring to the affective figures that the subject (viewed as an unstable mix of destructive 'subjectivation', and restorative 'subjective processes') moves across. This ethics is thus, first and foremost, immanent to the becoming of a subject—so how might it allow us to deepen our investigation of other, non-emancipatory subjects?

Given the centrality of radical novelty to Badiou's investigation, and what he has already indicated regarding the proletariat, born of a rotting bourgeoisie on the occasion of a social hysteria, the starting point for an ethics of subjectivity can only be *disorder*. What *affects* are borne by a subject that might try, by bringing itself into the world, to draw novelty out of this disorder? To begin with, a methodological proviso is required: like his theory of the subject, Badiou's theory of affect is also post-Cartesian, which is to say that it treats the subject as a formalization and an aleatory trajectory, meaning that 'affect' does not refer to an experience, a capacity, a spiritual or mental disposition. This ethics of affects, which principally concerns the subject's stance vis-à-vis the law of the world which is being destroyed, circulates through four concepts: anxiety, superego, courage and justice. 'These are categories of the subject-effect. What they allows us to know is a specific material region, at the basis [*principe*] of every destruction of what sustains it'. How these concepts are articulated to one another by the subject will determine its disposition with regard to the situation and its aptitude for the tasks of innovation.

Anxiety [*angoisse*] treats the given order as *dead*. It does not foresee the splitting and re-composition of the symbolic around a new law, but the simple 'killing' of the symbolic by the real. The consequence of this non-dialectical treatment of destruction as chaos and paralysis, abrogation of sense, is that 'the law, always undivided, glimmers in the distance of what it no longer supports' (TS 307). The excess over the law has no other symbols than those of its death, and remains in a sense hysterical, 'a question without an answer'.

The intervention of the *superego* is thus depicted as a response to the morbid paralysis of anxiety: 'As a figure of consistency, [superego] puts excess back in place *by distributing it over all the places*. The superego is the structural aspect of excess. Through it the algebrization of the topological

---

4. The philosophical notion of a 'Topics', concerned with the *topoi*, the places or locations of discourse, derives from Aristotle's eponymous treatise.

is effected, as if, filled with subjectivating anxiety, the place recomposed itself upon itself in the terrorizing prescription of placement. ... The superego is the subjective process of terror' (TS 308). The model here is provided by one of the crucial sources for Badiou's treatment of the dark side of subjectivity, Hegel's diagnosis of the Terror. Where anxiety signalled the chaos of a world without law, the superego determines a fixing of excess (and of death); a pitiless control of the situation by the forcible introduction of a new law, which, as Hegel shows, takes the shape of a purely negative and persecutory universality. But, foreshadowing the use of the same passages of Hegel in the more recent lessons on the twentieth century, for Badiou the superego-Terror 'is a phenomenon of the subject, and not of the State ... terror is a modality of politics and not the mechanical product of the modern State' (TS 309).[5] What does it mean to think terror as internal to the subject? For Badiou it means that the criminal ravages of terror (e.g. the Gulag) cannot be the object of an anti-statist moral critique, but must be rethought from within a (Marxist) politics that comprehends the superego as an internal, dialectical and 'restorative' figure. If terror is subjective it is only by understanding the ethical trajectory of subjects—from the inside—that it may be parried or limited. External critique, which excises or ignores the subjective element, merely prepares the return or repetition of terror.

The third ethical figure, *courage*, presents an important alternative to the subjectivity of terror qua antidote to the ravages of anxiety—where anxiety was a 'question without an answer', courage is presented as 'an answer without a question'. As an affect, courage qualifies the kind of subject capable of facing disorder and the anxiety that issues from it, without demanding the immediate restoration of the law. What is more, courage subtends the capacity to act, to traverse the chaos of anxiety, without the coordinates provided by the law. When gnawed by anxiety—so goes Badiou's recommendation—to act with courage is to do that very thing you think impossible, or before which you anxiously recoil. Or, as his motto has it: 'Find your indecency of the moment' (TS 310).

Possibly the most interesting ethical concept proposed in this 'topics' is that of *justice*, which is presented as basically the opposite of terror in its relationship to the law. While, inasmuch as its terroristic implementation

---

5. See also Alain Badiou, *The Century*, trans. and commentary by Alberto Toscano, London, Polity Press, 2007, especially Chapter 5: 'The passion for the real and the montage of semblance', where Hegel features as the principal philosophical reference for a reckoning with the molten core of the twentieth century.

is self-justifying, the superego absolutizes law, justice relativizes it, working by the criterion that the more Real and the less law, the better. But for this very reason, justice is a deeply unsettling affect, generating ever further anxiety as it casts doubt on the viability of rules for dealing with disorder. Insisting with a dialectical approach, this is why the institutive character of justice can never be wholly sundered from the restorative procedure of the superego, and why justice calls forth two stances which deny its autonomy: *dogmatism*, which demands the untrammelled supremacy of the superego over courage; and *scepticism*, in which the non-law of justice does not open up to the institution of new laws, but is merely the stand-in for the undecidability of law, which is to say, for anxiety. 'Justice is the *flux* [*flou*] *of places*, the opposite, therefore, of the right place [*la juste place*]' (TS 312).

What are the consequences of this quadripartite schema for a thinking of other subjects? I would like to focus on two. The first concerns the ideologization of subjects, the second Badiou's typology of ethical discourses.

Besides serving as a psychoanalytic clue to the functioning of Hegelian terror, the superego is also employed by Badiou to account for the immanent production of ideology out of the travails of subjectivation. Following a general methodological principle, which is that of following the vicissitudes of the subject without immediately imposing upon it the marks of structure, Badiou here proposes to see ideology as a product of something like an ethical failing within the subject itself. While 'true' subjectivation involves the real piercing into the symbolic, and the hazardous effort to recompose a new order after the destruction of the system of places, ideology is a question of the imaginary. Holding to the dialectical demand that organizes his ethics of the subject—the idea that faithful subjectivity must topologically adhere to its other—Badiou sees subjectivation and ideology as facets of the same process. He illustrates this with an example from an event, the German Peasants' War of 1525, which he had already touched upon in his earlier collaborative work on ideology: 'When Thomas Müntzer sets the German countryside aflame with an egalitarian communist aim, he subjectivates courageously, on a background of death, and calls for justice. When he names his courage on the basis of the absolute conviction that Christ wants the realization of this project, he imaginarily articulates the rebellious bravura on the superego whose allegory is the "kingdom of God"' (TS 314).[6] The same lesson can be drawn from

6. See also Alain Badiou and François Balmès, *De l'idéologie*, Paris, F. Maspéro, 1976.

the Cultural Revolution: it is the incapacity of the Red Guards to sustain their egalitarian programme, with courage and justice, that calls forth the imaginary and ideological guarantee, the ethical stop-gap provided by the superego-cult of Mao. The anxiety produced by egalitarian disorder is thus assuaged, not just through the idolatry of a new, if under-defined law (Mao-Tse-Tung-thought), but, following Hegel, through the persecution it gives rise to: the superego's manner of 'saturating places', which can only be occupied, without ambiguity, by revolutionaries or enemies. The imaginary dimension thus arises as a way of comforting the anxious subject, unable to sustain the uncertain discipline of courage and the undecidable measure of justice.

The terror exercised by the superego thus represents a weakness of the subject. But this does not exhaust the content of ethics. If ethics 'makes discourse of what cannot wait or be delayed', if it 'makes do with what there is', then its key problem, as Badiou explicitly draws from Lacan, is that 'the world only ever proposes the temptation to give up', 'to inexist in the service of goods' (TS 325, 328, 334). What an 'ethics of Marxism' would therefore need to confront are the various ways in which the temptation to give up on the labour of subjectivation, the labour of destruction, manifests itself. If 'subjectivation' names the destructive process whereby the subject subordinates place to excess, while 'subjective process' defines the contrary, conservative tendency, then the character of defeatism or even reaction involves giving up on subjectivation for the sake of an older subjective process. The source for this remains internal to the subject itself, in the failure of 'confidence' [confiance] ('the fundamental concept of the ethics of Marxism'). If the ethical subject is identified with the party pure and simple, then the ethical nemesis is surely the renegade, the traitor to be liquidated (thereby returning us to superego-Terror). But if we rein back this ferocious form of placement, what light can ethics shed on the existence of other subjects?

While Badiou had abandoned the idea of plural subjects when wrestling with the conundrum of the bourgeoisie, the issue seems to return once he declares ethics to be 'a naming of the subject as historically effectuated in the form of discourse'. For there is not just one, but *four* discourses of the subject for Badiou and thus, in a complex and problematic sense, if not four separate subjects, at least four tendencies within subjectivation and subjective processes. These four discourses are the discourse of praise, that of resignation, that of discordance, and the 'Promethean' discourse. Their fundamental affective tonalities are belief, fatalism, nihilism and confidence. Now, without delving into the detail of how these positions are derived from the prior distinction between superego, anxiety, courage and justice, it is important to note that the ethical subjects indexed to these discourses are intrinsically relational. In other words, they only exist by designating their others and the discourses of these others.

The discourse of praise and the Promethean discourse are the two that in a sense lie beyond anxiety. But they are diametrically opposed in their relations to the Whole (or space of placements, *esplace*) and the force of novelty (or the out of place, *horlieu*). It is a matter of belief (or confidence in the space of placements) versus confidence (or belief in the out-of-place). While belief opens up the possibility of salvation, and the potential eternity of the subject in a finally realized space of placements (without lack but determined by law), confidence, instead, works with fidelity to the innovative decision (courage), and a more porous recomposition of the real, less open to the law (justice). The subject of praise can here be recast in terms of something like the subject of the system itself, the believer and defender of its righteousness, a truly *conservative* subject. But the Promethean subject of destruction and recomposition, the universalist (proletarian) subject, has two other counterparts, mired in different forms of anxiety. These are the resigned fatalist and the nihilist. The resigned fatalist is most likely the one who has succumbed to the service of goods, who, though not beyond the pale, is in a sense a *passive* nihilist and something like an after-subject. It is the real nihilist instead who, plunged into the discordance of an anxious world, but without the safety of knowing scepticism, is the subject whom the Promethean discourse wishes to capture and persuade. For the nihilist is indeed imbued with a certain form of courage (the passion for the act, for excess) but is incapable of justice, of the right measurement of the relationship between the real and the law. He lacks the confidence which alone allows the organization and endurance of both courage and justice in a universal figure.

Thus, despite his arguments to the contrary when addressing the possibility of a bourgeois subject, Badiou already recognizes, in the *Théorie du sujet*, the need to think different subjective configurations, not all of which can be regarded as the ethical bearers of novelty and universality. Though his more recent work on ethics has been far more widely discussed than the earlier foray into an ethical 'topics', we can identify some manifest continuities, which bridge the theoretical caesura triggered by the introduction of the theory of the event and its metaontological, set-theoretical armature. In the first place, there is the idea that a subject is ethically defined by the manner in which it relates to other subjects within the space created by its confidence, or fidelity: 'Every fidelity to an authentic event names the adversaries of its perseverance'.[7] This *agonistic* dimension of subjectivation clearly relates to the relational character of the theory of ethical discourses (e.g. there is no Promethean subject without 'its' nihilist). Secondly, there is the idea that one can only rescind one's incorporation into a subject by *betrayal*. This theory of betrayal is in some respects akin to the discourse of resignation in the *Théorie du sujet*. The (ex-)subject of betrayal in fact *denies* having been seized by a truth, drowning his previous courage in deep scepticism and bowing to the imperative according to which we must avert the risks imposed by any truth procedure. Thirdly, there is the key tenet that the pathologies of subjectivity—more particularly the emergence of 'false' subjects that trade in *simulacra* of truth (e.g. Nazism) and the *terror* which exerts a full sovereignty of truth over all places—can only be understood from out of the possible impasses of a subject of truth.

The last is a persistent conviction underlying Badiou's treatment of what, for lack of better terms, we could refer to as 'non-universal' subjects. In other words, it is the irruption of a subject of truth which serves as the aleatory condition of possibility for the formation of other subjects. In the case of Nazism, for instance: 'Such a simulacrum is only possible thanks to the success of political revolutions that were genuinely eventual (and thus universally addressed)'. This is why it is only from the standpoint of fidelity to events of universal address—'the truth-processes whose simulacra they manipulate'—that these other, non- or anti-universal subjects, become intelligible.[8] Or, in Badiou's more classical terms, why Evil can only be understood from the standpoint of the Good.

STRUGGLES OVER SUBJECTIVE SPACE

The foregoing discussion suggests that the problem of other subjects—in its ethico-political, rather than epistemological sense—has been an abiding preoccupation and a thorny challenge for Badiou's thinking ever since the mid-seventies. In this regard, the treatment of the theory of the subject in *Being and Event*, wholly concerned with the subject of truth, seems to hark back to one of Badiou's theoretical tendencies, already encountered in the *Théorie*—the one which contends that, for a given situation (or space of placements) and for a given historical sequence, *there is only one subject*. As we observed with regard to the concept of the bour-

---

7. Alain Badiou, *Ethics*, trans. Peter Hallward, London, Verso, 2000, p. 75.
8. Badiou, *Ethics*, p. 77.

geoisie, there is something structural about this oscillation in the work of
Badiou. Are there one or many subjects? Prior to the recent publication
of the *Logiques des mondes*, which we will deal with below, Peter Hallward
already indicated, in his indispensable and lucid summary of Badiou's
1996-97 lectures on the axiomatic theory of the subject, that Badiou has
found it necessary to introduce a modicum of mediation[9] and plurality
into his account of the subject. As Hallward puts it, 'Badiou realizes that
an event can evoke a range of subjective responses. ... He now sees each
effect of truth as raising the possibility of a countereffect, no longer considered as simply external to the process of subjectivation, but as internal
to subjective space itself'.[10]

As I have already suggested however, this realization should not be
seen as a sudden innovation in Badiou's thinking, but as the recovery of a
problem intrinsic to his theory of the subject ever since his seminars of the
1970s. Besides the abiding preoccupation with the lessons of Hegel's phenomenology of terror, and the attempt to flesh out a theory of subjective
betrayal, Badiou has demonstrated an abiding concern with the possible
existence of subjects who veer from, react to or occlude the struggle for
transformative universality. In this respect, the *topique* presented in his ethics of Marxism, with its nihilists, fatalists and believers, is a clear precursor
of the theory of subjective space sketched out in his 1990s lectures and,
with some amendments, introduced in his 'meta-physics' of the subject in
the 2006 *Logiques des mondes*.[11] In other words, I think it is useful, especially
in order to survey the gamut of subjective possibilities investigated by Badiou's thought, to recognize that it is not just in the past few years that he
has come to consider 'the subjective realm precisely as a *space*—as something that no one figure can fully occupy and determine, as something
that every subject must traverse'.[12]

Given Hallward's exhaustive treatment of the earlier and unpublished
sketch of the theory of subjective space, I will focus here solely on the

---

9. 'To lend the event an implicative dimension is already to submit the process of its affirmation to a kind of logical mediation, as distinct from the immediacy of a pure nomination'. Peter Hallward, *Badiou: A Subject to Truth*, Minneapolis, University of Minnesota Press,
2003, p. 145.

10. Hallward, *Badiou*, pp. 144-5.

11. Among the differences between the two is that what appears as the 'faithful subject' in
the *Logiques des mondes* was split into two figures, the hysteric and the master, in the lectures
outlined by Hallward.

12. Hallward, *Badiou*, p. 145.

shape that this notion of subjective space takes on in Book I of the *Logiques des mondes*.

To begin with it is necessary briefly to outline the parameters of Badiou's recent finessing of his formal theory of the subject. Pitted against hermeneutic, moral, and ideological models of subjectivity, it is worth reiterating that Badiou's theory is not interested in the *experience* of subjectivity, but simply in its *form*. Nor is Badiou particularly concerned with the subject as a source of statements, a subject of enunciation capable of saying 'I' or 'we'. Rather, the subject is depicted as what *exceeds* the normal disposition and knowledge of 'bodies and languages'—the exclusive focus upon which defines Badiou's current ideological nemesis, what he calls 'democratic materialism'.[13] While the theory of the subject as a whole certainly tackles the 'subject-bodies' (political parties, scientific communities, artistic configurations…) that support truth procedures, the formal theory as such limits itself to the various formalizations of the effects of the 'body' of the subject. The theory propounded in Book I of the *Logiques* brackets the body (which is why Badiou dubs it a 'meta-physics'), providing the general parameters for thinking how subjects exceed the situations whence they arise. The notion of subject therefore 'imposes the readability of a unified orientation upon a *multiplicity* of bodies' (LM 54). This means that it also suspends a consideration of the specific historicity of a process of subjectivation, the manner in which the body of a subject is composed by incorporating certain elements of the situation and disqualifying others. The subject is thus viewed as an 'active and identifiable form of the production of truths'. The emphasis, evidently, is on 'form'.

But does this entail that the only subjects deserving of our theoretical attention are subjects of truth, of the *one* truth that may affect and dislocate any given situation? The particular inflection of Badiou's definition tells us otherwise: 'Saying "subject" or saying "subject with regard to truth" is redundant. For there is a subject only as the subject of a truth, at the service of this truth, of its denial, or of its occultation' (LM 58). This 'with regard to' already indicates that there are indeed, as Hallward suggests, different subjective positions or comportments, determined by a subject's stance towards the irruption of the event and the truths that may follow from it. Badiou himself presents this theory as a self-criticism of sorts, arguing that his earlier work (he is thinking of the *Théorie du sujet* in

---

13. Alain Badiou, 'Democratic Materialism and the Materialist Dialectic', trans. Alberto Toscano, *Radical Philosophy*, vol. 130, 2005, pp. 20–24. This is an excerpt from the preface to Alain Badiou, *Logiques des mondes*, Paris, Seuil, 2006 (henceforth LM).

particular) stipulated an all too firm and drastic opposition between the new and the old. In this new formal theory he wishes instead to confront the existence, amongst others, of what he calls '*reactionary novelties*' (LM 62-7). To resist the new, to deny it, one still requires arguments and subjective forms. In other words, the theory of the subject needs to countenance the fact that reactionary forms of subjectivation exist—which for Badiou unsurprisingly take the shape of the anti-communist anti-totalitarianism which spurred the backlash of revisionist historians (François Furet) and the renegade *nouveaux philosophes* (André Glucksmann) to the emancipatory innovations arising in the wake of May '68.

Now, as I suggested above, it is not entirely true that the *Théorie du sujet* foreclosed the possibility of reactionary novelties. The briefly-explored possibility of a bourgeois subject (not just in the French 'new bourgeoisie', but in the Soviet bureaucratic caste) definitely depended on its ability to generate some kind of novelty, however abject or corrupt. Similarly, the subjectivity of betrayal and resignation, or even that of active nihilism, as explored in Badiou's early 'ethics of Marxism', depend on the particular manner whereby they avoid or repress the courageous subjectivity and the just praxis of a revolutionary proletariat. They too are new by dint of how they respond (or better, *react*) to the disturbing irruption of that subjective figure. The fact that this formal theory of the subject comes after Badiou's formulation of a theory of evental subjectivity (first sketched in the 1985 book *Peut-on penser la politique?*) does make a difference to the account of 'other', non- or anti-universal subjects. For one, as we already intimated in our discussion of the *Ethics*, the dependency of subjectivation on the event permits Badiou to propose a philosophical argument as to why 'other' subjects are radically dependent on a subject of truth. As he writes: 'From a subjective point of view, it is not because there is reaction that there is revolution, it is because there is revolution that there is reaction' (LM 71).[14] This Maoist thesis of the primacy of revolt, which Badiou had already formulated as early as his 1975 *Théorie de la contradiction*, is now philosophically articulated in terms of the key 'temporal' category of Badiou's theory of the subject, that of the *present*. In responding to the *trace* of a supernumerary, illegal event, and in constructing the *body* that can bring the implications of this event to bear on a given world, a faithful subject is involved in the production of a present. Indeed, the only subjective tem-

---

14. This means, incidentally, that Badiou reiterates his intolerance for those, generally 'leftist' positions which base their notion of revolt on the prior reality of oppression, and for whom the political subject par excellence is therefore the *oppressed*.

porality, which is to say the only historicity, envisaged in Badiou's system derives from such an irruption of generic universality into the status quo.

But if the present, as a kind of rigorous and continued sequence of novelties (a permanent revolution...) belongs to the subject of truth, how can 'other subjects' partake in it? Badiou's contention is that they do so in a strictly derivative and parasitic (albeit by no means passive) manner. As he puts it, subjective 'destinations proceed in a certain order (to wit: production—denial—occultation), for reasons that formalism makes altogether clear: the denial of the present supposes its production, and its occultation supposes a formula of denial' (LM 71).

Given the arduous and ongoing production of a truth, *reactionary* subjects seek to deny the event that called it into being, and to disaggregate the body which is supposed to carry the truth of that event. It is for this reason that reaction, according to Badiou, involves the production of another, 'extinguished' present. The thesis of reaction, at base, is that all of the 'results' of a truth procedure (e.g. political equality in the French revolution) could be attained without the terroristic penchant of the faithful subject, and without the affirmation of a radically novel event. As Badiou recognizes, this constitutes an *active* denial of truth, which demands the creation of reactionary statements and indeed of what we could call reactionary anti-bodies. Think, for instance, of the elaborate strategies of cultural organization with which the CIA and its proxies sought to incorporate some of the innovations of aesthetic radicalism in order to deny their link with communist politics, invariably borrowing many formal traits and discursive dispositions from their nemeses.[15] Or consider the emergence, very evident nowadays among what some refer to as the 'pro-war left', of reactionary subjectivities. The resilience of such subjectivities was convincingly mapped by Georg Simmel when he set forth his portrait of the 'renegade'. Due to the drastic violence of his conversion, the renegade, according to Simmel, is in a sense a far more steadfast and loyal subject than a militant or partisan who, for whatever reason, might not have adhered to his camp with the same conscious resolve. As Simmel writes:

> The special loyalty of the renegade seems to me to rest on the fact that the circumstances, under which he enters the new relationship, have a longer and more enduring effect than if he had naïvely grown into it, so to speak, without breaking a previous one. ... It is as if

---

15. See Frances Stonor Saunders, *Who Paid the Piper? The CIA and the Cultural Cold War*, London, Granta, 2000.

he were repelled by the old relationship and pushed into the new
one, over and over again. Renegade loyalty is so strong because
it includes what loyalty in general can dispense with, namely, the
conscious continuance of the motives of the relationship.[16]

While the reactionary—and the renegade as one of its sub-spe-
cies—suspends or attenuates the present produced by an event, denying
its novelty but absorbing many of its traits, the second type of 'unfaithful'
subject, what Badiou calls the *obscure* subject, entertains a far more severe relation to the new present that the faithful subject had given rise to.
Rather than *denying* its novelty, the obscure subject is focussed on actually
negating the very existence of this new present. The *obscure* subject, in order
to occult novelty, 'systematically resorts to the invocation of a transcendent Body, full and pure, an ahistorical or anti-evental body (City, God,
Race...) whence it derives that the trace will be denied (here, the labour
of the reactive subject is useful to the obscure subject) and, by way of consequence, the real body, the divided body, will also be suppressed' (LM
68).[17] The obscure 'anti-body' is thus very different than the reactive one.
While the latter may be repressive, it is also aimed at persuading the faithful that 'it's just not worth it', that they should resign themselves to a 'lesser
present' and enjoy its diminished but secure rewards. The transcendent
body conjured up by the obscure subject is instead a kind of 'atemporal
fetish', writes Badiou, under whose weight novelty must be thoroughly
crushed and silenced.

Persisting with a conviction that dominates both the *topiques* of the
Théorie du sujet and the theory of evil in the *Ethics*, Badiou suggests that the
faithful subject, the subject that produces a new present by drawing the
worldly consequences of an event, must entertain a differentiated relationship to the other figures who inhabit the new subjective space that his
fidelity has opened up. Compared to the treatment of the fatalist and the
nihilist in the *Théorie*, in the *Logiques* Badiou strikes a more cautious note.
I will take the liberty of quoting at length the passage where he compares
the two figures of the reactionary and the obscurantist, in part because of
the literary flair with which he gives flesh to these formal figures:

> It is crucial to gauge the gap between the reactive formalism and
> the obscure formalism. As violent as it may be, reaction conserves

---

16. Georg Simmel, 'Faithfulness and Gratitude', in Kurt H. Wolff (ed.), *The Sociology of
Georg Simmel*, New York, The Free Press, 1964, pp. 385, 386.
17. Badiou links the theory of 'obscure' fascism to the 'production of imaginary macro-
scopic entities' and 'passive bodies of subjectivation' in *The Century*, Chapter 9.

the form of the faithful subject as its articulated unconscious. It does not propose to abolish the present, only to show that the faithful rupture (which it calls 'violence' or 'terrorism') is useless for engendering a moderate, that is to say extinguished, present (a present that it calls 'modern'). Moreover, this instance of the subject is itself borne by the debris of bodies: frightened and deserting slaves, renegades of revolutionary groups, avant-garde artists recycled into academicism, lovers asphyxiated by conjugal routine. Things are very different for the obscure subject. That is because it is the present that is directly its unconscious, its lethal disturbance, while it disarticulates within appearance the formal data of fidelity. The monstrous full Body to which it gives fictional shape is the atemporal filling of the abolished present. This means that what bears this body is directly linked to the past, even if the becoming of the obscure subject also immolates this past in the name of the sacrifice of the present: veterans of lost wars, failed artists, intellectuals perverted by rancour, dried up matrons, illiterate muscle-bound youths, shopkeepers ruined by Capital, desperate unemployed workers, rancid couples, bachelor informants, academicians envious of the success of poets, atrabilious professors, xenophobes of all stripes, mobsters greedy for decorations, vicious priests, and cuckolded husbands. To this hodgepodge of ordinary existence the obscure subject offers the chance of a new destiny, under the incomprehensible, but salvific, sign of an absolute body, which demands only that one serve it by entertaining everywhere and at all times the hatred of any living thought, of any transparent language and of every uncertain becoming (LM 67-70).

While the reactive or reactionary subject incorporates the form of faithfulness, the obscure subject seems be defined by the twofold movement of laying waste to the immanent production of the new and generating a transcendent, monolithic novelty, essentially indistinguishable from the most archaic past. Leaving aside the return of faithfulness in the fourth subjective figure, that of *resurrection*,[18] what changes does this theory of subjective space bring to the earlier theorization of non-universalist subjects, and what prospects for formal analysis does it harbour?

Most importantly, the theory of subjective space appears designed to resolve the conundrum about other subjects which, in the earlier work,

---

18. For some interesting comments on the figure of resurrection, and its introduction into Badiou's thought of a complex link between novelty and *repetition*, see Slavoj Žižek, 'Badiou: Notes from an Ongoing Debate', *International Journal of Žižek Studies*, vol. 2, no. 1, 2007, available at: <http://ics.leeds.ac.uk/zizek/article.cfm?id=21&issue=3>.

had been most acute in the figure of the bourgeoisie. In a sense, the new formal theory allows Badiou to affirm the relative autonomy of non- or anti-universalist subjects, whilst holding true, in his account of the sequence of subjects, to the primacy of revolt, in other words, to the primacy of the universalist subject. The new theory can thus be seen as a return, with the aid of a different formalism, of the 'topical' theory provided by the *Théorie du sujet*, though now instead of a discontinuous field of subjective affects we are presented with more clearly distinct subjects (faithful, reactive, obscure, resurrected). The relative exteriority of these figures to one another is also explained by the forsaking of the destructive-dialectical schema which, in *Théorie du sujet*, had portrayed the proletariat as an immanent purification of bourgeois space, a subjective torsion whose aim was to destroy the space of placements constituted by imperialist capitalism.

THE OBSCURE SUBJECT OF CURRENT AFFAIRS

What purchase can such a formal theory have on the identification and examination of contemporary political subjects? In his philosophical considerations on the facts of September 11, 2001, Badiou opted for the notion of 'nihilism' to capture the specular relationship between the 'infinite justice' of Bush's God-bothering 'capitalist-parliamentarian' regime and Bin Laden's pyrotechnic theological terror. The current situation would thus be framed by the 'disjunctive synthesis of two nihilisms'.[19] These nihilisms, unlike the youthful discordant nihilism courted by Badiou in the *Théorie du sujet*, are clearly not subjectively recoverable. What's more, it is rather opaque what relation, if any, they might entertain with faithful political subjects. So it is once again to the recent *Logiques des mondes* that we turn for some clarification.

One of the more striking features of this sequel to *Being and Event* for our aims is that, despite its formality, the meta-physics of the subject it deploys is marked by some extremely concrete examples. The most striking of these concerns Badiou's treatment of 'Islamism' as the present-day incarnation of the obscure subject:

> it is in vain that one tries to elucidate genealogically contemporary political Islamism, in particular its ultra-reactionary variants, which rival the Westerners for the fruits of the petrol cartel through

---

19. Alain Badiou, 'Philosophy and the "war against terrorism"', in *Infinite Thought*, ed. and trans. Justin Clemens and Oliver Feltham, London, Continuum, 2004, p. 143.

unprecedented criminal means. This political Islamism is a new manipulation of religion—from which it does not derive by any natural (or 'rational') inheritance—with the purpose of occulting the post-socialist present and countering, by means of a full Tradition or Law, the fragmentary attempts through which some try to reinvent emancipation. From this point of view, political Islamism is absolutely contemporary, both to the faithful subjects that produce the present of political experimentation, and to the reactive subjects that busy themselves with denying that ruptures are necessary in order to invent a humanity worthy of the name, and who moreover flaunt the established order as the miraculous bearer of a continuous emancipation. Political Islamism is nothing but one of the subjectivated names of today's obscurantism (LM 67-8).

Following the foundational thesis of the primacy of revolt (or primacy of the universal) Badiou is obliged to argue that if there is indeed an Islamist subject, then this subject is derivative (by way of occultation) of a faithful subject. Rather than a regurgitation of the past, Islamism is the contemporary of a politics of emancipation (which is why it is useless to engage in 'genealogical' explanations). Possibly the most important, and disputable, aspect of this argument is that the *purpose* (whether conscious or otherwise) of contemporary Islamism is 'occulting the post-socialist present'. Osama Bin Laden's jihadist piety is precisely depicted as a kind of sinister fetishism: 'the sole function of the God of conspiring Islam is to occult, at the heart of peoples, the present of the rational politics of emancipation, by dislocating the unity of their statements and their militant bodies' (LM 69). In what follows, I will briefly survey some of the debates about the nature of Islamism's relation to the politics of emancipation. For the moment, I want to indicate one of the most problematic aspects of Badiou's account, which inserts it directly into some bitter and vociferous recent debates. This has to do with the equation between Islamism and fascism.

In his response to the attacks on the Twin Towers and the Pentagon, Badiou had in fact already characterized those acts as 'conjuring up the fascist concept of action' and thus as 'formally fascistic'.[20] Moreover, the Islamist use of religion was judged to be akin to that of 'anti-capitalism' by the populist fascism of the thirties, a mere demagogic vocabulary cloaking Bin Laden's thirst for oil and political supremacy. At bottom then, the 2001 attacks signal the presence, under the instrumental facade of 'Islam'

---

20. Badiou, 'Philosophy and the "war against terrorism"', p. 143.

of 'a type of fascistic nihilism' typified by the 'sacralization of death; the absolute indifference to the victims; the transformation of oneself and others into instruments'.[21] In the *Logiques*, this verdict is corroborated by the inclusion of Islamism under the rubric of obscure subjectivity, which is by definition 'fascist'. Thus, according to Badiou's definition: 'The obscure subject engineers the destruction of the body: the appropriate word is *fascism*, in a broader sense than was given to this term in the thirties. One will speak of generic fascism to describe the destruction of the organized body through which there once transited the construction of the present (of the sequence)' (LM 81).

Besides the all too hurried identification of Bin Laden with Islamism (when many commentators indeed see him as a phenomenon which is subsequent to, and incompatible with, 'political Islam' proper), one cannot but register the unexpected convergence of this formal theory with one of the theses that have recently permitted the convergence between American neo-conservatives and left renegades, to wit, the existence of something like 'Islamic fascism' or 'Islamofascism' as the archenemy of today's democrats and progressives—a notion promoted by the likes of Christopher Hitchens, and very recently publicized, in some particularly incoherent speeches, by Bush himself. Leaving aside the dubious invocation of crimes of association, what is interesting about this congruence lies in its preconditions. It is indeed the short-circuit between a notion of 'generic fascism' (or of Ur-fascism)[22] and the specific subjective history of anti-fascist politics that has recently allowed members of the so-called left to sign up to the propaganda wing of the 'war on terror' as if they were joining the International Brigades. It is important to note in this respect that the historical and sociological debate on fascism has long been dominated by polemics regarding its specificity and extension, both historical and geographical. So it is rather peculiar to see Badiou, so adamant about thinking the subjective singularity of particular political sequences (e.g.

---

21. Badiou, 'Philosophy and the "war against terrorism"', p. 160.
22. For a recent treatment of (and intervention in) the scholarly debate on 'generic fascism', see Robert Griffin, 'The Palingenetic Core of Generic Fascist Ideology', in Alessandro Campi, ed., *Che cos'è il fascismo?*, Rome, Ideazione, 2003, pp. 97-122, also available at: <http://ah.brookes.ac.uk/history/staff/griffin/coreoffascism.pdf>. See also his *The Nature of Fascism*, London, Routledge, 1993. On 'Ur-fascism' or 'eternal fascism', see Umberto Eco, 'Ur-Fascism', *The New York Review of Books*, vol. 42, no. 11, 1995, pp. 12-15. It is worth noting that while those who advocate the concept of generic fascism tend to stress the modern and modernizing character of fascism, Eco regards the 'rejection of modernism' as a key feature of fascism. Badiou's formal notion of 'generic fascism' seems far more ample than either Griffin or Eco's proposals.

Nazism in *The Century*) sign up to a thesis, that of 'generic fascism', which, in its formality, seems to forestall an inquiry into that very singularity. By way of contrast, we can note that one of the more exhaustive recent studies of fascism, starting from the methodological imperative to, as it were, 'take the fascists at their word' (to treat their political thought and practice as a subjective form) concludes with a subtle repudiation of the notion of 'Islamic fascism'.[23]

But, as we have already intimated, at the core of Badiou's vision of the obscure subject as generically fascist there lies not a political taxonomy of the elements necessary for a fascist politics, but a formal evaluation of how this type of subjectivity relates to the subject which, by definition, opens the subjective space: the universalist subject of emancipation, the faithful subject. For Badiou's theory of the obscure subject to find its exemplification in Islamism it must be possible to argue that, in some sense or another, the relationship between Islamist obscurantism and the politics of emancipation is one where the purpose of the former is absolutely to negate the latter, through the production of a full subjective body and an archaic future. Now, in the case of Bin Laden, while it may be disputed whether the portrait of a cynical oil-fiend can withstand much scrutiny, it is indeed correct that, ideologically forged in the fight against the Soviet Satan, his relationship to communism bears all the hallmarks of the obscure subject. Consider this declaration, from Bin Laden's first public

---

23. For some useful references about this inevitably heated, and cliché-ridden debate, see the 'Wikipedia' entry at <http://en.wikipedia.org/wiki/Islamic_fascism>. According to Michael Mann, in none of the disparate, and often incompatible, instances of political Islam do we find 'the complete fascist package'. Rather, 'the term "Islamic fascism" is really just a particular instance of the word "Fascist!"—a term of abuse for our enemies ... the most powerful term of abuse in our world today'. As for Islamism and Hindu nationalism, he makes the following judgment: 'They most resemble fascism in deploying the means of moral murder, but the transcendence, the state, the nation, and the new man they seek are not this-worldly'. See his *Fascists*, Cambridge, Cambridge University Press, 2005, p. 374. While the polemical character of the appellation is obvious, and the point about the categorical differences well taken, I think it can be argued that most of the aims of Islamist politics, whether economic, legal or political, are remarkably 'this-worldly'. It is also worth noting that Badiou himself, contradicting his use of it in *Logiques des mondes*, has even disputed the political value of the term 'Islamism'. As he declared in a 2004 interview, 'words like "terrorism", "Islamism" and "crimes against humanity" are only destined to confuse situations and to create a kind of international political stupidity'. Alain Badiou, 'Las democracias están en guerra contra los pobres' (Democracies are at war against the poor), *Revista Ñ*, 23.10.2004. Available at: <http://www.clarin.com/suplementos/cultura/2004/10/23/u-854775.htm>.

statement, addressed to religious jurisprudents and spurred by the Saudi royals' support for the south Yemenis in the 1994 civil war:

> It is ludicrous to suggest that Communists are Muslims whose blood should be spared. Since when were they Muslims? Wasn't it you who previously issued a juridical decree calling them apostates and making it a duty to fight them in Afghanistan, or is there a difference between Yemeni Communists and Afghan Communists? Have doctrinal concepts and the meaning of God's unity become so confused? The regime is still sheltering some of these leaders of unbelief in a number of cities in the country, and yet we have heard no disapproval from you. The Prophet said, as related by Muslim, 'God cursed him who accommodates an innovator'.[24]

This ferocious hatred of innovation, of non-submissive secular equality, and of 'this torrential current of global unbelief',[25] seems to single out Bin Laden and his cohorts as sterling examples of Badiou's figure of the obscure subject.

But if we leave aside the not exactly representative figure of Bin Laden, with his anarchoid propaganda of the deed and kitsch fantasies of the caliphate, the relation between Islamism and emancipatory politics appears far more ambiguous. Taking the paradigmatic case of 'political Islam', the post-revolutionary Islamic Republic of Iran, we can see that the theocratic forces did not engage in a straightforward reaction to the mass revolts against the Shah—in which they, alongside the various groups of the radical left, instead played a mobilizing role—or in a simple occultation. It is certainly true that—as Badiou himself already noted in the *Théorie du sujet*—the Islamist superego in the figure of Khomeini played a

---

24. Osama Bin Laden, 'The Betrayal of Palestine' (December 29 1994), in Bruce Lawrence, ed., *Messages to the World: The Statements of Osama Bin Laden*, London, Verso, 2005, p. 8. Badiou's portrait, according to which Bin Laden's 'point of departure is a series of extraordinary complex manoeuvres in relation to the manna of oilfields in Saudi Arabia and that the character is, after all, a good American: someone for whom what matters is wealth and power, and for whom the means are of less concern' (Badiou, 'Philosophy and the "war on terrorism"', pp. 149-50), seems to underestimate the sinister sincerity of his conviction, and indeed the fact that, were wealth and power the objective, Bin Laden could have attained them with far greater ease without undertaking his peculiar brand of 'obscure' militancy.

25. Osama Bin Laden, 'Under Mullah Omar' (April 9 2001), *Messages to the World*, p. 98. It is worth noting that an 'obscure' notion of equality, the kind of equality by divine submission also favoured by Qutb, is part of Bin Laden's doctrinal arsenal. Thus, he writes in his declaration 'To the Americans' (October 6 2002), that Islam 'is the religion of unity and agreement on the obedience to God, and total equality between all people, without regard to their colour, sex, or language' (*Messages to the World*, p. 166).

role akin to that of the Mao, and the archaic and transcendent reference prepared the brutal occlusion of emancipatory trajectories. But the suppression of the left by theocratic forces worked, in the ideological arena, primarily by *borrowing* the left's prescriptions and 'Islamicizing' them, leaving the left the abject alternative of either abetting its own suppression or becoming traitor to the revolution. As Val Moghadam noted, in an incisive appraisal of the strategic and discursive failures of the Iranian left:

> The shared language of opposition had a further negative effect in that it obfuscated very real differences between the socio-political projects of the Left and the Religious Right ('national-popular government' versus political Islam/theocratic rule). Moreover, most of the Left seemed unaware in the 1970s that the religious forces were weaving a radical—populist Islamic discourse that would prove very compelling—a discourse which appropriated some concepts from the Left (exploitation, imperialism, world capitalism), made use of Third Worldist categories (dependency, the people) and populist terms (the toiling masses), and imbued certain religious concepts with new and radical meaning. For instance, *mostazafin*—meaning the wretched or dispossessed—now connoted and privileged the urban poor in much the same way that liberation theology refers to the poor. But in an original departure, the authors of the revolutionary Islamic texts, and especially Ayatollah Khomeini, declaimed that the *mostazafin* would rise against their oppressors and, led by the *ulama* or religious leaders, would establish the *umma* (community of believers) founded on *tauhid* (the profession of divine unity) and Islamic justice.[26]

Even if we accept that the 'purpose' of Iranian Islamism lay in the occultation (and indeed, the persecution and often slaughter) of any body that carried a promise of immanent universality—in what Achcar calls 'a permanent revolution in reverse' and a 'reactionary retrogression'[27]—it cannot be argued that it simply foreclosed the statements and organs of emancipatory politics. Rather, in a far more insidious and powerful move, it *incorporated* them, transcendentalizing, for instance, the concept of anti-imperialism into a religious duty bound to the defence of the *umma* rather than the creation of a truly generic humanity. Still remaining with the Iranian case, we can see that Islamism even produced a kind of revolution-

26. Val Moghadam, 'Socialism or Anti-Imperialism? The Left and Revolution in Iran', *New Left Review*, vol. 166, 1987, p. 14.
27. Gilbert Achcar, 'Eleven Theses on the Resurgence of Islamic Fundamentalism' (1981), in *Eastern Cauldron: Islam, Afghanistan, Palestine and Iraq in a Marxist Mirror*, London, Pluto Press, 2004, p. 57.

ary populism, in the figure of Ali Shari'ati, which, though posthumously manipulated by the clergy and its militias for their own rightist ends, is difficult to class simply as either reactive or obscure.

In Shari'ati we find an uneasy combination of the popular principle of rebellion, on the one hand, and an organicist vision of religious society, on the other. Via the likes of Fanon and Sartre, he incorporates an emancipatory drive into his political theology. For instance, he declares that 'Islam is the first school of social thought that recognizes the masses as the basis, the fundamental and conscious factor in determining history and society'[28]; that history is a struggle between the pole of Cain (of power, coercion, and most recently, imperialism) and the pole of Abel (a religiously oriented primitive communism); that 'it is the responsibility of every individual in every age to determine his stance in the constant struggle between the two wings we have described, and not to remain a spectator'.[29] But the very principles of the emancipatory politics which provides the obvious matrix for Shari'ati's thought (primitive communism, the classless society, rebellion...) are hypostasized into spiritual notions which, to use the language that the *Théorie du sujet* applied to the religious politics of the German Peasants' War, take equality into the *imaginary* domain of cosmopolitical unity, in the form of the opposition between unity (*tauhid*) and discordance or contradiction (*shirk*),[30] together with a radical reading of the notion of *umma* which nevertheless sees it, against the supposed shortcomings of socialism as 'the divine destiny of man in the plan of creation'.[31]

A related 'translation' of emancipatory themes can be found in the earlier and much more evidently revolutionary-conservative writings of Sayd Qutb, whose sombre anti-philosophy,[32] organicist vision of society, and definition of 'equality and freedom as common submission before

28. Shari'ati, 'Approaches to the Understanding of Islam', in *On the Sociology of Islam*, p. 49.

29. Shari'ati, 'The Philosophy of History: Cain and Abel', in *On the Sociology of Islam*, p. 109.

30. Shari'ati, 'The World-View of Tauhid', in *On the Sociology of Islam*, p. 82.

31. Shari'ati, 'The Ideal Society—the Umma', in *On the Sociology of Islam*, p. 120. It is worth noting that this umma is distinguished by Shari'ati in terms of its 'purity of leadership', which he explicitly juxtaposes to the 'fascist' purity of the leader, obviously sensitive to the potential confusion.

32. On Qutb's relationship to philosophy and modernity, see Roxanne L. Euben, *Enemies in the Mirror: Islamic Fundamentalism and the Limits of Modern Rationalism*, Princeton, Princeton University Press, 1999, p. 69.

God'[33] captured an authentic demand for justice and twisted it into an archaic and transcendent vision of a society finally free, not just of imperialism, but of the discordance and anxiety of modernity.

According to the group of theorists and activist RETORT, this dialectic of appropriation is also present in the most recent incarnations of 'revolutionary Islam'. This movement is characterized, in its diffuse and networked 'body' by a remarkable degree of organizational, theological and technological 'democratization', the invention of a new, post-Leninist (or post-anarchist[34]), articulation of vanguard and violence, and what they appositely refer to as 'a new, and malignant, universalism'.[35] While they too note the gestation of contemporary Islamism in the writings Qutb, and some of the 'proto-fascist' (but also 'crypto-communist') organizational models at the origins of the Muslim Brotherhood, they regard its causes as originating in 'the *crisis of secular nationalist development*—abetted by a specific (and poisonous) political-economic conjuncture whose vectors were oil, primitive accumulation, and Cold War geopolitics'.[36] A similar judgment was put forward in the wake of the Iranian Revolution by one of the more astute Marxist analysts of Middle East politics, Gilbert Achcar. His theses on Islamic fundamentalism, which provide a classical analysis of the petty-bourgeois roots of the Islamist phenomenon, echo the analysis of fascism—such as when he writes that 'the violence and rage of the petit bourgeois in distress are unparalleled'. Indeed, Achcar sees the bourgeoisie's relationship to the phenomenon of Islamism (particularly in Egypt) as typical of its customary stance towards far right movements and fascism in general—in other words, to borrow Badiou's terminology, reactionaries are always happy to use obscurantists against progressives, especially if the obscurantists can 'outbid the Left on the Left's two favourite issues: the national question and the social question; any gains made by Islamic reaction on these two issues mean equivalent losses for the Left'. Islamic fundamentalism in this sense represents 'an *auxiliary for the reactionary bourgeoisie*'.[37] But for Achcar this emergence of a petty bourgeois reaction is only possible because of the feebleness of the revolutionary proletariat

---

33. RETORT, Iain Boal, T.J. Clark, Joseph Matthews, Michael Watts, *Afflicted Powers: Capital and Spectacle in a New Age of War*, London, Verso, 2005, p. 146. See also *Enemies in the Mirror*, pp. 62-3.

34. 'For jihadist, read anarchist', *The Economist*, 18 August 2005, available at: <http://www.economist.com/displaystory.cfm?story_id=4292760>.

35. Boal, et. al., *Afflicted Powers*, p. 153.

36. Boal, et. al., *Afflicted Powers*, p. 162.

37. Achcar, 'Eleven Theses on the Resurgence of Islamic Fundamentalism', p. 56.

and the incapacity or unwillingness of the bourgeoisie to take on the aims of a national and democratic revolution.[38]

In this sense, the emergence of Islamism as a political subject does not necessarily represent an express reaction to emancipatory politics, but may rather constitute a capitalization on its absence, on the temporary incapacity of progressives to actually produce a present. Unlike Badiou, whose view of political subjectivation seems to preclude notions such as alliance or hegemony, Achcar does consider the possibility, which was of course the reality in Iran (his main point of reference in these reflections), that the proletarian subject might be obliged to struggle alongside Islamism against a common enemy, imperialism, and for 'national, democratic, and social issues'. And yet, this does not by any respects constitute a real alliance, since 'the duty of revolutionary socialists is to fight intransigently against the spell [Islamic fundamentalism] casts on the struggling masses'.[39] The least that can be said then, is that even from this classical

---

38. This position is corroborated by one of the most in-depth, revealing and sympathetic treatments of the subjective trajectories and resources of Islamism, François Burgat's *Face to Face with Political Islam*, London, I.B. Tauris, 2003. Burgat, while discounting the kind of socio-economic analysis favoured by Achcar and other Marxists, and refusing its characterization as *primarily* reactionary, violent or anti-democratic, places Islamism firmly in the history of emancipation from imperialism and colonialism: 'At first political, then economic, the distancing of the former colonizer through the rhetoric of oppositional Islam becomes ideological, symbolic and more broadly cultural, on the terrain where the shock of colonization has been most traumatic. In addition to its own language, local culture and history endow the dynamic of independence with something that has been missing for a long time: the precious attributes of a sort of ideological "autonomy" which perfects it, the right of those who propagate it to regain universality, without denouncing the structural elements of their "specificity" ... it is essentially in the old dynamic of decolonization that Islamism has taken root' (p. 49). While Burgat's sociological and anthropological focus on *identity* is deeply at odds with Badiou's theory of the subject, it is worth remarking the interest in this interpretation of Islamism as a tool for attaining a kind of universalizing autonomy. Without seconding Burgat's sympathies, it is important to note that such a demand for autochthonous universality is a sign of the failure of classical emancipatory discourses within the Muslim world to attain a truly 'generic' status and not be perceived as alien or imperial implantations. Moreover, Burgat's work is almost alone in providing detailed accounts, using numerous interviews and autobiographical texts, of the life-paths of north African Islamists—paths which, it should be noted, passed not only through Arab nationalism, but through Marxism too. For an attempt to delve into the subjectivity of extremist and terrorist variants of Islamism, see Juan Cole's intriguing study of the 'spiritual' documents left behind by the perpetrators of the attacks on the WTC and the Pentagon, 'Al-Qaeda's Doomsday Document and Psychological Manipulation' (2003), available at: <http://www.juancole.com/essays/qaeda.htm>. Cole's text provides a useful sketch of what a situated phenomenology of the obscure subject might look like.

39. Achcar, 'Eleven Theses on the Resurgence of Islamic Fundamentalism', p. 59.

Marxist position, the problem of other subjects—of how to confront re-actionaries and obscurantists whilst producing an emancipatory political present—appears as both urgent and inescapable.

CONCLUSION

So how does Badiou's theorization of 'untrue' subjects fare in the face of Islamism? The few cases and figures we have looked at point to the difficulties in formalizing the majority of politics that may be identified as 'Islamist' in terms of Badiou's theory of subjective space. Even if we accept the thesis of the primacy of the universal—the idea that 'other' subjects only arise in the wake of the emergence of a faithful subject and of the present it strives to produce—it is the specific relationship between the faithful subject and its two counterparts, reactive and obscure, that remains problematic.

First of all, the obscure subject—the subject that submits its action and statements to a transcendent, full body—does not necessarily have the oc-cultation of the faithful subject as its express purpose. One of the difficult lessons of the present conjuncture might be that, having vanquished the semblance or placeholder of communist politics, reactionaries and ob-scurantists are facing one another without necessarily passing through a direct opposition to faithful subjectivity. Or rather—at least at the spec-tacular level—what we are faced with is the struggle between slogans, be it 'freedom and democracy', or mythical and theological corruptions of anti-imperialism, which, whilst bearing the traces of emancipatory sub-jectivities, do not refer to them directly.

When its genesis was coeval with that of progressive subject, the ob-scure subject of Islamism did indeed crush anything that could have given body to a generic emancipatory subject, but it did not, contrary to what Badiou seems to intimate, erase all traces of the founding tenets of eman-cipatory politics. On the contrary, its tactic, largely effective against a left deluded by its own populism and strategic ineptitude, was to adopt and hypostasize the key principles of emancipation, making out as if their secular, communist version was merely a degenerate form of an archaic and eternal Islamic politics, with its submissive organicist egalitarianism. In this sense, the obscure subject is more a thief of the present than simply its destroyer.

When instead, as is mostly the case nowadays, Islamism is not in di-rect contact with figures of emancipation, it seems to operate with the ep-igones of capitalist reaction (Cold Warriors like Rumsfeld and Wolfowitz) as its counterparts, and entertains no univocal relationship to a politics of emancipation (aside from gloating at the defeat of its Soviet simulacrum, peddling theological variants of anti-imperialism and egalitarianism, or even, in today's Lebanon and Egypt, making tactical alliances with social-ist and communist groups). In a sense, this goes to corroborate Badiou's sequence, which moves from the production of the present, to its denial, to its occultation. But, for reasons very much having to do with the concrete strategic history of these movements, the phantasmagorical anti-bodies of Islamism (e.g. the caliphate) are more to be understood as the mythical filling-in of a political void produced by reaction than as a direct occul-tation of a subjectivized universal body. This is not to say that Islamism cannot be obscurantist, and indeed openly and virulently anti-communist (recall Bin Laden's exterminationist statement), but to note that our sub-jective space is currently dominated by struggles between non-universalist subjects far more than it is by their struggle against intelligible forms of 'post-socialist' subjectivity.

Having said that, the presence of a *gigantomachia*, a bloody and disjunc-tive synthesis, between reactionaries and obscurantists does not as such occlude the emergence of 'true' subjects. Which is why, in this grim inter-regnum, it is not a bad idea, not only to maintain open the possibility of universalist courage and justice, but to build on Badiou's several attempts to develop a muscular theory of the subjects of contemporary untruths and half-truths.

14

Philosophy and Revolution:
Badiou's Infidelity to the Event

Toula Nicolacopoulos and George Vassilacopoulos

INTRODUCTION

This paper offers some preliminary thoughts that spring from a first encounter with Badiou's philosophy.[1] They are also preliminary in a second, more fundamental sense, given that any encounter with genuine thinkers is always a deferral that takes the form of a promise for, and anticipation of, what will become a more radical and revealing engagement in some future reading. Indeed the practice of revisiting the intellectual landscapes of our fellow thinkers would not eventuate but for the recognition of the essentially preliminary and preparatory nature of previous visits.

This said, where do we encounter a philosopher philosophically and why do we do so in a certain way rather than some other? This is an unavoidable question especially when one tries to come to terms with the thought of philosophers like Badiou whose work addresses fundamental questions. It is unavoidable no less because Badiou's work encourages us to move beyond merely external or arbitrary encounters to what is properly philosophical. This is why the question we pose is also one of the hardest to answer.

Heidegger teaches that the encounter with other thinkers becomes necessary through the question of being and the thinking associated with it, irrespective of whether they belong to the 'first beginning' or whether they are the last metaphysicians. Hegel teaches that such an encounter

---

1. We would like to thank Paul Ashton for introducing us to the work of Alain Badiou.

takes place in the gathering of the 'we' whose very idea is paradigmati-
cally articulated by heroes of the pantheon of philosophy. In our encounter with Badiou we follow Hegel largely due to our political history, or
in Badiou's terms, due to our constitution as political subjects through
fidelity to the consequences of the event of the Russian Revolution. For
Badiou, of course, to become a political subject is to be constituted in
relation to an event—a self-founding or unfounded historical entity that
breaks radically with the situation from which it erupts—as the bearer of
a truth process who is called upon to maintain an enduring fidelity to the
event and its commands. But, we also follow Hegel as a result of a certain
experience not only of the constitution but also of the ultimate retreat
of the revolutionary project and of the collapse of the collective *as such*.
This experience situates us within—or perhaps, throws us into—what we
conceptualize as a speculative perspective. We read Hegel's thought as the
result and philosophical expression of a combination of the revolutionary
explosion of the gathering 'we' and the no less revolutionary implosion or
retreat of the project of unconditional solidarity that the French Revolution introduced.

It is from within the abovementioned particular form of philosophical
engagement with our political being that we come to explore the conceptual spaces that constitute Badiou's thinking. Here we find something at
once familiar and appealing but also something that we suspect ultimately
fails to do justice to the radical demands that the political event makes
upon us. Very briefly, our aim in this paper is to give reasons for thinking
that Badiou's philosophy does not seem prepared to follow through all
the consequences of the historical retreat of the political event. From our
perspective there does not seem to be enough room in his philosophy for
the accommodation of the 'darkness' often encountered in poetry that
directly relates the thinker to the historical retreat of the revolutionary
project. We want to suggest that it is important to come to terms with
the implications of this retreat as no less a revolutionary aspect of the
revolution. If, as Badiou insists, the event and one's loving relation to it
unconditionally demand an unconditional fidelity then, contrary to the
import of Badiou's account of evil, this would tell against any show of
eclecticism or any insistence on distinguishing between what is and what
is not acceptable from amongst the consequences of an event. Fidelity to
the event's retreat also points to a more direct relation of philosophy to the
event than Badiou allows. Rather than thinking the conditions that are
given to it from beyond itself, if philosophical thinking conceptualizes the
evental nature of the event then it must think itself as its own condition.

In what follows we will develop these points in four sections. Whereas the first section outlines the philosophical orientation that informs our encounter with Badiou's thought, the second examines the relationship between philosophy and the political event in order to set the context for the elaboration of our claim in the third section that fidelity to the event calls for attention not only to the demands of its emergence but also to those associated with the event's retreat. In the final section we indicate how the retreat of the political event might give rise to the philosophical subject and to the requirements of a philosophy of the event.

I. READING BADIOU WITH HEGEL

Bearing in mind our comments above concerning Hegel and the gathering of the 'we' as the condition of philosophy, we can begin by noting that Plato is possibly the first philosopher as such precisely because, in dramatizing Socrates' dialogical encounter with his friends, Plato identified the aim of philosophy with the problem of revealing the meaning of the gathering and its form with the gathering itself. It is no accident that in *The Republic* the gathering of Socrates and his friends presents justice as the very meaning of gathering, a gathering whose depth enables us to relate our collective being to the world as a whole. Of course Plato comes after Socrates, who is not only the one who does not write (Nietzsche) but is also the one who gathers in the public spaces of the city. In his uniqueness Socrates becomes a public thinker by creating the space of thinking within the city in which, his friends, the lovers of the philosopher, gather and dwell.

Still we have to wait until Aristotle for philosophical thought to leave behind Socrates' gathering in the actual space of the city, and Plato's theatrical dramatization of the gathering, in order to enter the genuine form of philosophy, the philosophical 'we' that identifies the soul of the thinker in exile from the city—an exile that Plato already highlighted in *The Republic*—as its proper and only place. We should stress that when in his deliberations the philosopher pronounces the 'we' he does not just reveal the inherently democratic or egalitarian space of philosophy. Rather, in the philosophical pronouncement of the 'we' by the singular subject whose horizon is the already alienated practice of the gathering of the collective from the democratic space of the city, the 'we' actually becomes or happens in its very idea or principle. Ultimately the philosopher produces the ideal of the collective as a direct articulation of the principle of the gathering 'we' and this process achieves a relation of critical understanding between the philosopher and reality. From the beginning then, philosophy explores the conceptual spaces beyond the positivity of the given world and attempts to make sense of the relation between the ideal of the revolutionary vision and the essentially lifeless reality of the polis. One can find traces of this tendency in Heraclitus' thought as well. So according to our story, under political conditions that deny the 'we' its reality, the exiled philosopher explores the 'mystery' associated with what is absolutely singular, namely the subject who can also pronounce and announce the 'we'. In the words of the poet, Tasos Livadites: 'the beautiful mystery of being alone, the mystery of the two, or the great mystery of the gathering of us all'.[2] How is it that the subject can make such an announcement? In our view this has to do with the power to withstand the tension between the 'I' and the 'we' that is indispensable for functioning as a genuine ego in the sense of being the place of dwelling and gathering of every other ego. Indeed, singularity, contra Levinas, is encountered as the power of universal love to accommodate a world, the world of the gathering 'we'. Elsewhere we have analysed this power in terms of the idea of (e)merging selves who unceasingly form as the collective in the processes of their merging/emerging.[3]

Since the Greeks, western history can be understood as the yet to be resolved tension between a world that produces the revolutionary idea of the gathering 'we' and at the same time constructs itself as the reality that denies the idea its actualization. Again Plato's *Republic* is the first philosophical work that registers this tension. In this history we can discern three stages that are characterized by three great commands of the gathering 'we'. The first and second stages are respectively associated with Greek philosophy and Christianity and they respectively invoke the commands 'know yourself' and 'love each other'. The third that was marked by the French Revolution invokes the command 'be as free and equal in a manner that is determined by solidarity' or what we can reformulate as 'be as a world'. What we want to suggest is that the constitution of the collective as such should be understood as the response of mutually encountering subjects to the command 'be as a world' that the encounter itself is. Here we have the ideal of the unconditional solidarity of people who dwell in each other and who equally and freely involve themselves in the project of creating a world. Other forms of encounter, for example

---

2. Tasos Livadites, *Small Book for Large Dreams (Greek)*, Athens, Kethros, 1987, p. 17.
3. Toula Nicolacopoulos and George Vassilacopoulos, 'Inquiry into Hope', *Critical and Creative Thinking: The Australasian Journal of Philosophy in Schools*, vol. 11, no. 2, 2003, pp. 1-7.

love, are equally important but limited responses and formulations of this command.

It is important to stress at this point that the essence of the command 'be as a world' is to be eternal, and eternally revolutionary, that is indeterminate or *skotinos* (dark). In its absolute indeterminacy or simplicity it helps to constitute the collective but it says nothing about how to actually create a world. In other words the collective that is constituted as a response to the command is the formless gathering of the 'we' whose aim is to create form out of such formlessness. This creation of form is a radically open process because its telos is not to overcome formlessness but to remain informed by it. In this sense the command is eternally revolutionary because it takes the collective beyond the created world in order for it to recognize its source and thus always to be creatively recreated as the sole responsibility of the participating subjects. Against this background we turn to Badiou's philosophy and to the questions that his thought raises for us.

II. PHILOSOPHY AND ITS POLITICAL CONDITION

According to Badiou,

> The specific role of philosophy is to propose a unified conceptual space in which naming takes place of events that serve as the point of departure for truth procedures. Philosophy seeks to *gather together all the additional-names*. It deals within thought with the compossable nature of the procedures that condition it. It does not establish any truth but it sets a locus of truths. It configurates the generic procedures, through a welcoming, a sheltering, built up with reference to their disparate simultaneity. Philosophy sets out to think its time by putting the state of procedures conditioning it into a common place. Its operations, whatever they may be, always aim to think 'together' to configurate within a unique exercise of thought the epochal disposition of the matheme, poem, political invention and love [...]. In this sense, philosophy's sole question is indeed that of the truth. Not that it produces any, but because it offers access to the unity of a moment of truths, a conceptual site in which the generic procedures are thought of as compossable.[4]

Badiou's philosophy belongs to the great modern tradition of theorizing the constitution and the historical significance of the collective, a collec-

---

4. Alain Badiou, *Manifesto for Philosophy*, trans. Norman Madarasz, Albany, State University of New York Press, 1999, p. 37 (henceforth MP).

tive that takes shape in response to a radical break with the status quo. For Badiou this theorizing is a matter of making possible the 'saying together' of the truths seized from philosophy's conditions. Indeed, 'philosophy is the locus of thinking within which 'there are' truths is stated along with their compossibility' (M 141-142). So it is the supply of just this sort of 'welcoming' space equally to all four conditions that distinguishes philosophical thought.

Yet, if we read Badiou's four conditions of philosophy—politics, love, art and science—as forms of the gathering, politics turns out to be primary for philosophy. Politics, according to Badiou, does have a special distinction as evidenced by those rare political orientations in recent history 'that have had or will have a connection with truth, a truth of the collective as such'.[5] In his *Metapolitics* Badiou notes that whereas 'science, love and art are aristocratic truth procedures' in that they require only 'the two', or no one in the case of the artist, 'politics is impossible without the statement that people, taken indistinctly, are capable of the thought that constitutes the post-evental political subject'.[6] Indeed, 'that the political event is collective prescribes that all are the virtual militants of the thought that proceeds on the basis of the event' (M 142). The political event is thus the event whose material is collective in an 'immediately universalizing' sense. In acknowledging that it 'belongs to all' the political event manifests the intrinsic universality peculiar to this condition: 'only politics is intrinsically required to declare that the thought that it is is the thought of all. This declaration is its constitutive pre-requisite' (M 141-142). So, in our terms we can say that even though love is no less a form of gathering it is radical politics that introduces and practices the very idea of the gathering 'we' as a universal collective. Here we are reminded once again of the words of the poet, Livadites cited above.

Now if we focus on philosophy in so far as it is thinking in relation to political thought and if thought is understood as a 'capacity which is specifically human' and defined as 'nothing other than that by which the path of a truth seizes and traverses the human animal' (IT 71), what is the precise relation between politics and philosophy? For Badiou philosophy depends upon the unfolding of radical politics (just as it does on the other three conditions) in order for it to think. However, radical political ori-

---

5. Alain Badiou, *Infinite Thought: Truth and the Return to Philosophy*, ed. and trans. Justin Clemens and Oliver Feltham, London, Continuum, 2003, p. 70 (henceforth IT).
6. Alain Badiou, *Metapolitics*, trans. Jason Barker, London, Verso, 2005, p. 142 (henceforth M).

entations can perform the role of a condition for philosophy's thinking, not because they 'trace a destiny' or because 'they construct a monumental history' but because they have 'a connection with a truth, a truth of the collective as such' (IT 70). If it is indeed correct that the political understood in terms of the procedure that generates 'a truth of the collective as such' is a paradigmatic expression of thought then there must be something more primordial in philosophy's association with politics as compared with its other three conditions. Philosophy's thinking can be practiced unconditionally only if it is directed to thought as such just as it is politics' association with philosophy that can affirm politics' thought as being universal or the thought of the collective as such. Badiou articulates the relation between politics and philosophy via a 'general axiom' that bears some resemblance with the command 'be as a world'. He insists 'for a political orientation to be worthy of submission to philosophy under the idea 'justice', its unique general axiom must be: people think, people are capable of truth' (IT 71). So, the specific political orientation is suitable to be elevated to a condition of philosophy in that it bears the general axiom. Through this association political thought can be affirmed in philosophy's thinking and presumably the criterion for submitting one political orientation to philosophy rather than some other must be a matter for philosophy rather than politics since the actual practice of radical politics does not depend upon philosophy. Indeed philosophy's evaluative role is its distinctive service to thought according to Badiou. In particular:

> the distinctive service that philosophy renders thought is the evaluation of time. The issue is whether we can say, and according to what principles, that this time, our time, has value.[7]

Now, if we can test the radicality of a political orientation by submitting it to philosophy's thinking this raises the question: what is the test for the radicality of philosophy's thinking? Badiou's own criterion of adequacy for philosophical thought seems modestly oriented. For him 'philosophical concepts weave a general space in which thought accedes to time, to its time, so long as the truth procedures of this time find shelter for their compossibility within it' (MP 38). So, Badiou's focus is on maintaining a certain relation between the truth procedures. We might say that philosophy does well when it ensures that truth procedures are not placed so as to cancel each other out.

---

7. Alain Badiou, & Lauren Sedofsky, 'Being by Numbers', *Artforum*, October 1994, http://www.highbeam.com/library/docFree.asp?DOCID=1G1:16315394

Yet, if we say with Badiou that philosophy activates its thinking when its conditions are available it must equally be correct to say that philosophy's thinking must nevertheless affirm the authenticity of its conditions as a precondition for its activation. So philosophy must already include within itself, quite apart from its conditions, criteria of adequacy for what is to be thought in order to prepare the space of the thinking 'together' of its conditions. Consequently just as philosophy depends upon the readiness of its conditions in order to think them, so too these conditions presuppose philosophy's prior readiness.

If this is correct then philosophy must have access to its adequacy criteria prior to engaging in the act of seizing its truths. This we suggest is possible when philosophy has direct access to the political event unmediated by its four conditions. The political event has primacy here in so far as philosophy's thinking is primarily the thinking of the collective as such in which case access to the command or the general axiom becomes crucial for the constitution of such thinking. In other words philosophy must have a more primordial relation to the political event, the event that harbours the 'great mystery', as a pre-requisite for its activation.

Accordingly, if philosophy is the general theory of the event, as Badiou insists, it must also be *of* the event in the sense that it belongs to the event. From our discussion so far we can note that any articulation of what happens in the practice of philosophical thinking presupposes some account of how this thinking is activated and where it takes place. That is, the question of philosophy's own site and the process of its own generation becomes a pressing issue. Here our attention is directed away from the conditions of philosophy whose compossibility philosophy must think to the condition of philosophy understood as that *in which* philosophy happens. So, in the first instance, the primary challenge is to determine not what philosophy thinks or how it 'welcomes' its multiple conditions but where one encounters philosophy or, in Badiou's terms, how the subject of philosophy is constituted.

Like Badiou we believe that radical philosophy, or a properly philosophical project, relates somehow to the radicality of the event. From our perspective the activation of a philosophical orientation is a matter of appreciating the command 'be as a world' and the indeterminate gathering 'we' that is constituted as a response to this command. This means that the collective as such—the collective that the political event manifests—must be available to philosophy as its place of activation. So, the would-be philosopher is somehow related to a real process of fidelity to a singular political event. This is important because it is only through such relating that one is exposed to the experience of the collective as such. One can participate in poetry by appreciating a poem someone else has written but one cannot have the fundamental sense of the collective without being engaged, at some level, with the being of the collective in its different manifestations.

To be sure, mere involvement in the usual forms of political activism is not sufficient. The radical personal transformation that Badiou rightly thinks is associated with revolutionary politics is directly connected, we believe, to a certain dynamic interaction between life and death. Ultimately fidelity to the political event, in Badiou's sense of thinking the situation according to the event, is grounded on one's deeply held belief that, if the need arises, one is prepared to die for the cause and one's comrades. To put it more dramatically, one is able truly to imagine that one has already died for the cause even if this might not actually eventuate when the opportunity arises. This is important for two reasons.

On the one hand, the political event and fidelity to it claim one as a whole. Consequently nothing, not even life itself, can be taken as a given. Life, in the radical sense of committed presence as such as a precondition for engagement with anything specific, is claimed through death. Thus the conviction that, given the need, one will die for the cause is the point of entry, so to speak, into the truth process. Indeed, with the poet Livadites we can say 'and if we don't die for each other we are already dead'.[8] This conviction decisively characterizes a fundamental aspect of the process of fidelity to the political event.

On the other hand, death is the ultimate site of gathering for the living. In the collective ethos of those who respond to any form of the command 'be as a world' sacrifice becomes the ultimate realization of the subject as a place of dwelling and of others' gathering. In these circumstances even one's absolute absence is significant as a place of gathering. It is no accident that the three commands we mentioned above are directly associated with sacrifice (Socrates, Christ, and so on). So, a certain political participation functions as a precondition for becoming philosophical in so far as the latter relies upon the experience of the collective as such. In order to elaborate our claim that the political subject becomes philosophical as an outcome of remaining faithful to the full implications of the emergence of the political event, in the next section we turn to an exploration of Badiou's claims regarding the ethic of perseverance that informs the political subject's fidelity to the event.

---

8. Livadites, *Small Book for Large Dreams*, p. 43.

III. THE RETREAT OF THE POLITICAL EVENT AND THE EVENT AS RETREAT

> There is always only one question in the ethic of truths: how will I, as some-one, *continue* to exceed my own being? How will I link the things I know, in a consistent fashion, via the effects of being seized by the not-known?[9]

> The Immortal that I am capable of being [...] must be *directly* seized by fidelity. That is to say: broken, in its multiple being, by the course of an immanent break, and convoked [*requis*], finally, with or without knowing it, by the evental supplement. To enter into the composition of a subject of truth can only be something that *happens to you* (E 51).

Once composed, the subject must struggle to maintain her infinite dimension, the dimension brought into being by a truth procedure, and for Badiou this struggle is informed by the maxim 'keep going' (E 52). Fidelity to the event, moreover, calls for a 'decision to relate henceforth to the situation from the perspective of its evental [...] supplement' (E 41). 'An evental fidelity is a real break (both thought and practiced) in the specific order in which the event took place', a break that produces a truth in the situation:

> Essentially, a truth is the material course traced, within the situation, by the evental supplementation. It is thus an *immanent break*. 'Immanent' because a truth proceeds *in* the situation, [...] 'Break' because what enables the truth- process—the event— meant nothing according to the prevailing language and established knowledge of the situation (E 42-43).

In introducing something new an event always emerges in a specific situation and is dependent for this on the edge of the void or more specifically what Badiou terms an 'evental site'. By this he means:

> an entirely abnormal multiple; that is, a multiple such that none of its elements are presented in the situation. The site, itself, is presented, but 'beneath' it nothing from which it is composed is presented.[10]

---

9. Alain Badiou, *Ethics: An Essay on the Understanding of Evil*, trans. Peter Hallward, London, Verso, 2001, p. 52 (henceforth E).
10. Alain Badiou, *Being and Event*, trans. Oliver Feltham, London, Continuum, 2005, p. 175.

Whilst it is the situation's evental site—in Badiou's sense of a site that at once belongs to the situation without also having discernable elements in common with the latter—that ensures its specificity, the unnameable of the situation, that which falls beyond its knowledge regime, ensures the continuation of truth processes.[11]

Accordingly, for Badiou fidelity to the political event calls, not only for perseverance in following through the consequences of the event, but also for an acceptance of the unnameable orientation of a truth such that the subject cannot properly define the collective as a matter of engaging in politics or thinking as the collective. For a subject to name the collective therefore is to practice an evil in Badiou's sense of a corruption of the truth of the given political sequence. By linking the occurrence of political evil to a specific subject's orientation through the specific relation to a truth, Badiou provides a rationale for his ethic of perseverance as expressed in the maxim 'keep going' that by-passes the worry that the political evils of recent history might be evidence of a flaw in the very character of the political event understood as the idea of the revolutionary project itself.

Now, if we can imagine the subject of politics, say the revolutionary party, to fail to remain faithful to the event to which it owes its origin, through an act of corruption of the truth of which it is the bearer, is it also conceivable that fidelity to the event may call for a faithful response to the fact of *the event's retreat* no less than to the overwhelming seizure associated with its emergence? If political truths escape the logic that structures the specific situation through processes of subtraction from the particularity of the known, as Badiou insists, they must nevertheless remain true to the event from which they originate even when the evental supplement has receded historically and not for want of willing truth bearers. We suspect that because Badiou's theory of the event does not propose an account of the political event's *retreat* in the sense of the collapse of the revolutionary project but only of its emergence, his discussion of the questions of fidelity in the circumstances of today's world ultimately leads him to lose sight of that which was at the heart of the revolutionary project, namely bringing about a new world in response to the current circumstances of the world. Instead, on his analysis the world is reduced to a stage, whatever the circumstances, for the perpetuation of the revolutionary subject's thinking (doing). We would like to lend some force to this critical observation by

---

11. See Peter Hallward, *Badiou: A Subject to Truth*, Minneapolis, University of Minnesota Press, 2003, pp. 255-70.

attempting to outline an account of the possibility of philosophy as a response to the retreat of the political event.

Bearing in mind our discussion in the first section of our paper we can pose the following question. What if in modern times, our times, in so far as it relies on an evental site in a specific situation every political event sequence also explicitly or implicitly invokes a tension between the source of the command 'be as a world' and that of the prevailing logic of the situation to which every political truth sequence poses its challenge? Let us follow through the implications of this suggestion along with Badiou. Viewed from the regime of knowledge that structures the specific situation of liberal-capitalism the political event and what this event signifies for its revolutionary subjects is nothing tangible, nothing that the cognitive net of the situation can get a hold of. But could the significance of this 'nothing' lie in the fact that instead of challenging the situation by way of an 'immanent break' this 'nothing' constitutes an integral part of the situation in the sense that the situation relies upon it for its completion? How might we differentiate between a challenge to the situation in Badiou's sense of an immanent break and the situation taken as posing to itself the historical challenge to accommodate that which presents to it as 'nothing'? If, as we suggested in the first section of our paper, we understand the political event as the gathering 'we' then from the perspective of the situation we can understand the evental site's 'abnormality' in terms of the form of gathering that the event is. If the situation is itself a response to a kind of gathering from whose perspective what the political event signifies is 'nothing', how can the specific situation of liberal-capitalism be understood, on the one hand, as a response to a certain idea of the gathering and, on the other, as consisting of sites that make possible the emergence of the gathering of the political event?

From our Hegelian perspective the idea of the gathering to which the situation of liberal-capitalism constitutes a response is to be understood in terms of Hegel's formulation of the abstract principle of the modern world:

> To start from the self, to live in the self, is the other extreme of formal subjectivity, when it is still empty, or rather has made itself to be empty; such is pure formalism, the abstract principle of the modern world.[12]

---

12. G. W. F. Hegel, *Lectures on the History of Philosophy*, trans. E. S. Haldane and Frances H. Simson, Vol. I Greek Philosophy to Plato, 3 vols., Lincoln, University of Nebraska Press, 1995, p. 152.

This pure formalism is expressed in the exchange relations of persons in their capacity as property owners. These relations are responses to the command 'be a person, and respect others as persons'.[13] In our terms they express what we can call the formless gathering of property owners. In the last few centuries we have witnessed the unceasing process of expansion and intensification of the gathering of property owners on a global scale. Accordingly, the situation of global capitalism amounts to a series of forms of gatherings—legal, economic, political, artistic and so on—that are informed by the formlessness of the global gathering of property owners perpetually responding to the command 'be as a person'. Participation in these processes has become an unconditionally democratic ritual. From this perspective the expansion and intensification of exchange relations has very little to do with capitalism's drive for profit. Quite the contrary, the need unceasingly to affirm the creation of form from the formless gathering of property owners feeds capitalism.

Now the revolutionary political event comes to challenge the very idea of the gathering of property owners responding to the command 'be as a person'. What is this challenge, precisely? To begin with, at the heart of the gathering of property owners is the mediation of what Hegel calls the 'thing' and the exchange relation that conforms to it. Because this purely negative relating captures only the individuality of the self it gives rise to the negative command concerning respect for persons. In contrast, the mediation of the thing is not relied upon in the gathering 'we' that responds to the command 'be as a world'. Here, the self is expanded, functioning as the place of dwelling of the other selves. This radical understanding of gathering understood in terms of the collective as such marks both a liberation from the conditioned form of the gathering of property owners and a new project, that of the creation of the world of solidarity. From its perspective the gathering of property owners is a particular form of gathering that misrepresents itself as the gathering as such. It is a false universal in this sense.

Yet from the perspective of the gathering of property owners, the 'collective as such' means 'nothing' in the sense that the claim to be a universal command that meaningfully informs a new world appreciation is incomprehensible. Indeed the idea of the collective as such can only be understood as informing a local form of life within the situation. This is because in so far as the gathering of property owners functions in the

---

13. G. W. F. Hegel, *The Philosophy of Right*, trans. T. M. Knox, New York, Oxford, 1980, p. 37.

situation as that which embodies the very idea of the gathering, the situation must be able to accommodate incompatible materially local forms of gathering. In this case the emphasis is placed on locality and not on universality.

To elaborate on this last point let us consider how evental sites become available in the situation that is informed by the formless gathering of property owners, the situation of liberal-capitalism. In so far as an evental site is an element of the situation it conforms to the logic of this situation. Elsewhere we have analysed this logic in terms of the operations of the formal universality of particularity.[14] According to this logic the modern individual (a group, a person, an institution, a system of knowledge) is negatively defined as not being identified with the universal as such, and thus it is distinct from that which gives the specific particular its specificity. Particularity is the mode of being of every modern particular individual irrespective of the content of its concrete existence. Particularity is, therefore universal in the sense that it explicitly supplies the mode of being of every modern particular. This points to a separation between form and content, since each particular emerges and becomes part of the situation through the indispensable moment of differentiation between its universal mode of being (form) and its particular substance (content). This kind of differentiation between the formal universal and the substantive particular translates into a dichotomous division as distinct from a mere differentiation. Firstly, because the substantive particular is defined only in its negative relation to the universal, the two are oppositionally defined. Secondly, given that the formal being of the differentiated universal is not dependent on any substantive particular, unlike the particular, the formal universal is self-determining. For both the above reasons the formal universal takes a privileged position relative to the substantive particular. The principle then of the situation can be appreciated in terms of the following negative imperative: be a particular in accordance with the logic of the formal universality of particularity. Basically this means that in the given form of gathering what really matters is not what happens within its confines but how, those who participate in it are representable in the situation. They must be representable in terms of the property-owning relations that this form makes possible, that is, as integral members of the gathering of formal subjects.

---

14. See Toula Nicolacopoulos and George Vassilacopoulos, *Hegel and the Logical Structure of Love: An Essay on Sexualities, Family and the Law*, Aldershot, Ashgate, 1999, pp. 9-24.

From the above it follows that through the principle of the formal universality of particularity the situation combines that which can be absolutely known and predicted, namely sites according to particularity as the mode of being of the particular, with that which cannot be known precisely because it need not be known, namely the content of the particular, or its internal elements. Take love as an example. We can understand the loving relation as a total disruption of each participant's being as a property owner. The form of subjectivity and recognition to which the relation of love gives rise does not conform to the logic governing property-owning subjects' relations, the logic that relies on the mediation of the property item. Love thus disrupts the command 'be as a person' by supplying its own, radically different imperative: be as the world of the unity that is the loving subject. Yet despite this radical difference and the radical rupture in the property-owning subjectivity of those who come together to form a loving subject, even the constitution of the loving subject ultimately depends on the structure of property ownership for its external recognition. It seems then that the situation demonstrates its strength the moment it is shown to determine what it cannot detect by its cognitive net. By providing the formal space of particularity the situation situates the unknowable in the space of its knowing.

We can extend this analysis to account for the political event and the truth procedures associated with it. Whereas the event of love is limited in the sense that two suffice for its emergence, the political event exhibits an in principle unrestricted universality that directly challenges the formal universality of the gathering of property owners. More specifically, whereas love disrupts only the subjectivity of those involved, the political event disrupts both the subjectivity of those involved and challenges the formal universality of particularity in so far as it counter-poses the command 'be as a world' to the command 'be as a person'. Moreover, it is the situation that provides the opportunity for this challenge to arise and to be contained, whether peacefully or violently, within the boundaries of its own logic. In this sense the political event can be said to complete the situation. So, we can explain the 'abnormality' of the evental site by noting that the event gives rise to something that cannot be known and hence incorporated into the situation in an evental site whose form is nevertheless presentable simply because the situation is interested only in this form and not in what this form accommodates. The fact that the situation cannot know the event means that the situation's horizon of knowing has already generated a 'space' within it for what cannot be known. A priori then the situation accommodates everything necessary for the event to happen.

From the above considerations something quite dramatic follows regarding the political event. In order to take shape that which is in essence formless and the source of the forms given to its truth processes, the collective as such, must rely upon a particular site. Here the form is not created out of what is formless since its own form—the form of the form—is already determined by the situation. So whereas the site as the form of the event expresses singularity, the form or mode of being of the site itself, of any site, expresses universality. In other words, the principle or law of the situation ultimately determines the site. Because of this historical restriction and the situatedness of the political event in an evental site, the event whose own logic it is to question the role of the indeterminate collective of property owners can only challenge what is determinate in the situation such as the state, the authoritarian party, the legal institution and so on.

This sort of challenge effectively overwhelms the political event and its command. Since challenging what is determinate in the situation replaces challenging the indeterminate that informs the situation, ultimately the event is subordinated to its truth processes. The truth of a political sequence, say the Leninist party, performs two roles. Firstly, as a response to the command 'be as a world' it expresses the effort to generate form out of the formless gathering 'we'. But, secondly, due to the fact that the political event depends upon its evental site, the truth process amounts to a challenge to the specific situation. Ultimately then truth processes are activated as this challenge and not as processes of creating forms out of what is otherwise indeterminate. Accordingly, the formless that is understood through and as the challenge of the situation comes to be named. As a result the indeterminacy of the gathering of property owners that informs the situation is lost sight of and its place is taken by specific formations, like the state and so on. Here the truth process comes to articulate the challenge to the situation rather than to the formlessness of the gathering 'we'. Even though the ultimate source of challenge is the gathering 'we' the truth process is forced to take its place or in Badiou's terms to name the collective as such. In this case what constitutes the collective is not the response to the command 'be as a world' but the response to the command linked to the particular truth process. Historically, the state's or the party's act of naming the unnameable constituted an inevitable aspect of an effective challenge to the situation. Of course, it amounted to a challenge of force precisely because, although it was informed by the logic of the formal universality of particularity, it nevertheless posited itself as all-determining.

The difference between the challenge implicit in the idea of the gathering 'we' that is posited to the indeterminate gathering of property owners and the challenge posited by truth processes to the situation, can also be understood as follows. Truth processes challenge the historical, whereas the political event challenges history. In so far as we are interested in overcoming the limits of the situation for our political emancipation, as revolutionary subjects we treat the determinations of the situation as historical, that is, as capable of change. However this is a serious limitation since what we want to change is already historical as an outcome of being structured by the logic of the formal universality of particularity and in this case historicality is associated not with future change but with the horizontal and fluid coexistence of particulars. Truth processes are historical in just this sense. Capitalism has replaced the time of the historical with the horizon of history and the indeterminate gathering of property owners marks this horizon along with the intensification of exchange relations for the reasons we already mentioned above. From this perspective change is meaningful if we can move from history to the eternal whose command is 'be as a world'. But since the situation of history totalizes itself by excluding the command and the corresponding indeterminate gathering 'we', the universal and unconditional release of this command demands the collapse, so to speak, of this totality. Precisely because the command is infinitely realisable in the emptiness that such a collapse will bring, the event that transforms us in the true spirit of the revolution must be just such a collapse. This said, for obvious reasons we do not have access to this idea of collapse and its implications in our capacity as political subjects but they are accessible to us through philosophy. We turn in the final section of our paper to the question of the relationship between the political event as retreat and the turn to speculative philosophy.

IV. THE EVENT'S RETREAT AND SPECULATIVE PHILOSOPHY

We have argued that in our times fidelity to the political event of the revolutionary project calls for a response to the fact of the event's retreat and not only to its emergence. This is a response that forms the basis for the constitution of philosophical subjectivity. Through the relation of the political subject as the bearer of a truth of the event, the would-be philosopher is exposed to the idea of the collective as such, a form of the gathering 'we' that the situation of liberal-capitalism denies in principle. Now, in our view we can appreciate the turn to speculative philosophy as a matter of fidelity to the event's retreat, that is, to the collapse of the revolutionary project as such, by following through the implications of what we can call the liberation of the event from dependence on some evental site.

To appreciate and accept the event's retreat in all its radicality is to insist upon the liberation of the event from the form of particularity that inevitably regulates the announcement of the gathering 'we' to which the political event gives rise. If such liberation is conceivable—we might think of this as a moment of radical skepticism in relation to all the significations that the situation makes possible—then through its retreat the event points to the situation as a whole as the world that denies the event. This is a denial not merely of the event's power to inform the world, but of the very idea that informs the political event.

Consequently, unlike the truth procedures that despite being constituted in response to the event's emergence are incapable of directly addressing the idea of gathering that informs the situation, namely the indeterminate gathering of property owners, through its retreat the event directs itself to precisely this idea. How is this possible? We have made the point that the gathering of property owners treats itself as the gathering that embodies the very principle of gathering subjects. Accordingly, it functions as the gathering whose command—'be as a person'—restricts the principle of subjectivity to that of formal subjectivity. From this it follows that the retreat of the event can be shown to free the event from what conditions it only if its very idea can become the practice/thought of a subject as the 'abyss' that stirs the world. In citing the words of Paul Celan to articulate the meaning of justice—'On inconsistencies Rest: two fingers are snapping in the abyss, a world is stirring in the scratch-sheets, it all depends on you'—Badiou emphasizes that 'it all depends on you' (E 78) to the detriment of the equally significant observation that for the poet the world's stirring is possible only in so far as everything—and, contra Badiou (E 72-73), not just the political truth procedure—is already situated in the abyss that justice is.

For the emergence of this kind of subject and thinking there need only be one instance of a revolutionary subject through the being of whom the all-determining power of property-owning subjectivity might ultimately be disrupted to the point of its implosion. In this intense moment we have the uttering of the 'we' by the single subject. This uttering is the moment of philosophy that relates directly to the event.

Understood in this way philosophy is activated in the battlefield that the self of the philosopher is, once this self is determined by the power to think of itself as that which has the power to disrupt the pure formalism of subjectivity and thereby to point to something more fundamental. This is a disruption in history itself since, as we noted in the previous section, history is constituted as the indeterminate gathering of property owners. Through this disruption the eternal invades history in a manner that renders it impossible for history to resist. In other words, the retreating event determines philosophy as its truth process that directly intervenes in history by thinking it. Ultimately only an event without evental site, posits the very idea of commanding to which philosophy responds. History is the situation of the event that does not depend on a site. Here, what is to be thought is not an object but the significance for the world of the very possibility of philosophy, since history is created by presupposing this very possibility. As Hegel notes, history is the emptying out of Spirit, that is, of the gathering 'we'. What we have here is the in principle implosion of the world that releases the very idea of the gathering 'we' an idea fully realized as philosophy. Philosophy is its own condition and thus philosophy thinks itself.

From this perspective Badiou's approach to philosophy appears, on the one hand, to refer us to the political event that no longer has the power to shatter us, and, on the other, it remains silent on that which does indeed have this power today, namely the collapse of the revolutionary project. Consequently, much like some of the philosophers he criticizes, his thinking remains caught in the in between.

Follysophy

Dominique Hecq

Poetic form is the innocence of the grandiose.
ALAIN BADIOU

Today I feel altogether unbuttoned.
I rejoice in these vast barrens of white
And, you will understand, transform them
In the expansive tracts of my genius.

> *If you were to try to flatter me*
> *With bardic vocables and sepia verse,*
> *I should object.*

I think I shall sing,
In a variety of forms, of light,
Of sincerity, and of love, of course.

> *Oh, please. I don't give a shit for love.*
> *Fashion for me a desolate confection.*
> *I feel the need of a substantial torte,*
> *Lightly powdered with desperation.*

Crooked gums under snow? The light falling
All afternoon? My large and tragic face
In the glass?

> *I am no longer young.*
> *My soul unravels to infinity as I contemplate*
> *The woman I loved in the naked presence*
> *Of a handsome fellow, come upon*
> *In silence and with joy.*

As in the dark
We are afraid. As we wake. Opening,
Again and again, our soft and empty hands.

> *I cannot move. For the moment I am draped*
> *In glacial distress. I can see the grand,*
> *Groundless abyss under the dispassionate eye*
> *Of vacant heaven. I can smell the nape*
> *Of the neck of despair. It is coming to fasten me*
> *In a tender embrace.*

How the banded lapwing
Whistles, fatherless, from the plain?

> *You know,*
> *Love seemed the grandest plan of them all.*
> *Perhaps the heart is simply too small.*

It may be. Tough I can't tell for real.
I find it hard to imagine the stark
Language of a large and foundering body.
What I see is an array of banks and streamers,
Patches of light, and hanging draperies.

> *I will expand, I think, at the last, through the sadness.*
> *See these slender rivers of ionospheric grief,*
> *The noctilucent clouds and the vast desolation.*

bibliography

Bibliography of Work on and
by Alain Badiou in English

Compiled by Paul Ashton

This bibliography presents a complete list of the work on and by Badiou currently available (as of 1/10/2006) in English. The bibliography separates the works by Badiou (further broken into the sub-sections: *Books*, *Collections of Essays*, and *Essays and Interviews*), from the 'Commentaries on Badiou's Work'.

Other works cited in this book, and works by Badiou that are as yet not translated, are listed at the end of this bibliography.

WORKS BY ALAIN BADIOU

BOOKS

MP   *Manifesto for Philosophy*, trans. Norman Madarasz, Albany, State University of New York Press, 1999.

D   *Deleuze: The Clamor of Being*, trans. Louise Burchill, Minneapolis, University of Minnesota Press, 2000.

E   *Ethics: An Essay on the Understanding of Evil*, trans. Peter Hallward, London, Verso, 2001.

SP   *Saint Paul: The Foundation of Universalism*, trans. Ray Brassier, Stanford, Stanford University Press, 2003.

BE   *Being and Event*, trans. Oliver Feltham, London, Continuum, 2005.

M   *Metapolitics*, trans. Jason Barker, London, Verso, 2005.

HI   *Handbook of Inaesthetics*, trans. Alberto Toscano, Stanford, Stanford University Press, 2005.

TO   *Briefings On Existence: A Short Treatise on Transitory Ontology*, trans. Norman Madarasz, Albany, State University of New York Press, 2006.

TC   *The Century*, trans. Alberto Toscano, London, Polity, 2007 (forthcoming).

COLLECTIONS OF ESSAYS

IT   *Infinite Thought: Truth and the Return to Philosophy*, ed. and trans. Justin Clemens and Oliver Feltham, London, Continuum, 2003.
>   Including:
>   'Philosophy and Desire', pp. 39-57.
>   'Philosophy and Truth', pp. 58-68.
>   'Philosophy and Politics', pp. 69-78.
>   'Philosophy and Psychoanalysis', pp. 79-90.
>   'Philosophy and Art', pp. 91-108 (from *Conditions*, Paris, Seuil, 1992, pp. 93-107).
>   'Philosophy and Cinema', pp. 109-125 (from *L'Art du Cinéma*, no. 24, 1999).
>   'Philosophy and the "Death of Communism"', pp. 126-140 (from *D'un désastre obscur*, Paris, Editions de L'Aube, 1998, pp. 7-25).
>   'Philosophy and the "War Against Terrorism"', pp. 141-164.
>   'The Definition of Philosophy', pp. 165-168 (from *Conditions*, Paris, Seuil, 1992, pp. 79-82).
>   'Ontology and Politics: An Interview with Alain Badiou', pp. 169-194.

OB   *On Beckett*, ed. and trans. Alberto Toscano and Nina Power, Manchester, Clinamen, 2003.
>   Including:
>   'The Writing of the Generic', pp. 1-36 (from *Conditions*, Paris, Seuil, 1992, pp. 329-66).
>   'Tireless Desire', pp. 37-78 (from *Beckett L'increvable désir*, 1995).
>   'Being, Existence, Thought: Pose and Concept', pp. 79-112 (from *Handbook of Inaesthesis*, pp. 89-121).
>   'What Happens', pp. 113-18.

TW   *Theoretical Writings*, ed. and trans. Ray Brassier and Alberto Toscano, London, Continuum Books, 2004.
>   Including:
>   'Mathematics and Philosophy: The Grand Style and the Little Style', pp. 3-20 (unpublished).
>   'Philosophy and Mathematics: Infinity and the End of

Romanticism', pp. 21-38 (from *Conditions*, Paris, Seuil, 1992, pp. 157-78).

'The Question of Being Today', pp. 39-48 (from *Briefings on Existence*, pp. 33-44).

'Platonism and Mathematical Ontology', 49-58 (from *Briefings on Existence*, pp. 89-100).

'The Being of Number', pp. 59-65 (from *Briefings on Existence*, pp. 125-132).

'One, Multiple, Multiplicities', pp. 67-80 (from *multitudes*, 1, 2000, pp. 195-211).

'Spinoza's Closed Ontology', pp. 81-93 (from *Briefings on Existence*, pp. 73-88).

'The Event as Trans-Being', pp. 97-102 (revised and expanded version of an essay of the same title from *Briefings on Existence*, pp. 59-62).

'On Subtraction', pp. 103-17 (from *Conditions*, Paris, Seuil, 1992, pp. 179-95).

'Truth: Forcing and the Unnamable', pp. 119-33 (from *Conditions*, Paris, Seuil, 1992, pp. 196-212).

'Kant's Subtractive Ontology', pp. 135-42 (from *Briefings on Existence*, pp. 133-142).

'Eight Theses on the Universal', pp. 143-52 (from Jelica Sumic (ed.), *Universal, Singulier, Subjet*, Paris, Kimé, 2000, pp. 11-20).

'Politics as a Truth Procedure', pp. 153-60 (from *Metapolitics*, pp. 141-52).

'Being and Appearance', pp. 163-75 (from *Briefings on Existence*, pp. 153-168).

'Notes Toward Thinking Appearance', pp. 177-87 (unpublished).

'The Transcendental', pp. 189-220 (from a draft manuscript [now published] of *Logiques des mondes*, Paris, Seuil).

'Hegel and the Whole', pp. 221-31 (from a draft manuscript [now published] of *Logiques des mondes*, Paris, Seuil).

'Language, Thought, Poetry', pp. 233-41 (unpublished).

P *Polemics*, trans. Steve Corcoran, London, Verso, 2006.

ESSAYS AND INTERVIEWS

'On a Finally Objectless Subject', trans. Bruce Fink, *Topoi*, no. 7, 1988, pp. 93-8. Reproduced as: Alain Badiou, 'On a Finally Objectless Subject', *Who Comes After the Subject?*, trans. Bruce Fink, Routledge, 1991, pp. 24-32.

'Gilles Deleuze, The Fold: Leibniz and the Baroque', in Constantin Boundas and Dorethea Olkowski (eds.), *Deleuze and Theatre of Philosophy*, trans. Thelma Sowley, New York, Columbia, 1994, pp. 51-69.

'Beckett's Generic Writing', trans. Alban Urbanas, *Journal of Beckett Studies*, vol. 4, no. 1, 1994, pp. 13-21.

'Descartes/Lacan', trans. Sigi Jöttkandt and Daniel Collins, *UMBR(a)*, no. 1, 1996, pp. 13-7.

'Psychoanalysis and Philosophy', trans. Raphael Comprone and Marcus Coelen, *UMBR(a)*, no. 1, 1996, pp. 19-26.

'Hegel', trans. Marcus Coelen and Sam Gillespie, *UMBR(a)*, no. 1, 1996, pp. 27-35.

'What is Love?' trans. Justin Clemens, *UMBR(a)*, no. 1, 1996, pp. 37-53.

'Is There a Theory of the Subject in Georges Canguilhem?' trans. Graham Burchell, *Economy and Society*, vol. 27, no. 2/3, 1998, pp. 225-33.

'Philosophy and Politics', trans. Thelma Sowley, *Radical Philosophy*, 1999, pp. 29-32.

'On a Contemporary Usage of Frege', trans. Justin Clemens and Sam Gillespe, *UMBR(a)*, no. 1, 2000, pp. 99-115.

'Metaphysics and the Critique of Metaphysics', trans. Alberto Toscano, *Pli: Warwick Journal of Philosophy*, no. 10, 2000, pp. 174-90.

'Of Life as a Name of Being, or, Deleuze's Vitalist Ontology ', *Pli: Warwick Journal of Philosophy*, no. 10, 2000.

'Art and Philosophy', trans. Jorge Jauregui, *Lacanian Ink*, no. 17, 2000.

'Who is Nietzsche?' trans. Alberto Toscano, *Pli: Warwick Journal of Philosophy*, no. 11, 2001, pp. 1-10.

'The Political as a Procedure of Truth', trans. Barbara P. Faulks, *Lacanian Ink*, no. 19, 2001, pp. 71-81.

'Highly Speculative Reasoning on the Concept of Democracy', trans. Jorge Jauregui, *Lacanian Ink*, no. 16, 2001.

'The Ethic of Truths: Construction and Potency', trans. Selma Sowley, *Pli: Warwick Journal of Philosophy*, no. 12, 2001, pp. 245-55.

'On Evil: An Interview with Alain Badiou', with Christoph Cox and Molly Whalen, *Cabinet*, no. 5, 2001-2.

'Philosophical Considerations of Some Recent Facts', trans. Steven Corcoran, *Theory & Event*, vol. 6, no. 2, 2002.

'Existence and Death', trans. Nina Power and Alberto Toscano, *Discourse: Journal for Theoretical Studies in Media and Culture*, vol. 24, no. 1, 2002, pp. 63-73.

'One Divides into Two', trans. Alberto Toscano, *Culture Machine*, no. 4, 2002.

'Beyond Formalisation: An Interview', with Peter Hallward and Bruno Bosteels, trans. Bruno Bosteels and Alberto Toscano, *Angelaki: Journal of Theoretical Humanities*, vol. 8, no. 2, 2003, pp. 111-36.

'Seven Variations on the Century', *Parallax*, vol. 9, no. 2, 2003, pp. 72-80.

'Philosophical Considerations of the Very Singular Custom of Voting: An Analysis Based on Recent Ballots in France', trans. Steven Corcoran, *Theory & Event*, vol. 6, no. 3, 2003.

'Logic of the Site', trans. Steve Corcoran and Bruno Bosteels, *Diacritics*, vol. 33, no. 3, 2003, pp. 141-50.

'The Scene of Two', trans. Barbara P. Faulks, *Lacanian Ink*, no. 21, 2003, pp. 42-55.

'Lack and Destruction', *UMBR(a)*, no. 1, 2003, pp. 39-61.

'A Conversation with Alain Badiou', with Goldenberg, *Lacanian Ink*, no. 23, 2004.

'Some Replies to a Demanding Friend', *Think Again: Alain Badiou and the Future of Philosophy*, Hallward, Peter, London, Continuum Books, 2004, pp. 232-7.

'Fifteen Theses on Contemporary Art', *Lacanian Ink*, no. 23, 2004, pp. 103-19.

'Of an Obscure Disaster', trans. Barbara P. Faulks, *Lacanian Ink*, no. 22, 2004.

'The Flux and the Party: In the Margins of Anti-Oedipus', trans. Laura Balladur and Simon Krysl, *Polygraph*, no. 15-16, 2004, pp. 75-92.

'Fragments of a Public Diary on the American War Against Iraq', *Contemporary French and Francophone Studies*, vol. 8, no. 3, 2004, pp. 223-38.

'Fifteen Theses on Contemporary Art', *Lacanian Ink*, no. 23, 2004, pp. 100-19.

'An Interview with Alain Badiou: Universal Truths & the Question of Religion', with Adam S. Miller, *Journal of Philosophy and Scripture*, vol. 3, no. 1, 2005, pp. 38-42.

'Democratic Materialism and the Materialist Dialectic', *Radical Philosophy*, vol. 130, 2005, pp. 20-4.

'The Adventure of French philosophy', *New Left Review*, no. 35, 2005, pp. 67-77.

'Selections from *Théorie du sujet* on the Cultural Revolution', trans. Alberto Toscano, Lorenzo Chiesa, and Nina Power, *positions: east asia cultures critique*, vol. 13, no. 3, 2005, pp. 635-48.

'The Cultural Revolution: The Last Revolution?' trans. Bruno Bosteels, *positions: east asia cultures critique*, vol. 13, no. 3, 2005, pp. 481-514.

'The Triumphant Restoration', trans. Alberto Toscano, *positions: east asia cultures critique*, vol. 13, no. 3, 2005, pp. 659-62.

'Further Selections from *Théorie du sujet* on the Cultural Revolution', trans. Lorenzo Chiesa, *positions: east asia cultures critique*, vol. 13, no. 3, 2005, pp. 649-58.

'An Essential Philosophical Thesis: "It Is Right to Rebel against the Reactionaries"', trans. Alberto Toscano, *positions: east asia cultures critique*, vol. 13, no. 3, 2005, pp. 669-77.

'Manifesto of Affirmationism', trans. Barbara P. Faulks, *Lacanian Ink*, no. 24/25, 2005, pp. 92-109.

'Lacan. Seminar, Book X: Anxiety', trans. Barbara P. Faulks, *Lacanian Ink*, no. 26, 2005.

'Anxiety', trans. Barbara P. Faulks, *Lacanian Ink*, no. 26, 2006, pp. 70-1.

'The Formulas of L'Étourdit', trans. Scott Savaiano, *Lacanian Ink*, no. 27, 2006, pp. 80-95.

'Lacan and the pre-Socratics', in Slavoj Žižek (ed.), *Lacan: The Silent Partners*, London, Verso, 2006, pp. 7-16.

'The Subject of Art', *The Symptom*, no. 6, Spring 2005.

'What is a Philosophical Institution? Or: Address, Transmission, Inscription', trans. A. J. Bartlett, *Cosmos and History*, vol. 1, no. 1-2, 2006, pp. 9-14.

COMMENTARIES ON BADIOU'S WORK

Alliez, Eric, 'Badiou: The Grace of the Universal', *Polygraph*, vol. 17, 2005, pp. 267-73.

Ashton, Paul, A. J. Bartlett and Justin Clemens, 'Masters & Disciples: Institution, Philosophy, Praxis', *Cosmos and History*, vol. 1, no. 1-2, 2006, pp. 1-8.

Azman, M., 'How to Think Science? How Does Science Think?' *Filozofski Vestnik*, vol. 26, no. 1, 2005.

Baldwin, Jon and Nick Haeffner, '"Fault Lines": Simon Critchley in Discussion on Alain Badiou', *Polygraph*, vol. 17, 2005, pp. 295-307.

Balibar, Etienne, 'The History of Truth: Alain Badiou in French Philosophy', *Radical Philosophy*, vol. 115, 2002, pp. 16-28.

Balibar, Etienne, 'The History of Truth: Alain Badiou in French Philosophy', in Peter Hallward (ed.), *Think Again: Alain Badiou and the Future of Philosophy*, London, Continuum Books, 2004, pp. 21-38.

Barker, Jason, *Alain Badiou: A Critical Introduction*, London, Pluto, 2002.

Barker, Jason, 'The Topology of Revolution', *Communication and Cognition*, vol. 36, no. 1-2, 2003, pp. 61-72.

Barker, Jason, 'Topography and Structure', *Polygraph*, vol. 17, 2005, pp. 93-104.

Bartlett, A. J., 'The Pedagogical Theme: Alain Badiou and an Eventless Education', *anti-THESIS*, vol. 16, 2006, pp. 129-47.

Bartlett, A. J., 'Conditional Notes on a New Republic?', *Cosmos and History*, vol. 1, no. 1-2, 2006, pp. 39-67.

Baumbach, Nico, 'Something Else Is Possible: Thinking Badiou on Philosophy and Art', *Polygraph*, vol. 17, 2005, pp. 157-73.

Beistegui, Miguel de, 'The Ontological Dispute: Badiou, Heidegger, and Deleuze', in Gabriel Riera (ed.), *Alain Badiou: Philosophy and Its Conditions*, trans. Ray Brassier, Albany, State University of New York, 2005, pp. 45-58.

Bell, V., 'On the Critique of Secular Ethics: An essay with Flannery O'Connor and Hannah Arendt', *Theory Culture & Society*, vol. 22, no. 2, 2005.

Bensaid, Daniel, 'Alain Badiou and the Miracle of the Event', in Peter Hallward (ed.), *Think Again: Alain Badiou and the Future of Philosophy*, London, Continuum Books, 2004, pp. 94-105.

Besana, Bruno, 'One or Several Events? The Knot between Event and Subject in the Work of Alain Badiou and Gilles Deleuze', *Polygraph*, vol. 17, 2005, pp. 245-66.

Bosteels, Bruno, 'Alain Badiou's Theory of the Subject: The Recommencement of Dialectical Materialism? (Part I)', *Pli: Warwick Journal of Philosophy*, no. 12, 2001, pp. 200-29.

Bosteels, Bruno, 'Alain Badiou's Theory of the Subject: The Recommencement of Dialectical Materialism? (Part II)', *Pli: Warwick Journal of Philosophy*, no. 13, 2002, pp. 173-208.

Bosteels, Bruno, 'On the Subject of the Dialectic', in Peter Hallward (ed.), *Think Again: Alain Badiou and the Future of Philosophy*, London, Continuum Books, 2004, pp. 150-64.

Bosteels, Bruno, 'Logics of Antagonism: In the Margins of Alain Badiou's "The Flux and the Party"', *Polygraph*, no. 15-16, 2004, pp. 93-107.

Bosteels, Bruno, 'Post-Maoism: Badiou and Politics', *positions: east asia cultures critique*, vol. 13, no. 3, 2005, pp. 575-634.

Bosteels, Bruno, 'The Speculative Left', *South Atlantic Quarterly*, vol. 104, no. 4, 2005, pp. 751-67.

Bosteels, Bruno, 'Badiou without Žižek', *Polygraph*, vol. 17, 2005, pp. 221-44.

Bosteels, Bruno, 'Can Change Be Thought? A Dialogue with Alain Badiou', in Gabriel Riera (ed.), *Alain Badiou: Philosophy and Its Conditions*, Albany, State University of New York, 2005, pp. 237-61.

Bosteels, Bruno, 'Alain Badiou's Theory of the Subject: The Recommencement of Dialectical Materialism?' in Slavoj Žižek (ed.), *Lacan: The Silent Partners*, London, Verso, 2006, pp. 115-68.

Bottomley, Anne, 'Shock to Thought: An Encounter (of a Third Kind) with Legal Feminism', *Feminist Legal Studies*, vol. 12, no. 1, 2004, pp. 29-65.

Brassier, Ray, 'Stellar Void or Cosmic Animal? Badiou and Deleuze', *Pli: Warwick Journal of Philosophy*, vol. 10, 2000.

Brassier, Ray, 'Nihil Unbound: Remarks on Subtractive Ontology and Thinking Capitalism', in Peter Hallward (ed.), *Think Again: Alain Badiou and the Future of Philosophy*, London, Continuum Books, 2004, pp. 50-8.

Brassier, Ray, 'Badiou's Materialist Epistemology of Mathematics', *Angelaki: Journal of Theoretical Humanities*, vol. 10, no. 2, 2005, pp. 135-50.

Brassier, Ray, 'Presentation as Anti-Phenomenon in Alain Badiou's *Being and Event*', *Continental Philosophy Review*, 2006.

Brassier, Ray and Alberto Toscano, 'Postface', in Ray Brassier and Alberto Toscano eds. and trans., *Theoretical Writings*, London, Continuum Books, 2005, pp. 233-41.

Brown, Nicholas, '{∅, 8} ∈ {$}? Or, Alain Badiou and Slavoj Žižek, Waiting for Something to Happen', *CR: The New Centennial Review*, vol. 4, no. 3, 2004, pp. 289-319.

Bryant, Levi R., 'A Lacanian Episteme?' *Communication and Cognition*, vol. 36, no. 1-2, 2003, pp. 121-7.

Byrne, Richard, 'Being M. Badiou: The French Philosopher Brings His Ideas to America, Creating a Buzz', *The Chronicle of Higher Education*, vol. 52, no. 29, 2006, pp. A. 20.

Calcagno, Antonio, 'Jacques Derrida and Alain Badiou: Is There a Relation between Politics and Time?' *Philosophy and Social Criticism*, vol. 30, no. 7, 2004, pp. 799-815.

Calcagno, Antonio, *Politics and its Time: Derrida, Lazarus and Badiou*, Ph.D.,

University of Guelph (Canada), 2004.

Calcagno, A., 'Can Alain Badiou's Notion of Time Account for Political Events?' *International Studies in Philosophy*, vol. 37, no. 2, 2005, pp. 1-14.

Chiesa, Lorenzo, 'Count-as-one, Forming-into-one, Unary Trait, S1', *Cosmos and History*, vol. 1, no. 1-2, 2006, pp. 68-93.

Clemens, Justin, 'The lalangue of Phalloi: Lacan versus Lacan', *UMBR(a)*, no. 1, 1996.

Clemens, Justin, 'Platonic Meditations', *Pli: Warwick Journal of Philosophy*, vol. 11, 2001, pp. 200-29.

Clemens, Justin, 'Letters As the Condition of Conditions for Alain Badiou', *Communication and Cognition*, vol. 36, no. 1-2, 2003, pp. 73-102.

Clemens, Justin, *The Romanticism of Contemporary Theory: Institution, Aesthetics, Nihilism*, Aldershot, Ashgate, 2003.

Clemens, Justin, 'Doubles of nothing: The Problem of Binding Truth to Being in the Work of Alain Badiou', *Filozofski Vestnik*, vol. 26, no. 2, 2005, pp. 21-35.

Clemens, Justin, 'Had We But Worlds Enough, and Time, this Absolute, Philosopher...', *Cosmos and History*, vol. 1, no. 1-2, 2006, pp. 277-310.

Clucas, Stephen, 'Poem, Theorem', *Parallax*, vol. 7, no. 4, 2001, pp. 48-65.

Cobussen, Marcel, 'Noise and Ethics: On Evan Parker and Alain Badiou', *Culture, Theory, and Critique*, vol. 46, no. 1, 2005, pp. 29-42.

Copjec, Joan, 'Gai Savoir Sera: The Science of Love and the Insolence of Chance', in Gabriel Riera (ed.), *Alain Badiou: Philosophy and Its Conditions*, Albany, State University of New York, 2005, pp. 119-35.

Critchley, Simon, 'Observations and Questions Regarding A. Badiou's Ethics Doctrine', *Filozofski Vestnik-Acta Philosophica*, vol. 19, no. 1, 1998, pp. 21-31.

Critchley, Simon, 'Demanding Approval: On the Ethics of Alain Badiou', *Radical Philosophy*, vol. 100, 2000, pp. 16-27.

Critchley, Simon, 'On the Ethics of Alain Badiou', in Gabriel Riera (ed.), *Alain Badiou: Philosophy and Its Conditions*, Albany, State University of New York, 2005, pp. 215-35.

Cunningham, Conor, 'Lacan, Philosophy's Difference, and Creation From No-One', *American Catholic Philosophical Quarterly*, vol. 78, no. 3, 2004, pp. 445-79.

De Kesel, Marc, 'Truth As Formal Catholicism on Alain Badiou, Saint Paul: La fondation de l'universalisme', *Communication and Cognition*, vol. 37, no. 3-4, 2004, pp. 167-97.

Desanti, Jean Toussaint, 'Some Remarks on the Intrinsic Ontology of Alain Badiou', in Peter Hallward (ed.), *Think Again: Alain Badiou and the Future of Philosophy*, London, Continuum Books, 2004, pp. 59-66.

Devisch, Ignaas, 'Democracy's Content Thinking Politics with Badiou and Schmitt', *Communication and Cognition*, vol. 36, no. 1-2, 2003, pp. 45-59.

Dews, Peter, 'Uncategorical Imperatives: Adorno, Badiou and the Ethical Turn', *Radical Philosophy*, vol. 111, 2002, pp. 33-7.

Dews, Peter, 'States of Grace: The Excess of the Demand in Badiou's Ethics of Truths', in Peter Hallward (ed.), *Think Again: Alain Badiou and the Future of Philosophy*, London, Continuum Books, 2004, pp. 106-19.

Dews, Peter, 'Disenchantment and the Persistence of Evil: Habermas, Jonas, Badiou', in Alan D. Schrift (ed.), *Modernity and the Problem of Evil*, Bloomington, Indiana University Press, 2005, pp. 51-65.

During, Elie, 'How Much Truth Can Art Bear? On Badiou's 'Inaesthetics'', *Polygraph*, vol. 17, 2005, pp. 143-55.

Düttmann, Alexander Garcia, 'What Remains of Fidelity after Serious Thought', in Peter Hallward (ed.), *Think Again: Alain Badiou and the Future of Philosophy*, London, Continuum Books, 2004, pp. 202-7.

Eagleton, Terry, 'Subjects and Truths', *New Left Review*, no. 9, 2001, pp. 155-60.

Eagleton, Terry, Figures of Dissent: Critical Essays on Fish, Spivak, Žižek and Others, London, Verso, 2003.

Feltham, Oliver, 'Singularity Happening in Politics: The Aboriginal Tent Embassy, Canberra 1972', *Communication and Cognition*, vol. 37, no. 3-4, 2004, pp. 225-45.

Feltham, Oliver, 'And Being and Event and ...: Philosophy and Its Nominations', *Polygraph*, vol. 17, 2005, pp. 27-40.

Feltham, Oliver, 'An Explosive Genealogy: Theatre, Philosophy and the Art of Presentation', *Cosmos and History*, vol. 1, no. 1-2, 2006, pp. 226-40.

Filewood, Alan, 'Impurity and the Postcolonial Subject', *Performance Research*, vol. 9, no. 4, 2004, pp. 95-8.

Fink, Bruce, 'Alain Badiou', *UMBR(a)*, no. 1, 1996.

Formis, Barbara, 'Event and Ready-Made: Delayed Sabotage', *Communication and Cognition*, vol. 37, no. 3-4, 2004, pp. 247-61.

Fraser, Zachary, 'The Law of the Subject: Alain Badiou, Luitzen Brouwer and the Kripkean Analyses of Forcing and the Heyting Calculus', *Cosmos and History*, vol. 1, no. 1-2, 2006, pp. 94-133.

Gibson, Andrew, 'Badiou, Beckett, Watt and the Event', *Journal of Beckett Studies*, vol. 12, no. 1-2, 2001, pp. 40-52.

Gibson, Andrew, 'Narrative Subtraction', in Jörg Helbig (ed.), *Erzählen und Erzähltheorie im 20. Jahrhundert*, Heidelberg, Carl Winter Universitätsverlag, 2001, pp. 213-31.

Gibson, Andrew, 'Three Dialogues and Beckett's Tragic Ethics', *Samuel Beckett Today / Aujourd'hui: An Annual Bilingual Review / Revue Annuelle Bilingue*, vol. 13, 2003, pp. 43-54.

Gibson, Andrew, 'Repetition and Event: Badiou and Beckett', *Communication and Cognition*, vol. 37, no. 3-4, 2004, pp. 263-78.

Gibson, Andrew, 'Badiou and Beckett: Actual Infinity, Event, Remainder', *Polygraph*, vol. 17, 2005, pp. 175-203.

Gibson, Andrew, *Beckett and Badiou: The Pathos of Intermittency*, Oxford, Oxford University Press, 2007 (forthcoming).

Gillespie, Sam, 'Subtractive', *UMBR(a)*, no. 1, 1996, pp. 7-10.

Gillespie, Sam, 'Hegel Unsutured (an Addendum to Badiou)', *UMBR(a)*, no. 1, 1996, pp. 57-69.

Gillespie, Sam, 'Neighborhood of Infinity: On Badiou's Deleuze: The Clamor of Being', *UMBR(a)*, no. 1, 2001, pp. 91-106.

Gillespie, S., 'Placing the Void – Badiou on Spinoza', *Angelaki: Journal of the Theoretical Humanities*, vol. 6, no. 3, 2001, pp. 63-77.

Gillespie, Sam, 'Beyond Being: Badiou's Doctrine of Truth', *Communication and Cognition*, vol. 36, no. 1-2, 2003, pp. 5-30.

Gillespie, Sam, The Mathematics of Novelty: Badiou's Minimalist Metaphysics, University of Warwick, Warwick, 2004.

Gillespie, Sam, 'Giving Form to Its Own Existence: Anxiety and the Subject of Truth', *Cosmos and History*, vol. 1, no. 1-2, 2006, pp. 161-85.

Glazener, Nancy, 'The Novel, the Social, and the Event: An International Ethical Encounter', in Anna Fahraeus (ed.), *Textual Ethos Studies: or Locating Ethics*, New York, Rodopi, 2005, pp. 35-52.

Grigg, Russell, 'Lacan and Badiou: Logic of the pas-tout', *Filozofski Vestnik*, vol. 26, no. 2, 2005.

Hair, Lindsey, "'I Love (U)": Badiou on Love, Logic, and Truth', *Polygraph*, vol. 17, 2005, pp. 127-42.

Hair, Lindsey, 'Ontology and Appearing: Documentary Realism as a Mathematical Thought', *Cosmos and History*, vol. 1, no. 1-2, 2006, pp. 241-62.

Hallward, Peter, 'Ethics Without Others: A Reply to Critchley on Badiou's Ethics', *Radical Philosophy*, vol. 102, 2000, pp. 27-30.

Hallward, Peter, 'The Singular and the Specific: Recent French Philosophy', *Radical Philosophy*, no. 99, 2000, pp. 6-18.

Hallward, Peter, 'Badiou's Politics: Equality and Justice', *Culture Machine: Generating Research in Culture and Theory*, no. 4, 2002.

Hallward, Peter, *Badiou: A Subject to Truth*, Minneapolis, University of Minnesota Press, 2003.

Hallward, Peter (ed.), *Think Again: Alain Badiou and the Future of Philosophy*, London, Continuum Books, 2004.

Hallward, Peter, 'Depending on Inconsistency: Badiou's Answer to the "Guiding Question of All Contemporary Philosophy"', *Polygraph*, vol. 17, 2005, pp. 11-25.

Helcinel, G., 'A Century Beyond Good and Evil: On "Siecle" by Alain Badiou', *Esprit*, no. 5, 2005, pp. 63-74.

Herbrechter, Stefan, 'Badiou, Derrida, and *The Matrix*: Cultural Criticism between Objectless Subjects and Subjectless Objects', *Polygraph*, vol. 17, 2005, pp. 205-20.

Hewlett, Nick, 'Engagement and Transcendence: The Militant Philosophy of Alain Badiou', *Modern & Contemporary France*, vol. 12, no. 3, 2004, pp. 335-52.

Hoens, Dominiek, 'The True Is Always New: Essays on Alain Badiou', *Communication and Cognition*, vol. 36, no. 1-2, 2003, pp. 3-4.

Hoens, Dominiek, 'Miracles Do Happen: Essays on Alain Badiou', *Communication and Cognition*, vol. 37, no. 3-4, 2004, pp. 165-6.

Hoens, Dominiek and Ed Pluth, 'Working Through as a Truth Procedure', *Communication and Cognition*, vol. 37, no. 3-4, 2004, pp. 279-92.

Holland, Christian Paul, *Time for Paul: Lyotard, Agamben, Badiou*, Ph.D., Emory University, Georgia, 2004.

Hopley, Vit and Yve Lomax, 'Immanent Trajectories', *Parallax*, vol. 7, no. 4, 2001, pp. 3-8.

Hyldgaard, Kirsten, 'Truth and Knowledge in Heidegger, Lacan, and Badiou', *UMBR(a)*, no. 1, 2001, pp. 79-90.

Ingram, James D., 'Can Universalism Still Be Radical? Alain Badiou's Politics of Truth', *Constellations*, vol. 12, no. 4, 2005, pp. 561-73.

James, Sarah, The Rudiments of Ornamental Composition / Constructed Works, 2005. Accessed.

Jenkins, Joseph Scott, *Inheritance Law as Constellation in Lieu of Redress: A Detour Through Exceptional Terrain*, Ph.D., University of California, Los Angeles, California, 2004.

Jenkins, Keith, 'Ethical Responsibility and the Historian: On the Possible End of a History "of a Certain Kind"', *History and Theory*, vol. 43, no.

4, 2004, pp. 43-60.

Johnston, A., 'Nothing is not always no-one: (a)voiding love', *Filozofski Vestnik*, vol. 26, no. 2, 2005, pp. 67-81.

Jones, S. H. and D. B. Clarke, 'Waging terror: The geopolitics of the real', *Political Geography*, vol. 25, no. 3, 2006, pp. 298-314.

Kaufman, Eleanor, 'Why the Family Is Beautiful (Lacan against Badiou)', *Diacritics*, vol. 32, no. 3/4, 2002, pp. 135-51.

Kaufman, Eleanor, 'Betraying well', *Criticism*, vol. 46, no. 4, 2004, pp. 651-9.

Kear, Adrian, 'Thinking out of Time: Theatre and the Ethic of Interruption', *Performance Research*, vol. 9, no. 4, 2004, pp. 99-110.

Kroeker, P. T., 'Whither Messianic Ethics? Paul as Political Theorist', *Journal of the Society of Christian Ethics*, vol. 25, no. 2, 2005, pp. 37-58.

Laclau, Ernesto, 'An Ethics of Militant Engagement', in Peter Hallward (ed.), *Think Again: Alain Badiou and the Future of Philosophy*, London, Continuum Books, 2004, pp. 120-37.

Laerke, Mogens, 'The Voice and the Name: Spinoza in the Badioudian Critique of Deleuze', *Pli: Warwick Journal of Philosophy*, no. 8, 1999, pp. 86-99.

Lecercle, Jean-Jacques, 'Alice and the Sphinx', *REAL: The Yearbook of Research in English and American Literature*, no. 13, 1997, pp. 25-47.

Lecercle, Jean-Jacques, 'Cantor, Lacan, Mao, Beckett, Meme Combat: The Philosophy of Alain Badiou', *Radical Philosophy*, no. 93, 1999, pp. 6-13.

Lecercle, Jean Jacques, 'Badiou's Poetics', in Peter Hallward (ed.), *Think Again: Alain Badiou and the Future of Philosophy*, London, Continuum Books, 2004, pp. 208-17.

Ling, Alex, 'Can Cinema Be Thought?: Alain Badiou and the Artistic Condition', *Cosmos and History*, vol. 1, no. 1-2, 2006, pp. 263-76.

MacCannell, Juliet Flower, 'Alain Badiou: Philosophical Outlaw', in Gabriel Riera (ed.), *Alain Badiou: Philosophy and Its Conditions*, Albany, State University of New York, 2005, pp. 137-84.

Macherey, Pierre, 'The Mallarmé of Alain Badiou', in Gabriel Riera (ed.), *Alain Badiou: Philosophy and Its Conditions*, trans. Marilyn Gaddis Rose and Gabriel Riera, Albany, State University of New York, 2005, pp. 109-15.

Madarasz, Norman, 'On Alain Badiou's Treatment of Category Theory in View of a Transitory Ontology', in Gabriel Riera (ed.), *Alain Badiou: Philosophy and Its Conditions*, Albany, State University of New York, 2005, pp. 23-43.

Marchart, *Oliver, Politics and the Political: An Inquiry into Post-Foundational Political Thought*, Ph.D., University of Essex (United Kingdom), 2003.

Marchart, Oliver, 'Nothing but a Truth: Alain Badiou's 'Philosophy of Politics' and the Left Heideggerians', *Polygraph*, vol. 17, 2005, pp. 105-25.

May, Todd, 'Badiou and Deleuze on the One and the Many', in Peter Hallward (ed.), *Think Again: Alain Badiou and the Future of Philosophy*, London, Continuum Books, 2004, pp. 67-76.

McNulty, Tracy, 'Feminine Love and the Pauline Universal', in Gabriel Riera (ed.), *Alain Badiou: Philosophy and Its Conditions*, Albany, State University of New York, 2005, pp. 185-212.

Meister, Bob, '"Never Again": The Ethics of the Neighbor and the Logic of Genocide', *Postmodern Culture: An Electronic Journal of Interdisciplinary Criticism*, vol. 15, no. 2, 2005.

Moreau, Pierre-François, 'Alain Badiou as a Reader of Spinoza', *Pli: Warwick Journal of Philosophy*, vol. 14, 2002.

Moreiras, Alberto, 'Children of Light: Neo-Paulinism and the Cathexis of Difference (Part I)', *Bible and Critical Theory*, vol. 1, no. 1, 2004, pp. 1-16.

Moreiras, Alberto, 'Children of Light: Neo-Paulinism and the Cathexis of Difference (Part II)', *Bible and Critical Theory*, vol. 1, no. 2, 2005, pp. 1-13.

Moulard, Valentine, 'Thought as Modern Art or the Ethics of Perversion', *Philosophy Today*, vol. 48, no. 3, 2004, pp. 288.

Mount, B. Madison, 'The Cantorian Revolution: Alain Badiou on the Philosophy of Set Theory', *Polygraph*, no. 17, 2005, pp. 41-91.

Murphet, Julian, 'Cultural Studies and Alain Badiou', in Gary Hall and Clare Birchall (eds.), *New Cultural Studies*, Edinburgh, Edinburgh University Press, 2006.

Nancy, Jean Luc, 'Philosophy without Conditions', in Peter Hallward (ed.), *Think Again: Alain Badiou and the Future of Philosophy*, London, Continuum Books, 2004, pp. 39-49.

Nicolacopoulos, Toula and George Vassilacopoulos, 'Philosophy and Revolution: Badiou's Infidelity to the Event', *Cosmos and History*, vol. 1, no. 1-2, 2006, pp. 210-25.

Noys, Benjamin, 'Badiou's Fidelities: Reading the Ethics', *Communication and Cognition*, vol. 36, no. 1-2, 2003, pp. 31-44.

Noys, Benjamin, 'The Provocations of Alain Badiou', *Theory, Culture and Society*, vol. 20, no. 1, 2003, pp. 123-32.

Ophir, Adi and Ariella Azoulay, 'The Contraction of Being: Deleuze After Badiou', *UMBR(a)*, no. 1, 2001, pp. 107-20.

Palti, E. J., 'Poststructuralist Marxism and the "Experience of the Disaster." On Alain Badiou's Theory of the (Non-)Subject', *The European Legacy*, vol. 8, no. 4, 2003, pp. 459-80.

Patel, Rajeev, 'Global Fascism Revolutionary Humanism and the Ethics of Food Sovereignty', *Development*, vol. 48, no. 2, 2005, pp. 79.

Pekerow, D., 'The Evental Site of Resistance: Badiou as Supplement to Foucault', *International Studies in Philosophy*, vol. 37, no. 2, 2005, pp. 57-80.

Pluth, Ed and Dominiek Hoens, 'What if the Other Is Stupid? Badiou and Lacan on 'Logical Time", in Peter Hallward (ed.), *Think Again: Alain Badiou and the Future of Philosophy*, London, Continuum Books, 2004, pp. 182-90.

Power, Nina, 'Towards an Anthropology of Infinitude: Badiou and the Political Subject', *Cosmos and History*, vol. 1, no. 1-2, 2006, pp. 186-209.

Rabaté, Jean-Michel, 'Unbreakable B's: From Beckett and Badiou to the Bitter End of Affirmative Ethics', in Gabriel Riera (ed.), *Alain Badiou: Philosophy and Its Conditions*, Albany, State University of New York, 2005, pp. 87-108.

Ramond, C. and A. Badiou, 'Poetry as a Condition of Philosophy: Interview with Alain Badiou', *Europe-Revue Litteraire Mensuelle*, vol. 78, no. 849-50, 2000, pp. 65-75.

Rancière, Jacques, 'Aesthetics, Inaesthetics, Anti-Aesthetics', in Peter Hallward (ed.), *Think Again: Alain Badiou and the Future of Philosophy*, London, Continuum Books, 2004, pp. 218-31.

Regard, F., 'The Ethics of Biographical Reading: A Pragmatic Approach', *Cambridge Quarterly*, vol. 29, no. 4, 2000, pp. 394-408.

Reinelt, J., 'Theatre and Politics: Encountering Badiou', *Performance Research*, vol. 9, no. 4, 2004, pp. 87-94.

Reinhard, Kenneth, 'Universalism and the Jewish Exception: Lacan, Badiou, Rozenzweig', *UMBR(a)*, no. 1, 2005.

Revault d'Allones, M., 'Who is Afraid of Politics? A Response to a Recent Book by Alain Badiou', *Esprit*, no. 12, 1998, pp. 236-42.

Riera, Gabriel, 'Alain Badiou After the "Age of Poets"', *(a): a journal of culture and the unconscious*, vol. 1, no. 1, 2000, pp. 10-33.

Riera, Gabriel, 'For an "Ethics of Mystery": Philosophy and the Poem', in Gabriel Riera (ed.), *Alain Badiou: Philosophy and Its Conditions*, Albany, State University of New York, 2005, pp. 61-85.

Badiou, Alain and L. Sedofsky, 'Being by Numbers: Interview with Artists and Philosopher Alain Badiou', *Artforum*, vol. 33, no. 2, 1994, pp. 84-90.

Skidelsky, Edward, 'Bogus Philosophy', *New Statesman*, vol. 14, no. 657, 2001, pp. 51.

Smith, A. M. Sheridan, 'Three New Novelists: JMG Le Clezio, Didier Coste and Alain Badiou', *London Magazine*, no. 4, 1964, pp. 61-4.

Smith, Daniel W., 'Mathematics and the Theory of Multiplicities: Badiou and Deleuze Revisited', *Southern Journal of Philosophy*, vol. 41, no. 3, 2003, pp. 411-49.

Smith, Daniel W., 'Badiou and Deleuze on the Ontology of Mathematics', in Peter Hallward (ed.), *Think Again: Alain Badiou and the Future of Philosophy*, London, Continuum Books, 2004, pp. 77-93.

Smith, Brian Anthony, 'The Limits of The Subject in Badiou's Being and Event', *Cosmos and History*, vol. 1, no. 1-2, 2006, pp. 134-58.

Stavrakakis, Yannis, 'Re-Activating the Democratic Revolution: The Politics of Transformation beyond Reoccupation and Conformism', *Parallax*, vol. 9, no. 2, 2003, pp. 56-71.

Strathausen, Carsten, 'The Badiou-Event', *Polygraph*, no. 17, 2005, pp. 275-93.

Stuart Fisher, Amanda, 'Developing an Ethics of Practice in Applied Theatre: Badiou and Fidelity to the Truth of the Event', *Research in Drama Education*, vol. 10, no. 2, 2005, pp. 247-52.

Tassone, Giuseppe, 'Amoral Adorno: Negative Dialectics Outside Ethics', *European Journal of Social Theory*, vol. 8, no. 3, 2005, pp. 251-67.

Tormey, Simon, 'A 'Creative Power'?: The Uses of Deleuze. A Review Essay', *Contemporary Political Theory*, vol. 4, no. 4, 2005, pp. 414.

Toscano, Alberto, 'From the State to the World? Badiou and Anti-Capitalism', *Communication and Cognition*, vol. 37, no. 3-4, 2004, pp. 199-223.

Toscano, Alberto, 'Communism As Separation', in Peter Hallward (ed.), *Think Again: Alain Badiou and the Future of Philosophy*, London, Continuum Books, 2004, pp. 138-49.

Toscano, Alberto, 'The Bourgeois and the Islamist, or, The Other Subjects of Politics', *Cosmos and History*, vol. 1, no. 1-2, 2006, pp. 15-38.

Widder, Nathan, 'The Rights of Simulacra: Deleuze and the Univocity of Being', *Continental Philosophy Review*, vol. 34, no. 4, 2001, pp. 437-53.

Wilkens, Matthew, 'Introduction: The Philosophy of Alain Badiou', *Polygraph*, no. 17, 2005, pp. 1-9.

Žižek, Slavoj, 'Psychoanalysis in Post-Marxism: The Case of Alain Badiou',

The South Atlantic Quarterly, vol. 97, no. 2, 1998, pp. 235-61.

Žižek, Slavoj, *The Ticklish Subject: The Absent Centre of Political Ontology*, New York, Verso, 2000.

Žižek, Slavoj, 'Is There a Politics of Subtraction? Badiou versus Lacan', *Communication and Cognition*, vol. 36, no. 1-2, 2003, pp. 103-19.

Žižek, Slavoj, 'From Purification to Subtraction: Badiou and the Real', in Peter Hallward (ed.), *Think Again: Alain Badiou and the Future of Philosophy*, London, Continuum Books, 2004, pp. 165-81.

Žižek, Slavoj, 'Notes on a Debate "From Within the People"', *Criticism*, vol. 46, no. 4, 2004.

Žižek, Slavoj, *Lacan: The Silent Partners*, London, Verso, 2006.

Žižek, Slavoj, 'Badiou: Notes From an Ongoing Debate', *International Journal of Žižek Studies*, vol. 1, 2006.

Zupančič, Alenka, 'The Fifth Condition', in Peter Hallward (ed.), *Think Again: Alain Badiou and the Future of Philosophy*, London, Continuum Books, 2004, pp. 191-201.

NON-ENGLISH WORKS BY BADIOU CITED IN THIS VOLUME

CM *Le Concept de modèle*, Paris, Maspero, 1967.

DI with François Balmès, *De l'idéologie*, Paris, F. Maspéro, 1976

S 'Jean-Paul Sartre' (pamphlet), Paris, Potemkine, 1980.

TS *Théorie du sujet*, Paris, Seuil, 1982.

EE *L'être et l'événement*, Paris, Éditions du Seuil, 1988.

NN *Le Nombre et les nombres*, Paris, Éditions du Seuil, 1990.

C *Conditions*, Paris, Seuil, 1992.

CT *Court traité d'ontologie transitoire*, Paris, Éditions du Seuil, 1998.

CI *Circonstances, 2: Irak, foulard*, Allemagne/France, Paris, Léo Scheer, 2004.

LS *Le Siècle*, Paris, Seuil, 2005.

LM/LOW *Logiques des mondes: l'être et l'événement, 2*, Paris, Seuil, 2006.

'Las democracias están en guerra contra los pobres', *Revista Ñ*, 23.10.2004.

'Marque et manque: à propos du zero', *Cahiers pour l'analyse*, vol. 10, 1969, pp. 150-73.

Un, Deux, Trois, Quatre, et aussi Zéro, unpublished.

OTHER WORKS CITED

Achcar, Gilbert, 'Eleven Theses on the Resurgence of Islamic Fundamentalism', in *Eastern Cauldron: Islam, Afghanistan, Palestine and Iraq in a Marxist Mirror*, London, Pluto Press, 2004.

Althusser, Louis , 'Ideology and the State', in *Lenin and Philosophy and Other Essays*, trans. Ben Brewster, New York, Monthly Review Press, 2000.

Atten, Mark van, 'Brouwer, as Never Read by Husserl', *Synthese*, vol. 137, no. 1-2, pp. 3-19.

Artaud, Antonin, *Oeuvres Complètes*, vol. XIII, Paris, Gallimard, 1974

Balibar, Etienne, 'Citizen Subject', *Who Comes After the Subject?*, Eduardo Cadava, Peter Connor, Jean-Luc Nancy (eds.), London, Routledge, 1991.

Barkhine, Mikhail, and Serge Vakhtangov 'Le batiment théâtral moderne vu par Meyerhold', *Revue d'Histoire du Théâtre*, 1967-4.

Bazin, Andre, 'In Defence of Rossellini: A letter to Guido Aristarco, editor-in-chief of Cinema Nuovo', *What is Cinema?*, trans. Hugh Gray, Berkeley, University of California Press, 1971.

Bishop, Errett, *Foundations of Constructive Analysis*, New York, McGraw-Hill, 1967.

Brecht, Bertolt *Brecht on Theatre*, ed. and trans. J. Willett, London, Methuen, 1964

Brouwer, Luitzen Egbertus Jan, *Collected Works, vol. 1*, Arend Heyting (ed.), Amsterdam, North-Holland Publishing, 1975.

Burgat, François, *Face to Face with Political Islam*, London, I.B. Tauris, 2003.

Butler, Judith, 'Competing Universalities', in Judith Butler, Ernesto Laclau, and Slavoj Žižek (eds.), *Contingency, Hegemony, Universality*, London, Verso, 2000, pp. 136-81.

Cantor, Georg, *Contributions to the Founding of the Theory of Transfinite Numbers*, trans. Philip Jourdain, New York, Dover, 1915.

Potter, Michael, *Set Theory and its Philosophy*, Oxford, Oxford University Press, 2004.

Callinicos, Alex, *The Resources of Critique*, Cambridge, Polity, 2006.

Cavaillès, Jean, 'On Logic and the Theory of Science', in Joseph J. Kockelmans and Theodore J. Kisiel (eds.), *Phenomenology and the Natural Sciences*, trans. Theodore J. Kisiel, Evanston, Northwestern University Press, 1970.

Chiesa, Lorenzo, *Lacan and Subjectivity: A Philosophical Introduction*, Cambridge, MIT Press, 2007.

Chiesa, Lorenzo and Alberto Toscano, 'Ethics and Capital, Ex Nihilo', *Umbr(a): A Journal of the Unconscious*, no. 1, 2005, pp. 9-25.

Clemens, Justin and Russell Grigg (eds.), *Jacques Lacan and the Other Side of Psychoanalysis*, Durham, Duke University Press, 2006.

Cohen, Paul J, *Set Theory and the Continuum Hypothesis*, New York, W.A. Benjamin, 1966.

Cole, Juan, 'Al-Qaeda's Doomsday Document and Psychological Manipulation', 2003.

Copjec, Joan, *Read My Desire: Lacan Against the Historicists*, Cambridge, MIT Press, 1994.

Copjec, Joan, *Imagine There's No Woman: Ethics and Sublimation*, Cambridge, MIT Press, 2002.

Cornford, F. M., 'Mathematics and Dialectic in the Republic VI.-VII. (I.)', *Mind*, vol. 41, no. 161, 1932, pp. 37-52.

Cornford, F. M., 'Mathematics and Dialectic in the Republic VI.-VII. (II.)', *Mind*, vol. 41, no. 162, 1932, pp. 173-90.

Cunningham, Conor, *A Genealogy of Nihilism: Philosophies of Nothing and the Difference of Theology*, London, Routledge, 2002.

Daubier, Jean, *History of the Chinese Cultural Revolution*, trans. Richard Sever, New York, Vintage Books, 1974.

Deleuze, Gilles, *Expressionism in Philosophy: Spinoza*, trans. Martin Joughin, New York, Zone Books, 1991.

Deleuze, Gilles, *The Fold*, trans. Tom Conley, London, Continuum, 2001.

Deleuze, Gilles, *Negotiations: 1972-1990*, trans. Martin Joughin, New York, Columbia University Press, 1995.

Deleuze, Gilles, *Cinema 2: The Time-Image*, trans. Hugh Tomlinsom & Robert Galeta, London, Continuum, 2005.

Deleuze, Gilles, 'The Brain is the Screen', in David Lapoujade (ed.) *Two Regimes of Madness: Texts and Interviews 1975-1995*, trans. Ames Hodges & Mike Taormina, New York, MIT Press, 2006, pp. 282-291.

Dummett, Michael, *Elements of Intuitionism*, Oxford, Clarendon Press, 1977.

Dunayevskaya, Raya, 'Marxist-Humanism's concept of "Subject"', letter to young members of News and Letters Committees, *The Raya Dunayevskaya Collection, Supplement*, 1971. Available at http://www.marxists.org/archive/dunayevskaya/works/1971/subject.htm.

Eco, Umberto, 'Ur-Fascism', *The New York Review of Books*, vol. 42, no. 11,

1995.

Education QLD 2010, 'New Basics Research Program', 2003.

Feltham, Oliver, 'Enjoy your stay: Structural Change in Seminar XVII', in J. Clemens and R. Grigg (eds.), *Jacques Lacan and the Other Side of Psychoanalysis*, Durham, Duke University Press, 2006.

Feuerbach, Ludwig, *The Essence of Christianity*, trans. George Eliot, New York, London, Harper and Row, 1957.

Feuerbach, Ludwig, *The Fiery Brook: Selected Writings of Ludwig Feuerbach*, ed. and trans. Zawar Hanfi, New York, Anchor Books, 1972.

'For jihadist, read anarchist', *The Economist*, 18 August 2005.

Frege, Gottlob, *The Foundations of Arithmetic*, trans. J.L. Austin, New York, Harper and Bros., 1960.

Freud, Sigmund, 'Civilization and its Discontents', in Albert Dickson (ed.), *Civilization, Society and Religion*, trans. James Strachey, vol. XII Penguin Freud Library, London, Penguin, 1991, pp. 243-340.

Freud, Sigmund, 'Group Psychology and the Analysis of the Ego', *The Standard Edition of the Complete Psychological Work of Sigmund Freud*, vol. XVIII, London, The Hogarth Press and the Institute of Psychoanalysis, 2001.

Euben, Roxanne L., *Enemies in the Mirror: Islamic Fundamentalism and the Limits of Modern Rationalism*, Princeton, Princeton University Press, 1999.

Gramsci, Antonio, *Selections from the Prison Notebooks*, trans. Quentin Hoare and Geoffrey Nowell-Smith, New York, International Publishers, 1971.

Gillespie, Sam, 'Slavoj Your Symptom!', *UMBR(a)*, no. 1, 1995, pp. 115-9.

Gillespie, Sam, 'Subtractive', *UMBR(a)*, no. 1, 1996, pp. 7-10, (available from CSeARCH).

Gillespie, Sam, 'Get Your Lack On', *UMBR(a)*, no. 1, 2004, pp. 9-19.

Goldberg, Rosa Lee, *Performance Art: From Futurism to the Present*, revised ed., London, Thames and Hudson, 1988.

Griffin, Roger, *The Nature of Fascism*, London, Routledge, 1993.

Griffin, Roger, 'The Palingenetic Core of Generic Fascist Ideology', in Alessandro Campi, ed., *Che cos'è il fascismo?*, Rome, Ideazione, 2003.

Hardt, Michael and Antonio Negri, *Empire*, Cambridge, Harvard University Press, 2001.

Hegel, G.W. F., *The Science of Logic*, trans. A.V. Miller, Atlantic Highlands NJ, Humanities Press International, 1996.

Hegel, G. W. F., *Lectures on the History of Philosophy*, trans. E. S. Haldane and Frances H. Simson, vol. I Greek Philosophy to Plato, 3 vols.,

Lincoln, University of Nebraska Press, 1995.

Hegel, G. W. F., *The Philosophy of Right*, trans. T. M. Knox, New York, Oxford, 1980.

Heidegger, Martin, *Hegel's Phenomenology of Spirit*, trans. P. Emad and K. Maly, Bloomington, Indiana University Press, 1988.

Heidegger, Martin, *Contributions to Philosophy: from Enowning*, trans. Parvis Emad and Kenneth Maly, Bloomington, Indiana University Press, 1999.

Heyting, Arend, *Intuitionism: An Introduction*, 3rd ed., Amsterdam, North-Holland Publishing, 1971.

Kant, Immanuel, *Critique of Practical Reason*, trans. T.K. Abbott, Amherst, Prometheus Books, 1996.

Kripke, Saul, 'Semantical Analysis of Intuitionistic Logic I', in J.N. Crossley and M.A.E. Dummett (eds.), *Formal Systems and Recursive Functions, Proceedings of the Eighth Logic Colloquium, Oxford, July, 1963*, Amsterdam, North-Holland Publishing Co., 1965, pp. 92-130.

Lacan, Jacques, *Seminar IX (1961-1962): 'L'identification'*, unpublished.

Lacan, Jacques, *Seminar VI (1958-1959), 'Le désir et son interpretation'*, unpublished.

Lacan, Jacques, *Seminar XIX (1971-1972), '...Ou pire'*, unpublished.

Lacan, Jacques, *The Four Fundamental Concepts of Psychoanalysis*, trans. Alan Sheridan, New York, Norton, 1978.

Lacan, Jacques, *The Seminar of Jacques Lacan. Book I, Freud's Papers on Technique, 1953-1954*, Jacques-Alain Miller (ed.), trans. John Forrester, 1st American ed., New York, W.W. Norton, 1988.

Lacan, Jacques, 'Kant avec Sade', trans. James Swenson, *October*, vol. 51, 1989, pp. 55-104.

Lacan, Jacques, *The Ethics of Psychoanalysis, 1959-1960*, trans. Dennis Porter, New York, Norton, 1992.

Lacan, Jacques, *Le séminaire livre IV. La relation d'objet, 1956-1957*, Paris, Seuil, 1994.

Lacan, Jacques, *On Feminine Sexuality: The Limits of Love and Knowledge, The Seminar of Jacques Lacan, Book XX, Encore*, trans. Bruce Fink, New York, Norton, 1998.

Lacan, Jacques, *Seminar VII*, The *Ethics of Psychoanalyses*, ed. Jacques-Alain Miller, trans. Dennis Porter, London, W.W. Norton, 1997.

Lacan, Jacques, *Le séminaire livre V. Les formations de l'inconscient, 1957-1958*, Paris, Seuil, 1998.

Lacan, Jacques, *The Four Fundamental Concepts of Psychoanalysis*, London, Vintage, 1998.

Lacan, Jacques, 'L'étourdit', *Autres écrits*, Paris, Seuil, 2001.

Lacan, Jacques, *Le séminaire livre X. L'angoisse, 1962-1963*, Paris, Seuil, 2004.

Lacan, Jacques, *Ecrits*, trans. Bruce Fink with Heloise Fink and Russell Grigg, New York, W.W. Norton & Company, 2006.

Lawrence, Bruce (ed.), *Messages to the World: The Statements of Osama Bin Laden*, London, Verso, 2005.

Lawvere, F. W. and S. H. Schanuel, *Conceptual Mathematics: A First Introduction to Categories*, Cambridge, Cambridge University Press, 1997.

Leibniz, Gottfried Wilhelm Freiherr von, 'On Freedom', in G.H.R. Parkinson (ed.), *Philosophical Writings*, trans. Mary Morris and G.H.R. Parkinson, London, J.M. Dent and Sons, Ltd., pp. 106-115.

Lenin, V. I., *What is to be Done?*, trans. S.V. and Patricia Utechin, Oxford, Oxford University Press, 1963.

Lipscome, James., 'Correspondence and Controversy: Cinéma Vérité', *Film Quarterly*, vol. 18, 1964, pp. 62-3.

Livadites, Tasos, *Small Book for Large Dreams (Greek)*, Athens, Kethros, 1987.

Lutkehaus, Nancy and Jenny Cool, 'Paradigms Lost and Found', in Jane Gaines and Michael Renov (eds.), *Collecting Visible Evidence*, Minneapolis, University of Minnesota Press, 1999.

Maistre, Joseph de, *The Works of Joseph de Maistre*, trans. and with an introduction by Jack Lively, London, Allen and Unwin, 1965.

Malevich, Kazimir, 'And Visages Are Victorious on the Screen', in Oksana Bulgakowa (ed.), *Kazimir Malevich: The White Rectangle; Writings on Film*, San Francisco, Potemkin Press, 2002.

Mallarmé, Stéphane, *Collected Poems*, trans. Henry Weinfield, Berkeley, University of California Press, 1994.

Mancosu, Paolo (ed.), *From Brouwer to Hilbert*, New York, Oxford University Press, 1998.

Mao Zedong, *Combat Liberalism*, Peking, Foreign Languages Press, 1954.

McClarty, C., *Elementary Categories, Elementary Toposes*, Oxford, Oxford University Press, 1992.

Metz, Christian, *Psychoanalysis and Cinema: The Imaginary Signifier*, trans. Celia Britton, Annwyl Williams, Ben Brewster & Alfred Guzzetti, London, Macmillan Press, 1983.

Miller, Jacques-Alain, 'Suture (Elements of the Logic of the Signifier)', *Screen*, vol. 18, no. 4, 1977-8, pp. 24-34.

Moghadam, Val, 'Socialism or Anti-Imperialism? The Left and Revolution in Iran', *New Left Review*, vol. 166, 1987.

Meyerhold, Vsevolod, *Meyerhold on Theatre*, trans. E. Braun, London, Metheun, 1969

Nancy, Jean-Luc, *Les Muses*, Paris, Gallimard, 2001.

Neumann, John Von, 'An Axiomatization of Set Theory', in Jean Van Heijenoort (ed.), *From Frege to Gödel: A Source Book in Mathematical Logic, 1879-1931*, Cambridge, Harvard University Press, 1967, pp. 393-413.

Nicolacopoulos, Toula and George Vassilacopoulos, *Hegel and the Logical Structure of Love: An Essay on Sexualities, Family and the Law*, Aldershot, Ashgate, 1999.

Nicolacopoulos, Toula and George Vassilacopoulos, 'Inquiry into Hope', *Critical and Creative Thinking: The Australasian Journal of Philosophy in Schools*, vol. 11, no. 2, 2003, pp. 1-7.

Plato, *The Republic of Plato*, trans. F.M. Cornford, London, Oxford University Press, 1941.

Plato, 'Sophist', in *Plato's Theory of Knowledge: The Theaetetus and the Sophist*, trans. F. M. Cornford, Mineola, Dover Publications, 2003.

Plato, *Plato and Parmenides: Parmenides' Way of Truth and Plato's Parmenides*, trans. F.M. Cornford, London, Routledge & Kegan Paul, 1939.

Plato, *The Collected Dialogues of Plato, Including the Letters*, Edith Hamilton, Huntington Cairns and Lane Cooper (eds.), New York, Princeton University Press, 1996.

Von Plato, Jan, 'Review of Dirk van Dalen, *Mystic, Geometer, and Intuitionist, The Life of L.E.J. Brouwer, Vol. 1. The Dawning Revolution'. Bulletin of Symbolic Logic*, vol. 7, no. 1, March, 2001. pp. 63-64.

Pourciau, Bruce, 'Intuitionism as a (Failed) Kuhnian Revolution in Mathematics', *Studies in the History and Philosophy of Science*, vol. 31, no. 2, 2000, pp. 297-339.

Rancière, Jacques, *The Ignorant Schoolmaster: Five lessons in intellectual emancipation*, trans. Kristin Ross, Stanford: Stanford University Press 1991.

RETORT (Iain Boal, T.J. Clark, Joseph Matthews, Michael Watts), *Afflicted Powers: Capital and Spectacle in a New Age of War*, London, Verso, 2005.

Rony, Fatimah Tobing, *The Third Eye: Race: Cinema and the Ethnographic Spectacle*, Durham, Duke University Press, 1996.

Rosen, Philip, *Change Mummified: Cinema, Historicity, Theory*, Minneapolis, University of Minnesota Press, 2001.

Rose, Jacqueline, 'We are all afraid, but of what exactly?', *The Guardian*, 20 March 2003, ‹http://www.guardian.co.uk/comment/story/0,3604,917712,00.html›, accessed July 6, 2004.

Rousseau, Jean-Jacques, *The Social Contract*, trans. Maurice Cranston, London, Penguin, 1968.

Russell, Bertrand, *Introduction to Mathematical Philosophy*, London, George Allen, 1963.

Safouan, M., *Lacaniana: Les séminaires de Jacques Lacan * 1953-1963*, Paris, Seuil, 2001.

Sartre, Jean-Paul, *Being and Nothingness, An Essay in Phenomenological Ontology*, trans. Hazel Barnes, New York, Philosophical Library, 1956.

Saunders, Frances Stonor, *Who Paid the Piper? The CIA and the Cultural Cold War*, London, Granta, 2000.

Schmitt, Carl, *Political Theology: Four Chapters on the Concept of Sovereignty*, trans. George Schwab, Cambridge, The MIT Press, 1985.

Schuster, A., *Commentary on Lacan Seminar IX L'Identification, 20 December 1961*, unpublished.

Shari'ati, Ali, *On the Sociology of Islam*, trans. Hamid Algar, Oneonta, Mizan Press, 1979.

Shivas, Mark 'New Approach', *Movie 8*, no. 13, April 1963.

Tasíc, Vladimir, *The Mathematical Roots of Postmodern Thought*, Oxford, Oxford University Press, 2001.

Tiles, Mary, *The Philosophy of Set Theory, An Introduction to Cantor's Paradise*, Oxford, Basil Blackwell, 1989.

Vainqueur, Bernard, 'De quoi "sujet" est-il le nom pour Alain Badiou?', *Penser le Multiple*, Paris, L'Harmattan, 2002, pp. 313-38, p. 314.

Virmaux, Alain, *Antonin Artaud et le théâtre*, Paris, Seghers, 1970.

Virno, Paolo, *A Grammar of the Multitude*, New York, Semiotext(e), 2004.

Wittgenstein, Ludwig, *Tractatus Logico-Philosophicus*, trans. C.K. Ogden, London, Routledge and Kegan Paul, 1922.

Wolff, Kurt H. (ed.), *The Sociology of Georg Simmel*, New York, The Free Press, 1964.

Žižek, Slavoj, *The Sublime Object of Ideology*, London, Verso, 1989.

Žižek, Slavoj, *Tarrying with the Negative: Kant, Hegel and the Critique of Ideology*, Durham, Duke University Press, 1993.

Žižek, Slavoj, *The Ticklish Subject: The Absent Centre of Political Ontology*, New York, Verso, 2000.

Žižek, Slavoj, *For They Know Not What They Do: Enjoyment as a Political Factor*, 2nd ed., London, Verso, 2002.

Žižek, Slavoj, 'Foreword to the Second Edition: Enjoyment within the Limits of Reason Alone', *For They Know Not What They Do: Enjoyment as a Political Factor*, 2nd ed., London, Verso, 2002, pp. xi-cvii.

Zupančič, Alenka, 'The Splendor of Creation: Kant, Lacan, Nietzsche',

Umbr(a): A Journal of the Unconscious, no. 1, 1999, pp. 35-42.

Zupančič, Alenka, *Ethics of the Real: Kant, Lacan*, London, Verso, 2000.

Contributors

Paul Ashton teaches in the Liberal Arts at Victoria University and is completing his PhD at LaTrobe University.

Alain Badiou teaches at Ecole Normale Supérieure and at the Collège international de philosophie in Paris.

A. J. Bartlett teaches at Deakin University and is completing his PhD at the University of Melbourne.

Lorenzo Chiesa teaches in the Department of European Languages and Culture, University of Kent at Canterbury.

Justin Clemens teaches at the University of Melbourne.

Oliver Feltham teaches at the American University of Paris.

Zachary Fraser teaches at University of Kings College, Halifax, NS.

Sam Gillespie completed his dissertation in philosophy at the University of Warwick.

Lindsey Hair is a graduate student at the Department of Comparative Literature, SUNY Buffalo.

Dominique Hecq teaches creative writing at Swinburne University.

Sigi Jöttkandt is a Flanders Research Fellow at Ghent University, Belgium.

Alex Ling is a PhD candidate, School of Art History, Cinema, Classics & Archaeology, the University of Melbourne.

Brian Anthony Smith is a PhD research student in the philosophy department at the University of Dundee.

Alberto Toscano teaches at Goldsmiths College, University of London.

Toula Nicolacopoulos teaches philosophy at LaTrobe University.

Nina Power teaches philosophy at Roehampton University, London.

George Vassilacopoulos teaches philosophy at LaTrobe University.

Index

421

Printed in the United Kingdom by
Lightning Source UK Ltd., Milton Keynes
138256UK00001B/119/A